Diaries, 1910–1923

FRANZ KAFKA

Diaries, 1910-1923

Edited by
MAX BROD

Schocken Books

NEW YORK

This translation of *Tagebücher von Kafka* was originally
published in the United States in two separate volumes
by Schocken Books Inc. in 1948 and 1949. This one-volume
edition first published in Great Britain by Peregrine Books,
an imprint of Penguin Books Ltd., London, in 1964.

The Diaries of Franz Kafka 1910–13 translated from the German by Joseph Kresh
The Diaries of Franz Kafka 1914–23 translated from the German by
Martin Greenberg with the cooperation of Hannah Arendt

Manufactured in the United States of America

28th Printing

CONTENTS

*Only longer compositions, or those of a
finished nature, are listed here.*

CONTENTS

Die Zuschauer erstarren, wenn der Zug vorbeifährt.

"Wenn er mich immer fragt' das ä losgelöst vom Satze flog dahin wie ein Ball auf der Wiese.

Sein Ernst bringt mich um. Den Kopf im Kragen, die Haare unbeweglich um den Schädel geordnet, die Muskeln unten an den Wangen an ihrem Platze gespannt

Ist der Wald noch immer da? Der Wald war noch ungefähr da. Kaum aber war mein Blick zehn Schritte weit, ließ ich ab wieder eingefangen vom langweiligen Gespräch.

Im dunklen Wald im durchweichten Boden fand ich mich nur durch das Weiß seines Kragens zurecht.

Ich bat im Traum die Tänzerin Eduardowa sie möchte doch den Csardas noch einmal tanzen. Sie hatte einen breiten Streifen Schatten oder Licht mitten

Manuscript of the first page of the *Diaries*.

DIARIES 1910

The onlookers go rigid when the train goes past.

'If he should forever ahsk me.' The *ah*, released from the sentence, flew off like a ball on the meadow.

His gravity is the death of me. His head in its collar, his hair arranged immovably on his skull, the muscles of his jowels below, tensed in their places –

Are the woods still there? The woods were still almost there. But hardly had my glance gone ten steps farther when I left off, again caught up in the tedious conversation.

In the dark woods, on the sodden ground, I found my way only by the whiteness of his collar.

In a dream I asked the dancer Eduardova[1] to dance the Czardas just one time more. She had a broad streak of shadow or light across the middle of her face between the lower part of her forehead and the cleft of her chin. Just then someone with the loathsome gestures of an unconscious intriguer approached to tell her the train was leaving immediately. The manner in which she listened to this announcement made it terribly clear to me that she would not dance again. 'I am a wicked, evil woman, am I not?' she said. 'Oh no,' I said, 'not that,' and turned away aimlessly.

Before that I had questioned her about the many flowers that were stuck into her girdle. 'They are from all the princes of Europe,' said she. I pondered as to what this might mean – that all those fresh flowers stuck in her girdle had been presented to the dancer Eduardova by all the princes of Europe.

The dancer Eduardova, a lover of music, travels in the tram, as everywhere else, in the company of two vigorous violinists whom she

9

makes play often. For there is no known reason why one should not play in the tram if the playing is good, pleasing to the fellow passengers, and costs nothing; i.e., if the hat is not passed round afterwards. Of course, at first it is a little surprising and for a short while everybody finds it improper. But at full speed, in a strong breeze and on a silent street, it sounds quite nice.

The dancer Eduardova is not as pretty in the open air as on the stage. Her faded colour, her cheekbones which draw her skin so taut that there is scarcely a trace of motion in her face and a real face is no longer possible, the large nose, which rises as though out of a cavity, with which one can take no liberties – such as testing the hardness of the point or taking it gently by the bridge and pulling it back and forth while one says, 'But now you come along.' The large figure with the high waist in skirts with too many pleats – whom can that please? – she looks like one of my aunts, an elderly lady; many elderly aunts of many people look like that. In the open air Eduardova really has nothing to compensate for these disadvantages, moreover, aside from her very good feet; there is actually nothing that would give occasion for enthusiasm, astonishment, or even for respect. And so I have actually seen Eduardova very often treated with a degree of indifference that even gentlemen, who were otherwise very adroit, very correct, could not conceal, although they naturally made every effort to do so in the presence of so famous a dancer as Eduardova still was.

The auricle of my ear felt fresh, rough, cool, succulent as a leaf, to the touch.

I write this very decidedly out of despair over my body and over a future with this body.

When despair shows itself so definitely, is so tied to its object, so pent up, as in a soldier who covers a retreat and thus lets himself be torn to pieces, then it is not true despair. True despair overreaches its goal immediately and always, (at this comma it became clear that only the first sentence was correct).

Do you despair?

Yes? You despair?

Ich schreibe das ganz bestimmt aus Verzweiflung über meinen
Körper und über die Zukunft mit diesem Körper

Wenn sich die Verzweiflung so bestimmt gibt
so an ihren Gegenstand gebunden ist, so zurückgehalten
wie von einem Soldaten, der den Rückzug deckt und sich
dafür zerreissen lässt, dann ist es nicht die richtige
Verzweiflung. Die richtige Verzweiflung hat ihr
Ziel gleich und immer überholt. (Bei diesem Beistrich
zeigte es sich, dass nur der erste (satz richtig war)

A Manuscript page of the *Diaries* (see page 10).

You run away? You want to hide?

I passed by the brothel as though past the house of a beloved.

Writers speak a stench.

The seamstresses in the downpour of rain.[2]

Finally, after five months of my life during which I could write nothing that would have satisfied me, and for which no power will compensate me, though all were under obligation to do so, it occurs to me to talk to myself again. Whenever I really questioned myself, there was always a response forthcoming, there was always something in me to catch fire, in this heap of straw that I have been for five months and whose fate, it seems, is to be set afire during the summer and consumed more swiftly than the onlooker can blink his eyes. If only that would happen to me! And tenfold ought that to happen to me, for I do not even regret this unhappy time. My condition is not unhappiness, but it is also not happiness, not indifference, not weakness, not fatigue, not another interest — so what is it then? That I do not know this is probably connected with my inability to write. And without knowing the reason for it, I believe I understand the latter. All those things, that is to say, those things which occur to me, occur to me not from the root up but rather only from somewhere about their middle. Let someone then attempt to seize them, let someone attempt to seize a blade of grass and hold fast to it when it begins to grow only from the middle.

There are some people who can do this, probably, Japanese jugglers, for example, who scramble up a ladder that does not rest on the ground but on the raised soles of someone half lying on the ground, and which does not lean against a wall but just goes up into the air. I cannot do this — aside from the fact that my ladder does not even have those soles at its disposal. This, naturally, isn't all, and it isn't such a question that prompts me to speak. But every day at least one line should be trained on me, as they now train telescopes on comets. And if then I should appear before that sentence once, lured by that sentence, just as, for instance, I was last Christmas, when I was so far gone that I was barely able to control myself and when I seemed really

meiner Leiter nicht einmal jene Sohlen zur Ver-
fügung stehn. Es ist das natürlich nicht alles
und eine solche Anfrage bringt mich noch nicht zum
Reden. Aber jeden Tag soll zumindest eine Zeile
gegen mich gerichtet werden wie man die
Fernrohre jetzt gegen den Kometen richtet. Und
Wenn ich dann einmal vor jenem Satze erscheinen
würde hergelockt von jenem Satze so wie ich
z. B. letzte Weihnachten gewesen bin und wo
ich so weit war, dass ich mich nur noch gerade
fassen konnte und wo ich wirklich auf
der letzten Stufe meiner Leiter schien, die
aber ruhig auf dem Boden stand und an
der Wand. Aber was für ein Boden! was für
eine Wand! Und doch fiel jene Leiter nicht,
so drückten sie meine Füsse an den Boden,
so hoben sie meine Füsse an die Wand.

A Manuscript page of the *Diaries* (see page 12).

on the last rung of my ladder, which, however, rested quietly on the ground and against a wall. But what ground, what a wall! And yet that ladder did not fall, so strongly did my feet press it against the ground, so strongly did my feet raise it against the wall.

Today, for instance, I acted three pieces of insolence, towards a conductor, towards someone introduced to me – well, there were only two, but they hurt like a stomach-ache. On the part of anyone they would have been insolent, how much the more so on my part. Therefore I went outside myself, fought in the air amid the mist, and, worst of all, no one noticed that I was even insolent to my companions, a piece of insolence as such, and had to be, and had to assume the proper manner for it and the responsibility; but the worst was when one of my acquaintances took this insolence not even as the indication of a personality but rather as a personality itself, called my attention to my insolence and admired it. Why don't I stay within myself? To be sure, I now say to myself: Look, the world submits to your blows, the conductor and the person introduced to you remained undisturbed; as you left, the latter even said good-bye. But that means nothing. You can achieve nothing if you forsake yourself; but what do you miss, aside from this, in your circle? To this appeal I answer only: I too would rather submit to blows within the circle than myself deal the blows outside it – but where the devil is this circle? For a time, indeed, I did see it lying on the earth, as if sprayed in lime, but now it just seems to hover about me, indeed does not even hover.

Night of comets, 17–18 May.

Together with Blei, his wife and child, from time to time listened to myself outside of myself, it sounded like the whimpering of a young cat.

How many days have again gone silently by; today is 28 May. Have I not even the resolution to take this penholder, this piece of wood, in my hand every day? I really think I do not. I row, ride, swim, lie in the sun. Therefore my calves are good, my thighs not bad, my belly will pass muster, but my chest is very shabby and if my head set low between my shoulders –

Sunday, 19 July, slept, awoke, slept, awoke, miserable life.

When I think about it, I must say that my education has done me great harm in some respects. I was not, as a matter of fact, educated in any out-of-the-way place, in a ruin, say, in the mountains – something against which in fact I could not have brought myself to say a word of reproach. In spite of the risk of all my former teachers not understanding this, I should prefer most of all to have been such a little dweller in the ruins, burnt by the sun which would have shone for me there on the tepid ivy between the remains on every side; even though I might have been weak at first under the pressure of my good qualities, which would have grown tall in me with the might of weeds.

When I think about it, I must say that my education has done me great harm in some respects. This reproach applies to a multitude of people – that is to say, my parents, several relatives, individual visitors to our house, various writers, a certain particular cook who took me to school for a year, a crowd of teachers (whom I must press tightly together in my memory, otherwise one would drop out here and there – but since I have pressed them together so, the whole mass crumbles away bit by bit anyhow), a school inspector, slowly walking passersby; in short, this reproach twists through society like a dagger. And no one, I repeat, unfortunately no one, can be sure as to whether the point of the dagger won't suddenly appear sometimes in front, at the back, or from the side. I do not want to hear this reproach contradicted; since I have already heard too many contradictions, and since most of the contradictions, moreover, have refuted me, I include these contradictions in my reproach and now declare that my education and this refutation have done me great harm in many respects.

Often I think it over and then I always have to say that my education has done me great harm in some ways. This reproach is directed against a multitude of people; indeed, they stand here together and, as in old family photographs, they do not know what to do about each other, it simply does not occur to them to lower their eyes, and out of anticipation they do not dare smile. Among them are my parents, several relatives, several teachers, a certain particular cook, several girls at dancing school, several visitors to our house in earlier times, several writers, a swimming teacher, a ticket-seller, a school inspector, then

15

some people that I met only once on the street, and others that I just cannot recall and those whom I shall never again recall, and those, finally, whose instruction, being somehow distracted at the time, I did not notice at all; in short, there are so many that one must take care not to name anyone twice. And I address my reproach to them all, introduce them to one another in this way, but tolerate no contradiction. For honestly I have borne enough contradictions already, and since most of them have refuted me, all I can do is include these refutations, too, in my reproach, and say that aside from my education these refutations have also done me great harm in some respects.

Does one suspect, perhaps, that I was educated in some out-of-way place? No, I was educated in the middle of the city, in the middle of the city. Not, for example, in a ruin in the mountains or beside the lake. My reproach had until now covered my parents and their retinue and made them grey; but now they easily push it aside and smile, because I have drawn my hands away from them to my forehead and am thinking: I should have been that little dweller in the ruins, hearkening to the cries of the crows, soared over by their shadows, cooling under the moon, burnt by the sun which would have shone for me from all sides on my bed of ivy, even though I might have been a little weak at first under the pressure of my good qualities, which would have had to grow in me with the might of weeds.

Often I think it over and give my thoughts free rein, without interfering, and always, no matter how I turn or twist it, I come to the conclusion that in some respects my education has done me terrible harm. There inheres in the recognition of this a reproach directed against a multitude of people. There are my parents and my relatives, a certain particular cook, my teachers, several writers – the love with which they harmed me makes their guilt even greater, for how much [good] they could have [done] me with their love – several families friendly with my family, a swimming teacher, natives of summer resorts, several ladies in the city park of whom this would not at all have been expected, a hairdresser, a beggarwoman, a helmsman, the family doctor, and many more besides; and there would be still more if I could and wanted to name them all; in short, there are so many that one must be careful not to name anyone in the lot twice.

Now one might think that these great numbers would make a reproach lose its firmness, that it would simply have to lose its firmness, because a reproach is not an army general, it just goes straight ahead and does not know how to distribute its forces. Especially in this case, when it is directed against persons in the past. Forgotten energy may hold these persons fast in memory, but they would hardly have any ground left under them and even their legs would have already turned to smoke. And how expect it to be of any use to throw up to people in such a condition the mistakes they once made in earlier times in educating a boy who is as incomprehensible to them now as they to us. But indeed one cannot even do as much as make them remember those times, no person can compel them to do so; obviously one cannot mention compulsion at all, they can remember nothing, and if you press them, they push you dumbly aside, for most probably they do not even hear the words. Like tired dogs they stand there, because they use up all their strength in remaining upright in one's memory.

But if you actually did make them hear and speak, then your ears would only hum with counter-reproaches, for people take the conviction of the venerability of the dead together with them into the beyond and uphold it ten times as much from there. And if perhaps this opinion is not correct and the dead do stand in especially great awe of the living, then they would side with their own living past all the more – after all, it's closest to them – and again our ears would hum. And if this opinion, too, is not correct and the dead are after all very impartial, even then they could never sanction their being disturbed by unverifiable reproaches. For such reproaches are unverifiable even as between one person and another. The existence of past mistakes in education cannot be proved, so how much the less the original responsibility for them. And now let me see a reproach that in such a situation would not be transformed into a sigh.

That is the reproach that I have to make. It has a sound core, theory supports it. That which really has been spoiled in me, however, I forget for the moment or excuse, and don't as yet make any fuss about it. On the other hand, I can prove at any time that my education tried to make another person out of me than the one I became. It is for the harm, therefore, that my educators could have done me in accordance with their intentions that I reproach them; I demand from their hands

the person I now am, and since they cannot give him to me, I make of
my reproach and laughter a drumbeat sounding into the world beyond.
But all this only serves a different purpose. The reproach for having
after all spoiled a part of me – for having spoiled a good, beautiful
part (in my dreams sometimes it appears to me the way a dead bride
appears to others) – this reproach that is forever on the point of becoming a sigh, this reproach should before all else reach there undamaged
as an honest reproach, which is what it is, too. Thus it happens that the
great reproach, to which nothing can happen, takes the small one by
the hand, if the great one walks, the small one hops, but when the small
one gets there, it distinguishes itself – which is what we have always
expected – and sounds the trumpet for the drummer.

Often I think it over and give my thoughts free rein, without interfering, but I always come to the conclusion that my education has
spoiled me more than I can understand. Externally I am a man like
others, for my physical education kept as close to the ordinary as my
body itself was ordinary, and even if I am pretty short and a little
stout, I still please many, even girls. There is nothing to be said about
that. Only recently one of them said something very intelligent: 'Ah,
if I could only see you naked once, then you ought to be really pretty
and kissable.' But if I lacked an upper lip here, there an ear, here a
rib, there a finger, if I had hairless spots on my head and pockmarks on
my face, this would still be no adequate counterpart to my inner imperfection. This imperfection is not congenital and therefore so much the
more painful to bear. For like everyone, I too have my centre of gravity
inside me from birth, and this not even the most foolish education
could displace. This good centre of gravity I still have, but to a certain
extent I no longer have the corresponding body. And a centre of gravity
that has no work to do becomes lead, and sticks in the body like a
musket ball. But this imperfection is not earned either, I have suffered
its emergence through no fault of my own. This is why I can find
nowhere within myself any repentance, much as I may seek it. For
repentance would be good for me, it cries itself out all by itself, it takes
the pain to one side and settles everything alone like an affair of
honour; we remain upright because it relieves us.

My imperfection is, as I said, not congenital, not earned, nevertheless I bear it better than others, by means of great labour of the imagination and sought-out expedients, bear much smaller misfortunes – a horrible wife, for instance, poverty, a miserable profession – and am at the same time not at all black in the face with despair, but rather white and red.

I would not be so, if my education had penetrated into me as deeply as it wanted to. Perhaps my youth was too short for that, in which case, now in my forties,[3] I still rejoice over its shortness with all my heart. That alone made it possible for me to have enough strength left to become conscious of the deprivations of my youth; further, to suffer through these deprivations; further, to reproach the past in all respects; and, finally, to have left a remnant of strength for myself. But all these strengths are, again, only a remnant of those I possessed as a child, which exposed me more than others to the corruptors of youth, yes, a good racing chariot is the first to be pursued and overtaken by dust and wind, and its wheels fly over obstacles so that one might almost believe in love.

What I still am now is revealed most clearly to me by the strength with which the reproaches urge their way out of me. There were times when I had nothing else inside me except reproaches driven by rage, so that, although physically well, I would hold on to strangers in the street because the reproaches inside me tossed from side to side like water in a basin that was being carried rapidly.

Those times are past. The reproaches lie around inside me like strange tools that I hardly have the courage to seize and lift any longer. At the same time the corruption left by my old education seems to begin to affect me again more and more; the passion to remember, perhaps a general characteristic of bachelors of my age, opens my heart again to those people who should be the objects of my reproaches; and an event like that of yesterday, formerly as frequent as eating, is now so rare that I make a note of it.

But even above and beyond that, I myself, I who have just now put down my pen in order to open the window, am perhaps the best aid of my assailants. For I underestimate myself, and that in itself means an overestimation of others; but even aside from that I overestimate them. And aside from that I also do harm to myself directly. If I am overcome by the desire to make reproaches, I look out of the window. Who could deny that the fishermen sit there in their boats like pupils who have been taken out to the river from school; good, their immobility is often incomprehensible, like that of flies on window-panes. And over the bridge go the trams, naturally as always with a roaring rude as the wind's, and they sound like spoiled clocks; and the policeman, no doubt, black from head to foot, with the yellow light of the badge on his chest, reminds one of nothing else but hell when now, with thoughts similar to mine, he contemplates a fisherman who suddenly – is he crying, has he seen an apparition, or is his float bobbing? – bends down to the side of his boat. All this is all right, but in its own time; now only my reproaches are right.

They are directed against a multitude of people; this is really frightening and not only I at the open window but everyone else as well would rather look at the river. There are my parents and relatives. That they have done me harm out of love makes their guilt all the greater, for how much good they could have done me out of love; then friendly families with the evil eye, out of their sense of guilt they make themselves heavy and refuse to rise up into memory; then a crowd of nurses, teachers, and writers and among them a certain particular cook; then, their punishment being that they fade into one another, a family doctor, a hairdresser, a helmsman, a beggarwoman, a newspaper vendor, a park watchman, a swimming teacher, then strange ladies in the city park of whom one would not have expected it at all, natives of summer resorts, an insult to the innocence of nature, and many others; but there were still more, if I could and wanted to name them all; in short, there are so many that one must take care not to name any one of them twice.

I often think it over and give my thoughts free rein without interfering, but I always come to the same conclusion: that my education has spoiled me more than all the people I know and more than I can conceive. Yet only once in a long while can I say this, for if I am asked immediately after, 'Really? Is that possible? Are you supposed to believe that?' out of nervous fear I immediately try to restrict it.

Externally I look like everybody else; have legs, body and head, trousers, coat, and hat; they put me through a thorough course of gymnastics and if I have nevertheless remained rather short and weak, that just could not be helped. Besides, I am agreeable to many people, even young girls, and those to whom I am not agreeable still find me bearable.

It is reported, and we are inclined to believe it, that when men are in danger they have no consideration even for beautiful strange women; they shove them against walls, shove them with head and hands, knees and elbows, if these women happen only to be in the way of their flight from the burning theatre. At this point our chattering women fall silent, their endless talking reaches a verb and period, their eyebrows rise out of their resting places, the rhythmic movement of their thighs and hips is interrupted; into their mouths, only loosely closed by fear, more air than usual enters and their cheeks seem a little puffed out.[4]

'You,' I said, and gave him a little shove with my knee (at this sudden utterance some saliva flew from my mouth as an evil omen), 'don't fall asleep!'

'I'm not falling asleep,' he answered, and shook his head while opening his eyes. 'If I were to fall asleep, how could I guard you then? And don't I have to do that? Isn't that why you grabbed hold of me then in front of the church? Yes, it was a long time ago, as we know it, just leave your watch in your pocket.'

'It's really very late,' I said. I had to smile a little and in order to conceal it I looked intently into the house.

'Does it really please you so much? So you would like to go up, very much like to? Then just say so, after all, I won't bite you. Look, if you think that it will be better for you up there than down here, then just go up there at once without thinking of me. It's my opinion – therefore the opinion of a casual passer-by – that you will soon come down again and that it would then be very good if somehow someone should be standing here whose face you won't even look at, but who'll take you under the arm, strengthen you with wine in a near-by tavern, and then lead you to his room which, miserable as it is, still has a few panes of glass between itself and the night; for the time being you don't have to give a damn about this opinion. True it is, and I can repeat that in front of anyone you like, that it goes badly with us here below; yes, it's even a dog's life, but there's no help for me now; whether I lie here in the gutter and stow away the rain water or drink champagne with the same lips up there under the chandelier makes no difference to me. Besides, I don't even have so much as a choice between the two things; indeed, anything that attracts people's attention never happens to me, and how could it happen within the framework of the ceremonies that are necessary for me, within which indeed I can only crawl on, no better than some sort of vermin. You, to be sure, who know all that may be hidden in yourself, you have courage, at least you think you have. Try it anyhow, what do you have to lose, after all – often you can already recognize yourself, if you pay attention, in the face of the servant at the door.'

'If I just knew definitely that you were being sincere with me, I should have been up there long ago. But how could I even tell whether you were sincere with me? You're looking at me now as though I were a little child, that doesn't help me at all, that indeed makes it even worse. But perhaps you want to make it worse. At the same time I can no longer stand the air in the street, so I already belong with the company up there. When I pay attention there's a scratching in my throat, there you have it. Besides, I cough. And have you any idea how I'll get along up there? The foot with which I step into the hall will already be transformed before I can draw the other one after it.'

'You are right, I am not sincere with you.'

'I want to leave, want to mount the steps, if necessary, by turning somersaults. From that company I promise myself everything that I lack, the organization of my strength, above all, for which the sort of intensification that is the only possibility for this bachelor on the street is insufficient. The latter would be satisfied just to maintain his – really – shabby physique, protect his few meals, avoid the influence of other people, in short, to preserve only as much as is possible in the disintegrating world. But if he loses anything, he seeks to get it back by force, though it be transformed, weakened, yes, even though it be his former property only in seeming (which it is for the most part). His nature is suicidal, therefore, it has teeth only for his own flesh and flesh only for his own teeth. For without a centre, without a profession, a love, a family, an income; i.e. without holding one's own against the world in the big things – only tentatively, of course – without, therefore, making to a certain extent an imposing impression on it by a great complex of possessions, one cannot protect oneself from losses that momentarily destroy one. This bachelor with his thin clothes, his art of prayer, his enduring legs, his lodgings that he is afraid of, with his otherwise patched-up existence now brought out again after a long period – this bachelor holds all this together with his two arms and can never pick up any unimportant chance object without losing two others of his own. The truth, naturally, lies in this, the truth that is nowhere so clearly to be seen. For whoever appears as a complete citizen, that is, travels over the sea in a ship with foam before him and wake behind, that is, with much effect round about, quite different from the man in the waves on a few planks of wood that even bump against and submerge each other – he, this gentleman and citizen, is in no lesser danger. For he and his property are not one, but two, and whoever destroys the connexion destroys him at the same time. In this respect we and our acquaintances are indeed unknowable, for we are entirely concealed; I, for instance, am now concealed by my profession, by my imagined or actual sufferings, by literary inclinations, etc., etc. But it is just I who feel my depth much too often and much too strongly to be able to be even only half-way satisfied. And this depth I need but feel uninterruptedly for a quarter of an hour and the poisonous world flows into my mouth like water into that of a drowning man.

'There is at the moment scarcely any difference between me and the bachelor, only that I can still think of my youth in the village and perhaps, if I want to, perhaps even if my situation alone demands it, can throw myself back there. The bachelor, however, has nothing before him and therefore nothing behind him. At the moment there is no difference, but the bachelor has only the moment. He went astray at that time – which no one can know today, for nothing can be so annihilated as that time – he went astray at that time when he felt his depth lastingly, the way one suddenly notices an ulcer on one's body that until this moment was the least thing on one's body – yes, not even the least, for it appeared not yet to exist and now is more than everything else that we had bodily owned since our birth. If until now our whole person had been oriented upon the work of our hands, upon that which was seen by our eyes, heard by our ears, upon the steps made by our feet, now we suddenly turn ourselves entirely in the opposite direction, like a weather-vane in the mountains.

'Now, instead of having run away at that moment, even in this latter
direction, for only running away could have kept him on the tips of his
toes and only the tips of his toes could have kept him on the earth,
instead of that he lay down, as children now and then lie down in the
snow in winter in order to freeze to death. He and these children, they
know of course that it is their fault for having lain down or yielded in
some other way, they know that they should not have done it at any
cost, but they cannot know that after the transformation that is taking
place in them on the fields or in the cities they will forget every former
fault and every compulsion and that they will move about in the new
element as if it were their first. But forgetting is not the right word
here. The memory of this man has suffered as little as his imagination.
But they just cannot move mountains; the man stands once and for all
outside our people, outside our humanity, he is continually starved, he
has only the moment, the everlasting moment of torment which is followed by no glimpse of a moment of recovery, he has only one thing
always: his pain; in all the circumference of the world no second thing
that could serve as a medicine, he has only as much ground as his two
feet take up, only as much of a hold as his two hands encompass, so
much the less, therefore, than the trapeze artist in a variety show, who
still has a safety net hung up for him below.

'We others, we, indeed, are held in our past and future. We pass
almost all our leisure and how much of our work in letting them bob
up and down in the balance. Whatever advantage the future has in
size, the past compensates for in weight, and at their end the two are
indeed no longer distinguishable, earliest youth later becomes distinct,
as the future is, and the end of the future is really already experienced
in all our sighs, and thus becomes the past. So this circle along whose
rim we move almost closes. Well, this circle indeed belongs to us, but
belongs to us only so long as we keep to it, if we move to the side just
once, in any chance forgetting of self, in some distraction, some fright,
some astonishment, some fatigue, we have already lost it into space,
until now we had our noses stuck into the tide of the times, now we
step back, former swimmers, present walkers, and are lost. We are
outside the law, no one knows it and yet everyone treats us accordingly.'

'You mustn't think of me now. And how can you want to compare

yourself with me? I have been here in the city for more than twenty
years already. Can you even imagine what that means? I have spent
each season here twenty times' – Here he shook his slack fist over our
heads – 'The trees have been growing here for twenty years, how small
should a person become under them. And all these nights, you know,
in all the houses. Now you lie against this, now against that wall, so
that the window keeps moving around you. And these mornings, you
look out of the window, move the chair away from the bed and sit down
to coffee. And these evenings, you prop up your arm and hold your ear
in your hand. Yes, if only that weren't all! If only you at least acquired
a few new habits such as you can see here in the streets every day –
Now it perhaps seems to you as though I wanted to complain about it?
But no, why complain about it, after all neither the one nor the other
is permitted me. I must just take my walks and that must be sufficient,
but in compensation there is no place in all the world where I could
not take my walks. But now it looks again as though I were being vain
of it.'

'I have it easy, then. I shouldn't have stopped here in front of the
house.'

'Therefore don't compare yourself in that with me and don't let me
make you doubtful. You are after all a grown man, are besides, as it
seems, fairly forsaken here in the city.'

I am indeed close to being so. Already, what protected me seemed to
dissolve here in the city. I was beautiful in the early days, for this
dissolution takes place as an apotheosis, in which everything that holds
us to life flies away, but even in flying away illumines us for the last
time with its human light. So I stand before my bachelor and most
probably he loves me for it, but without himself really knowing why.
Occasionally his words seem to indicate that he knows himself thoroughly, that he knows whom he has before him and that he may therefore allow himself anything. No, it is not so, however. He would rather
meet everyone this same way, for he can live only as a hermit or a
parasite. He is a hermit only by compulsion, once this compulsion is
overcome by forces unknown to him, at once he is a parasite who
behaves insolently whenever he possibly can. Of course, nothing in the
world can save him any longer and so his conduct can make one think
of the corpse of a drowned man which, borne to the surface by some

current, bumps against a tired swimmer, lays its hands upon him and would like to hold on. The corpse does not come alive, indeed is not even saved, but it can pull the man down.

'You,' I said, and gave him a little shove with my knee (at this sudden utterance some saliva flew from my mouth as an evil omen), 'now you're falling asleep.'

'I haven't forgotten you,' he said, and shook his head while he was still opening his eyes.

'I wasn't afraid of it either,' I said. I ignored his smile and looked down on the pavement. 'I just wanted to tell you that now, come what may, I am going up. For, as you know, I have been invited up there, it is already late and the company is waiting for me. Perhaps some arrangements have been put off until I come. I don't insist it is so, but it is always possible. You will now ask me whether I could not perhaps forgo the company altogether.'

'I won't, for in the first place you are burning to tell me, and in the second place it doesn't interest me at all, down here and up there are all the same to me. Whether I lie here in the gutter and stow away the rain water or drink champagne up there with the same lips makes no difference to me, not even in the taste, for which, besides, I easily console myself, for neither the one nor the other is permitted me and therefore it is not right for me to compare myself to you. And you! How long really have you been in the city? How long have you been in the city, I ask?'

'Five months. But still, I know it well enough already. You, I have given myself no rest. When I look back like this I don't know at all whether there have been any nights, everything looks to me, can you imagine, like one day without any mornings, afternoons, and evenings, even without any differences in light.'

6 November. Lecture by a Madame Ch. on Musset. Jewish women's habit of lip-smacking. Understand French through all the preliminaries and complications of the anecdote, until, right before the last word, which should live on in the heart on the ruins of the whole anecdote, the French disappears before our eyes, perhaps we have strained ourselves too much up to that point, the people who understand French leave before the end, they have already heard enough, the others

haven't yet heard nearly enough, acoustics of the hall which favour the coughing in the boxes more than the words of the lecturer. Supper at Rachel's, she is reading Racine's *Phèdre* with Musset, the book lies between them on the table upon which in addition there is everything else imaginable lying.

Consul Claudel,[5] brilliance in his eyes, which his broad face picks up and reflects, he keeps wanting to say good-bye, he succeeds in part too, but not entirely, for when he says good-bye to one, another is standing there who is joined again by the one to whom good-bye has already been said. Over the lecture platform is a balcony for the orchestra. All possible sorts of noise disturb. Waiters from the corridor, guests in their rooms, a piano, a distant string orchestra, hammering, finally a squabble that is irritating because of the difficulty of telling where it is taking place. In a box a lady with diamonds in her ear-rings that sparkle almost uninterruptedly. At the box office young, black-clothed people of a French Circle. One of them makes a sharp bow in greeting that causes his eyes to sweep across the floor. At the same time he smiles broadly. But he does this only before girls, immediately after he looks the men straight in the face with his mouth solemnly pursed, by which he at the same time declares the former greeting to be perhaps a ridiculous but in any case unavoidable ceremony.

7 November. Lecture by Wiegler[6] on Hebbel. Sits on the stage against a set representing a modern room as if his beloved will bound in through a door to begin the play at last. No, he lectures. Hunger of Hebbel. Complicated relationship with Elisa Lensing. In school he has an old maid for a teacher who smokes, takes snuff, thrashes, and gives the good ones raisins. He travels everywhere (Heidelberg, Munich, Paris) with no real apparent purpose. Is at first a servant of a parish bailiff, sleeps in the same bed with the coachman under the steps.

Julius Schnorr von Carolsfeld – drawing by Friedrich Olivier, he is sketching on a slope, how pretty and earnest he is there (a high hat like a flattened clown's cap with a stiff, narrow brim extends over his face, curly, long hair, eyes only for his picture, quiet hands, the board on his knees, one foot has slipped down a little on the slope). But no, that is Friedrich Olivier, drawn by Schnorr.

10 o'clock, 15 November. I will not let myself become tired. I'll jump into my story even though it should cut my face to pieces.

12 o'clock, 16 November. I'm reading *Iphigenie auf Tauris*. Here, aside from some isolated, plainly faulty passages, the dried-up German language in the mouth of a pure boy is really to be regarded with absolute amazement. The verse, at the moment of reading, lifts every word up to the heights where it stands in perhaps a thin but penetrating light.

27 November. Bernard Kellermann read aloud. 'Some unpublished things from my pen,' he began. Apparently a kind person, an almost grey brush of hair, painstakingly close-shaven, a sharp nose, the flesh over his cheekbones often ebbs and flows like a wave. He is a mediocre writer with good passages (a man goes out into the corridor, coughs, and looks around to see if anyone is there), also an honest man who wants to read what he promised, but the audience wouldn't let him; because of the fright caused by the first story about a hospital for mental disorders, because of the boring manner of the reading, the people, despite the story's cheap suspense, kept leaving one by one with as much zeal as if someone were reading next door. When, after the first third of the story, he drank a little mineral water, a whole crowd of people left. He was frightened. 'It is almost finished,' he lied outright. When he was finished everyone stood up, there was some applause that sounded as though there were one person in the midst of all the people standing up who had remained seated and was clapping by himself. But Kellermann still wanted to read on, another story, perhaps even several. But all he could do against the departing tide was to open his mouth. Finally, after he had taken counsel, he said, 'I should still like very much to read a little tale that will take only fifteen minutes. I will pause for five minutes.' Several still remained, whereupon he read a tale containing passages that were justification for anyone to run out from the farthest point of the hall right through the middle of and over the whole audience.

15 December. I simply do not believe the conclusions I have drawn from my present condition, which has already lasted almost a year, my

condition is too serious for that. Indeed, I do not even know whether I can say that it is not a new condition. My real opinion, however, is that this condition is new – I have had similar ones, but never one like this. It is as if I were made of stone, as if I were my own tombstone, there is no loophole for doubt or for faith, for love or repugnance, for courage or anxiety, in particular or in general, only a vague hope lives on, but no better than the inscriptions on tombstones. Almost every word I write jars against the next, I hear the consonants rub leadenly against each other and the vowels sing an accompaniment like Negroes in a minstrel show. My doubts stand in a circle around every word, I see them before I see the word, but what then! I do not see the word at all, I invent it. Of course, that wouldn't be the greatest misfortune, only I ought to be able to invent words capable of blowing the odour of corpses in a direction other than straight into mine and the reader's face. When I sit down at the desk I feel no better than someone who falls and breaks both legs in the middle of the traffic of the Place de l'Opéra. All the carriages, despite their noise, press silently from all directions in all directions, but that man's pain keeps better order than the police, it closes his eyes and empties the Place and the streets without the carriages having to turn about. The great commotion hurts him, for he is really an obstruction to traffic, but the emptiness is no less sad, for it unshackles his real pain.

16 December. I won't give up the diary again. I must hold on here, it is the only place I can.

I would gladly explain the feeling of happiness which, like now, I have within me from time to time. It is really something effervescent that fills me completely with a light, pleasant quiver and that persuades me of the existence of abilities of whose non-existence I can convince myself with complete certainty at any moment, even now.

Hebbel praises Justinus Kerner's *Reiseschatten*. 'And a book like this hardly exists, no one knows it.'

Die Strasse der Verlassenheit by W. Fred. How do such books get written? A man who on a small scale produces something fairly good here blows up his talent to the size of a novel in so pitiful a manner

29

that one becomes ill even if one does not forget to admire the energy with which he misuses his own talent.

This pursuit of the secondary characters I read about in novels, plays, etc. This sense of belonging together which I then have! In the *Jungfern vom Bischofsberg* (is that the title?), there is mention made of two seamstresses who sew the linen for the play's one bride. What happens to these two girls? Where do they live? What have they done that they may not be part of the play but stand, as it were, outside in front of Noah's ark, drowning in the downpour of rain, and may only press their faces one last time against a cabin window, so that the audience in the stalls sees something dark there for a moment?

17 December. Zeno, pressed as to whether anything is at rest, replied: Yes, the flying arrow rests.

If the French were German in their essence, then how the Germans would admire them!

That I have put aside and crossed out so much, indeed almost everything I wrote this year, that hinders me a great deal in writing. It is indeed a mountain, it is five times as much as I have in general ever written, and by its mass alone it draws everything that I write away from under my pen to itself.

18 December. If it were not absolutely certain that the reason why I permit letters (even those that may be foreseen to have insignificant contents, like this present one) to lie unopened for a time is only weakness and cowardice, which hesitate as much to open a letter as they would hesitate to open the door of a room in which someone, already impatient, perhaps, is waiting for me, then one could explain this allowing of letters to lie even better as thoroughness. That is to say, assuming that I am a thorough person, then I must attempt to protract everything pertaining to the letter to the greatest possible extent. I must open it slowly, read it, slowly and often, consider it for a long time, prepare a clean copy after many drafts, and finally delay even the posting. All this lies within my power, only the sudden receipt of the

letter cannot be avoided. Well, I slow even that down in an artificial manner, I do not open it for a long time, it lies on the table before me, it continuously offers itself to me, continuously I receive it but do not accept it.

11.30 p.m. That I, so long as I am not freed of my office, am simply lost, that is clearer to me than anything else, it is just a matter, as long as it is possible, of holding my head so high that I do not drown. How difficult that will be, what strength it will necessarily drain me of, can be seen already in the fact that today I did not adhere to my new time schedule, to be at my desk from 8 to 11 p.m., that at present I even consider this as not so very great a disaster, that I have only hastily written down these few lines in order to get into bed.

19 December. Started to work in the office. Afternoon at Max's.

Read a little in Goethe's diaries. Distance already holds this life firm in tranquillity, these diaries set fire to it. The clarity of all the events makes it mysterious, just as a park fence rests the eye when looking at broad tracts of turf, and yet inspires inadequate respect in us.

Just now my married sister[7] is coming to visit us for the first time.

20 December. How do I excuse yesterday's remark about Goethe (which is almost as untrue as the feeling it describes, for the true feeling was driven away by my sister)? In no way. How do I excuse my not yet having written anything today? In no way. Especially as my disposition is not so bad. I have continually an invocation in my ear: 'Were you to come, invisible judgement!'

In order that these false passages which refuse to leave the story at any price may at last give me peace, I write down two here:

'His breathing was loud like sighs in a dream, where unhappiness is more easily borne than in our world so that simple breathing can serve as sighs.'

'Now I look him over as aloofly as one looks over a small puzzle about which one says to oneself: What does it matter if I cannot get the pellets into their holes, it all belongs to me, after all, the glass, the case,

31

the pellets, and whatever else there is; I can simply stick the whole affair into my pocket.'

21 December. Curiosities from *Taten des grossen Alexander* by Michail Kusmin:

'Child whose upper half dead, lower alive, child's corpse with moving little red legs.'

'The four kings God and Magog, who were nourished on worms and flies, he drove into riven cliffs and sealed them in until the end of the world with the seal of Solomon.'

'Rivers of stone, where in place of water stones rolled with a great din past the brooks of sand that flow for three days to the south and for three days to the north.'

'Amazons, women with their right breasts burned away, short hair, male footgear.'

'Crocodiles who with their urine burned down trees.'

Was at Baum's,[8] so heard nice things. I, frail as before and always. To have the feeling of being bound and at the same time the other, that if one were unbound it would be even worse.

22 December. Today I do not even dare to reproach myself. Shouted into this empty day, it would have a disgusting echo.

24 December. I have now examined my desk more closely and have seen that nothing good can be done on it. There is so much lying about, it forms a disorder without proportion and without that compatibility of disordered things which otherwise makes every disorder bearable. Let disorder prevail on the green baize as it will, the same is true of the orchestras of old theatres. But that (25 December) wads of old newspapers, catalogues, picture postcards, letters, all partly torn, partly open, should stick out from the standing-room – the open pigeonhole under the centrepiece – in the shape of a staircase, this unseemly state of affairs spoils everything. Individual, relatively huge things in the orchestra appear in the greatest possible activity, as though it were permissible for the merchant to audit his books in the theatre, the carpenter to hammer, the officer to brandish his sabre, the cleric to speak

to the heart, the scholar to the reason, the politician to the sense of citizenship, the lovers not to restrain themselves, etc. Only the shaving mirror stands erect on my table, in the way it is used for shaving, the clothes-brush lies with its bristles on the cloth, the wallet lies open in case I want to make a payment, from the key ring a key sticks out in readiness and the tie still twines itself partly around the collar I have taken off. The next higher open pigeonhole, already hemmed in by the small closed drawers, is nothing but a lumber-room, as though the first balcony of the auditorium, really the most visible part of the theatre, were reserved for the most vulgar people, for old men-about-town in whom the dirt gradually moves from the inside to the outside, rude fellows who let their feet hang down over the balcony railing. Families with so many children that one merely glances at them without being able to count them here set up the filth of poor nurseries (indeed, it is already running into the orchestra), in the dark background sit the incurably sick, fortunately one sees them only when one shines a light in there, etc. In this pigeonhole lie old papers that I should long ago have thrown away if I had a waste-paper basket, pencils with broken points, an empty match-box, a paperweight from Karlsbad, a ruler with an edge the unevenness of which would be awful even for a country road, a lot of collar buttons, used razor blades (for these there is no place in the world), tie clips and still another heavy iron paperweight. In the pigeonhole above –

Wretched, wretched, and yet with good intentions. It is midnight, but since I have slept very well, that is an excuse only to the extent that by day I would have written nothing. The burning electric light, the silent house, the darkness outside, the last waking moments, they give me the right to write even if it be only the most miserable stuff. And this right I use hurriedly. That's the person I am.

26 December. Two and a half days I was, though not completely, alone, and already I am, if not transformed, at any rate on the way. Being alone has a power over me that never fails. My interior dissolves (for the time being only superficially) and is ready to release what lies deeper. A slight ordering of my interior begins to take place and I need nothing more, for disorder is the worst thing in small talents.

27 December. My strength no longer suffices for another sentence. Yes, if it were a question of words, if it were sufficient to set down one word and one could turn away in the calm consciousness of having entirely filled this word with oneself.

I slept part of the afternoon away, while I was awake I lay on the sofa, thought about several love experiences of my youth, lingered in a pique over a neglected opportunity (at the time I was lying in bed with a slight cold and my governess read me *The Kreutzer Sonata*, which enabled her to enjoy my agitation), imagined my vegetarian supper, was satisfied with my digestion, and worried whether my eyesight would last all my life.

28 December. When I have acted like a human being for a few hours, as I did today with Max and later at Baum's, I am already full of conceit before I go to sleep.

≱ ≱ ≱

3 January. 'You,' I said, and then gave him a little shove with my knee, 'I want to say good-bye.' At this sudden utterance some saliva flew from my mouth as an evil omen.

'But you've been considering that for a long time,' he said, stepped away from the wall and stretched.

'No, I haven't been considering it at all.'

'Then what have you been thinking about?'

'For the last time I have been preparing myself a little more for the company. Try as you may, you won't understand that. I, an average man from the country, whom at any moment one could exchange for one of those who wait together by the hundreds in railway stations for particular trains.'

4 January. *Glaube und Heimat* by Schönherr.
The wet fingers of the balconyites beneath me who wipe their eyes.

6 January. 'You,' I said, aimed, and gave him a little shove with my knee, 'but now I'm going. If you want to see it too, open your eyes.'

'Really, then?' he asked, at the same time looking at me from wide-open eyes with a direct glance that nevertheless was so weak that I could have fended it off with a wave of my arm. 'You're really going, then? What shall I do? I cannot keep you. And if I could, I still wouldn't want to. By which I simply want to make clear to you your feeling that you could still be held back by me.' And immediately he assumed that inferior servants' face by means of which they are permitted within an otherwise regulated state to make the children of their masters obedient or afraid.

7 January. N.'s sister who is so in love with her fiancé that she manoeuvres to speak with each visitor individually, since one can better express and repeat one's love to a single person.

As though by magic, since neither external nor internal circumstances – which are now more friendly than they have been for a year – prevented me, I was kept from writing the entire holiday, it is a Sunday. – Several new perceptions of the unfortunate creature that I am have dawned upon me consolingly.

12 January. I haven't written down a great deal about myself during these days, partly because of laziness (I now sleep so much and so soundly during the day, I have greater weight while I sleep) but also partly because of the fear of betraying my self-perception. This fear is justified, for one should permit a self-perception to be established definitively in writing only when it can be done with the greatest completeness, with all the incidental consequences, as well as with entire truthfulness. For if this does not happen – and in any event I am not capable of it – then what is written down will, in accordance with its own purpose and with the superior power of the established, replace what has been felt only vaguely in such a way that the real feeling will disappear while the worthlessness of what has been noted down will be recognized too late.

A few days ago Leonie Frippon, cabaret girl, Stadt Wien. Hair dressed in a bound-up mass of curls. Bad girdle, very old dress, but very pretty with tragic gestures, flutterings of the eyelids, thrusts of the long legs, skilful stretching of the arms along the body, significance of the rigid throat during ambiguous passages. Sang: Button Collection in the Louvre.

Schiller, as drawn by Schadow in 1804 in Berlin, where he had been greatly honoured. One cannot grasp a face more firmly than by this nose. The partition of the nose is a little pulled down as a result of the habit of pulling on his nose while working. A friendly, somewhat hollow-cheeked person whom the shaven face has probably made senile.

14 January. Novel, *Eheleute*, by Beradt. A lot of bad Jewishness. A sudden, monotonous, coy appearance of the author; for instance: All were gay, but one was present who was not gay. Or: Here comes a Mr Stern (whom we already know to the marrow of his novelistic bones). In Hamsun too there is something like this, but there it is as natural as the knots in wood, here, however, it drips into the plot like a fashionable medicine on to sugar. Odd turns of expression are clung to interminably, for instance: He was busy about her hair, busy and again busy. Individual characters, without being shown in a new light, are brought out well, so well that even faults here and there do not matter. Minor characters mostly wretched.

17 January. Max read me the first act of *Abschied von der Jugend*. How can I, as I am today, come up to this? I should have to look for a year before I found a true emotion in me, and am supposed, in the face of so great a work, in some way to have a right to remain seated in my chair in the coffee-house late in the evening, plagued by the passing flatulence of a digestion which is bad in spite of everything.

19 January. Every day, since I seem to be completely finished – during the last year I did not wake up for more than five minutes at a time – I shall either have to wish myself off the earth or else, without my being able to see even the most moderate hope in it, I shall have to start afresh like a baby. Externally, this will be easier for me than before. For in those days I still strove with hardly a suspicion after a description in which every word would be linked to my life, which I would draw to my heart, and which would transport me out of myself.

With what misery (of course, not to be compared with the present) I began! What a chill pursued me all day long out of what I had written! How great the danger was and how uninterruptedly it worked, that I did not feel that chill at all, which indeed on the whole did not lessen my misfortune very much.

Once I projected a novel in which two brothers fought each other, one of whom went to America while the other remained in a European prison. I only now and then began to write a few lines, for it tired me at once. So once I wrote down something about my prison on a Sunday afternoon when we were visiting my grandparents and had eaten an especially soft kind of bread, spread with butter, that was customary there. It is of course possible that I did it mostly out of vanity, and by shifting the paper about on the tablecloth, tapping with my pencil, looking around under the lamp, wanted to tempt someone to take what I had written from me, look at it, and admire me. It was chiefly the corridor of the prison that was described in the few lines, above all its silence and coldness; a sympathetic word was also said about the brother who was left behind, because he was the good brother. Perhaps I had a momentary feeling of the worthlessness of my description, but before that afternoon I never paid much attention to such feelings when among relatives to whom I was accustomed (my timidity was so great that the accustomed was enough to make me half-way happy), I sat at the round table in the familiar room and could not forget that I was young and called to great things out of this present tranquillity. An uncle who liked to make fun of people finally took the page that I was holding only weakly, looked at it briefly, handed it back to me, even without laughing, and only said to the others who were following him with their eyes, 'The usual stuff,' to me he said nothing. To be sure, I remained seated and bent as before over the now useless page of mine, but with one thrust I had in fact been banished from society, the judgement of my uncle repeated itself in me with what amounted almost to real significance and even within the feeling of belonging to a family I got an insight into the cold space of our world which I had to warm with a fire that first I wanted to seek out.

19 February. When I wanted to get out of bed this morning I simply folded up. This has a very simple cause, I am completely overworked.

Not by the office but my other work. The office has an innocent share in it only to the extent that, if I did not have to go there, I could live calmly for my own work and should not have to waste these six hours a day which have tormented me to a degree that you cannot imagine, especially on Friday and Saturday, because I was full of my own things. In the final analysis, I know, that is just talk, the fault is mine and the office has a right to make the most definite and justified demands on me. But for me in particular it is a horrible double life from which there is probably no escape but insanity. I write this in the good light of the morning and would certainly not write it if it were not so true and if I did not love you like a son.

For the rest, I shall certainly be myself again by tomorrow and come to the office where the first thing I hear will be that you want to have me out of your department.

The special nature of my inspiration in which I, the most fortunate and unfortunate of men, now go to sleep at 2 a.m. (perhaps, if I can only bear the thought of it, it will remain, for it is loftier than all before), is such that I can do everything, and not only what is directed to a definite piece of work. When I arbitrarily write a single sentence, for instance, 'He looked out of the window', it already has perfection.

'Will you stay here for a long time?' I asked. At my sudden utterance some saliva flew from my mouth as an evil omen.

'Does it disturb you? If it disturbs you or perhaps keeps you from going up, I will go away at once, but otherwise I should still like to remain, because I'm tired.'

But finally he had every right to be satisfied too, and to become continually more satisfied the better I knew him. For he continually knew me even better, apparently, and could certainly stick me, with all my perceptions, in his pocket. For how otherwise could it be explained that I still remained on the street as though no house but rather a fire were before me. When one is invited into society, one simply steps into the house, climbs the stairs, and scarcely notices it, so engrossed is one in thought. Only so does one act correctly towards oneself and towards society.[9]

20 February. Mella Mars in the Cabaret Lucerna. A witty trage-dienne who, so to speak, appears on a stage turned wrong side out in the way tragediennes sometimes show themselves behind the scenes. When she makes her appearance she has a tired, indeed even flat, empty, old face, which constitutes for all famous actors a natural be-ginning. She speaks very sharply, her movements are sharp too, begin-ning with the thumb bent backwards, which instead of bone seems to be made of stiff fibre. Unusual changeability of her nose through the shifting highlights and hollows of the playing muscles around it. Despite the eternal flashing of her movements and words she makes her points delicately.

Small cities also have small places to stroll about in.

The young, clean, well-dressed youths near me on the promenade reminded me of my youth and therefore made an unappetizing im-pression on me.

Kleist's early letters, twenty-two years old. Gives up soldiering. They ask him at home: Well, how are you going to earn a living, for that was something they considered a matter of course. You have a choice of jurisprudence or political economy. But then do you have connexions at court? 'I denied it at first in some embarrassment, but then declared so much the more proudly that I, even if I had con-nexions, should be ashamed, with my present ideas, to count on them. They smiled, I felt that I had been too hasty. One must be wary of expressing such truths.'

21 February. My life here is just as if I were quite certain of a second life, in the same way, for example, I got over the pain of my unsuccessful visit to Paris with the thought that I would try to go there again very soon. With this, the sight of the sharply divided light and shadows on the pavement of the street.[10]

For the length of a moment I felt myself clad in steel.
How far from me are – for example – my arm muscles.

Marc Henry – Delvard. The tragic feeling bred in the audience by the empty hall increases the effect of the serious songs, detracts from that of the merry ones. Henry does the prologue, while Delvard, behind a curtain that she doesn't know is translucent, fixes her hair. At poorly attended performances, W., the producer, seems to wear his Assyrian beard – which is otherwise deep black – streaked with grey. Good to have oneself blown upon by such a temperament, it lasts for twenty-four hours, no, not so long. Much display of costumes, Breton costumes, the undermost petticoat is the longest, so that one can count the wealth from a distance – Because they want to save an accompanist, Delvard does the accompaniment first, in a very low-cut green dress, and freezes – Parisian street cries. Newsboys are omitted – Someone speaks to me; before I draw a breath I have been dismissed – Delvard is ridiculous, she has the smile of an old maid, an old maid of the German cabaret. With a red shawl that she fetches from behind the curtain, she plays revolution. Poems by Dauthendey in the same tough, unbreakable voice. She was charming only at the start, when she sat in a feminine way at the piano. At the song 'À Batignolles' I felt Paris in my throat. Batignolles is supposed to live on its annuities, even its Apaches. Bruant wrote a song for every section of the city.

THE URBAN WORLD

Oscar M., an older student – if one looked at him closely one was frightened by his eyes – stopped short in the middle of a snowstorm on an empty square one winter afternoon, in his winter clothes with his winter coat, over it a shawl around his neck and a fur cap on his head. His eyes blinked reflectively. He was so lost in thought that once he took off his cap and stroked his face with its curly fur. Finally he seemed to have come to a conclusion and turned with a dancing movement on to his homeward path.

When he opened the door to his parental living-room he saw his father, a smooth-shaven man with a heavy, fleshy face, seated at an empty table facing the door.

'At last,' said the latter, when Oscar had barely set foot in the room. 'Please stay by the door, I am so furious with you that I don't know what I might do.'

'But father,' said Oscar, and became aware only when he spoke how he had been running.

'Silence,' shouted the father and stood up, blocking a window. 'Silence, I say. And keep your "buts" to yourself, do you understand?' At the same time he took the table in both hands and carried it a step nearer to Oscar. 'I simply won't put up with your good-for-nothing existence any longer. I'm an old man. I hoped you would be the comfort of my old age, instead you are worse than all my illnesses. Shame on such a son, who through laziness, extravagance, wickedness, and – why shouldn't I say so to your face – stupidity, drives his old father to his grave!' Here the father fell silent, but moved his face as though he were still speaking.

'Dear Father,' said Oscar, and cautiously approached the table, 'calm yourself, everything will be all right. Today I have had an idea that will make an industrious person out of me, beyond all your expectations.'

'How is that?' the father asked, and gazed towards a corner of the room.

'Just trust me, I'll explain everything to you at supper. Inwardly I was always a good son, but the fact that I could not show it outwardly embittered me so, that I preferred to vex you if I couldn't make you happy. But now let me go for another short walk so that my thoughts may unfold more clearly.'

The father, who, becoming attentive at first, had sat down on the edge of the table, stood up. 'I do not believe that what you just said makes much sense, I consider it only idle talk. But after all you are my son. Come back early, we will have supper at home and you can tell me all about this matter then.'

'This small confidence is enough for me, I am grateful to you from my heart for it. But isn't it evident in my very appearance that I am completely occupied with a serious matter?'

'At the moment, no, I can't see a thing,' said the father. 'But that could be my fault too, for I have got out of the habit of looking at you at all.' With this, as was his custom, he called attention to the passage of time by regularly tapping on the surface of the table. 'The chief thing, however, is that I no longer have any confidence at all in you, Oscar. If I sometimes yell at you – when you came in I really did yell at you, didn't I? – then I do it not in the hope that it will improve you, I do it only for the sake of your poor, good mother who perhaps doesn't yet feel any immediate sorrow on your account, but is already slowly going to pieces under the strain of keep off such sorrow, for she thinks she can help you in some way by this. But after all, these are really things which you know very well, and out of consideration for myself alone I should not have mentioned them again if you had not provoked me into it by your promises.'

During these last words the maid entered to look after the fire in the stove. She had barely left the room when Oscar cried out, 'But Father! I would never have expected that. If in the past I had had only one little idea, an idea for my dissertation, let's say, which has been lying in my trunk now for ten years and needs ideas like salt, then it is possible, even if not probable, that, as happened today, I would have come running from my walk and said: "Father, by good fortune I have such-and-such an idea." If with your venerable voice you had then thrown into my face the reproaches you did, my idea would simply have been blown away and I should have had to march off at once with some sort of apology or without one. Now just the contrary! Everything you say against me helps my ideas, they do not stop, becoming stronger, they fill my head. I'll go, because only when I am alone can I bring them into order.' He gulped his breath in the warm room.

'It may be only a piece of rascality that you have in your head,' said the father with his eyes opened wide in surprise. 'In that case I am ready to believe that it has got hold of you. But if something good has lost its way into you, it will make its escape overnight. I know you.'

Oscar turned his head as though someone had him by the throat. 'Leave me alone now. You are worrying me more than is necessary. The bare possibility that you can correctly predict my end should really not induce you to disturb me in my reflections. Perhaps my past gives you the right to do so, but you should not make use of it.'

'There you see best how great your uncertainty must be when it forces you to speak to me so.'

'Nothing forces me,' said Oscar, and his neck twitched. He also stepped up very close to the table so that one could no longer tell to whom it belonged. 'What I said, I said with respect and even out of love for you, as you will see later, too, for consideration for you and Mama plays the greatest part in my decisions.'

'Then I must thank you right now,' the father said, 'as it is indeed very improbable that your mother and I will still be capable of it when the time comes.'

'Please, Father, just let tomorrow sleep on as it deserves. If you awaken it before its time, then you will have a sleepy day. But that your son must say this to you! Besides, I really didn't intend to convince you yet, but only to break the news to you. And in that, at least, as you yourself must admit, I have succeeded.'

'Now, Oscar, there is only one thing more that really makes me wonder: why haven't you been coming to me often with something like this business of today. It corresponds so well with your character up to now. No, really, I am being serious.'

'Yes, wouldn't you have thrashed me, then, instead of listening to me? I ran home, God knows, in a hurry to give you a little pleasure. But I can't tell you a thing as long as my plan is not complete. Then why do you punish me for my good intentions and demand explanations from me that at this time might still injure the execution of my plan?'

'Keep quiet, I don't want to know a thing. But I have to answer you very quickly because you are retreating towards the door and apparently have something very urgent in hand: You have calmed my first anger with your trick, but now I am even sadder in spirit than before and therefore I beg you – if you insist, I can even fold my hands – i t least say nothing to your mother of your ideas. Be satisfied with me.'

'This can't be my father speaking to me,' cried Oscar, who already had his arm on the door latch. 'Something has happened to you since noon, or I'm meeting a stranger now for the first time in my father's room. My real father' – Oscar was silent for a moment with his mouth open – 'he would certainly have had to embrace me, he would have called my mother. What is wrong with you, Father?'

'Then you ought to have supper with your real father, I think. It would be more fun.'

'He will come, you can be sure of that. In the end he can't stay away. And my mother must be there. And Franz, whom I am now going to fetch. All.' Thereupon Oscar pressed his shoulder against the door – it opened easily – as though he were trying to break it down.

Having arrived in Franz's home, he bowed to the little landlady and said, 'The Herr Engineer is asleep, I know, it doesn't matter.' And without bothering about the woman, who because she was displeased by the visit walked aimlessly up and down in the ante-room, he opened the glass door – it quivered under his hand as though it had been touched in a sensitive spot – and called, paying no heed to the interior of the room into which he could scarcely see, 'Franz, get up. I need your expert advice. But I can't stand it here in the room, we must go for a little walk, you must also have supper with us. Quick, then.'

'Gladly,' said the engineer from his leather sofa, 'but which first? Get up, have supper, go for a walk, give advice? And some of it I probably haven't caught.'

'Most important, Franz, don't joke. That's the most important thing, I forgot that.'

'I'll do you that favour at once. But to get up! I would rather have supper for you twice than get up once.'

'Get up now! No arguments.' Oscar grabbed the weak man by the front of his coat and sat him up.

'You're mad, you know. With all due respect. Have I ever pulled you off a sofa like that?' He wiped his closed eyes with his two little fingers.

'But Franz,' said Oscar with a grimace. 'Get dressed now. After all, I'm not a fool, to have waked you without a reason.'

'Just as I wasn't sleeping without a reason, either. Yesterday I worked the night shift, after that I'm done out of my afternoon nap, also because of you.'

'Why?'

'Oh, well, it annoys me how little consideration you have for me. It isn't the first time. Naturally, you are a free student and can do whatever you want. Not everyone is so fortunate. So you really must have some consideration, damn it! Of course, I'm your friend, but they haven't taken my profession away yet because of that.' This he indicated by shaking his hands up and down, palm to palm.

'But to judge by your present jabbering don't I have to believe that you've had more than your fill of sleep?' said Oscar, who had drawn himself up against a bedpost whence he looked at the engineer as though he now had somewhat more time than before.

'Well, what is it you really want of me? Or rather, why did you wake me?' the engineer asked, and rubbed his neck hard under his goatee in that more intimate relationship which one has to one's body after sleep.

'What I want of you,' said Oscar softly, and gave the bed a kick with the heel of his foot. 'Very little. I already told you what I want while I was still in the ante-room: that you get dressed.'

'If you want to point out by that, Oscar, that your news interests me very little, then you are quite right.'

'All the better. Then the interest my news will kindle in you will burn entirely on its own account, without our friendship adding to it. The information will be clearer too. I need clear information, keep that in mind. But if you are perhaps looking for your collar and tie, they are lying there on the chair.'

'Thanks,' said the engineer, and started to fasten his collar and tie. 'A person can really depend on you after all.'

26 March. Theosophical lectures by Dr Rudolf Steiner, Berlin. Rhetorical effect: Comfortable discussion of the objections of opponents, the listener is astonished at this strong opposition, further development and praise of these objections, the listener becomes worried, complete immersion in these objections as though they were nothing else, the listener now considers any refutation as completely impossible and is more than satisfied with a cursory description of the possibility of a defence.

Continual looking at the palm of the extended hand. – Omission of the period. In general, the spoken sentence starts off from the speaker with its initial capital letter, curves in its course, as far as it can, out to the audience, and returns with the period to the speaker. But if the period is omitted then the sentence, no longer held in check, falls upon the listener immediately with full force.

Before that, lecture by Loos and Kraus.

In Western European stories, as soon as they even begin to include any groups of Jews, we are now almost used immediately to hunting for and finding under or over the plot the solution to the Jewish question too. In the *Jüdinnen,* however, no such solution is indicated, indeed not even conjectured, for just those characters who busy themselves with such questions stand farthest from the centre of the story at a point where events are already revolving more rapidly, so that we can, to be sure, still observe them closely, but no longer have an opportunity to get from them a calm report of their efforts. Offhand, we recognize in this a fault in the story, and feel ourselves all the more entitled to such a criticism because today, since Zionism came into being, the possibilities for a solution stand so clearly marshalled about the Jewish problem that the writer would have had to take only a few last steps in order to find the possibility of a solution suitable to his story.

This fault, however, has still another origin. The *Jüdinnen* lacks non-Jewish observers, the respectable contrasting persons who in other stories draw out the Jewishness so that it advances towards them in amazement, doubt, envy, fear, and finally, finally is transformed into self-confidence, but in any event can draw itself up to its full height only before them. That is just what we demand, no other principle for the organization of this Jewish material seems justified to us. Nor do we appeal to this feeling in this case alone, it is universal in at least one respect. In the same way, too, the convulsive starting up of a lizard under our feet on a footpath in Italy delights us greatly, again and again we are moved to bow down, but if we see them at a dealer's by hundreds crawling over one another in confusion in the large bottles in which otherwise pickles are usually packed, then we don't know what to do.

Both faults unite into a third. The *Jüdinnen* can do without that most prominent youth who usually, within his story, attracts the best to himself and leads it nicely along a radius to the borders of the Jewish circle. It is just this that we will not accept, that the story can do without this youth, here we sense a fault rather than see it.

28 March. P. Karlin the artist, his wife, two large, wide upper front teeth that gave a tapering shape to the large, rather flat face, Frau Hofrat B., mother of the composer, in whom old age so brings out her heavy skeleton that she looks like a man, at least when she is seated.

Dr Steiner is so very much taken up with his absent disciples. At the lecture the dead press so about him. Hunger for knowledge? But do they really need it? Apparently, though – Sleeps two hours. Ever since someone once cut off his electric light he has always had a candle with him – He stood very close to Christ – He produced his play in Munich (you can study it all year there and won't understand it), he designed the costumes, composed the music – He instructed a chemist. Löwy Simon, soap dealer on Quai Moncey, Paris, got the best business advice from him. He translated his works into French. The wife of the Hofrat therefore has in her notebook, 'How Does One Achieve Knowledge of the Higher Worlds?'[11] At S. Löwy's in Paris.'

In the Vienna lodge there is a theosophist, sixty-five years old, strong as a giant, a great drinker formerly, and a blockhead, who constantly believes and constantly has doubts. It is supposed to have been very funny when once, during a congress in Budapest, at a dinner on the Blocksberg one moonlit evening, Dr Steiner unexpectedly joined the company; in fear he hid behind a beer barrel with his beer mug (although Dr Steiner would not have been angered by it).

He is, perhaps, not the greatest contemporary psychic scholar, but he alone has been assigned the task of uniting theosophy and science. And that is why he knows everything too. Once a botanist came to his native village, a great master of the occult. He enlightened him.

That I would look up Dr Steiner was interpreted to me by the lady as the beginning of recollection. The lady's doctor, when the first signs of influenza appeared in her, asked Dr Steiner for a remedy, prescribed this for the lady, and restored her to health with it immediately. A French woman said good-bye to him with '*Au revoir*'. Behind her back he shook his head. In two months she died. A similar case in Munich. A Munich doctor cures people with colours decided upon by Dr Steiner. He also sends invalids to the picture gallery with instructions to concentrate for half an hour or longer before a certain painting.

End of the Atlantic world, lemuroid destruction, and now through egoism. We live in a period of decision. The efforts of Dr Steiner will succeed if only the Ahrimanian forces do not get the upper hand.

He eats two litres of emulsion of almonds and fruits that grow in the air.

He communicates with his absent disciples by means of thought-forms which he transmits to them without bothering further about them after they are generated. But they soon wear out and he must replace them.

Mrs F.: 'I have a poor memory.' Dr St.: 'Eat no eggs.'

MY VISIT TO DR STEINER

A woman is already waiting (upstairs on the third floor of the Victoria Hotel on Jungmannstrasse), but urges me to go in before her. We wait. The secretary arrives and gives us hope. I catch a glimpse of him down the hall. Immediately thereafter he comes toward us with arms half spread. The woman explains that I was there first. So I walk behind him as he leads me into his room. His black Prince Albert which on those evenings when he lectures looks polished (not polished but just shining because of its clean blackness) is now in the light of day (3 p.m.) dusty and even spotted, especially on the back and elbows.

In his room I try to show my humility, which I cannot feel, by seeking out a ridiculous place for my hat, I lay it down on a small wooden stand for lacing boots. Table in the middle, I sit facing the window, he on the left side of the table. On the table papers with a few drawings which recall those of the lectures dealing with occult physiology. An issue of the *Annalen für Naturphilosophie* topped a small pile of the books which seemed to be lying about in other places as well. However, you cannot look around because he keeps trying to hold you with his glance. But if for a moment he does not, then you must watch for the return of his glance. He begins with a few disconnected sentences. So you are Dr Kafka? Have you been interested in theosophy long?

But I push on with my prepared address: I feel that a great part of my being is striving toward theosophy, but at the same time I have the greatest fear of it. That is to say, I am afraid it will result in a new confusion which would be very bad for me, because even my present unhappiness consists only of confusion. This confusion is as follows: My happiness, my abilities, and every possibility of being useful in any way have always been in the literary field. And here I have, to be sure, experienced states (not many) which in my opinion correspond very closely to the clairvoyant states described by you, Herr Doktor, in which I completely dwelt in every idea, but also filled every idea, and in which I not only felt myself at my boundary, but at the boundary of the human in general. Only the calm of enthusiasm, which is probably characteristic of the clairvoyant, was still lacking in those states, even if not completely. I conclude this from the fact that I did not write the best of my works in those states. I cannot now devote myself completely to this literary field, as would be necessary and indeed for various reasons. Aside from my family relationships, I could not live by literature if only, to begin with, because of the slow maturing of my work and its special character; besides, I am prevented also by my health and my character from devoting myself to what is, in the most favourable case, an uncertain life. I have therefore become an official in a social insurance agency. Now these two professions can never be reconciled with one another and admit a common fortune. The smallest good fortune in one becomes a great misfortune in the other. If I have written something good one evening, I am afire the next day in the office and can bring nothing to completion. This back and forth continually becomes worse. Outwardly, I fulfil my duties satisfactorily in the office, not my inner duties, however, and every unfulfilled inner duty becomes a misfortune that never leaves. And to these two never-to-be-reconciled endeavours shall I now add theosophy as a third? Will it not disturb both the others and itself be disturbed by both? Will I, at present already so unhappy a person, be able to carry the three to completion? This is what I have come to ask you, Herr Doktor, for I have a presentiment that if you consider me capable of this, then I can really take it upon myself.

He listened very attentively without apparently looking at me at all, entirely devoted to my words. He nodded from time to time, which he seems to consider an aid to strict concentration. At first a quiet head cold disturbed him, his nose ran, he kept working his handkerchief deep into his nose, one finger at each nostril.

Since in contemporary Western European stories about Jews the reader has become used immediately to hunting for and finding under or over the story the solution to the Jewish question too, and since in the *Jüdinnen* no such solution is indicated or even conjectured, therefore it is possible that offhand the reader will recognize in this a fault of the *Jüdinnen*, and will look on only unwillingly if Jews go about in the light of day without political encouragement from the past or the future. He must tell himself in regard to this that, especially since the rise of Zionism, the possibilities for a solution stand marshalled so clearly about the Jewish problem that in the end all the writer has to do is turn his body in order to find a definite solution, suitable to the part of the problem under discussion.

27 May. Today is your birthday, but I'm not even sending you the usual book, for it would be only pretence; at bottom I am after all not even in a position to give you a book. I am writing only because it is so necessary for me today to be near you for a moment, even though it be only by means of this card, and I have begun with the complaint only so that you may recognize me at once.

15 August. The time which has just gone by and in which I haven't written a word has been so important for me because I have stopped being ashamed of my body in the swimming pools in Prague, Königs-saal, and Czernoschitz. How late I make up for my education now, at the age of twenty-eight, a delayed start they would call it at the race track. And the harm of such a misfortune consists, perhaps, not in the fact that one does not win; this is indeed only the still visible, clear, healthy kernel of the misfortune, progressively dissolving and losing its boundaries, that drives one into the interior of the circle, when after all the circle should be run around. Aside from that I have also observed a great many other things in myself during this period which was to some extent also happy, and will try to write it down in the next few days.

20 August. I have the unhappy belief that I haven't the time for the least bit of good work, for I really don't have time for a story, time to expand myself in every direction in the world, as I should have to do. But then I once more believe that my trip will turn out better, that I shall comprehend better if I am relaxed by a little writing, and so try it again.

From his appearance I had a suspicion of the exertions which he had taken upon himself for my sake and which now, perhaps only because he was tired, gave him this certainty. A little more effort might have sufficed and the deception would have succeeded, it succeeded per-haps even now. Did I defend myself, then? Indeed, I stood stiff-necked here in front of the house, but – just as stiff-necked – I hesitated to go up. Was I waiting until the guests came to fetch me with a song? [12]

I have been reading about Dickens. Is it so difficult and can an out-sider understand that you experience a story within yourself from its beginning, from the distant point up to the approaching locomotives of steel, coal, and steam, and you don't abandon it even now, but want to be pursued by it and have time for it, therefore are pursued by it and of your own volition run before it wherever it may thrust and wherever you may lure it.

I can't understand it and can't believe it. I live only here and there in a small word in whose vowel ('thrust' above, for instance) I lose my useless head for a moment. The first and last letters are the beginning and end of my fishlike emotion.

24 August. Sitting with acquaintances at a coffee-house table in the open air and looking at a woman at the next table who has just arrived, breathing heavily beneath her heavy breasts, and who, with a heated, brownish, shining face, sits down. She leans her head back, a heavy down becomes visible, she turns her eyes up, almost in the way in which she perhaps sometimes looks at her husband, who is now reading an illustrated paper beside her. If one could only persuade her that one may read at most a newspaper but never a magazine beside one's wife in a coffee-house. After a moment she becomes aware of the fullness of her body and moves back from the table a little.

26 August. Tomorrow I am supposed to leave for Italy. Father has been unable to fall asleep these evenings because of excitement, since he has been completely caught up in his worries about the business and in his illness, which they have aggravated. A wet cloth on his heart, vomiting, suffocation, walking back and forth to the accompaniment of sighs. My mother in her anxiety finds new solace. He was always after all so energetic, he got over everything, and now . . . I say that all the misery over the business could after all last only another three months, then everything will have to be all right. He walks up and down, sigh-ing and shaking his head. It is clear that from his point of view his

worries will not be taken from his shoulders and will not even be made lighter by us, but even from our point of view they will not, even in our best intentions there is something of the sad conviction that he must provide for his family – By his frequent yawning or his poking into his nose (on the whole not disgusting) Father engenders a slight reassurance as to his condition, which scarcely enters his consciousness, despite the fact that when he is well he usually does not do this. Ottla confirmed this for me – Poor Mother will go to the landlord tomorrow to beg.[13]

It had already become a custom for the four friends, Robert, Samuel, Max, and Franz, to spend their short holidays every summer or autumn on a trip together. During the rest of the year their friendship consisted mostly of the fact that they all four liked to come together one evening every week, usually at Samuel's, who, as the most well-to-do, had a rather large room, to tell each other various things and to accompany it by drinking a moderate amount of beer. They were never finished with the telling of things when they separated at midnight; since Robert was secretary of an association, Samuel an employee in a business office, Max a Civil Service official, and Franz an employee in a bank, almost everything that anyone had experienced in his work during the week was not only unknown to the other three and had to be told to them quickly, but it was also incomprehensible without rather lengthy explanations. But more than anything else the consequence of the difference of these professions was that each was compelled to describe his profession to the others again and again, since the descriptions (they were all only weak people, after all) were not thoroughly understood, and for that very reason and also out of friendship were demanded again and again.

Talk about women, on the other hand, was seldom engaged in, for even if Samuel for his part would have found it to his liking he was still careful not to demand that the conversation adapt itself to his requirements, in this regard the old maid who brought up the beer often appeared to him as an admonition. But they laughed so much during these evenings that Max said on the way home that this eternal laughing is really to be regretted, because of it one forgets all the serious concerns of which everyone, after all, really has enough. While one laughs one thinks there is still time enough for seriousness. That isn't correct, however, for seriousness naturally makes greater demands on a person, and after all it is clear that one is also able to satisfy greater demands in the society of friends than alone. One should laugh in the office because there is nothing better to be accomplished there. This opinion was aimed at Robert, who worked hard in the art association he was putting new life into and at the same time observed in the old the most comical things with which he entertained his friends.

As soon as he began, the friends left their places, stood around him or sat down on the table, and laughed so self-obviously, especially Max and Franz, that Samuel carried all the glasses over to a side-table. If they tired of talking Max sat down at the piano with suddenly renewed strength and played, while Robert and Samuel sat beside him on the bench; Franz, on the other hand, who understood nothing of music, stood alone at the table and looked through Samuel's collection of picture postcards or read the paper. When the evenings became warmer and the window could be left open, all four would perhaps come to the window and with their hands behind their backs look down into the street without letting themselves be diverted from their conversation by the light traffic outside Now and then one returned to the table to take a swallow of beer, or pointed to the curls of two girls who sat downstairs in front of their wine-shop, or to the moon that quietly surprised them, until finally Franz said it was getting cool, they ought to close the window.

In summer they sometimes met in a public garden, sat at a table off to one side where it was darker, drank to one another, and, their heads together in conversation, hardly noticed the distant brass band. Arm in arm and in step, they then walked home through the park. The two on the outside twirled their canes or struck at the shrubs, Robert called on them to sing, but then he sang alone, well enough for four, the other one in the middle felt himself made especially comfortable by this.

On one such evening, Franz, drawing his two neighbours more closely to him, said it was really so beautiful to be together that he couldn't understand why they met only once a week when they could certainly arrange without difficulty to see each other, if not often, then at least twice a week. They all were in favour of it, even the fourth one on the end, who had heard Franz's soft words only indistinctly. A pleasure of this sort would certainly be worth the slight effort which it would now and then cost one of them. It seemed to Franz as though he had a hollow voice as punishment for speaking uninvited for all of them. But he did not stop. And if sometimes one of them couldn't come, that's his loss and he can be consoled for it the next time, but do the others then have to give each other up, aren't three enough for each other, even two, if it comes to that? Naturally, naturally, they all said. Samuel disengaged himself from the end of the line and stood close in front of the three others, because in this way they were closer to each other. But then it didn't seem so, and he preferred to link up with the others again.

Robert made a proposal. 'Let's meet every week and study Italian. We are determined to learn Italian, last year already we saw in the little part of Italy where we were that our Italian was only sufficient to ask the way when we got lost, remember, among the vineyard walls of the Campagna. And even then it managed to do only thanks to the greatest efforts on the part of those we asked. We'll have to study it if we want to go to Italy again this year. We simply have to. And so isn't it best to study together?'

'No,' said Max, 'we shall learn nothing together. I am as certain of that as you, Samuel, are certain that we ought to study together.'

'Am I!' Samuel said. 'We shall certainly learn very well together, I always regret that we weren't together even at school. Do you realize that we've known each other only two years?' He bent forward to look at all three. They had slowed down their steps and let go their arms.

'But we haven't studied anything together yet,' said Franz. 'I like it very well that way, too. I don't want to learn a thing. But if we have to learn Italian, then it is better for each one to learn it by himself.'

'I don't understand that,' Samuel said. 'First you want us to meet every week, then you don't want it.'

'Come now,' Max said. 'Franz and I, after all, just don't want our being together to be disturbed by studying, or our studying by being together, nothing else.'

'Yes,' said Franz.

'And indeed there isn't much time,' said Max. 'It is June now and in September we want to leave.'

54

'That's the very reason why I want us to study together,' Robert said, and stared in surprise at the two who opposed him. His neck became especially flexible when someone contradicted him.[14]

One thinks that one describes him correctly, but it is only approximate and is corrected by the diary.

It probably lies in the essence of friendship and follows it like a shadow – one will welcome it, the second regret it, the third not notice it at all –

26 September. The artist Kubin recommends Regulin as a laxative, a powdered seaweed that swells up in the bowels, shakes them up, is thus effective mechanically in contrast to the unhealthy chemical effect of other laxatives which just tear through the excrement and leave it hanging on the walls of the bowels.

He met Hamsun at Langen. He (Hamsun) grins mockingly for no reason. During the conversation, without interrupting it, he put one foot on his neck, took a large pair of paper-shears from the table, and trimmed the frayed edges of his trousers. Shabbily dressed, with one or so rather expensive details, his tie, for example.

Stories about an artist's pension in Munich where painters and veterinaries lived (the latters' school was in the neighbourhood) and where they acted in such a debauched way that the windows of the house across the way, from which a good view could be had, were rented out. In order to satisfy these spectators, one of the residents in the pension would sometimes jump up on the window sill in the posture of a monkey and spoon his soup out of the pot.

A manufacturer of fraudulent antiques who got the worn effect by means of buckshot and who said of a table: 'Now we must drink coffee on it three more times, then it can be shipped off to the Innsbruck Museum.'

Kubin himself: very strong, but somewhat monotonous facial expression, he describes the most varied things with the same movement of muscles. Looks different in age, size, and strength according to whether he is sitting, standing, wearing just a suit, or an overcoat.

27 September. Yesterday on the Wenzelsplatz met two girls, kept

my eye too long on one while it was just the other, as it proved too late, who wore a plain, soft, brown, wrinkled, ample coat, open a little in front, had a delicate throat and delicate nose, her hair was beautiful in a way already forgotten – Old man with loosely hanging trousers on the Belvedere. He whistles; when I look at him he stops; if I look away he begins again; finally he whistles even when I look at him – The beautiful large button, beautifully set low on the sleeve of a girl's dress. The dress worn beautifully too, hovering over American boots. How seldom I succeed in creating something beautiful, and this unnoticed button and its ignorant seamstress succeeded – The woman talking on the way to the Belvedere, whose lively eyes, independent of the words of the moment, contentedly surveyed her story to its end – The powerful half-turn of the neck of a strong girl.

29 September. Goethe's diaries. A person who keeps none is in a false position in the face of a diary. When for example he reads in Goethe's diaries: '1/11/1797. All day at home busy with various affairs,' then it seems to him that he himself had never done so little in one day.

Goethe's observations on his travels different from today's because made from a mail-coach, and with the slow changes of the region, develop more simply and can be followed much more easily even by one who does not know those parts of the country. A calm, so-to-speak pastoral form of thinking sets in. Since the country offers itself unscathed in its indigenous character to the passengers in a wagon, and since highways too divide the country much more naturally than the railway lines to which they perhaps stand in the same relationship as do rivers to canals, so too the observer need do no violence to the landscape and he can see systematically without great effort. Therefore there are few observations of the moment, mostly only indoors, where certain people suddenly and hugely bubble up before one's eyes; for instance, Austrian officers in Heidelberg, on the other hand the passage about the men in Wiesenheim is closer to the landscape, 'They wear blue coats and white vests ornamented with woven flowers' (quoted from memory). Much written down about the falls of the Rhine at Schaffhausen, in the middle in larger letters: 'Excited ideas.'

Cabaret Lucerna. Lucie König showing photographs with old hairstyles. Threadbare face. Sometimes, with her turned-up nose, with her arm held aloft and a turn of all her fingers, she succeeds in something. A milksop face – Longen[15] (the painter Pittermann), mimic jokes. A production that is obviously without joy and yet cannot be considered so, for if it were, then it couldn't be performed every evening, particularly since it was so unhappy a thing even at the moment it was created that no satisfactory pattern has resulted which would dispense with frequent appearances of the whole person. Pretty jump of a clown over a chair into the emptiness of the wings. The whole thing reminds one of a private production where, because of social necessity, one vigorously applauds a wretched, insignificant performance in order to get something smooth and rounded from the minus of the production by means of the plus of the applause.

The singer Vaschata. So bad that one loses oneself in his appearance. But because he is a powerful person he holds the attention of the audience with an animal force of which certainly I am consciously aware.

Grünbaum is effective with what is apparently only the seeming inconsolability of his existence.

Odys, dancer. Stiff hips. Real fleshlessness. Red knees only suit the 'Moods of Spring' dance.

30 September. The girl in the adjoining room yesterday. I lay on the sofa and, on the point of dozing off, heard her voice. She seemed to me in my mind to be overdressed not only because of the clothes she wore, but also because of the entire room; only her shapely, naked, round, strong, dark shoulders which I had seen in the bath prevailed against her clothes. For a moment she seemed to me to be steaming and to be filling the whole room with her vapours. Then she stood up in her ash-grey-coloured bodice that stood off from her body so far at the bottom that one could sit down on it and after a fashion ride along.

More on Kubin: The habit always of repeating in an approving tone someone else's last words, even if it appears from his own words added on that he by no means agrees with the other person. Provoking – When you listen to his many stories it is easy to forget his importance.

Suddenly you are reminded of this and become frightened. Someone said that a place we wanted to go to was dangerous; he said he wouldn't go there, then; I asked him whether he was afraid to, and he answered (moreover, his arm was passed through mine): 'Naturally, I am young and have a lot in front of me yet.'

All evening he spoke often and – in my opinion – entirely seriously about my constipation and his. Towards midnight, however, when I let my hand hang over the edge of the table, he saw part of my arm and cried: 'But you are really sick.' Treated me from then on even more indulgently and later also kept off the others who wanted to talk me into going to the brothel with them. When we had already said good-bye he called to me again from the distance: 'Regulin!'

Tucholsky and Szafranski. The aspirated Berlin dialect in which the voice makes use of intervals consisting of '*nich*'. The former, an entirely consistent person of twenty-one. From the controlled and powerful swing of his walking-stick that gives a youthful lift to his shoulders to the deliberate delight in and contempt for his own literary works. Wants to be a defence lawyer, sees only a few obstacles and at the same time how they may be overcome: his clear voice that after the manly sound of the first half-hour of talk pretends to become revealingly girlish – doubt of his own capacity to pose, which, however, he hopes to get with more experience of the world – fear, finally, of changing into a melancholic, as he has seen happen in older Berlin Jews of his type, in any event for the time being he sees no sign of this. He will marry soon.

Szafranski, a disciple of Bernhardt's, grimaces while he observes and draws in a way that resembles what is drawn. Reminds me that I too have a pronounced talent for metamorphosing myself, which no one notices. How often I must have imitated Max. Yesterday evening, on the way home, if I had observed myself from the outside I should have taken myself for Tucholsky. The alien being must be in me, then, as distinctly and invisibly as the hidden object in a picture-puzzle, where, too, one would never find anything if one did not know that it is there. When these metamorphoses take place, I should especially like to believe in a dimming of my own eyes.

1 October. The Altneu Synagogue yesterday. Kol Nidre.[16] Suppressed murmur of the stock market. In the entry, boxes with the inscription: 'Merciful gifts secretly left assuage the wrath of the bereft.' Churchly inside. Three pious, apparently Eastern Jews. In socks. Bowed over their prayer books, their prayer shawls drawn over their heads, become as small as they possibly can. Two are crying, moved only by the holy day. One of them may only have sore eyes, perhaps, to which he fleetingly applies his still-folded handkerchief, at once to lower his face to the text again. The words are not really, or chiefly, sung, but behind them arabesque-like melodies are heard that spin out the words as fine as hairs. The little boy without the slightest conception of it all and without any possibility of understanding, who, with the clamour in his ears, pushes himself among the thronging people and is pushed. The clerk (apparently) who shakes himself rapidly while he prays, which is to be understood only as an attempt at putting the strongest possible – even if possibly incomprehensible – emphasis on each word, by means of which the voice, which in any case could not attain a large, clear emphasis in the clamour, is spared. The family of a brothel owner. I was stirred immeasurably more deeply by Judaism in the Pinkas Synagogue.

The day before the day before yesterday. The one, a Jewish girl with a narrow face – better, that tapers down to a narrow chin, but is loosened by a broad, wavy hair-do. The three small doors that lead from the inside of the building into the salon. The guests as though in a police station on the stage, drinks on the table are scarcely touched.

Several girls here dressed like the marionettes for children's theatres that are sold in the Christmas market, i.e. with ruching and gold stuck on and loosely sewn so that one can rip them with one pull and they then fall apart in one's fingers. The landlady with the pale blonde hair drawn tight over doubtless disgusting pads, with the sharply slanting nose the direction of which stands in some sort of geometric relation to the sagging breasts and the stiffly held belly, complains of headaches which are caused by the fact that today, Saturday, there is so great an uproar and there is nothing in it.

More on Kubin: The story about Hamsun is suspect. One could tell such stories as one's own experiences by the thousand from his works.

More on Goethe: 'Excited ideas' are only the ideas which the Rhine Falls excite. One sees this from a letter to Schiller – The isolated momentary observation, 'Castanet rhythms of the children in wooden shoes,' made such an impression, is so universally accepted, that it is unthinkable that anyone, even if he had never read this remark, could feel this observation as an original idea.

2 October. Sleepless night. The third in a row. I fall asleep soundly, but after an hour I wake up, as though I had laid my head in the wrong hole. I am completely awake, have the feeling that I have not slept at all or only under a thin skin, have before me anew the labour of falling asleep and feel myself rejected by sleep. And for the rest of the night, until about five, thus it remains, so that indeed I sleep but at the same time vivid dreams keep me awake. I sleep alongside myself, so to speak, while I myself must struggle with dreams. About five the last trace of sleep is exhausted, I just dream, which is more exhausting than wakefulness. In short, I spend the whole night in that state in which a healthy person finds himself for a short time before really falling asleep. When I awaken, all the dreams are gathered about me, but I am careful not to reflect on them. Towards morning I sigh into the pillow, because for this night all hope is gone. I think of those nights at the end of which I was raised out of deep sleep and awoke as though I had been folded in a nut.

The horrible apparition last night of a blind child, apparently the daughter of my aunt in Leitmeritz who, however, has no daughter but only sons, one of whom once broke his leg. On the other hand there were resemblances between this child and Dr M.'s daughter who, as I have recently seen, is in the process of changing from a pretty child into a stout, stiffly dressed little girl. This blind or weak-sighted child had both eyes covered by a pair of glasses, the left, under a lens held at a certain distance from the eye, was milky-grey and bulbous, the other receded and was covered by a lens lying close against it. In order that this eyeglass might be set in place with optical correctness it was necessary, instead of the usual support going behind the ears, to make use of a lever, the head of which could be attached to no place but the cheek-bone, so that from this lens a little rod descended to the cheek, there disappeared into the pierced flesh and ended on the bone, while another small wire rod came out and went back over the ear.

I believe this sleeplessness comes only because I write. For no matter how little and how badly I write, I am still made sensitive by these minor shocks, feel, especially towards evening and even more in the morning, the approaching, the imminent possibility of great moments which would tear me open, which could make me capable of anything, and in the general uproar that is within me and which I have no time to command, find no rest. In the end this uproar is only a suppressed, restrained harmony, which, left free, would fill me completely, which could even widen me and yet still fill me. But now such a moment arouses only feeble hopes and does me harm, for my being does not have sufficient strength or the capacity to hold the present mixture, during the day the visible word helps me, during the night it cuts me to pieces unhindered. I always think in this connexion of Paris, where at the time of the siege and later, until the Commune, the population of the northern and eastern suburbs, up to that time strangers to the Parisians, for a period of months moved through the connecting streets into the centre of Paris, dawdling like the hands of a clock.

My consolation is – and with it I now go to bed – that I have not written for so long, that therefore this writing could find no right place within my present circumstances, that nevertheless, with a little fortitude, I'll succeed, at least temporarily.

I was so weak today that I even told my chief the story of the child. I remembered that the glasses in the dream derive from my mother, who in the evening sits next to me and, while playing cards, looks across at me not very pleasantly under her eyeglasses. Her glasses even have, which I do not remember having noticed before, the right lens nearer the eye than the left.

3 October. The same sort of night, but fell asleep with even more difficulty. While falling asleep a vertically moving pain in my head over the bridge of the nose, as though from a wrinkle too sharply pressed into my forehead. To make myself as heavy as possible, which I consider good for falling asleep, I had crossed my arms and laid my

hands on my shoulders, so that I lay there like a soldier with his pack. Again it was the power of my dreams, shining forth into wakefulness even before I fall asleep, which did not let me sleep. In the evening and the morning my consciousness of the creative abilities in me is more than I can encompass. I feel shaken to the core of my being and can get out of myself whatever I desire. Calling forth such powers, which are then not permitted to function, reminds me of my relationship with B. Here too there are effusions which are not released but must instead spend themselves in being repulsed, but here – this is the difference – it is a matter of more mysterious powers which are of an ultimate significance to me.

On the Josefsplatz a large touring car with a family sitting crowded together drove by me. In the wake of the car, with the smell of petrol, a breath of Paris blew across my face.

While dictating a rather long report to the district Chief of Police, towards the end, where a climax was intended, I got stuck and could do nothing but look at K., the typist, who, in her usual way, became especially lively, moved her chair about, coughed, tapped on the table and so called the attention of the whole room to my misfortune. The sought-for idea now has the additional value that it will make her be quiet, and the more valuable it becomes the more difficult it becomes to find it. Finally I have the word 'stigmatize' and the appropriate sentence, but still hold it all in my mouth with disgust and a sense of shame as though it were raw meat, cut out of me (such effort has it cost me). Finally I say it, but retain the great fear that everything within me is ready for a poetic work and such a work would be a heavenly enlightenment and a real coming-alive for me, while here, in the office, because of so wretched an official document, I must rob a body capable of such happiness of a piece of its flesh.

4 October. I feel restless and vicious. Yesterday, before falling asleep, I had a flickering, cool little flame up in the left side of my head. The tensions over my left eye has already settled down and made itself at home. When I think about it, it seems to me that I couldn't hold out in the office even if they told me that in one month I'd be free. And most of the time in the office I do what I am supposed

to, am quite calm when I can be sure that my boss is satisfied, and do not feel that my condition is dreadful. By the way, last night I purposely made myself dull, went for a walk, read Dickens, then felt a little better and had lost the strength for sorrow. I still regarded the sorrow as justified but it seemed to have withdrawn somewhat, I looked at it from a distance and therefore hoped for better sleep. It was a little deeper too, but not enough, and often interrupted. I told myself, as consolation, that I had indeed once more repressed the great agitation in me but that I did not wish to succumb at once, as I had always done in the past after such occasions; rather, I wished to remain entirely conscious of the final flutterings of that agitation, which I had never done before. Perhaps in this way I would find hidden steadfastness in myself.

Towards evening, in the dark of my room on the sofa. Why does one take a rather long time to recognize a colour, but then, after the understanding has reached the decisive turning-point, quickly become all the more convinced of the colour. If the light from the ante-room and the kitchen shines on the glass door simultaneously from the outside, then greenish – or rather, not to detract from the definiteness of the impression – green light pours down almost the length of the panes. If the light in the ante-room is turned off and only the kitchen light remains, then the pane nearer the kitchen becomes deep blue, the other whitish blue, so whitish that all the drawings on the frosted glass (stylized poppies, tendrils, various rectangles, and leaves) dissolve.

The lights and shadows thrown on the walls and the ceiling by the electric lights in the street and the bridge down below are distorted, partly spoiled, overlapping, and hard to follow. When they installed the electric arc-lamps down below and when they furnished this room, there was simply no housewifely consideration given to how my room would look from the sofa at this hour without any lights of its own.

The glare thrown on the ceiling by the tram passing down below moves whitely, wraithlike and with mechanical pauses along the one wall and ceiling, broken in the corner. The globe stands on the linen chest in the first, fresh, full reflection of the street lights, a greenishly clean light on top, has a highlight on its roundness and gives the impression that the glare is really too strong for it, although the light

passes over its smoothness and goes off leaving it rather brownish like
a leather apple. The light from the ante-room throws a large patch of
glare on the wall over the bed. This patch is bounded by a curved
line beginning at the head of the bed, gives the illusion that the bed
is pressed down, widens the dark bedposts, raises the ceiling over the
bed.

5 October. Restlessness again for the first time in several days, even
now that I am writing. Rage at my sister who comes into the room and
sits down at the table with a book. Waiting for the next trifling occasion
to let this rage explode. Finally she takes a visiting card from the tray
and fiddles around with it between her teeth. With departing rage, of
which only a stinging vapour remains behind in my head, and dawning
relief and confidence, I begin to work.

Last night Café Savoy. Yiddish troupe.[17] Mrs K., 'male impersonator'. In a caftan, short black trousers, white stockings, from the
black shirt a thin white woollen waistcoat emerges that is held in front
at the throat by a knot and then flares into a wide, loose, long, spreading collar. On her head, confining her woman's hair but necessary
anyhow and worn by her husband as well, a dark, brimless skullcap,
over it a large, soft black hat with a turned-up brim.

I really don't know what sort of person it is that she and her husband
represent. If I wanted to explain them to someone to whom I didn't
want to confess my ignorance, I should find that I consider them
sextons, employees of the temple, notorious lazybones with whom the
community has come to terms, privileged shnorrers for some religious
reason, people who, precisely as a result of their being set apart, are
very close to the centre of the community's life, know many songs as a
result of their useless wandering about and spying, see clearly to the
core the relationship of all the members of the community, but as a
result of their lack of relatedness to the workaday world don't know
what to do with this knowledge, people who are Jews in an especially
pure form because they live only in the religion, but live in it without
effort, understanding, or distress. They seem to make a fool of everyone, laugh immediately after the murder of a noble Jew, sell themselves
to an apostate, dance with their hands on their earlocks in delight when

the unmasked murderer poisons himself and calls upon God, and yet all this only because they are as light as a feather, sink to the ground under the slightest pressure, are sensitive, cry easily with dry faces (they cry themselves out in grimaces), but as soon as the pressure is removed haven't the slightest specific gravity but must bounce right back up in the air.

They must have caused a lot of difficulty in a serious play, such as *Der Meshumed*[18] by Lateiner is, for they are forever – large as life and often on tiptoe or with both feet in the air – at the front of the stage and do not unravel but rather cut apart the suspense of the play. The seriousness of the play spins itself out, however, in words so compact, carefully considered even where possibly improvised, so full of the tension of a unified emotion, that even when the plot is going along only at the rear of the stage, it always keeps its meaning. Rather, the two in caftans are suppressed now and then which befits their nature, and despite their extended arms and snapping fingers one sees behind them only the murderer, who, the poison in him, his hand at his really too large collar, is staggering to the door.

The melodies are long, one's body is glad to confide itself to them. As a result of their long-drawn-out forward movement, the melodies are best expressed by a swaying of the hips, by raising and lowering extended arms in a calm rhythm, by bringing the palms close to the temples and taking care not to touch them. Suggests the *šlapák*.[19]

Some songs, the expression 'yiddische kinderlach', some of this woman's acting (who, on the stage, because she is a Jew, draws us listeners to her because we are Jews, without any longing for or curiosity about Christians) made my cheeks tremble. The representative of the government, with the exception of a waiter and two maids standing to the left of the stage, perhaps the only Christian in the hall, is a wretched person, afflicted with a facial tic that – especially on the left side of his face, but spreading also far on to the right – contracts and passes from his face with the almost merciful quickness, I mean the haste but also the regularity, of a second hand. When it reaches the left eye it almost obliterates it. For this contraction new, small, fresh muscles have developed in the otherwise quite wasted face.

The talmudic melody of minute questions, adjurations, or explanations. The air moves into a pipe and takes the pipe along, and a great screw, proud in its entirety, humble in its turns, twists from small, distant beginnings in the direction of the one who is questioned.

6 October. The two old men up front at the long table near the stage. One leans both his arms on the table and has only his face (whose false, bloated redness with an irregular, square, matted beard beneath it sadly conceals his old age) turned up to the right towards the stage, while the other, directly opposite the stage, holds his face, which old age has made quite dry, back away from the table on which he leans only with his left arm, holding his right arm bent in the air in order better to enjoy the melody that his fingertips follow and to which the short pipe in his right hand weakly yields. 'Tateleben, come on and sing,' cries the woman now to one, now to the other, at the same time stooping a little and stretching her arms forward encouragingly.

The melodies are made to catch hold of every person who jumps up and they can, without breaking down, encompass all his excitement even if one won't believe they have inspired it. The two in caftans are particularly in a hurry to meet the singing, as though it were stretching their body according to its most essential needs, and the clapping of the hands during the singing is an obvious sign of the good health of the man in the actor. The children of the landlord, in a corner of the stage, remain children in their relationship to Mrs K. and sing along, their mouths, between their pursed lips, full of the melody.

The play: Twenty years ago Seidemann, a rich Jew, obviously having marshalled all his criminal instincts towards that end, had himself baptized, poisoning his wife at the same time, since she would not let herself be forced into baptism. Since then he has made every effort to forget the jargon that unintentionally echoes in his speech, especially at first so that the audience can notice it and because the approaching events still leave time for it, and continually expresses great disgust for everything Jewish. He has promised his daughter to the officer, Dragomirow, while she, who is in love with her cousin, young Edelmann, in a big scene, drawing herself up in an unusual stony position, broken only at the waist, declares to her father that she holds fast to Judaism and ends a whole act with contemptuous laughter for the violence done her. (The Christians in the play are: an honest Polish servant of Seidemann's who later contributes to his unmasking, honest chiefly because

66

Seidemann must be ranged round with contrasts; the officer with whom
the play – aside from portraying his guilt – concerns itself little, because as a distinguished Christian he interests no one, just the same as
a presiding judge who appears later; and finally a court attendant
whose malice does not exceed the requirements of his position and the
mirth of the two in caftans, although Max calls him a pogromist.)
Dragomirow, however, for some reason or other can marry only if his
notes, which old Edelmann holds, are taken up, but which the latter,
although he is about to leave for Palestine and although Seidemann
wants to pay them in cash, will not hand over. The daughter acts
haughtily towards the enamoured officer and boasts of her Judaism
although she has been baptized, the officer does not know what to do,
and, his arms slack, his hands loosely clasped at the ends of them,
looks beseechingly at the father. The daughter runs away to Edelmann,
she wants to be married to her beloved, even if for the time being in
secret, since according to civil law a Jew cannot marry a Christian
woman and she obviously cannot convert to Judaism without the consent of her father. The father arrives, sees that without some stratagem
all is lost, and outwardly gives his blessing to this marriage. They all
forgive him, yes, begin to love him as though they had been in the
wrong, even old Edelmann, and especially he, although he knows that
Seidemann had poisoned his sister. (These inconsistencies arose perhaps
through cutting, but perhaps also because the play is passed on orally
most of the time, from one troupe of actors to another.) Through his
reconciliation Seidemann gets hold, first of all, of Dragomirow's notes –
'You know,' he says, 'I don't want this Dragomirow to speak badly
of the Jews' – and Edelmann gives them to him for nothing, then
Seidemann calls him to the portière in the background, ostensibly to
show him something, and from behind gives him a fatal thrust with a
knife through his dressing-gown into his back. (Between the reconciliation and the murder Seidemann was removed from the stage for a time
to think out the plan and buy the knife.) In this way he intends to bring
young Edelmann to the gallows, for it is he whom suspicion must fall
upon, and his daughter will become free for Dragomirow. He runs
away, Edelmann lies behind the portière. The daughter, wearing her
bridal veil, enters on the arm of young Edelmann, who has put
on his prayer shawl. The father, they see, unfortunately is not yet

there. Seidemann enters and seems happy at the sight of the bridal couple.

8 October. Then a man appears, perhaps Dragomirow himself, perhaps only an actor, but actually a detective unknown to us, and explains that he has to search the house since 'your life isn't safe in this house'. Seidemann: 'Children, don't worry, this is of course an obvious mistake. Everything will be straightened out.' Edelmann's body is found, young Edelmann torn from his beloved and arrested. For a whole act Seidemann, with great patience and very well-stressed little asides (Yes, yes, very good. No, that's wrong. Yes, now that's better. Of course, of course), instructs the two in caftans how they are to testify in court concerning the alleged enmity that has existed between old and young Edelmann for years. They get going with difficulty, there are many misunderstandings (they come forward at an improvised rehearsal of the court scene and declare that Seidemann had commissioned them to represent the affair in the following way), until finally they immerse themselves in that enmity so thoroughly that even Seidemann can no longer restrain them – they now know how the murder itself took place and the man stabs the woman to death with a French bread. This of course is again more than will be required of them. But Seidemann is satisfied enough with the two and hopes with their help for a favourable outcome to the trial. Here, for the spectator who is religious, without its having been expressed because it is self-evident, God himself reaches into the play in place of the author and strikes the villain blind.

In the last act the presiding judge is again the eternal Dragomirow actor (in this, too, contempt is revealed for the Christian, one Jewish actor can play three Christian roles well, and if he plays them badly, it doesn't matter either) and beside him, as defence attorney, with great display of hair and moustache, recognized at once, Seidemann's daughter. Of course, you recognize her easily, but in view of Dragomirow you assume for a long time that she is playing a second part until, towards the middle of the act, you realize that she has disguised herself to save her beloved. The two caftans are each supposed to testify individually, but that is very difficult for them as they have rehearsed it together. Also, they don't understand the judge's High German, although it is true that the defence attorney helps him out when he gets too involved, as he has to prompt him in other respects as well. Then comes Seidemann, who had already tried to direct the two in caftans by tugging at their clothes, and by his fluent, decisive speech, by his reasonable bearing, by correctly addressing the presiding judge in contrast to the former witnesses, makes a good impression which is in terrible contrast to what we know of him. His testimony is pretty much without content, unfortunately he knows very little about the whole case. But the last witness, the servant, is, though not entirely aware of it, Seidemann's real accuser. He had seen Seidemann buy the knife, he knows that at the crucial time Seidemann was at Edelmann's, he knows, finally, that Seidemann hates the Jews and especially Edelmann and wanted his notes. The two in caftans jump up and are happy to be able to confirm all this. Seidemann defends himself as a somewhat confused man of honour. Then the discussion turns to his daughter. Where is she? At home, naturally, and she'll bear him out. No, that she won't do, insists the defence attorney, and he will prove it, turns to the wall, takes off the wig, and turns toward the horrified Seidemann in the person of his daughter. The clean whiteness of her upper lip looks threatening when she takes off the moustache. Seidemann has taken poison in order to escape the justice of this world, confesses his misdeeds, but hardly any longer to the people, rather to the Jewish God whom he now professes. Meanwhile the piano player has struck up a tune, the two in caftans feel moved by it and must start dancing. In the background stands the reunited bridal pair, they sing the melody, especially the serious bridegroom, in the customary old way.

First appearance of the two in caftans. They enter Seidemann's empty room with collection boxes for the temple, look around, feel ill at ease, look at each other. Feel along the doorposts with their hand, don't find a *mezuzah*.[20] None on the other doors, either. They don't want to believe it and jump up beside doors as if they were catching flies, jumping up and falling back, slapping the very tops of the doorposts again and again. Unfortunately all in vain. Up to now they haven't spoken a word.

Remembrance between Mrs K and last year's Mrs W. Mrs K. has a personality perhaps a trifle weaker and more monotonous, to make up for it she is prettier and more respectable. Mrs W.'s standing joke was to bump her fellow players with her large behind. Besides, she had a worse singer with her and was quite new to us.

'Male impersonator' is really a false title. By virtue of the fact that she is stuck into a caftan, her body is entirely forgotten. She only reminds one of her body by shrugging her shoulder and twisting her back as though she were being bitten by fleas. The sleeves, though short, have to be pulled up a little every minute; this the spectator enjoys and even watches for it to happen, anticipating the great relief it will be for this woman who has so much to sing and to explain in the talmudic manner.

Would like to see a large Yiddish theatre as the production may after all suffer because of the small cast and inadequate rehearsal. Also, would like to know Yiddish literature, which is obviously characterized by an uninterrupted tradition of national struggle that determines every work. A tradition, therefore, that pervades no other literature, not even that of the most oppressed people. It may be that other peoples in times of war make a success out of a pugnacious national literature, and that other works, standing at a greater remove, acquire from the enthusiasm of the audience a national character too, as is the case with *The Bartered Bride*, but here there appear to be only works of the first type, and indeed always.

The appearance of the simple stage that awaits the actors as silently as we. Since, with its three walls, the chair, and the table, it will have to suffice for all the scenes, we expect nothing from it, rather with all our energy await the actors and are therefore unresistingly attracted by the singing from behind the blank walls that introduces the performance.

9 October. If I reach my fortieth year, then I'll probably marry an old maid with protruding upper teeth left a little exposed by the upper lip. The upper front teeth of Miss K., who was in Paris and London, slant towards each other a little like legs which are quickly crossed at the knees. I'll hardly reach my fortieth birthday, however; the frequent

tension over the left half of my skull, for example, speaks against it – it feels like an inner leprosy which, when I only observe it and disregard its unpleasantness, makes the same impression on me as the skull cross-section in textbooks, or as an almost painless dissection of the living body where the knife – a little coolingly, carefully, often stopping and going back, sometimes lying still – splits still thinner the paper-thin integument close to the functioning parts of the brain.

Last night's dream which in the morning I myself didn't even consider beautiful except for a small comic scene consisting of two counter-remarks which resulted in that tremendous dream satisfaction but which I have forgotten.

I walked – whether Max was there right at the start I don't know – through a long row of houses at the level of the first or second floor, just as one walks through a tunnel from one carriage to another. I walked very quickly, perhaps also because the house was so rickety that for that reason alone one hurried. The doors between the houses I did not notice at all, it was just a gigantic row of rooms, and yet not only the differences between the individual apartments but also between the houses were recognizable. They were perhaps all rooms with beds through which I went. One typical bed has remained in my memory. It stood at the side to the left of me against the dark or dirty wall, which sloped like an attic's, perhaps had a low pile of bedclothes, and its cover, really only a coarse sheet crumpled by the feet of the person who had slept here, hung down in a point. I felt abashed to walk through people's rooms at a time when many of them were still lying in their beds, therefore took long strides on tiptoes, by which I somehow or other hoped to show that I was passing through only by compulsion, was as considerate of everything as was at all possible, walked softly, and that my passing through did not, as it were, count at all. Therefore, too, I never turned my head in any one room and saw only either what lay on the right towards the street or on the left towards the back wall.

The row of houses was often interrupted by brothels; and although I was making this journey seemingly because of them, I walked through them especially quickly so that I remember nothing except that they were there. However, the last room of all the houses was again a brothel, and here I remained. The wall across from the door through which I entered, therefore the last wall of the row of houses, was either of glass or merely broken through, and if I had walked on I should have fallen. It is even more probable that it was broken through, for the whores lay towards the edge of the floor. Two I saw clearly on the ground, the head of one hung down a little over the edge into the open air. To the left was a solid wall, on the other hand the wall on the right was not finished, you could see down into the court, even if not to the bottom of it, and a ramshackle grey staircase led down in several flights. To judge by the light in the room the ceiling was like that in the other rooms.

I occupied myself chiefly with the whore whose head was hanging down, Max with the one lying beside her on the left. I fingered her legs and then for a long time pressed the upper parts of her thighs in regular rhythm. My pleasure in this was so great that I wondered that for this entertainment, which was after all really the most beautiful kind, one still had to pay nothing. I was convinced that I (and I alone) deceived the world. Then the whore, without moving her legs, raised the upper part of her body and turned her back to me, which to my horror was covered with large sealing-wax-red circles with paling edges, and red splashes scattered among them. I now noticed that her whole body was full of them, that I was pressing my thumb to her thighs in just such spots, and that there were these little red particles – as though from a crumbled seal – on my fingers too.

I stepped back among a number of men who seemed to be waiting against the wall near the opening of the stairway, on which there was a small amount of traffic. They were waiting in the way men in the country stand together in the market place on Sunday morning. Therefore it was Sunday too. It was here that the comic scene took place, when a man I and Max had reason to be afraid of went away, then came up the stairs, then stepped up to me, and while I and Max anxiously expected some terrible threat from him, put a ridiculously simple-minded question to me. Then I stood there and with apprehension watched Max, who, without fear in this place, was sitting on the ground somewhere to the left eating a thick potato soup out of which the potatoes peeped like large balls, especially one. He pushed them down into the soup with his spoon, perhaps with two spoons, or just turned them.

10 October. Wrote a sophistic article for the *Tetschen-Bodenbacher Zeitung* for and against my insurance institute.

Yesterday evening on the Graben. Three actresses coming towards me from a rehearsal. It is so difficult quickly to become familiar with the beauty of three women when in addition you also want to look at two actors who are approaching behind them with that too-swinging actors' walk. The two – of whom the one on the left, with his fat, youthful face and open overcoat wrapped around his strong body, is representative enough of both – overtake the ladies, the one on the left on the pavement, the one on the right down in the roadway. The one on the left grasps his hat high up near the top, seizes it with all five fingers, raises it high and calls (the one on the right recollects himself only now): Good-bye! Good night! But while this overtaking and greeting has separated the gentlemen, the ladies addressed, as though led by the one nearest the roadway who seems to be the weakest and tallest but also the youngest and most beautiful, continue on their way quite undisturbed, with an easy greeting which scarcely interrupts their harmonious conversation. The whole thing seemed to me at the moment to be strong proof that theatrical affairs here are orderly and well conducted.

Day before yesterday among the Jews in Café Savoy. *Die Sedernacht* by Feimann. At times (at the moment the consciousness of this pierced me) we did not interfere in the plot only because we were too moved, not because we were mere spectators.

12 October. Yesterday at Max's wrote in the Paris diary.[21] In the half-darkness of Rittergasse, in her autumn outfit, fat, warm R. whom we have known only in her summer blouse and thin, blue summer jacket, in which a girl with a not entirely faultless appearance is, after all, worse than naked. Then you really were able to see the large nose in her bloodless face and the cheeks to which you could have pressed your hands for a long time before any redness appeared, the heavy

blonde down which heaped itself up on the cheek and upper lip, the railway dust which had strayed between the nose and cheek, and the sickly whiteness where her blouse was cut away. Today, however, we ran after her respectfully, and when I had to make my farewells at the entrance to a house that went through to Ferdinandstrasse (I was unshaven and otherwise shabby in appearance), I afterward felt a few slight impulses of affection for her. And when I considered why, I had to keep telling myself: because she was so warmly dressed.

13 October. Inaesthetic transition from the taut skin of my boss's bald spot to the delicate wrinkles of his forehead. An obvious, very easily imitated fault of nature, bank notes should not be made so.

I didn't consider the description of R. good, but nevertheless it must have been better than I thought, or my impression of R. the day before yesterday must have been so incomplete that the description was adequate to it or even surpassed it. For when I went home last night the description came to my mind for a moment, imperceptibly replaced the original impression and I felt that I had seen R. only yesterday, and indeed without Max, so that I prepared myself to tell him about her just as I have described her here for myself.

Yesterday evening on Schützen Island, did not find my colleagues and left immediately. I made some stir in my short jacket with my crushed soft hat in my hand, because it was cold out, but too hot inside from the breath of the beer drinkers, smokers, and the wind-instrument players of the military band. This band was not very high up, could not be, either, because the hall is pretty low, and filled the one end of the hall to the side-walls. The mass of musicians was crowded into this end of the room as though cut to size. This crowded impression was then lost a little in the hall, as the places near the band were pretty empty and the hall filled up only towards the middle.

Talkativeness of Dr K. Walked around with him for two hours behind the Franz-Josef railway station, begged him from time to time to let me leave, had clasped my hands in impatience and listened as little as possible. It seemed to me that a person who is good at his job, when he has got himself involved in talking shop, must become irresponsible; he becomes conscious of his proficiency, there are associations with every story, and indeed several, he surveys them all because he has experienced them, must in haste and out of consideration for me suppress many, some I also destroy by asking questions but remind him by these of others, show him thereby that he is also in control deep into my own thinking, he himself plays in most of the stories a handsome role which he just touches upon, because of which the suppressed seems even more significant to him, now he is however so certain of my admiration that he can also complain, for even in his misfortune, his trouble, his doubt, he is admirable, his opponents are also capable people and worth talking about; in an attorney's office which had four clerks and two chiefs there was a controversy in which he alone opposed this office, for weeks the daily subject of discussion of the six lawyers. Their best speaker, a sharp lawyer, opposed him – to this is attached the Supreme Court whose decisions are allegedly bad, contradictory; in a tone of farewell I say a word of defence for this court, now he produces proofs that the court cannot be defended, and once more we must walk up and down the street, I am immediately surprised at the badness of this court, whereupon he explains to me why it must be so, the court is overburdened, why and how, well, I must leave, but now the Court of Appeals is better and the Court of Administration much better still, and why and how, finally I can't be detained any longer, whereupon he brings in my own affairs (setting up the factory), which is what I come to him about and which we had already fully discussed, he unconsciously hopes in this way to trap me and to be able to tempt me back to his stories again. I say something, but while speaking I hold out my hand in farewell and so escape.

He is a very good storyteller, by the way, in his stories the detailed expansiveness of the brief is mixed with the vivacious speech that one often finds in such fat, black Jews, healthy for the present, of medium height, excited by continuous smoking of cigarettes. Legal expressions give the speech steadiness, paragraphs are numbered to a high count that seems to banish them into a distance. Each story is developed from its very beginning, speech and counter-speech are produced and, as it were, shuffled up by personal asides, matters that are beside the point, that no one would think of, are first mentioned, then called beside the point and set aside ('A man, his name is beside the point'), the listener is personally drawn in, questioned, while alongside the plot of the story thickens, sometimes, preliminary to a story which cannot interest him at all, the listener is even questioned, uselessly of course, in order to establish some sort of provisional connexion, the listener's interjected remarks are not immediately introduced, which would be annoying (Kubin), but are shortly put in the right place as the story goes on, so that the listener is flattered and drawn into the story and given a special right to be a listener.

14 October. Yesterday evening at the Savoy. *Sulamith* by A. Gold-faden. Really an opera, but every sung play is called an operetta, even this trifle seems to me to point to an artistic endeavour that is stubborn, hasty, and passionate for the wrong reasons, that cuts across European art in a direction that is partly arbitrary.

The story: A hero saves a girl who is lost in the desert ('I pray thee, great, almighty God') and because of the torments of thirst has thrown herself into a well. They swear to be true to each other ('My dear one, my loved one, my diamond found in the desert') by calling upon the well and a red-eyed desert cat in witness. The girl, Sulamith (Mrs Ts.), is taken back to Bethlehem to her father, Manoach (Ts.), by Cingitang, the savage servant of Absalom (P.), while Absalom (K.) goes on another journey to Jerusalem; there, however, he falls in love with Abigail, a rich girl of Jerusalem (Mrs K.), forgets Sulamith, and marries. Sula-mith waits for her lover at home in Bethlehem. 'Many people go to *Yerusholaim* and arrive *beshulim.*' 'He, the noble one, will be untrue to me!' By means of despairing outbursts she gains a confidence pre-pared for anything and determines to feign insanity in order not to have to marry and to be able to wait. 'My will is of iron, my heart I make a fortress.' And even in the insanity which she now feigns for years she enjoys sadly and aloud all her memories of her lover, for her insanity is concerned only with the desert, the well, and the cat. By means of her insanity she immediately repels her three suitors with whom Manoach was able to get along in peace only by organizing a lottery: Joel Gedoni (U.), 'I am the most powerful Jewish hero,' Avidanov, the landowner (R.P.), and the potbellied priest, Nathan (Löwy), who feels superior to everyone, 'Give her to me, I die for her.'

Absalom suffered a misfortune, one of his children was bitten to death by a desert cat, the other falls into a well. He remembers his guilt, confesses all to Abigail. 'Restrain your crying.' 'Cease with your words to split my heart.' 'Alas, it is all *emes* that I speak.' Some ideas seem on the point of taking shape around the two and then disappear. Is Absalom to return to Sulamith and desert Abigail? Sulamith too deserves *rachmones*. Finally Abigail releases him. In Bethlehem Manoach laments over his daughter: 'Alas, oh, the years of my old age.' Absalom cures her with his voice. 'The rest, Father, I will tell thee later.' Abigail collapses there in the Jerusalem vineyard, Absalom has as justification only his heroism.

At the end of the performance we still expect the actor Löwy, whom I would admire in the dust. He is supposed, as is customary, 'to announce': 'Dear guests, I thank you in all our names for your visit and cordially invite you to tomorrow's performance, when the world-famous masterpiece — by — will be produced. Until we meet again!' Exit with a flourish of his hat. Instead, we see the curtain first held tightly closed, then tentatively drawn apart a little. This goes on quite a while. Finally it is drawn wide open, in the middle a button holds it together, behind it we see Löwy walking towards the footlights and, his face turned to us, the audience, defending himself with his hands against someone who is attacking him from behind, until suddenly the whole curtain with its wire supports on top is pulled down by Löwy who is looking for something to hold on to. Before our eyes P., who had played the savage and who is still bowed down as if the curtain were drawn, grabs Löwy (who is on his knees) by his head and pushes him sideways off the stage. Everyone runs together into the wing of the theatre. 'Close the curtain!' they shout on the almost completely exposed stage on which Mrs Ts., with her pale Sulamith face, is standing pitiably. Little waiters on tables and chairs put the curtain somewhat in order, the landlord tries to calm the government representative who, however, wants only to get away and is being held back by this attempt to calm him, behind the curtain one hears Mrs Ts.: 'And we who claim to preach morals to the public from the stage. . . .' The association of Jewish office workers, Zukunft, which took over the next night under its own direction and before tonight's performance had held a regular membership meeting, decides because of this occurrence to call a special meeting within half an hour, a Czech member of the association prophesies complete ruin for the actors as a result of their scandalous behaviour. Then suddenly one sees Löwy, who seemed to have disappeared, pushed towards a door by the head-waiter, R., with his hands, perhaps also with his knees. He is simply being thrown out. This head-waiter, who before and later stands before every guest, before us as well, like a dog, with a doglike muzzle which sags over a large mouth closed by humble wrinkles on the side, has his –

16 October. Strenuous Sunday yesterday. The whole staff gave Father notice. By soft words, cordiality, effective use of his illness, his size and former strength, his experience, his cleverness, he wins almost all of them back in group and individual discussions. An important clerk, F., wants time until Monday to think it over because he has given his word to our manager who is stepping out and would like to take the whole staff along into his newly-to-be-established business. On Sunday the book-keeper writes he cannot remain after all, R. will not release him from his promise.

I go to see him in Žižkov. His young wife with round cheeks, longish face, and a small, thick nose of the sort that never spoils Czech faces. A too-long, very loose, flowered and spotted housecoat. It seems especially long and loose because she moves especially hurriedly in order to greet me, to place the album properly on the table in a final straightening of the room and to disappear in order to have her husband called. The husband enters with similar hurried movements, perhaps imitated by his very dependent wife, the upper part of his body bent forward and his arms swinging rapidly like pendulums while the lower part is noticeably behind it. Impression of a man you have known for ten years, seen often, regarded little, with whom you suddenly come into a closer relationship. The less success I have with my Czech arguments (indeed, he already had a signed contract with R., he was just so embarrassed by my father Saturday evening that he had not mentioned the contract), the more catlike his face becomes. Towards the end I act a little with a very pleasurable feeling, so I look silently around the room with my face drawn rather long and my eyes narrowed, as though I were pursuing something significant into the ineffable. Am, however, not unhappy when I see that it has little effect and that I, instead of being spoken to by him in a new tone, must begin afresh to persuade him. The conversation was begun with the fact that on the other side of the street another T. lives, it was concluded at the door with his surprise at my thin clothes in the cold weather. Indicative of my first hopes and final failure. I made him promise, however, to come to see Father in the afternoon. My arguments in places too abstract and formal. Mistake not to have called his wife into the room.

Afternoon to Radotin to keep the clerk. Miss, as a result, the meeting with Löwy of whom I think incessantly. In the carriage: pointed nose of the old woman with still almost youthful, taut skin. Does youth therefore end at the tip of the nose and death begin there? The swallowing of the passengers that glides down their throats, the widening of their mouths as a sign that in their judgement the railway journey, the combination of the other passengers, their seating arrangements, the temperature in the carriage, even the copy of *Pan* that I hold on my knees and that several glance at from time to time (as it is after all something that they would not have expected in the compartment), are harmless, natural, unsuspicious, while at the same time they still believe that everything could have been much worse.

Up and down in Mr H.'s yard, a dog puts his paw on the tip of my foot which I shake. Children, chickens, here and there adults. A children's nurse, occasionally leaning on the railing of the *Pawlatsche*[22] or hiding behind a door, has her eye on me. Under her eyes I do not know just what I am, whether indifferent, embarrassed, young or old, impudent or devoted, holding my hands behind or before me, animal lover or man of affairs, friend of H. or supplicant, superior to those gathered at the meeting who sometimes go from the tavern to the *pissoir* and back in an unbroken line, or ridiculous to them because of my thin clothes, Jew or Christian, etc. The walking around, wiping my nose, occasional reading of *Pan*, timid avoiding of the *Pawlatsche* with my eyes only suddenly to see that it is empty, watching the poultry, being greeted by a man, seeing through the tavern window the flat faces of the men set crookedly close together and turned towards a speaker, everything contributes to it. Mr H. leaves the meeting from time to time and I ask him to use his influence for us with the clerk whom he had brought into our office. Black-brown beard growing around cheeks and chin, black eyes, between eyes and beard the dark shadings of his cheeks. He is a friend of my father's, I knew him even as a child and the idea that he was a coffee-roaster always made him even darker and more manly for me than he was.

17 October. I finish nothing because I have no time and it presses so within me. If the whole day were free and this morning restlessness could mount within me until midday and wear itself out by evening, then I could sleep. This way, however, there is left for this restlessness only an evening twilight hour at most, it gets somewhat stronger, is then suppressed, and uselessly and injuriously undermines the night for me. Shall I be able to bear it long? And is there any purpose in bearing it, shall I, then, be given time?

Napoleon is reminiscing at the royal table in Erfurt: When I was still a mere lieutenant in the Fifth Regiment . . . (the royal highnesses look at each other in embarrassment, Napoleon notices it and corrects himself), when I still had the honour to be a mere lieutenant . . . When I think of this anecdote the arteries in my neck swell with the pride that I can easily feel with him and that vicariously thrills through me.

Again in Radotin: freezing, I then walked around alone in the garden, then recognized in an open window the children's nurse who had walked to this side of the house with me.

20 October. The 18th at Max's; wrote about Paris. Wrote badly, without really arriving at that freedom of true description which releases one's foot from the experienced. I was also dull after the great exaltation of the previous day that had ended with Löwy's lecture. During the day I was not yet in any unusual frame of mind, went with Max to meet his mother who was arriving from Gablonz, was in the coffee-house with them and then at Max's, who played a gipsy dance from *La Jolie Fille de Perth* for me. A dance in which for pages only the hips rock gently in a monotonous ticking and the face has a slow, cordial expression. Until finally, towards the end, briefly and late, the inner wildness that has been tempted outward arrives, shakes the body, overpowers it, compresses the melody so that it beats into the heights

and depths (unusually bitter, dull tones are heard in it) and then comes to an unheeded close. At the beginning, and unmistakable through it all, a strong feeling of closeness to gipsydom, perhaps because a people so wild in the dance shows its tranquil side only to a friend. Impression of great truth of the first dance. Then leafed through *Aussprüche Napoleons*. How easily you become for the moment a little part of your own tremendous notion of Napoleon! Then, already boiling, I went home, I couldn't withstand one of my ideas, disordered, pregnant, dishevelled, swollen, amidst my furniture which was rolling about me; overwhelmed by my pains and worries, taking up as much space as possible, for despite my bulk I was very nervous, I entered the lecture hall. From the way in which I was sitting, for instance, and very truly sat, I should as a spectator immediately have recognized my condition.

Löwy read humorous sketches by Sholom Aleichem, then a story by Peretz, the *Lichtverkäuferin* by Rosenfeld, a poem by Bialik (the one instance where the poet stooped from Hebrew to Yiddish, himself translating his original Hebrew poem into Yiddish, in order to popularize this poem which, by making capital out of the Kishinev pogrom, sought to further the Jewish cause). A recurrent widening of the eyes, natural to the actor, which are then left so for awhile, framed by the arched eyebrows. Complete truth of all the reading; the weak raising of the right arm from the shoulder, the adjusting of the pince-nez that seems borrowed for the occasion, so poorly does it fit the nose; the position under the table of the leg that is stretched out in such a way that the weak joint between the upper and lower parts of the leg is particularly in motion; the crook of the back, weak and wretched-looking since the unbroken surface of a back cannot deceive an observer in the way that a face does, with its eyes, the hollows and projections of its cheeks, or even with some trifle be it only a stubble of beard. After the reading, while still on my way home, I felt all my abilities concentrated, and on that account complained to my sisters, even to my mother, at home.

On the 19th at Dr K.'s about the factory. The little theoretical hostility that is bound to arise between contracting parties when contracts are being made. The way my eyes searched H.'s face, which was turned toward the lawyers. This hostility is bound to arise all the more between two people who otherwise are not accustomed to think through their mutual relationship and therefore make difficulties about every trifle. Dr K.'s habit of walking diagonally up and down the room with the tense, forward rocking of the upper part of his body, as though in a drawing-room, at the same time telling stories and frequently, at the end of a diagonal, shaking off the ash of his cigarette into one of the three ash-trays placed about the room.

This morning at N. N. Co. The way the boss leans back sideways in his armchair in order to get room and support for the Eastern Jewish gestures of his hand. The inter-action and reciprocal reinforcement of the play of his hands and face. Sometimes he combines the two, either by looking at his hands, or for the convenience of the listener, holding them close to his face. Temple melodies in the cadence of his speech; the melody is led from finger to finger as though through various registers, especially when enumerating several points. Then met Father at the Graben with Mr Pr., who raises his hand to make his sleeve fall back a little (since he doesn't himself want to draw back the sleeve) and there in the middle of the Graben makes powerful screwing motions by opening up his hand and letting it fall away with the fingers spread.

I am probably sick, since yesterday my body has been itching all over. In the afternoon my face was so hot and blotched that I was afraid the assistant giving me a haircut, who could see me and my reflected image all the time, would recognize that I had a serious disease. Also the connexion between stomach and mouth is partly disturbed, a lid the size of a gulden moves up or down, or stays down below from where it exerts an expanding effect of light pressure that spreads upward over my chest.

More on Radotin: Invited her to come down. The first answer was serious although until then, together with the girl entrusted to her, she had giggled and flirted across at me in a way she would never have dared from the moment we became acquainted. We then laughed a great deal together although I was freezing down below and she up above at the open window. She pressed her breasts against her crossed arms and, her knees apparently bent, pressed her whole body against the window sill. She was seventeen years old and took me to be fifteen or sixteen;[23] I couldn't make her change her mind throughout our entire conversation. Her small nose was a little crooked and threw an unusual shadow across her cheek, which, to be sure, wouldn't help me to recognize her again. She was not from Radotin but from Chuchle (the next station on the way to Prague), which she wouldn't let me forget.

Then a walk with the clerk (who even without my trip would have remained with our firm) in the dark out of Radotin on the highway and back to the railway station. On one side waste hills used by a cement factory for its supply of chalky sand. Old mills. Story of a poplar whirled out of the earth by a tornado. Face of the clerk: dough-like reddish flesh on heavy bones, looks tired but robust within his limits. Does not show surprise even by his voice that we are walking here together. A clear moon over a large field, the chimney smoke looking like clouds in the light; the field, right in the middle of the town, bought up as a precaution by a factory but left unused for the time being, surrounded by factory buildings which were strongly but only partly lit up by electric lights. Train signals. Scuffling of rats near the path worn across the field by the townspeople in defiance of the will of the factory.

Examples of the way this writing, which is on the whole trivial, strengthens me after all:

Monday, the 16th, I was with Löwy at the National Theatre to see *Dubrovačka Trilogjia*. Play and production were hopeless. Of the first act I remember the beautiful chime of a mantel clock; the singing of the 'Marseillaise' by Frenchmen marching outside the window, the fading song is repeatedly taken up by the newcomers and rises again; a girl dressed in black carries her shadow through the streak of light that the setting sun throws on the parquet floor. Of the second act only the delicate throat of a girl, which rises out of shoulders dressed in red-brown, expands from between puffed sleeves, and lengthens into a small head. Of the third act the crushed Prince Albert, the dark fancy vest of an old, stooped descendant of the former gospodars with the gold watch-chain drawn diagonally across it. So it is not much. The seats were expensive, I was a poor benefactor to have thrown money away here while L. was in need; finally he was even somewhat more bored than I. In short, I had again demonstrated the misfortune that follows every undertaking that I begin by myself. But while I usually unite myself indivisibly with this misfortune, attract all earlier cases of misfortune up to me, all later ones down to me, I was this time almost completely independent, bore everything quite easily as something that happens just once, and for the first time in the theatre even felt my head, as the head of a spectator, raised high out of the collective darkness of the seat and the body into a distinct light, independent of the bad occasion of this play and this production.

A second example: Yesterday evening I simultaneously held out both my hands to my two sisters-in-law on Mariengasse with a degree of adroitness as if they were two right hands and I a double person.

21 October. A counter-example: When my boss confers with me about office matters (today the filing-cabinet), I cannot look him in the eye for long without there coming into my eyes against my will a slight bitterness which forces either my look or his away. His look yields more briefly but more often to every impulse to look away, since he is not aware of the reason, but his glance immediately returns as he considers it all only a momentary fatigue of his eyes. I defend myself against it more vigorously, therefore hasten the zigzagging of my glance, look by preference along his nose and across to the shadows of his cheeks, often only keep my face towards him by the aid of the teeth and tongue in my tight-shut mouth – when I must, I lower my eyes, to be sure, but never farther than to his tie, but get the most direct look immediately after he turns his eyes away, when I follow him closely and without consideration.

The Jewish actors. Mrs Tschissik has protuberances on her cheeks near her mouth. Caused in part by hollow cheeks as a result of the pains of hunger, childbed, journeys, and acting, in part by the relaxed unusual muscles she had to develop for the actor's movements of her large, what originally must have been a heavy mouth. Most of the time, as Sulamith, she wore her hair loose, which covered her cheeks so that her face sometimes looked like the face of a girl out of the past. She has a large, bony, moderately robust body and is tightly laced. Her walk easily takes on a solemnity since she has the habit of raising, stretching and slowly moving her long arms. Especially when she sang the Jewish national anthem, gently rocked her large hips and moved her arms, bent parallel to her hips, up and down with hands cupped as though she were playing with a slowly flying ball.

22 October. Yesterday with the Jews. *Kol Nidre* by Scharkansky, pretty bad play with a good, witty letter-writing scene, a prayer by the lovers standing up beside each other with hands clasped, the converted Grand Inquisitor pressing himself against the curtain of the Ark of the Covenant, he mounts the stairs and remains standing there, his head bowed, his lips against the curtain, holds the prayer book before his chattering teeth. For the first time on this fourth evening my distinct inability to get a clear impression. Our large company and the visits at my sisters' table were also responsible for it. Nevertheless, I needn't have been so weak. With my love for Mrs Ts., who only thanks to Max sat beside me, I behaved wretchedly. I'll recover again, however, even now I feel better.

Mrs Tschissik (I enjoy writing the name so much) likes to bow her head at the table even while eating roast goose, you believe you can get in under her eyelids with your glance if you first carefully look along her cheeks and then, making yourself small, slip in, in doing which you don't even first have to raise the lids, for they are raised and even let a bluish gleam through which lures you on to the attempt. Out of her truthful acting flourishes of her fist now and then emerge, turns of her arm that drape invisible trains about her body; she places her outspread fingers on her breast because the artless shriek does not suffice. Her acting is not varied: the frightened look at her antagonist, the seeking for a way out on the small stage, the soft voice that, without being raised, mounts heroically in even, short ascents aided only by a greater inner resonance, the joy that spreads through her face across her high forehead into her hair; the self-sufficiency and independence of all other means when she sings solos, the holding herself erect when she resists that compels the spectator to devote his attention to her whole body – but not much more. But there is the truth of the whole and as a result the conviction that the least of her effects cannot be taken from her, that she is independent of the play and of us.

The sympathy we have for these actors who are so good, who earn nothing and who do not get nearly enough gratitude and fame is really only sympathy for the sad fate of many noble strivings, above all of our own. Therefore, too, it is so immoderately strong, because on the surface it is attached to strangers and in reality belongs to us. Nevertheless, in spite of everything, it is so closely bound up with the actors that I cannot disengage it even now. Because I recognize this and in spite of it this sympathy attaches itself even more closely to them.

The striking smoothness of Mrs Tschissik's cheeks alongside her muscular mouth. Her somewhat shapeless little girl.

Walking with Löwy and my sister for three hours.

23 October. The actors by their presence always convince me to my horror that most of what I've written about them until now is false. It is false because I write about them with steadfast love (even now, while I write it down, this too becomes false) but varying ability, and this varying ability does not hit off the real actors loudly and correctly but loses itself dully in this love that will never be satisfied with the ability and therefore thinks it is protecting the actors by preventing this ability from exercising itself.

Quarrel between Tschissik and Löwy. Ts.: Edelstatt is the greatest Jewish writer. He is sublime. Rosenfeld is of course also a great writer, but not the foremost. Löwy: Ts. is a socialist and because Edelstatt writes socialist poems, because he is editor of a Jewish socialist newspaper in London, therefore Ts. considers him the greatest. But who is Edelstatt, his party knows him, no one else, but the world knows Rosenfeld. – Ts.: It is not a question of recognition. Everything of Edelstatt's is sublime. – L.: Of course, I'm well acquainted with him too. The *Selbstmörder*, for example, is very good. – Ts.: What's the use of arguing. We won't agree. I'll repeat my opinion until tomorrow and you the same. – L.: I until the day after tomorrow.

Goldfaden, married, spendthrift, even if terribly badly off. About a hundred pieces. Stolen liturgical melodies made popular. The whole people sings them. The tailor at his work (is imitated), the maid, etc.

With so little room for dressing you are bound, as Ts. says, to get into quarrels. You come off the stage excited, everyone considers himself the greatest actor, then if someone, for example, steps on someone else's foot, which cannot be avoided, not only a quarrel but a good battle is ready to break out. But in Warsaw there were seventy-five small, individual dressing-rooms, each one with light.

At six o'clock I met the actors in their coffee-house seated around two tables, divided into the two hostile groups. A book by Peretz was on the table of the Ts. group. Löwy had just shut it and stood up to leave with me.

Until the age of twenty Löwy was a *bocher* who studied and spent the money of his well-to-do father. There was a society of young people of the same age who met in a locked tavern precisely on Saturday and, dressed in their caftans, smoked and otherwise sinned against the Sabbath commandments.

'The great Adler' from New York, the most famous Yiddish actor, who is a millionaire, for whom Gordin wrote *Der Wilde Mensch* and whom Löwy in Karlsbad had asked not to come to the performance because he didn't have the courage to act in his presence on their poorly equipped stage. – Real sets, not this miserable stage on which you cannot move. How shall we play the wild man! You need a sofa for it. In the Crystal Palace in Leipzig it was magnificent. Windows you could open, the sun shone in, you needed a throne in the play, good, there was a throne, I walked towards it through the crowd and was really a king. It is much easier to act there. Here everything confuses you.

24 October. Mother works all day, is merry and sad as the fancy strikes her, without taking advantage of her own condition in the slightest, her voice is clear, too loud for ordinary speech but does you good when you are sad and suddenly hear it after some time. For a long time now I have been complaining that I am always ill, but never have any definite illness that would compel me to go to bed. This wish certainly goes back chiefly to the fact that I know how comforting

Mother can be when, for example, she comes from the lighted living-room into the twilight of the sick-room, or in the evening, when the day begins to change monotonously into night, returns from business and with her concerns and hurried instructions once more causes the day, already so late, to begin again and rouses the invalid to help her in this. I should wish that for myself once more, because then I should be weak, therefore convinced by everything my mother did, and could enjoy childish pleasure with age's keener capacity for gratification. Yesterday it occurred to me that I did not always love my mother as she deserved and as I could, only because the German language prevented it. The Jewish mother is no 'Mutter', to call her 'Mutter' makes her a little comic (not to herself, because we are in Germany), we give a Jewish woman the name of a German mother, but forget the contradiction that sinks into the emotions so much the more heavily, 'Mutter' is peculiarly German for the Jew, it unconsciously contains, together with the Christian splendour Christian coldness also, the Jewish woman who is called 'Mutter' therefore becomes not only comic but strange. Mama would be a better name if only one didn't imagine 'Mutter' behind it. I believe that it is only the memories of the ghetto that still preserve the Jewish family, for the word 'Vater' too is far from meaning the Jewish father.

Today I stood before Counsellor L., who asked about my illness unexpectedly, uninvited, childishly, lyingly, ridiculously and to the point where I lost patience. We hadn't spoken so intimately for a long time, or perhaps never at all – I felt my face, which had never before been so closely observed by him, reveal parts to him in spurious frankness that he hardly understood but that nevertheless surprised him. I was unrecognizable to myself. I know him quite well.

26 October. Thursday. All afternoon yesterday Löwy read from *Gott, Mensch, Teufel* by Gordin and then from his own Paris diaries. The day before yesterday I saw the performance of *Der Wilde Mensch* by Gordin. Gordin is better than Lateiner, Scharkansky, Feimann, etc., because he has more detail, more order, and more logical sequence in this order, he therefore somehow lacks the immediate Jewishness that is always being improvised in other plays, the clamour of this Jewish-

ness rings more dully and therefore in less detail. Of course, concessions are made to the audience and sometimes you believe you must
stretch in order to see the play over the heads of the Jewish theatre
audience of New York (the character of the wild man, the whole story
of Mrs Selde), but worse is the fact that palpable concessions are made
also to some vaguely felt art; for example, in *Der Wilde Mensch* the
plot rambles as a result of hesitancy, the wild man delivers speeches
humanly unintelligible but dramatically so clumsy that one would
prefer to close one's eyes, the same is true of the older girl in *Gott,
Mensch, Teufel*. Parts of the plot of *Der Wilde Mensch* are very
spirited. A young widow marries an old man with four children and
immediately brings her lover, Vladimir Vorobeitchik, along into the
marriage. The two proceed to ruin the whole family, Shmul Leiblich
(Pipes) must hand over all his money and becomes sick, the oldest son,
Simon (Klug), a student, leaves the house, Alexander becomes a
gambler and drunkard, Lise (Tschissik) becomes a prostitute, and
Lemech (Löwy), the idiot, is driven to idiotic insanity by hate of Mrs
Selde, because she takes the place of his mother, and by love, because
she is the first young woman to whom he feels close. At this point the
plot reaches a climax with the murder of Selde by Lemech. All the
others remain incomplete and helpless in the spectator's memory. The
conception of this woman and her lover, a conception that asks no one's
opinion, gave me a vague, different self-confidence.

The discreet impression made by the playbill. One learns not only
the names but a little more, yet only so much as the audience has to
know, even a very cool audience with the best intentions, about a
family exposed to their judgement. Shmul Leiblich is a 'rich merchant',
however, it is not said that he is old and infirm, that he is a ridiculous
ladies' man, a bad father, and an irreverent widower who remarries on
the anniversary of his wife's death. And yet all these characterizations
would be more accurate than that on the playbill, for at the end of the
play he is no longer rich, because the Selde woman has thoroughly
robbed him, he is also hardly a merchant any longer, since he has
neglected his business. Simon is 'a student' on the playbill, therefore
something very vague, something we know many sons of our most
distant acquaintances are. Alexander, this characterless young man, is
just 'Alexander'; of Lise, the home-loving girl, we know also only that

she is 'Lise'. Lemech is unfortunately 'an idiot', for that is something that cannot be hushed up. Vladimir Vorobeitchik is only 'Selde's lover', but not the corrupter of a family, not a drunkard, gambler, wastrel, idler, parasite. In the characterization, 'Selde's lover', much of course is betrayed, but considering his behaviour it is the least that can be said. In addition to this the scene of action is Russia, the scarcely assembled characters are scattered over a tremendous area, or assembled in a small, unrevealed place in this area, in short, the play has become impossible, the spectator will get to see nothing.

– Nevertheless, the play begins, the obviously great powers of the author begin to work, things come to light which one would not expect of the characters on the playbill but which fall to their lot with the greatest inevitability if one can only persuade oneself to believe in all the whipping, snatching away, beating, slapping on the shoulder, fainting, throat-cutting, limping, dancing in Russian topboots, dancing with raised skirts, rolling on the sofa, which are after all things that it does no good to contradict. Yet not even the climax of the spectator's excitement, remembered afterward, is necessary in order to recognize that the discreet impression made by the playbill is a false impression which can originate only in some tired outsider, since for one who judges honestly no decent relationship can be seen between the playbill and the play after its performance.

From the dash on, written in despair, because today they are playing cards with unusual uproar, I must sit at the common table, O. laughs with all her mouth, gets up, sits down, reaches across the table, speaks to me, and I, to complete the misfortune, write so badly and must think of Löwy's Paris recollections, well written with an uninterrupted feeling, which come out of an independent fire while I, at least now (mostly, I am certain, because I have so little time), am almost entirely under Max's influence, which sometimes, to cap it all, even spoils my enjoyment of his work as well. Because it consoles me I write down an autobiographical remark of Shaw's, although it actually is the opposite of consoling: As a boy he was apprentice in the office of an estate agent's in Dublin. He soon gave up this position, went to London, and became a writer. In the first nine years, from 1876 to 1885, he earned 140 kronen in all. 'But although I was a strong young man and my family found itself in poor circumstances, I did not throw myself into the struggle for a livelihood; I threw my mother in and let her support me. I was no support for my old father; on the contrary, I hung on to his coat-tails.' In the end this is little consolation for me. The free years he spent in London are already past for me, the possible happiness becomes ever more impossible, I lead a horrible synthetic life and am cowardly and miserable enough to follow Shaw only to the extent of having read the passage to my parents. How this possible life flashes before my eyes in colours of steel, with spanning rods of steel and airy darkness between!

27 October. Löwy's stories and diaries: How Notre Dame frightens him, how the tiger in the Jardin des Plantes affects him as an image of one who despairs and hopes, appeasing his despair and hope with food, how his pious father in misapprehension questions him as to whether he can now go for walks on Saturday, whether he now has time to read modern books, whether he now may eat on the fast days, while as a matter of fact he must work on Saturdays, has no time for anything, and fasts more than any religion prescribed. When he walks through the streets chewing his black beard it looks from a distance as though he were eating chocolate. The work in the cap factory and his friend the socialist who considers everyone a bourgeois who does not work exactly the way he does – such as Löwy with his fine hands – who is bored on Sundays, who despises reading as something luxurious, cannot read himself and ironically asks Löwy to read him a letter that he had received.

The Jewish ritual bath that every Jewish community in Russia has, which I picture to myself as a cabin with a basin of exactly determined outline, with arrangements appointed and supervised by the rabbi, which must only wash the earthly dirt from the soul, whose external condition is therefore a matter of indifference, that is, a symbol, therefore can be, and is, filthy and stinking, but still fulfils its purpose. The woman comes here to purify herself of her period, the Torah scribe to purify himself of all sinful thoughts before writing the last verse of a book of the Torah.

Custom, immediately after awakening, to dip the fingers three times in water, as the evil spirits have settled during the night on the second and third joints of the fingers. Rationalist explanation: To prevent the fingers directly touching the face, since, uncontrolled during sleep and dreams, they could after all have touched every possible part of the body, the armpits, the behind, the genitals.

The dressing-room behind their stage is so narrow that if by chance you are standing in front of the mirror behind the portière on the set and someone else wants to pass by, he must raise the curtain and willy-nilly show himself for a moment to the audience.

Superstition: The evil spirits gain entry into a person who drinks out of an imperfect glass.

How bruised the actors appeared to me after the performance, how I feared to touch them with a word. How instead I quickly left after a hasty handshake, as though I were angry and dissatisfied, because the truth of my impression was so impossible to express. Everyone seemed false to me except Max, who quietly made some meaningless remark. And the person who asked about some irrelevant detail was false, the person who gave a facetious reply to a remark by an actor, the ironic one and the one who began to explain his varied impressions, all the rabble that had been crowded into the back of the auditorium where it belonged and now, late at night, got up and once more became aware of its importance. (Very far from correct.)

28 October. Of course, I had a similar feeling, but neither acting nor play came anywhere near seeming perfect to me that evening. For that very reason I owed the actors particular respect. When there are small, even if many deficiencies in one's impression, who knows whose fault they are? Mrs Tschissik once stepped on the hem of her dress and tottered for a moment in her princess-style hussy's dress like a massive pillar; once she made a mistake in her lines and, in order to calm her tongue, turned in great agitation towards the back wall, despite the fact that this did not quite suit the words; it irritated me, but it did not prevent the sudden flutter of a shudder upon my cheekbone, which I always feel when I hear her voice. But because my acquaintances had got a much less pure impression than I, they seemed to me to owe

even greater respect, because in my opinion their respect would have been much more effective than mine, so that I had double reason to curse their behaviour.

'Axioms for the Drama' by Max in the *Schaubühne*. Has quite the character of a dream truth, which the expression 'axioms' suits too. The more dreamlike it inflates itself, all the more coolly must you seize it. The following principles are formulated:

The thesis is, that the essence of the drama lies in a lack.

The drama (on the stage) is more exhaustive than the novel, because we see everything about which we otherwise just read.

It only seems to be, for in the novel the author can show us only what is important, in the drama, on the other hand, we see everything, the actor, the settings, and so not just what is important, therefore less. From the point of view of the novel, therefore, the best drama would be entirely unstimulating, for example, a philosophical drama that would be read by seated actors in any set at all that represented a room.

And yet the best drama is that which is the most stimulating in time and space, frees itself of all the demands of life, limits itself only to the speeches, to the thoughts in the monologues, to the main points of what happens; everything else is left to the stimulation that has been aroused, and, raised high on a shield borne by the actors, painters, directors, obeys only its most extreme inspirations.

Error in this chain of reasoning: It changes its point of view without indicating it, sees things now from the writer's room, now from the audience. Granted that the audience does not see everything from the point of view of the author, that even he is surprised by the performance (29 October, Sunday), it is still the author who had the play with all its details within himself, who moved along from detail to detail, and who only because he assembled all the details in the speeches has given them dramatic weight and force. Because of this the drama in its highest development achieves an unbearable humanization which it is the task of the actor – with his role blowing loosely and in tatters about him – to draw down, to make bearable. The drama therefore hovers in the air, but not like a roof carried along on a storm, rather like a whole building whose foundation walls have been torn up out of the earth with a force which today is still close to madness.

Sometimes it seems that the play is resting up in the flies, the actors have drawn down strips of it the ends of which they hold in their hands or have wound about their bodies for the play, and that only now and then a strip that is difficult to release carries an actor, to the terror of the audience, up in the air.

I dreamed today of a donkey that looked like a greyhound, it was very cautious in its movements. I looked at it closely because I was aware how unusual a phenomenon it was, but remember only that its narrow human feet could not please me because of their length and uniformity. I offered it a bunch of fresh, dark-green cypress leaves which I had just received from an old Zürich lady (it all took place in Zürich), it did not want it, just sniffed a little at it; but then, when I left the cypress on a table, it devoured it so completely that only a scarcely recognizable kernel resembling a chestnut was left. Later there was talk that this donkey had never yet gone on all fours but always held itself erect like a human being and showed its silvery shining breast and its little belly. But actually that was not correct.

Besides this, I dreamed about an Englishman whom I met at a meeting like the one the Salvation Army held in Zürich. There were seats there like those in school, under the blackboard there was even an open shelf; once when I reached in to straighten something I wondered at the ease with which one makes friends on a trip. By this apparently was meant the Englishman, who shortly thereafter approached me. He had loose, light clothes in very good condition, but high up on the back of the arms, instead of the material of the clothing, or at least sewn on over it, there was a grey, wrinkled material, hanging a little, torn in strips, stippled as though by spiders, that reminded one as much of the leather reinforcements on riding-breeches as of the sleeve protectors of seamstresses, sales-girls, clerks. His face was also covered with a grey material that had very clever slits for mouth, eyes, probably also for the nose. But this material was new, napped, rather like flannel, very flexible and soft, of excellent English manufacture. All this pleased me so, that I was eager to become acquainted with the man. He wanted to invite me to his house too, but since I had to leave as soon as the day after tomorrow, that came to nothing. Before he left the meeting he put on several more apparently very practical pieces of clothing that made him look quite inconspicuous after he had buttoned them. Although he could not invite me to his home, he nevertheless asked me to go into the street with him. I followed him, we stopped across the street from the meeting-place on the curb, I below, he above, and found again after some discussion that nothing could be done about the invitation.

Then I dreamed that Max, Otto,[24] and I had the habit of packing our trunks only when we reached the railway station. There we were, carrying our shirts, for example, through the main hall to our distant trunks. Although this seemed to be a general custom, it was not a good one in our case, especially since we had begun to pack only shortly before the arrival of the train. Then we were naturally excited and had hardly any hope of still catching the train, let alone getting good seats.

Although the regular guests and employees of the coffee-house are fond of the actors, they cannot remain respectful amid the depressing impressions, and despise the actors as starvellings, tramps, fellow Jews, exactly as in the past. Thus, the head-waiter wanted to throw Löwy out of the hall, the doorman, who used to work in a brothel and is now a pimp, shouted little Tschissik down when she, in the excitement of her sympathy during *Der Wilde Mensch*, wanted to pass something to the actors, and the day before yesterday, when I accompanied Löwy back to the coffee-house after he had read me the first act of Gordin's *Eliezar ben Schevia* in the City Café, that fellow called to him (he squints, and between his crooked, pointed nose and his mouth there is a hollow out of which a small moustache bristles): 'Come on, idiot. (Allusion to the role in *Der Wilde Mensch*.) Someone's waiting. There's a visitor you really don't deserve. An officer candidate in the artillery is here. Look.' And he points to one of the curtained coffee-house windows behind which the officer candidate is allegedly sitting. Löwy passes his hand over his forehead: 'From Eliezar ben Schevia to this.'

The sight of stairs moves me so today. Early in the day already, and several times since, I have enjoyed the sight from my window of the triangular piece cut out of the stone railing of the staircase that leads down on the right from the Czech Bridge to the quay level. Very steep, as though it were giving only a hasty suggestion. And now, over there across the river, I see a step-ladder on the slope that leads down to the water. It has always been there, but is revealed only in the autumn and winter by the removal of the swimming school in front of it, and it lies there in the dark grass under the brown trees in the play of perspective.

Löwy: Four young friends became great Talmud scholars in their old age. But each had a different fate. One became mad, one died, Rabbi Eliezar became a free-thinker at forty and only the oldest one, Akiva, who had not begun his studies until the age of forty, achieved complete knowledge. The disciple of Rabbi Eliezar was Rabbi Meyer, a pious man whose piety was so great that he was not harmed by what the free-thinker taught him. He ate, as he said, the kernel of the nut, the shell he threw away. Once, on Saturday, Eliezar went for a ride, Rabbi Meyer followed on foot, the Talmud in his hand, of course only for two thousand paces, for you are not permitted to go any farther on Saturday. And from this walk emerged a symbolic demand and the reply to it. Come back to your people, said Rabbi Meyer. Rabbi Eliezar refused with a pun.

30 October. This craving that I almost always have, when for once I feel my stomach is healthy, to heap up in me notions of terrible deeds of daring with food. I especially satisfy this craving in front of pork butchers. If I see a sausage that is labelled as an old, hard sausage; I bite into it in my imagination with all my teeth and swallow quickly, regularly, and thoughtlessly, like a machine. The despair that this act, even in the imagination, has as its immediate result, increases my haste. I shove the long slabs of rib meat unbitten into my mouth, and then pull them out again from behind, tearing through stomach and intestines. I eat dirty delicatessen stores completely empty. Cram myself with herrings, pickles, and all the bad, old, sharp foods. Bonbons are poured into me like hail from their tin boxes. I enjoy in this way not only my healthy condition but also a suffering that is without pain and can pass at once.

It is an old habit of mine, at the point when an impression has reached its greatest degree of purity, whether of joy or pain, not to allow it to run its salutary course through all my being, but rather to cloud and dispel its purity by new, unexpected, weak impressions. It is not that I evilly intend my own harm, I am only too weak to bear the purity of that impression. Instead of admitting this weakness, which alone would be right, because in revealing itself it calls forth other forces to its support, I rather quietly and with seeming arbitrariness try to evoke new impressions in an effort to help myself.

On Saturday evening, for example, after hearing Miss T.'s[25] excellent story, which after all belongs more to Max, at least belongs to him to a greater extent than one of his own stories, and later after hearing the excellent play *Konkurrenz* by Baum, in which dramatic force can be seen in the work and in the effect quite as uninterruptedly as in the production of a living craftsman, after the hearing of both these works I was so cast down and my insides, already fairly empty for several days, quite without warning filled with such deep sorrow that I declared to Max on the way home that nothing can come of *Richard and Samuel*. For this declaration too, not the smallest courage was needed at the time, as far as either I or Max was concerned. The discussion that followed confused me a little, as *Richard and Samuel* was then far from being my chief concern and I therefore did not find the right answers to Max's objections. But later, when I was alone, and not only the disturbance of my sorrow by the conversation but also the almost effective consolation of Max's presence had disappeared, my hopelessness grew to such an extent that it began to dissolve my thinking (at this point, while I am stopping for dinner, Löwy comes to the house and interrupts me and delights me from seven to ten o'clock). Still, instead of waiting at home for what would happen next, I carelessly read two issues of *Aktion*, a little in *Die Missgeschickten*,[26] finally also in my Paris notes, and went to bed, really more content than before, but obdurate. It was the same several days ago when I returned from a walk and found myself imitating Löwy to such a degree that the force of his enthusiasm, externally, worked towards my goal. Then, too, I read and spoke a great deal in confusion at home and slowly collapsed.

31 October. Despite the fact that today I have read here and there in the Fischer catalogue, in the *Insel Almanach*, in the *Rundschau*, I am now pretty sure that, whether I have assimilated everything either thoroughly or casually, I have in any case defended myself against all

harm. And I should have enough self-confidence tonight if I didn't have to go out with Löwy again.

When on Sunday afternoon, just after passing three women, I stepped into Max's house, I thought: There are still one or two houses in which I have something to do, there are still women walking behind me who can see me turn in on a Sunday afternoon at a house door in order to work, talk, purposefully, hurriedly, only occasionally looking at the matter in this way. This must not remain so for long.

I read the stories of Wilhelm Schäfer, especially when aloud, with the same attentive enjoyment that I should get from drawing a piece of twine over my tongue. At first I did not like Valli[27] very much yesterday afternoon, but after I had lent her *Die Missgeschickten* and she had already read it a little while and must already have been properly under the influence of the story, I loved her because of this influence and caressed her.

In order not to forget it, should my father once again call me a bad son, I write it down that, in the presence of several relatives, without special occasion, whether it may have been simply to put me in my place, whether it was supposedly to rescue me, he called Max a '*meshuggener ritoch*',[28] and that yesterday, when Löwy was in my room, ironically shaking his body and contorting his mouth, he referred to these strange people who were being let into the house, what could interest one in a strange person, why one enters into such useless relationships, etc. After all, I should not have written it down, for I have written myself almost into a hatred of my father, for which after all he has given no occasion today and which, at least as far as Löwy is concerned, is out of all proportion to what I have written down as having been said by my father, and which even increases because I cannot remember what was really wicked in my father's behaviour yesterday.

1 November. Today, eagerly and happily began to read the *History of the Jews* by Graetz. Because my desire for it had far outrun the reading, it was at first stranger to me than I thought, and I had to stop

here and there in order by resting to allow my Jewishness to collect itself. Towards the end, however, I was already gripped by the imperfection of the first settlements in the newly conquered Canaan and the faithful handing down of the imperfections of the popular heroes (Joshua, the Judges, Elijah).

Last night, good-bye to Mrs Klug. We, I and Löwy, ran alongside the train and saw Mrs Klug looking out from the darkness behind a closed window in the last coach. She quickly stretched her arm towards us while still in her compartment, stood up, opened the window, filling it for a moment with her unbuttoned cloak, until the dark Mr Klug (all he can do is open up his mouth wide and bitterly and then snap it shut, as though forever) got up opposite her. During the fifteen minutes I spoke very little to Mr Klug and looked at him for perhaps only two seconds, otherwise I could not, during the weak, uninterrupted conversation, turn my eyes away from Mrs Klug. She was completely under the domination of my presence, but more in her imagination than in reality. When she turned to Löwy with the repeated introductory phrase, 'You, Löwy,' she spoke to me, when she leaned close against her husband who sometimes left her with only her right shoulder showing at the window and pressed against her dress and her baggy overcoat, she was attempting in that way to make me an empty sign.

The first impression I had at the performances, that she did not like me especially, was probably correct, she seldom invited me to sing with her; when, without real feeling, she asked me something, I unfortunately answered incorrectly ('Do you understand that?' 'Yes,' I said, but she wanted 'No' in order to reply, 'Neither do I'); she did not offer me her picture postcards a second time, I preferred Mrs Tschissik, to whom I wanted to give some flowers in order to spite Mrs Klug. To this disinclination, however, was joined a respect for my doctorate which was not impaired by my childish appearance, indeed, it was even increased by it. This respect was so great and it became so articulate in her frequent but by no means particularly stressed way of addressing me – 'You know, Herr Doktor' – that I half unconsciously regretted that I deserved it so little and asked myself whether I had a right to be addressed like that by everyone. But while I was so respected by her as a person, as a spectator I was even more respected. I beamed when she sang, I laughed and looked at her all the time while she was on the stage, I sang the tunes with her, later the words, I thanked her after several performances; because of this, again, she naturally liked me very well. But if she spoke to me out of this feeling I was so embarrassed that she undoubtedly fell back into her original disinclination and remained there. She had to exert herself all the more to reward me as a spectator, and she was glad to do it because she is a vain actress and a good-natured woman.

She looked at me, especially when she was silent up there in the window of the compartment, with a mouth rapturously contorted by embarrassment and slyness and with twinkling eyes that swam on the wrinkles spreading from her mouth. She must have believed I loved her, as was indeed true, and with these glances she gave me the sole fulfilment that a young but experienced woman, a good wife and mother, could give a doctor of her imagination. These glances were so urgent, and were supported by expressions like 'There were such nice guests here, especially some of them', that I defended myself, and those were the moments when I looked at her husband. I had, when I compared the two, an unjustified sense of astonishment at the fact that they should depart from us together and yet concern themselves only with us and have no glance for one another. Löwy asked whether they had good seats. 'Yes, if it remains as empty as this,' Mrs Klug answered, and looked casually into the inside of the compartment the warm air of which her husband will spoil with his smoking. We spoke of their children for whose sake they were leaving; they have four children, three boys among them, the oldest is nine years old, they haven't seen them for eighteen months now. When a gentleman got hurriedly into a near-by compartment, the train seemed about to leave, we quickly said good-bye, shook each other's hands, I tipped my hat and then held it against my chest, we stepped back as one does when trains leave, by which one means to show that everything is finished and one has come to terms with it. The train did not leave yet, however, we stepped up close again, I was rather happy about it, she asked after my sisters. Surprisingly, the train began to move slowly. Mrs Klug prepared to wave her handkerchief, I must write to her, she called, do I know her address, she was already too far away for me to be able to answer her, I pointed to Löwy from whom I could get the address, that's good, she nodded to me and him quickly, and let her handkerchief float in the wind, I tipped my hat, at first awkwardly, then, the farther away she was, the more freely.

Later I remembered that I had had the impression that the train was not really leaving but only moving the short length of the railway station in order to put on a play for us, and then was swallowed up. In a doze that same evening, Mrs Klug appeared to me unnaturally short, almost without legs, and wrung her hands with her face distorted as though a great misfortune had befallen her.

This afternoon the pain occasioned by my loneliness came upon me so piercingly and intensely that I became aware that the strength which I gain through this writing thus spends itself, a strength which I certainly have not intended for this purpose.

As soon as Mr Klug comes to a new city one can see how his and his wife's jewels disappear into the pawnshop. As their departure draws near he gradually redeems them again.

Favourite saying of the wife of the philosopher Mendelssohn: *Wie mies ist mir vor tout l'univers!*

One of the most important impressions at the departure of Mrs Klug: I was always forced to think that, as a simple middle-class woman, she holds herself by force below the level of her true human destiny and requires only a jump, a tearing open of the door, a turned-up light, in order to be an actress and to subjugate me. Actually, even, she stood above and I below, as in the theatre – She married at sixteen, is twenty-six years old.

2 November. This morning, for the first time in a long time, the joy again of imagining a knife twisted in my heart.

In the newspapers, in conversation, in the office, the impetuosity of language often leads one astray, also the hope, springing from temporary weakness, for a sudden and stronger illumination in the very next moment, also mere strong self-confidence, or mere carelessness, or a great present impression that one wishes at any cost to shift into the future, also the opinion that true enthusiasm in the present justifies any future confusion, also delight in sentences that are elevated in the middle by one or two jolts and open the mouth gradually to its full size even if they let it close much too quickly and tortuously, also the slight possibility of a decisive and clear judgement, or the effort to give further flow to the speech that has really ended, also the desire to escape from the subject in a hurry, one's belly if it must be, or despair that seeks a way out for its heavy breath, or the longing for a light without shadow – all this can lead one astray to sentences like: 'The book which I have just finished is the most beautiful I have ever read,' or, 'is more beautiful than any I have ever read'.

In order to prove that everything I write and think about them is false, the actors (aside from Mr and Mrs Klug) have again remained here, as Löwy, whom I met yesterday evening, told me; who knows whether for the same reason they will not depart again today, for Löwy did not call at the office despite the fact that he promised to.

3 November. In order to prove that both things that I wrote were false, a proof that seems almost impossible, Löwy himself came yesterday evening and interrupted me while I was writing.

N.'s habit of repeating everything in the same tone of voice. He tells someone a story about his business, of course not with so many details that it would in itself completely kill the story, but nevertheless in a slow manner, thorough only because of that, it is a communication which is not intended to be anything else and is therefore done with when it is finished. A short time passes with something else, suddenly he finds a transition to his story and produces it again in its old form, almost without additions, but also almost without omissions, with the innocence of a person who carries about the room a ribbon that someone has treacherously tied to his back. Now my parents like him particularly, therefore feel his habit more strongly than they notice it, and so it happens that they, especially my mother, unconsciously give him opportunities to repeat. If some evening the moment for repeating a story cannot quite be found, then Mother is there, she asks a question, and indeed with a curiosity that does not end even after the question is asked, as one might expect. As for stories that have already been repeated and could not return again by their own strength, Mother hunts after them with her questions even several evenings later. N.'s habit is, however, so obsessive that it often has the power to justify itself completely. No one else gets with such regular frequency into the position of having to tell members of the family individually a story that basically concerns all of them. The story must then be told, almost as often as there are persons, to the family circle that in such cases assembles slowly, at intervals, one person at a time. And because I am the one who alone has recognized N.'s habit, I am also usually the one who hears the story first and for whom the repetitions provide only the small pleasure of confirming an observation.

Envy at nominal success of Baum whom I really like so much. With this, the feeling of having in the middle of my body a ball of wool that quickly winds itself up, its innumerable threads pulling from the surface of my body to itself.

Löwy. My father about him: 'Whoever lies down with dogs gets up with fleas.' I could not contain myself and said something uncontrolled. To which Father with unusual quietness (to be sure, after a long interval which was otherwise occupied): 'You know that I should not get excited and must be treated with consideration. And now you speak to me like that. I really have enough excitement, quite enough. So don't bother me with such talk.' I say: 'I make every effort to restrain myself,' and sense in my father, as always in such extreme moments, the existence of a wisdom of which I can grasp only a breath.

Death of Löwy's grandfather, a man who had an open hand, knew several languages, had made long journeys deep into Russia, and who once on a Saturday refused to eat at the house of a wonder-rabbi in Ekaterinoslav because the long hair and coloured neckerchief of the rabbi's son made him suspect the piety of the house.

The bed was set up in the middle of the room, the candlesticks were borrowed from friends and relatives, the room therefore full of the light and smoke of the candles. Some forty men stood around his bed all day to receive inspiration from the death of a pious man. He was conscious until the end and at the right moment, his hand on his breast, he began to repeat the death prayers. During his suffering and after his death the grandmother, who was with the women gathered in the next room, wept incessantly, but while he was dying she was completely calm because it is a commandment to ease the death of the dying man as much as one can. 'With his own prayers he passed away.' He was much envied for this death that followed so pious a life.

Pesach festival. An association of rich Jews rents a bakery, its members take over for the heads of the families all the tasks of producing the so-called eighteen-minute matzos: the fetching of water, the koshering, the kneading, the cutting, the piercing.

5 November. Yesterday slept, with Löwy after *Bar Kokhba* from seven on, read a letter from his father. Evening at Baum's.

I want to write, with a constant trembling on my forehead. I sit in my room in the very headquarters of the uproar of the entire house. I hear all the doors close, because of their noise only the footsteps of those running between them are spared me, I hear even the slamming of the oven door in the kitchen. My father bursts through the doors of my room and passes through in his dragging dressing-gown, the ashes are scraped out of the stove in the next room, Valli asks, shouting into the indefinite through the ante-room as though through a Paris street, whether Father's hat has been brushed yet, a hushing that claims to be friendly to me raises the shout of an answering voice. The house door is unlatched and screeches as though from a catarrhal throat, then opens wider with the brief singing of a woman's voice and closes with a dull manly jerk that sounds most inconsiderate. My father is gone, now begins the more delicate, more distracted, more hopeless noise led by the voices of the two canaries. I had already thought of it before, but with the canaries it comes back to me again, that I might open the door a narrow crack, crawl into the next room like a snake and in that way, on the floor, beg my sisters and their governess for quiet.

The bitterness I felt yesterday evening when Max read my little motor-car story at Baum's. I was isolated from everyone and in the face of the story I kept my chin pressed against my breast, as it were. The disordered sentences of this story with holes into which one could stick both hands; one sentence sounds high, one sentence sounds low, as the case may be, one sentence rubs against another like the tongue against a hollow or false tooth; one sentence comes marching up with so rough a start that the entire story falls into sulky amazement; a sleepy imitation of Max (reproaches muffled – stirred up) seesaws in, sometimes it looks like a dancing course during its first quarter-hour. I explain it to myself by saying that I have too little time and quiet to draw out of me all the possibilities of my talent. For that reason it is only disconnected starts that always make an appearance, disconnected starts, for instance, all through the motor-car story. If I were ever able to write something large and whole, well shaped from beginning to end, then in the end the story would never be able to detach itself from me and it would be possible for me calmly and with open eyes, as a blood relation of a healthy story, to hear it read, but as it is every little piece of the story runs around homeless and drives me away from it in the opposite direction. – At the same time I can still be happy if this explanation is correct.

Performance of Goldfaden's *Bar Kokhba*. False judgement of the play throughout the hall and on the stage.

I had brought along a bouquet for Mrs Tschissik, with an attached visiting card inscribed 'in gratitude', and waited for the moment when I could have it presented to her. The performance had begun late, Mrs Tschissik's big scene was promised me only in the fourth act, in impatience and fear that the flowers might wilt I had them unwrapped by the waiter as early as during the third act (it was eleven o'clock), they lay on a table, the kitchen help and several dirty regular guests handed them from one to another and smelled them, I could only look on worriedly and angrily, nothing else, I loved Mrs Tschissik during her big scene in the prison, but still, I was anxious for her to bring it to its end, finally the act, unnoticed by me in my distraction, was finished, the head-waiter handed up the flowers, Mrs Tschissik took them between final curtains, she bowed in a narrow opening of the curtains and did not return again. No one noticed my love and I had intended to reveal it to all and so make it valuable in the eyes of Mrs Tschissik; the bouquet was hardly noticed. Meanwhile it was already past two o'clock, everyone was tired, several people had already left, I should have enjoyed throwing my glass at them.

With me was Comptroller P. from our firm, a Gentile. He, whom I usually like, disturbed me. My worry was the flowers, not his affairs. At the same time I knew that he understood the play incorrectly, while I had no time, desire, or ability to force upon him assistance which he did not think he needed. Finally I was ashamed of myself before him because I myself was paying so little attention. Also he disturbed me in my conversation with Max and even by the recollection that I had liked him before, would again like him afterwards, and that he could take my behaviour today amiss.

But not only I was disturbed. Max felt responsible because of his laudatory article in the paper. It was getting too late for the Jews in Bergmann's convoy. The members of the Bar Kokhba Association had come because of the name of the play and could not help being disappointed. From what I know of Bar Kokhba from this play, I would not have named any association after him. In the back of the hall there were two shop-girls in their best clothes with their sweethearts who had to be silenced by loud shouts during the death scenes. Finally people on the street struck the huge panes in annoyance that they saw so little of the stage.

The two Klugs were missing from the stage. Ridiculous extras. 'Vulgar Jews,' as Löwy said. Travelling salesmen who weren't paid. Most of the time they were concerned only with concealing their laughter or enjoying it, even if aside from this they meant well. A round-cheeked fellow with a blond beard at the sight of whom you could scarcely keep from laughing looked especially funny when he laughed. His false beard shook unnaturally, because of his laughter it was no longer pasted in its right place on his cheeks. Another fellow laughed only when he wanted to, but then a lot. When Löwy died, singing, in the arms of these two elders and was supposed to slip slowly to earth with the fading song, they put their heads together behind his back in order finally to be able to laugh their fill for once, unseen by the audience (as they thought). Yesterday, when I remembered it at lunch, I still had to laugh.

Mrs Tschissik in prison must take the helmet off the drunken Roman governor (young Pipes) who is visiting her and then put it on herself.

When she takes it off, a crushed towel falls out which Pipes had apparently stuffed in because the helmet pinched too much. Although he certainly must have known that the helmet would be taken off his head on the stage, he looks reproachfully at Mrs Tschissik, forgetting his drunkenness.

Beautiful: the way Mrs Tschissik, under the hands of the Roman soldiers (whom, however, she first had to pull to her, for they obviously were afraid to touch her), writhed while the movements of the three actors by her care and art almost, only almost, followed the rhythm of the singing; the song in which she proclaims the appearance of the Messiah, and, without destroying the illusion, sheerly by the spell she casts, represents the playing of a harp by the motions of bowing a violin; in the prison where at the frequent approach of footsteps she breaks off her song of lamentation, hurries to her treadmill and turns it to the accompaniment of a work song, then again escapes to her song and again to the mill, the way she sings in her sleep when Papus visits her and her mouth is open like a twinkling eye, the way in general the corners of her mouth in opening remind one of the corners of her eyes. In the white veil, as in the black, she was beautiful.

New among her familiar gestures: pressing her hand deep into her not very good bodice, abrupt shrug of her shoulders and hips in scorn, especially when she turns her back on the one scorned.

She led the whole performance like the mother of a family. She prompted everyone but never faltered herself; she instructed the extras, implored them, finally shoved them if need be; her clear voice, when she was off stage, joined in the ragged chorus on stage; she held up the folding screen (which in the last act was supposed to represent a citadel) that the extras would have knocked down ten times.

I had hoped, by means of the bouquet of flowers, to appease my love for her a little, it was quite useless. It is possible only through literature or through sleeping together. I write this not because I did not know it, but rather because it is perhaps well to write down warnings frequently.

7 November. Tuesday. Yesterday the actors and Mrs Tschissik finally left. I went with Löwy to the coffee-house in the evening, but waited outside, did not want to go in, did not want to see Mrs Tschissik.

But while I was walking up and down I saw her open the door and come out with Löwy, I went towards them with a greeting and met them in the middle of the street. Mrs Tschissik thanked me for my bouquet in the grand but natural vocables of her speech, she had only just now learned that it was from me. This liar Löwy had therefore said nothing to her. I was worried about her because she was wearing only a thin, dark blouse with short sleeves and I asked her – I almost touched her in order to force her – to go into the restaurant so that she would not catch cold. No, she said, she does not catch cold, indeed she has a shawl, and she raised it a little to show it and then drew it together more closely about her breast. I could not tell her that I was not really concerned about her but was rather only happy to have found an emotion in which I could enjoy my love, and therefore I told her again that I was worried.

Meanwhile her husband, her little girl, and Mr Pipes had also come out and it turned out that it had by no means been decided that they would go to Brünn as Löwy had convinced me, on the contrary, Pipes was even determined to go to Nuremberg. That would be best, a hall would be easy to get, the Jewish community is large, moreover, the trip to Leipzig and Berlin very comfortable. Furthermore they had discussed it all day and Löwy, who had slept until four, had simply kept them waiting and made them miss the seven-thirty for Brünn. Amidst these arguments we entered the tavern and sat down at a table, I across from Mrs Tschissik. I should so have liked to distinguish myself, this would not have been so difficult, I should just have had to know several train connexions, tell the railway stations apart, bring about a choice between Nuremberg and Brünn, but chiefly shout down Pipes who was behaving like his Bar Kokhba. To Pipes's shouting Löwy very reasonably, if unintentionally, counterposed a very quick, uninterruptable chatter in his normal voice that was, at least for me, rather incomprehensible at the time. So instead of distinguishing myself I sat sunk in my chair, looked from Pipes to Löwy, and only now and then caught Mrs Tschissik's eye on the way, but when she answered me with her glance (when she smiled at me because of Pipes's excitement, for instance) I looked away. This had its sense. Between us there could be no smiling at Pipes's excitement. Facing her, I was too serious for this, and quite tired by this seriousness. If I wanted to laugh at something I could look across her shoulder at the fat woman who had played the governor's wife in *Bar Kokhba*. But really I could not look at her seriously either. For that would have meant that I loved her. Even young Pipes behind me, in all his innocence, would have had to recognize that. And that would have been really unheard of. A young man whom everyone takes to be eighteen years old declares in the presence of the evening's guests at the Café Savoy, amidst the surrounding waiters, in the presence of the table full of actors, declares to a thirty-year-old woman whom hardly anyone even considers pretty, who has two children, ten and eight years old, whose husband is sitting beside her, who is a model of respectability and economy – declares to this woman his love to which he has completely fallen victim and, now comes the really remarkable part which of course no one else would have observed, immediately renounces the woman, just as he would renounce her if she were young and single. Should I be grateful or should I curse the fact that despite all misfortune I can still feel love, an unearthly love but still for earthly objects.

Mrs Tschissik was beautiful yesterday. The really normal beauty of small hands, of light fingers, of rounded forearms which in themselves are so perfect that even the unaccustomed sight of this nakedness does not make one think of the rest of the body. The hair separated into two waves, brightly illumined by the gaslight. Somewhat bad complexion around the right corner of her mouth. Her mouth opens as though in childish complaint, running above and below into delicately shaped curves, one imagines that the beautiful shaping of words, which spreads the light of the vowels throughout the words and preserves their pure contours with the tip of the tongue, can succeed only once, and admires how everlasting it is. Low, white forehead. The powdering that I have so far seen I hate, but if this white colour, this somewhat cloudy milk-coloured veil hovering low over the skin is the result of powder, then every woman should powder. She likes to hold two fingers to the right corner of her mouth, perhaps she even stuck the tips of her fingers into her mouth – yes, perhaps she even put a toothpick into her mouth; I didn't look closely at these fingers, but it seemed almost as though she were poking in a hollow tooth with a toothpick and let it stay there a quarter of an hour.

8 November. All afternoon at the lawyer's about the factory.

The girl who only because she was walking arm in arm with her sweetheart looked quietly around.

The clerk in N.'s office reminded me of the actress who played Manette Salomon at the Odéon in Paris a year and a half ago. At least when she was sitting. A soft bosom, broader than it was high, encased in a woolly material. A broad face down to the mouth, but then rapidly narrowing. Neglected, natural curls in a flat hair-do. Zeal and calm in a strong body. The resemblance was strengthened too, as I see now, because she worked on unmoved (the keys flew – Oliver system – on her typewriter like old-time knitting needles), also walked about, but scarcely spoke two words in half an hour, as though she had Manette Salomon within her.

When I was waiting at the lawyer's I looked at the one typist and thought how hard it was to make out her face even while looking at it. The relationship between a hair-do standing out almost at the same distance all around her head, and the straight nose that most of the time seemed too long, was especially confusing. When the girl who was reading a document made a more striking movement, I was almost confounded by the observation that through my contemplation I had remained more of a stranger to the girl than if I had brushed her skirt with my little finger.

When the lawyer, in reading the agreement [about the shares in the factory] to me, came to a passage concerning my possible future wife and possible children, I saw across from me a table with two large chairs and a smaller one around it. At the thought that I should never be in a position to seat in these or any other three chairs myself, my wife, and my child, there came over me a yearning for this happiness so despairing from the very start that in my excitement I asked the lawyer the only question I had left after the long reading, which at once revealed my complete misunderstanding of a rather long section of the agreement that had just been read.

Continuation of the farewell: In Pipes, because I felt oppressed by him, I saw first of all the jagged and darkly spotted tips of his teeth.

Finally I got half an idea: 'Why go as far as Nuremberg in one jump?' I asked. 'Why not give one or two performances at a smaller local station?'

'Do you know one?' asked Mrs Tschissik, not nearly as sharply as I write it, and in this way forced me to look at her. All that part of her body which was visible above the table, all the roundness of shoulders, back, and breast, was soft despite her (in European dress, on the stage) bony, almost coarse build. Ridiculously I mentioned Pilsen. Some regular guests at the next table very reasonably mentioned Teplitz. Mr Tschissik would have been in favour of any local station, he has confidence only in small undertakings, Mrs Tschissik agreed without their having consulted much with one another, aside from that she asks around about the fares. Several times they said that if they just earned enough for *parnusse*,[29] it would be sufficient. Her daughter rubs her cheek against her arm; she certainly does not feel it, but to the adult there comes the childish conviction that nothing can happen to a child who is with its parents, even if they are travelling actors, and that if you think about it, real troubles are not to be met with so close to the earth but only at the height of an adult's face. I was very much in favour of Teplitz because I could give them a letter of recommendation to Dr P. and so use my influence for Mrs Tschissik. In the face of the objection of Pipes, who himself prepared the lots to be drawn for the three possible cities and conducted the drawing with great liveliness, Teplitz was drawn for the third time. I went to the next table and excitedly wrote the letter of recommendation. I took my leave with the excuse that I had to go home to get the exact address of Dr P., which was not necessary, however, and which they didn't know at home, either. In embarrassment, while Löwy prepared to accompany me, I played with the hand of the woman, the chin of her little girl.

9 November. A dream the day before yesterday: Everything theatre, I now up in the balcony, now on the stage, a girl whom I had liked a few months ago was playing a part, tensed her lithe body when she held on to the back of a chair in terror; from the balcony I pointed to the girl who was playing a male role, my companion did not like her. In one act the set was so large that nothing else was to be seen, no stage, no auditorium, no dark, no footlights; instead, great crowds of

spectators were on the set which represented the Altstädter Ring, probably seen from the opening of Niklasstrasse. Although one should really not have been able to see the square in front of the Rathaus clock and the small Ring, short turns and slow rockings of the stage floor nevertheless made it possible to look down, for example, on the small Ring from Kinsky Palace. This had no purpose except to show the whole set whenever possible, since it was already there in such perfection anyhow, and since it would have been a crying shame to miss seeing any of this set which, as I was well aware, was the most beautiful set in all the world and of all time. The lighting was that of dark, autumnal clouds. The light of the dimmed sun was scatteredly reflected from one or another stained-glass window on the south-east side of the square. Since everything was executed in life size and without the smallest false detail, the fact that some of the casement windows were blown open and shut by the slight breeze without a sound because of the great height of the houses, made an overwhelming impression. The square was very steep, the pavement almost black, the Tein Church was in its place, but in front of it was a small imperial castle in the courtyard of which all the monuments that ordinarily stood in the square were assembled in perfect order: the Pillar of St Mary, the old fountain in front of the Rathaus that I myself have never seen, the fountain before the Niklas Church, and a board fence that has now been put up round the excavation for the Hus memorial.

They acted – in the audience one often forgets that it is only acting, how much truer is this on the stage and behind the scenes – an imperial fête and a revolution. The revolution, with huge throngs of people sent back and forth, was probably greater than anything that ever took place in Prague; they had apparently located it in Prague only because of the set, although really it belonged in Paris. Of the fête one saw nothing at first, in any event, the court had ridden off to a fête, meanwhile the revolution had broken out, the people had forced its ways into the castle, I myself ran out into the open right over the ledges of the fountain in the churchyard, but it was supposed to be impossible for the court to return to the castle. Then the court carriages came from Eisengasse at so wild a pace that they had to brake while still far from the castle entrance, and slid across the pavement with locked wheels. They were the sort of carriages – one sees them at festivals and processions – on which living tableaux are shown, they were therefore flat, hung with garlands of flowers, and from the carriage floors a coloured cloth covering the wheels hung down all around. One was all the more aware of the terror that their speed indicated. As though unconsciously, the horses, which reared before the entrance, pulled the carriages in a curve from Eisengasse to the castle. Just then many people streamed past me out into the square, mostly spectators whom I knew from the street and who perhaps had arrived this very moment. Among them there was also a girl I know, but I do not know which; beside her walked a young, elegant man in a yellowish-brown ulster with small checks, his right hand deep in his pocket. They walked toward Niklasstrasse. From this moment on I saw nothing more.

Schiller some place or other: The chief thing. is (or something similar) 'to transform emotion into character'.

11 November. Saturday. Yesterday all afternoon at Max's. Decided on the sequence of the essays for *The Beauty of Ugly Pictures*. Without good feeling. It is just then, however, that Max loves me most, or does it only seem so because then I am so clearly conscious how little deserving I am. No, he really loves me more. He wants to include my 'Brescia' in the book too.[80] Everything good in me struggles against it. I was supposed to go to Brünn with him today. Everything bad and weak in me held me back. For I cannot believe that I shall really write something good tomorrow.

The girls, tightly wrapped up in their work aprons, especially behind. One at Löwy's and Winterberg's this morning whose apron flaps, which closed only on her behind, did not tie together as they usually do, but instead closed over each other so that she was wrapped up like a child in swaddling clothes. Sensual impression like that which, even unconsciously, I always had of children in swaddling clothes who are so squeezed in their wrappings and beds and so laced with ribbons, quite as though to satisfy one's lust.

Edison, in an American interview, told of his trip through Bohemia, in his opinion the relatively higher development of Bohemia (in the suburbs there are broad streets, gardens in front of the houses, in travelling through the country you see factories being built) is due to the fact that the emigration of Czechs to America is so large, and that those returning from there one by one bring new ambition back.

As soon as I become aware in any way that I leave abuses undisturbed which it was really intended that I should correct (for example, the extremely satisfied, but from my point of view dismal, life of my married sister), I lose all sensation in my arm muscles for a moment.

I will try, gradually, to group everything certain in me, later the credible, then the possible, etc. The greed for books is certain in me. Not really to own or to read them, but rather to see them, to convince myself of their actuality in the stalls of a bookseller. If there are several copies of the same book somewhere, each individual one delights me. It is as though this greed came from my stomach, as though it were a perverse appetite. Books that I own delight me less, but books belonging to my sisters do delight me. The desire to own them is incomparably less, it is almost absent.

12 November. Sunday. Yesterday lecture by Richepin: 'La Légende de Napoléon' in the Rudolphinum. Pretty empty. As though on sudden inspiration to test the manners of the lecturer, a large piano is standing in the way between the small entrance door and the lecturer's table. The lecturer enters, he wants, with his eyes on the audience, to reach his table by the shortest route, therefore comes close to the piano, is startled, steps back and walks around it softly without looking at the audience again. In the enthusiasm at the end of his speech and in the loud applause, he naturally forgot the piano, as it did not call attention to itself during the lecture. With his hands on his chest, he wants to turn his back on the audience as late as possible, therefore takes several elegant steps to the side, naturally bumps gently into the piano and, on tiptoe, must arch his back a little before he gets into the clear again. At least that is the way Richepin did it.

A tall, powerful man of fifty with a waistline. His hair is stiff and tousled (Daudet's, for example) although pressed fairly close to his skull. Like all old Southerners with their thick nose and the broad, wrinkled face that goes with it, from whose nostrils a strong wind can blow as from a horse's muzzle, and of whom you know very well that this is the final state of their faces, it will not be replaced but will endure for a long time; his face also reminded me of the face of an elderly Italian woman wearing a very natural, definitely not false beard.

The freshly painted light grey of the podium rising behind him was distracting at first. His white hair blended with the colour and there was no outline to be seen. When he bent his head back the colour was set in motion, his head almost sank in it. Only towards the middle of the lecture, when your attention was fully concentrated, did this disturbance come to an end, especially when he raised his large, black-clad body during a recitation and, with waving hands, conducted the verses and put the grey colour to flight – In the beginning he was embarrassing, he scattered so many compliments in all directions. In telling about a Napoleonic soldier whom he had known personally and who had had fifty-seven wounds, he remarked that the variety of colours on the torso of this man could have been imitated only by a great colourist such as his friend Mucha, who was present.

I observed in myself a continual increase in the degree to which I am affected by people on a podium. I gave no thought to my pains and cares. I was squeezed into the left corner of my chair, but really into the lecture, my clasped hands between my knees. I felt that Richepin had an effect upon me such as Solomon must have felt when he took young girls into his bed. I even had a slight vision of Napoleon who, in a connected fantasy, also stepped through the little entrance door although he could really have stepped out of the wood of the podium or out of the organ. He overwhelmed the entire hall, which was tightly packed at that moment. Near as I actually was to him, I had and would have had even in reality never a doubt of his effect. I should perhaps have noticed any absurdity in his dress, as in the case of Richepin as well, but noticing it would not have disturbed me. How cool I had been, on the other hand, as a child! I often wished to be brought face to face with the Emperor to show him how little effect he had. And that was not courage, it was just coolness.

He recited poems as though they were speeches in the Chamber. An impotent onlooker at battles, he pounded the table, he flung out his outstretched arms to clear a path for the guards through the middle of the hall, '*Empereur!*' he shouted, with his raised arm become a banner, and in repeating it made it echo as though an army was shouting down in the plain. During the description of a battle, a little foot kicked against the floor somewhere, the matter was looked into, it was his foot that had had too little confidence in itself. But it did not disturb him. After 'The Grenadiers', which he read in a translation by Gérard de Nerval and which he thought very highly of, there was the least applause.

In his youth the tomb of Napoleon had been opened once a year and the embalmed face was displayed to disabled soldiers filing past in procession; the face was bloated and greenish, more a spectacle of terror than of admiration; this is why they later stopped opening the tomb. But nevertheless Richepin saw the face from the arm of his grand-uncle, who had served in Africa and for whose sake the Commandant opened the tomb.

He announces long in advance that a poem he intends to recite (he has an infallible memory, which a strong temperament must really always have), discusses it, the coming verses already cause a small earthquake under his words, in the case of the first poem he even said he would recite it with all his fire. He did.

He brought things to a climax in the last poem by getting imperceptibly into the verses (by Victor Hugo), standing up slowly, not sitting down again even after he finished the verses, picking up and carrying on the sweeping movements of the recitation with the final force of his own prose. He closed with the vow that even after a thousand years each grain of dust of his corpse, if it should have consciousness, would be ready to answer the call of Napoleon.

The French, short-winded from the quick succession of its escaping breaths, withstood even the most unskilful improvisations, did not break down even under his frequent talking about poets who beautify everyday life, about his own imagination (eyes closed) being that of a poet's, about his hallucinations (eyes reluctantly wrenched open on the distance) being those of a poet's, etc. At the same time he sometimes covered his eyes and then slowly uncovered them, taking away one finger after another.

He served in the army, his uncle in Africa, his grandfather under

116

Napoleon, he even sang two lines of a battle song. 13 November. And this man is, I learned today, sixty-two years old.

14 November. Tuesday. Yesterday at Max's who returned from his Brünn lecture.

In the afternoon while falling asleep. As though the solid skull-cap encircling the insensitive cranium had moved more deeply inwards and left a part of the brain exposed to the free play of light and muscles.

To awaken on a cold autumn morning full of yellowish light. To force your way through the half-shut window and while still in front of the panes, before you fall, to hover, arms extended, belly arched, legs curved backwards, like the figures on the bows of ships in old times.

Before falling asleep.

It seems so dreadful to be a bachelor, to become an old man struggling to keep one's dignity while begging for an invitation whenever one wants to spend an evening in company, having to carry one's meal home in one's hand, unable to expect anyone with a lazy sense of calm confidence, able only with difficulty and vexation to give a gift to someone, having to say good night at the front door, never being able to run up a stairway beside one's wife, to lie ill and have only the solace of the view from one's window when one can sit up, to have only side-doors in one's room leading into other people's living-rooms, to feel estranged from one's family, with whom one can keep on close terms only by marriage, first by the marriage of one's parents, then, when the effect of that has worn off, by one's own, having to admire other people's children and not even being allowed to go on saying: 'I have none myself,' never to feel oneself grow older since there is no family growing up around one, modelling oneself in appearance and behaviour on one or two bachelors remembered from our youth.

This is all true, but it is easy to make the error of unfolding future sufferings so far in front of one that one's eye must pass beyond them and never again return, while in reality, both today and later, one will stand with a palpable body and a real head, a real forehead that is, for smiting on with one's hand.[31]

Now I'll try a sketch for the introduction to *Richard and Samuel*.

15 November. Yesterday evening, already with a sense of foreboding, pulled the cover off the bed, lay down, and again became aware of all my abilities as though I were holding them in my hand; they tightened my chest, they set my head on fire, for a short while, to console myself for not getting up to work, I repeated: 'That's not healthy, that's not healthy,' and with almost visible purpose tried to draw sleep over my head. I kept thinking of a cap with a visor which, to protect myself, I pulled down hard over my forehead. How much did I lose yesterday, how the blood pounded in my tight head, capable of anything and restrained only by powers which are indispensable for my very life and are here being wasted.

It is certain that everything I have conceived in advance, even when I was in a good mood, whether word for word or just casually, but in specific words, appears dry, wrong, inflexible, embarrassing to everybody around me, timid, but above all incomplete when I try to write it down at my desk, although I have forgotten nothing of the original conception. This is naturally related in large part to the fact that I conceive something good away from paper only in a time of exaltation, a time more feared than longed for, much as I do long for it; but then the fullness is so great that I have to give up. Blindly and arbitrarily I snatch handfuls out of the stream so that when I write it down calmly, my acquisition is nothing in comparison with the fullness in which it lived, is incapable of restoring this fullness, and thus is bad and disturbing because it tempts to no purpose.

16 November. This noon, before falling asleep, but I did not fall asleep, the upper part of the body of a wax woman lay on top of me. Her face was bent back over mine, her left forearm pressed against my breast.

No sleep for three nights, at the slightest effort to do anything my strength is immediately exhausted.

From an old notebook: 'Now, in the evening, after having studied since six o'clock in the morning, I noticed that my left hand had already for some time been sympathetically clasping my right hand by the fingers.'[32]

18 November. Yesterday in the factory. Rode back on the trolley, sat in a corner with legs stretched out, saw people outside, lights in stores, walls of viaducts through which we passed, backs and faces over and over again, a highway leading from the business street of the suburb with nothing human on it save people going home, the glaring electric lights of the railway station burned into the darkness, the low, tapering chimneys of a gasworks, a poster announcing the guest appearance of a singer, de Treville, that gropes its way along the walls as far as an alley near the cemeteries, from where it then returned with me out of the cold of the fields into the liveable warmth of the city. We accept foreign cities as a fact, the inhabitants live there without penetrating our way of life, just as we cannot penetrate theirs, a comparison must be made, it can't be helped, but one is well aware that it has no moral or even psychological value, in the end one can often even omit the comparison because the difference in the condition of life is so great that it makes it unnecessary.

The suburbs of our native city, however, are also foreign to us, but in this case comparisons have value, a half-hour's walk can prove it to us over and over again, here live people partly within our city, partly on the miserable, dark edge of the city that is furrowed like a great ditch, although they all have an area of interest in common with us that is greater than any other group of people outside the city. For this reason I always enter and leave the suburb with a weak mixed feeling of anxiety, of abandonment, of sympathy, of curiosity, of conceit, of joy in travelling, of fortitude, and return with pleasure, seriousness, and calm, especially from Žižkov.

19 November. Sunday. Dream: In the theatre. Performance of *Das Weite Land* by Schnitzler, adapted by Utitz.[33] I sit right up at the front, think I am sitting in the first row until it finally appears that it is the second. The back of the row is turned towards the stage so that one can see the auditorium comfortably, the stage only by turning. The author is somewhere near by, I can't hold back my poor opinion of the play which I seem to know from before, but add that the third act is supposed to be witty. With this 'supposed to be', however, I mean to say that if one is speaking of the good parts, I do not know the play and must rely on hearsay; therefore I repeat this remark once more,

not just for myself, but nevertheless it is disregarded by the others. There is a great crush around me. The audience seems to have come in its winter clothes, everyone fills his seat to overflowing. People beside me, behind me, whom I do not see, interrupt me, point out new arrivals, mention their names, my attention is called especially to a married couple forcing their way along a row of seats, since the woman has a dark-yellow, mannish, long-nosed face, and besides, as far as one can see in the crowd out of which her head towers, is wearing men's clothes; near me, remarkably free, the actor Löwy, but very unlike the real one, is standing and making excited speeches in which the word '*principium*' is repeated, I keep expecting the words '*tertium comparationis*', they do not come. In a box in the second tier, really only in a right-hand corner (seen from the stage) of the balcony that connects with the boxes there, a third son of the Kisch family,[34] dressed in a beautiful Prince Albert with its flaps opened wide, stands behind his mother, who is seated, and speaks out into the theatre. Löwy's speeches have a connexion with these speeches. Among other things, Kisch points high up to a spot on the curtain and says, 'There sits the German Kisch,' by this he means my schoolmate who studied Germanics. When the curtain goes up the theatre begins to darken, and Kisch, in order to indicate that he would disappear in any case, marches up and away from the balcony with his mother, again with all his arms, coats, and legs spread wide.

The stage is somewhat lower than the auditorium, you look down with your chin on the back of the seat. The set consists chiefly of two low, thick pillars in the middle of the stage. The scene is a banquet in which girls and young men take part. Despite the fact that when the play began many people in the first rows left, apparently to go backstage, I can see very little, for the girls left behind block the view with their large, flat hats, most of which are blue, that move back and forth along the whole length of the row. Nevertheless, I see a small ten- to fifteen-year-old boy unusually clearly on the stage. He has dry, parted, straight-cut hair. He cannot even place his napkin properly on his lap, must look down carefully when he does, and is supposed to be a man-about-town in this play. In consequence, I no longer have much confidence in this theatre. The company on the stage now waits for various newcomers who come down onto the stage from the first rows of the auditorium. But the play is not well rehearsed, either. Thus, an actress named Hackelberg has just entered, an actor, leaning back in his chair like a man of the world, addresses her as 'Hackel', then becomes aware of his mistake and corrects himself. Now a girl enters whom I know (her name is Frankel, I think), she climbs over the back of the seat right where I am sitting, her back, when she climbs over, is entirely naked, the skin not very good, over the right hip there is even a scratched, bloodshot spot the size of a doorknob. But then, when she turns around on the stage and stands there with a clean face, she acts very well. Now a singing horseman is supposed to approach out of the distance at a gallop, a piano reproduces the clatter of hoofs, you hear the stormy song approaching, finally I see the singer too, who, to give the singing the natural swelling that takes place in a rapid approach, is running along the balcony up above towards the stage. He is not yet at the stage or through with the song and yet he has already passed the climax of haste and shrieking song, and the piano too can no longer reproduce distinctly the sound of hoofs striking against the stones. Both stop, therefore, and the singer approaches quietly, but he makes himself so small that only his head rises above the railing of the balcony, so that you cannot see him very clearly.

With this, the first act is over, but the curtain doesn't come down, the theatre remains dark too. On the stage two critics sit on the floor, writing, with their backs resting against a piece of scenery. A dramatic coach or stage manager with a blond, pointed beard jumps on to the stage, while still in the air he stretches one hand out to give some instructions, in the other hand he has a bunch of grapes that had been in a fruit dish on the banquet table and which he now eats.

Again facing the auditorium I see that it is lit by simple paraffin lamps that are stuck up on simple chandeliers, like those in the streets, and now, of course, burn only very low. Suddenly, impure paraffin or a damaged wick is probably the cause, the light spurts out of one of these lanterns and sparks pour down in a broad gush on the crowded audience that forms a mass as black as earth. Then a gentleman rises up out of this mass, walks on it towards the lamp, apparently wants to fix the lamp, but first looks up at it, remains standing near it for a short while, and, when nothing happens, returns quietly to his place in which he is swallowed up. I take him for myself and bow my face into the darkness.

I and Max must really be different to the very core. Much as I admire his writings when they lie before me as a whole, resisting my and anyone else's encroachment (a few small book reviews even today), still, every sentence he writes for *Richard and Samuel* is bound up with a reluctant concession on my part which I feel painfully to my very depths. At least today.

This evening I was again filled with anxiously restrained abilities.

20 November. Dream of a picture, apparently by Ingres. The girls in the woods in a thousand mirrors, or rather: the virgins, etc. To the right of the picture, grouped in the same way and airily drawn like the pictures on theatre curtains, there was a more compact group, to the left they sat and lay on a gigantic twig or flying ribbon, or soared by their own power in a chain that rose slowly towards the sky. And now they were reflected not only towards the spectator but also away from him, became more indistinct and multitudinous; what the eye lost in detail it gained in fullness. But in front stood a naked girl untouched by the reflections, her weight on one leg, her hip thrust forward. Here Ingres's draftsmanship was to be admired, but I actually found with satisfaction that there was too much real nakedness left in this girl even for the sense of touch. From behind her came a gleam of pale, yellowish light.

My repugnance for antitheses is certain. They are unexpected, but do not surprise, for they have always been there; if they were unconscious, it was at the very edge of consciousness. They make for thoroughness, fullness, completeness, but only like a figure on the 'wheel of life',[35] we have chased our little idea around the circle. They are as undifferentiated as they are different, they grow under one's hand as though bloated by water, beginning with the prospect of infinity, they always end up in the same medium size. They curl up, cannot be straightened out, are mere clues, are holes in wood, are immobile assaults, draw antitheses to themselves, as I have shown. If they would only draw all of them, and forever.

For the drama: Weise, English teacher, the way he hurried by with squared shoulders, his hands deep in his pockets, his yellowish over-coat tightly folded, crossing the tracks with powerful strides right in front of the trolley that still stood there but was already signalling its departure with its bell. Away from us.

E: Anna!
A [*looking up*]: Yes.
E: Come here.
A [*long, quiet steps*]: What do you want?
E: I wanted to tell you that I have been dissatisfied with you for some time.
A: Really!
E: It is so.
A: Then you must certainly give me notice, Emil.
E: So quickly? And don't you even ask the reason?
A: I know it.
E: You do?
A: You don't like the food.
E [*stands up quickly, loud*]: Do you or don't you know that Kurt is leaving this evening?
A [*inwardly undisturbed*]: Why yes, unfortunately he is leaving, you didn't have to call me here for that.

21 November. My former governess, the one with the black-and-yellow face, with the square nose and a wart on her cheek which used to delight me so, was at our house today for the second time recently to see me. The first time I wasn't home, this time I wanted to be left in peace and to sleep and made them tell her I was out. Why did she bring me up so badly, after all I was obedient, she herself is saying so now to the cook and the governess in the ante-room, I was good and had a quiet disposition. Why didn't she use this to my advantage and prepare a better future for me? She is a married woman or a widow, has children, has a lively way of speaking that doesn't let me sleep, thinks I am a tall, healthy gentleman at the beautiful age of twenty-eight who likes to remember his youth and in general knows what to do with himself. Now, however, I lie here on the sofa, kicked out of

the world, watching for the sleep that refuses to come and will only graze me when it does, my joints ache with fatigue, my dried-up body trembles toward its own destruction in turmoils of which I dare not become fully conscious, in my head are astonishing convulsions. And there stand the three women before my door, one praises me as I was, two as I am. The cook says I shall go straight – she means without any detour – to heaven. This it shall be.

Löwy: A rabbi in the Talmud made it a principle, in this case very pleasing to God, to accept nothing, not even a glass of water, from anyone. Now it happened, however, that the greatest rabbi of his time wanted to make his acquaintance and therefore invited him to a meal. To refuse the invitation of such a man, that was impossible. The first rabbi therefore set out sadly on his journey. But because his principle was so strong, a mountain raised itself up between the two rabbis.

> [ANNA *sits at the table, reading the paper.*
> KARL *walks round the room, when he comes to the window he stops and looks out, once he even opens the inner window.*]

ANNA: Please leave the window closed, it's really freezing.

KARL [*closes the window*]: Well, we have different things to worry about.

(22 November) ANNA: No, but you have developed a new habit, Emil, one that's quite horrible. You know how to catch hold of every trifle and use it to find something bad in me.

KARL [*rubs his fingers*]: Because you have no consideration, because in general you are incomprehensible.

It is certain that a major obstacle to my progress is my physical condition. Nothing can be accomplished with such a body. I shall have to get used to its perpetual balking. As a result of the last few nights spent in wild dreams but with scarcely a few snatches of sleep, I was so incoherent this morning, felt nothing but my forehead, saw a half-way bearable condition only far beyond my present one, and in sheer readiness to die would have been glad simply to have curled up in a ball on the cement floor of the corridor with the documents in my hand. My body is too long for its weakness, it hasn't the least bit of fat to engender a blessed warmth, to preserve an inner fire, no fat on which the spirit could occasionally nourish itself beyond its daily need without damage to the whole. How shall the weak heart that lately has troubled me so often be able to pound the blood through all the length of these legs? It would be labour enough to the knees, and from there it can only spill with a senile strength into the cold lower parts of my legs. But now it is already needed up above again, it is being waited for, while it is wasting itself down below. Everything is pulled apart throughout the length of my body. What could it accomplish then, when it perhaps wouldn't have enough strength for what I want to achieve even if it were shorter and more compact.

From a letter of Löwy's to his father: When I come to Warsaw I will walk about among you in my European clothes like 'a spider before your eyes, like a mourner at a wedding'.

Löwy tells a story about a married friend who lives in Postin, a small town near Warsaw, and who feels isolated in his progressive interests and therefore unhappy.

'Postin, is that a large city?'

'This large,' he holds out the palm of his hand to me. It is covered by a rough yellow-brown glove and looks like a wasteland.

23 November. On the 21st, the hundredth anniversary of Kleist's death, the Kleist family had a wreath placed on his grave with the epitaph: 'To the best of their house.'

On what circumstances my way of life makes me dependent! Tonight I slept somewhat better than in the past week, this afternoon even fairly well, I even feel that drowsiness which follows moderately good sleep, consequently I am afraid I shall not be able to write as well, feel individual abilities turning more deeply inward, and am prepared for any surprise, that is, I already see it.

24 November. *Shechite* (one who is learning the slaughterer's art). Play by Gordin. In it quotations from the Talmud, for example: If a great scholar commits a sin during the evening or the night, by

morning you are no longer permitted to reproach him with it, for in his scholarship he has already repented of it himself.

If you steal an ox then you must return two, if you slaughter the stolen ox then you must return four, but if you slaughter a stolen calf then you must return only three because it is assumed that you had to carry the calf away, therefore had done hard work. This assumption influences the punishment even if the calf was led away without any difficulty.

Honesty of evil thoughts. Yesterday evening I felt especially miserable. My stomach was upset again. I had written with difficulty. I had listened with effort to Löwy's reading in the coffee-house (which at first was quiet so that we had to restrain ourselves, but which then became full of bustle and gave us no peace), the dismal future immediately before me seemed not worth entering, abandoned, I walked through Ferdinandstrasse. Then at the junction with the Bergstein I once more thought about the more distant future. How would I live through it with this body picked up in a lumber room? The Talmud too says: A man without a woman is no person. I had no defence this evening against such thoughts except to say to myself: 'It is now that you come, evil thoughts, now, because I am weak and have an upset stomach. You pick this time for me to think you. You have waited for your advantage. Shame on you. Come some other time, when I am stronger. Don't exploit my condition in this way.' And, in fact, without even waiting for other proofs, they yielded, scattered slowly and did not again disturb me during the rest of my walk, which was, naturally, not too happy. They apparently forgot, however, that if they were to respect all my evil moments, they would seldom get their chance.

The odour of petrol from a motor-car driving towards me from the theatre made me notice how visibly a beautiful home life (and were it lit by a single candle, that is all one needs before going to bed) is waiting for the theatre-goers coming towards me who are giving their cloaks and dangling opera glasses a last tug into place, but also how it seems that they are being sent home from the theatre like subordinates before whom the curtain has gone down for the last time and behind whom the doors have opened through which – full of pride because of some ridiculous worry or another – they had entered the theatre before the beginning of or during the first act.

28 November. Have written nothing for three days.

Spent all afternoon of the 25th in the Café City persuading M. to sign a declaration that he was just a clerk with us, therefore not covered by insurance, so that Father would not be obliged to make the large payment on his insurance. He promises it, I speak fluent Czech, I apologize for my mistakes with particular elegance, he promises to send the declaration to the office Monday, I feel that if he does not like me then at least he respects me, but on Monday he sends nothing, nor is he any longer in Prague, he has left.

Dull evening at Baum's without Max. Reading of *Die Hässliche*, a story that is still too disorganized, the first chapter is rather the building-site of a story.

On Sunday, 26 November. *Richard and Samuel* with Max morning and afternoon until five. Then to N., a collector from Linz, recommended by Kubin, fifty, gigantic, towerlike movements; when he is silent for any length of time one bows one's head, for he is entirely silent, while when he speaks he does not speak entirely; his life consists of collecting and fornicating.

Collecting: He began with a collection of postage stamps, then turned to drawings, then collected everything, then saw the aimlessness of this collection which could never be completed and limited himself to amulets, later to pilgrimage medals and pilgrimage tracts from lower Austria and southern Bavaria. These are medals and tracts which are issued anew for each pilgrimage, most of them worthless in their material and also artistically, but often have nice pictures. He now also began industriously to write about them, and indeed was the first to write on this subject, for the systematization of which he first established the points of reference. Naturally, those who had been collecting these objects and had put off publishing were furious, but had to put up with it nevertheless. Now he is an acknowledged expert on these pilgrimage medals, requests come from all over for his opinion and decision on these medals, his voice is decisive. Besides, he collects everything else as well, his pride is a chastity belt that, together with his amulets, was exhibited at the Dresden Hygienic Exhibition. (He has just been there to have everything packed for shipment.) Then a beautiful knight's sword of the Falkensteiners. His relationship to art is unambiguous and clear in that bad way which collecting makes possible.

From the coffee-house in the Hotel Graf he takes us up to his over-heated room, sits down on the bed, we on two chairs around him, so that we form a quiet group. His first question: 'Are you collectors?'

'No, only poor amateurs.'

'That doesn't matter.' He pulls out his wallet and practically showers us with book-plates, his own and others', jumbled with announcements of his next book, *Magic and Superstition in the Mineral Kingdom*. He has already written much, especially on 'Motherhood in Art', he considers the pregnant body the most beautiful, for him it is also the most pleasant to f—. He has also written about amulets. He was also in the employ of the Vienna Court Museum, was in charge of excavations in Braila at the mouth of the Danube, invented a process, named after him, for restoring excavated vases, is a member of thirteen learned societies and museums, his collection is willed to the Germanic Museum in Nuremberg, he often sits at his desk until one or two o'clock at night and is back at eight o'clock in the morning. We have to write something in a lady friend's album which he has brought along to fill up on his journey. Those who themselves create come first. Max writes a complicated verse which Mr N. tries to render by the proverb, 'Every cloud has a silver lining.' Before this, he had read it aloud in a wooden voice. I write down:

> Little Soul,
> Boundest in dancing, etc.

He reads aloud again, I help, finally he says: 'A Persian rhythm? Now what is that called? Ghazel? Right.' We are not in a position to agree with this nor even to guess at what he means. Finally he quotes a '*ritornello* by Rückert'. Yes, he meant *ritornello*. However, it is not that either. Very well, but it has a certain melody.

He is a friend of Halbe. He likes to talk about him. We would much rather talk about Blei. There is not much to say about him, however, Munich literary society does not think much of him because of his intellectual double-crossing, he is divorced from his wife who had had a large practice as a dentist and supported him, his daughter, sixteen,

blonde, with blue eyes, is the wildest girl in Munich. In Sternheim's
Hose – N. was at the theatre with Halbe – Blei played an ageing man-
about-town. When N. met him the next day he said: 'Herr Doktor,
yesterday you played Dr Blei.'

'What? What?' he said in embarrassment, 'but I was playing so-
and-so.'

When we leave he throws open the bed so that it may thoroughly take
on the warmth of the room, he arranges for additional heating besides.

29 November. From the Talmud: When a scholar goes to meet his
bride, he should take an *am ha-aretz*[36] along, he is too deeply sunk in
his scholarliness, he would not observe what should be observed.

As a result of bribery the telephone and telegraph wires around
Warsaw were put up in a complete circle, which in the sense of the
Talmud makes the city a bounded area, a courtyard, as it were, so that
on Saturday it is possible even for the most pious person to move
about, carry trifles (like handkerchiefs) on his person, within this circle.

The parties of the Hasidim where they merrily discourse on talmudic
problems. If the entertainment runs down or if someone does not take
part, they make up for it by singing. Melodies are invented, if one is a
success, members of the family are called in and it is repeated and
rehearsed with them. At one such entertainment a wonder-rabbi who
often had hallucinations suddenly laid his face on his arms, which were
resting on the table, and remained in that position for three hours while
everyone was silent. When he awoke he wept and sang an entirely new,
gay, military march. This was the melody with which the angels of the
dead had just escorted to heaven the soul of a wonder-rabbi who had
died at this time in a far-off Russian city.

On Friday, according to the Kabbalah, the pious get a new, more
delicate soul, entirely divine, which remains with them until Saturday
evening.

On Friday evening two angels accompany each pious man from the
synagogue to his home; the master of the house stands while he greets
them in the dining-room; they stay only a short time.

The education of girls, their growing up, getting used to the ways of
the world, was always especially important to me. Then they no longer

run so hopelessly out of the way of a person who knows them only casually and would like to speak casually with them, they have begun to stop for a moment, even though it be not quite in that part of the room in which you would have them, you need no longer hold them with glances, threats, or the power of love; when they turn away they do so slowly and do not intend any harm by it, then their backs have become broader too. What you say to them is not lost, they listen to the whole question without your having to hurry, and they answer, jokingly to be sure, but directly to the point. Yes, with their faces lifted up they even ask questions themselves, and a short conversation is not more than they can stand. They hardly ever let a spectator disturb them any more in the work they have just undertaken, and therefore pay less attention to him, yet he may look at them longer. They withdraw only to dress for dinner. This is the only time when you may be insecure. Apart from this, however, you need no longer run through the streets, lie in wait at house doors, and wait over and over again for a lucky chance, even though you have really long since learned that such chances can't be forced.

But despite this great change that has taken place in them it is no rarity for them to come towards us with mournful faces when we meet them unexpectedly, to put their hands flatly in ours and with slow gestures invite us to enter their homes as though we were business acquaintances. They walk heavily up and down in the next room; but when we penetrate there too, in desire and spite, they crouch in a window-seat and read the paper without a glance to spare for us.

3 December. I have read a part of Schäfer's *Karl Stauffers Lebensgang. Eine Chronik der Leidenschaft*, and am so caught up and held fast by this powerful impression forcing its ways into that inner part of me which I listen to and learn from only at rare intervals, but at the same time am driven to such a pass by the hunger imposed on me by my upset stomach and by the usual excitements of the free Sunday, that I must write, just as one can get relief from external excitement forced upon one from the outside only by flailing one's arms.

The unhappiness of the bachelor, whether seeming or actual, is so easily guessed at by the world around him that he will curse his decision, at least if he has remained a bachelor because of the delight he takes in secrecy. He walks around with his coat buttoned, his hands in the upper pockets of his jacket, his arms akimbo, his hat pulled down over his eyes, a false smile that has become natural to him is supposed to shield his mouth as his glasses do his eyes, his trousers are tighter than seem proper for his thin legs. But everyone knows his condition, can detail his sufferings. A cold breeze breathes upon him from within and he gazes inward with the even sadder half of his double face. He moves incessantly, but with predictable regularity, from one apartment to another. The farther he moves away from the living, for whom he must still – and this is the worst mockery – work like a conscious slave who dare not express his consciousness, so much the smaller a space is considered sufficient for him. While it is death that must still strike down the others, though they may have spent all their lives in a sick-bed – for even though they would have gone down by themselves long ago from their own weakness, they nevertheless hold fast to their loving, very healthy relatives by blood and marriage – he, this bachelor, still in the midst of life, apparently of his own free will resigns himself to an ever smaller space, and when he dies the coffin is exactly right for him.

My recent reading of Mörike's autobiography to my sisters began well enough but improved as I went on, and finally, my fingertips together, it conquered inner obstacles with my voice's unceasing calm, provided a constantly expanding panorama for my voice, and finally the whole room round about me dared admit nothing but my voice. Until my parents, returning from business, rang.

Before falling asleep felt on my body the weight of the fists on my light arms.

8 December. Friday, have not written for a long time, but this time it was really in part because of satisfaction, as I have finished the first chapter of *Richard and Samuel* and consider it, particularly the original description of the sleep in the train compartment, a success. Even more, I think that something is happening within me that is very close to Schiller's transformation of emotion into character. Despite all the resistance of my inner being I must write this down.

Walk with Löwy to the Lieutenant-Governor's castle, which I called Fort Zion. The entrance gates and the colour of the sky matched very well.

Another walk to Hetz Island. Story about Mrs Tschissik, how they took her into the company in Berlin out of pity, at first an insignificant singer of duets in an antiquated dress and hat. Reading of a letter from Warsaw in which a young Warsaw Jew complains about the decline of the Jewish theatre and writes that he prefers to go to the 'Nowosti', the Polish operetta theatre, rather than to the Jewish one, for the miserable equipment, the indecencies, the 'mouldy' couplets, etc., are unbearable. Just imagine the big scene of a Jewish operetta in which the prima donna, with a train of small children behind her, marches through the audience on to the stage. Each of them is carrying a small scroll of the Torah and is singing: *Toire iz di beste s'khoire* – the Torah is the best merchandise.

Beautiful lonely walk over the Hradschin and the Belvedere after those successful parts of *Richard and Samuel*. In the Nerudagasse a sign: Ann Křižová, Dressmaker, Trained in France by the Aid of the Dowager Duchess Ahrenberg, née Princess Ahrenberg – In the middle of the first castle court I stood and watched the calling out of the castle guard.

The last section I wrote hasn't pleased Max, probably because he regards it as unsuitable for the whole, but possibly also because he considers it bad in itself. This is very probable because he warned me against writing such long passages and regards the effect of such writing as somewhat jellylike.

In order to be able to speak to young girls I need older persons near me. The slight disturbance emanating from them enlivens my speech, I immediately feel that the demands made on me are diminished; what I speak out of myself without previous consideration can always, if it is not suitable for the girl, be directed to the older person, from whom I can also, if it becomes necessary, draw an abundance of help.

Miss H. She reminds me of Mrs Bl., only her long, slightly double-curved, and relatively narrow nose looks like the ruined nose of Mrs Bl.

132

But apart from that there is also in her face a blackness, hardly caused externally, that can be driven into the skin only by a strong character. Broad back, well on the way to being a woman's swelling back; heavy body that seems thin in the well-cut jacket and on which the narrow jacket is even loose. She raises her head freely to show that she has found a way out of the embarrassing moments of the conversation. Indeed, I was not put down in this conversation, had not surrendered even inwardly, but had I just looked at myself from the outside, I should not have been able to explain my behaviour in any other way. In the past I could not express myself freely in the company of new acquaintances because the presence of sexual wishes unconsciously hindered me, now their conscious absence hinders me.

Ran into the Tschissik couple at the Graben. She was wearing the hussy's dress she wore in *Der Wilde Mensch*. When I break down her appearance into its details as I saw it then at the Graben, she becomes improbable. (I saw her only for a moment, for I became frightened at the sight of her, did not greet her, nor did she see me, and I did not immediately dare to turn around.) She seemed much smaller than usual, her left hip was thrust forward, not just at the moment, but permanently, her right leg was bent in at the knee, the movements of her throat and head, which she brought close to her husband, were very quick, with her right arm crooked outwards she tried to take the arm of her husband. He was wearing his little summer hat with the brim turned down in front. When I turned they were gone. I guessed that they had gone to the Café Central, waited awhile on the other side of the Graben, and was lucky enough after a long interval to see her come to the window. When she sat down at the table only the rim of her cardboard hat, covered with blue velvet, was visible.

I then dreamed that I was in a very narrow but not very tall glass-domed house with two entrances like the impassable passageways in the paintings of Italian primitives, also resembling from the distance an arcade leading off from the rue des Petits Champs that we saw in Paris. Except that the one in Paris was really wider and full of stores, but this one ran along between blank walls, appeared to have scarcely enough room for two people to walk side by side, but when one really entered it, as I did with Mrs Tschissik, there was a surprising amount of room, which did not really surprise us. While I left by one exit with Mrs Tschissik in the direction of a possible observer of all this, and Mrs Tschissik at the same time apologized for some offence or other (it seemed to be drunkenness) and begged me not to believe her detractors, Mr Tschissik, at the second of the house's two exits, whipped a shaggy, blond St Bernard which stood opposite him on its hind legs. It was not quite clear whether he was just playing with the dog and neglected his wife because of it, or whether he had himself been attacked by the dog in earnest, or whether he wished to keep the dog away from us.

With L. on the quay. I had a slight spell of faintness that stifled all my being, got over it and remembered it after a short time as something long forgotten.

Even if I overlook all other obstacles (physical condition, parents, character), the following serves as a very good excuse for my not limiting myself to literature in spite of everything: I can take nothing on myself as long as I have not achieved a sustained work that satisfies me completely. That is of course irrefutable.

I have now, and have had since this afternoon, a great yearning to write all my anxiety entirely out of me, write it into the depths of the paper just as it comes out of the depths of me, or write it down in such a way that I could draw what I had written into me completely. This is no artistic yearning. Today, when Löwy spoke of his dissatisfaction with and of his indifference to everything that the troupe does, I explained his condition as due to homesickness, but in a sense did not give him this explanation even though I voiced it, instead kept it for myself and enjoyed it in passing as a sorrow of my own.

9 December. Stauffer-Bern: 'The sweetness of creation begets illusions about its real value.'

If one patiently submits to a book of letters or memoirs, no matter by whom, in this case it is Karl Stauffer-Bern, one doesn't make him one's own by main strength, for to do this one has to employ art, and art is its own reward; but rather one suffers oneself to be drawn away –

this is easily done, if one doesn't resist – by the concentrated otherness of the person writing, and lets oneself be made into his counterpart. Thus it is no longer remarkable, when one is brought back to one's self by the closing of the book, that one feels the better for this excursion and this recreation, and, with a clearer head, remains behind in one's own being, which has been newly discovered, newly shaken up and seen for a moment from the distance. Only later are we surprised that these experiences of another person's life, in spite of their vividness, are faithfully described in the book – our own experience inclines us to think that nothing in the world is further removed from an experience (sorrow over the death of a friend, for instance) than its description. But what is right for us is not right for the other person. If our letters cannot match our own feelings – naturally, there are varying degrees of this, passing imperceptibly into one another in both directions – if even at our best, expressions like 'indescribable', 'inexpressible', or 'so sad', or 'so beautiful', followed by a rapidly collapsing 'that' clause, must perpetually come to our assistance, then as if in compensation we have been given the ability to comprehend what another person has written with at least the same degree of calm exactitude which we lack when we confront our own letter-writing. Our ignorance of those feelings which alternately make us crumple up and pull open again the letter in front of us, this very ignorance becomes knowledge the moment we are compelled to limit ourselves to this letter, to believe only what it says, and thus to find it perfectly expressed and perfect in expression, as is only right, if we are to see a clear road into what is most human. So Karl Stauffer's letters contain only an account of the short life of an artist –

10 December. Sunday. I must go to see my sister and her little boy. When my mother came home from my sister's at one o'clock at night the day before yesterday with the news of the boy's birth, my father marched through the house in his nightshirt, opened all the doors, woke me, the maid, and my sisters and proclaimed the birth as though the child had not only been born, but as though it had already lived an honourable life and been buried too.

13 December. Because of fatigue did not write and lay now on the

sofa in the warm room and now on the one in the cold room, with sick
legs and disgusting dreams. A dog lay on my body, one paw near my
face. I woke up because of it but was still afraid for a little while to
open my eyes and look at it.

Biberpelz. Bad play, flowing along without climax. Scenes with the
police superintendent not true. Delicate acting by the Lehmann woman
of the Lessing Theatre. The way her skirt folds between her thighs
when she bends. The thoughtful look of the people when she raises her
two hands, places them one under the other on the left in front of her
face, as though she wanted to weaken the force of the denying or pro-
testing voice. Bewildered, coarse acting of the others. The comedian's
impudence towards the play (draws his sabre, exchanges hats). My
cold aversion. Went home, but while still there sat with a feeling of
admiration that so many people take upon themselves so much excitement for an evening (they shout, steal, are robbed, harass, slander,
neglect), and that in this play, if one only looks at it with blinking eyes,
so many disordered human voices and exclamations are thrown together. Pretty girls. One with a flat face, unbroken surfaces of skin,
rounded cheeks, hair beginning high up, eyes lost in this smoothness
and protruding a little – Beautiful passages of the play in which the
Wulffen woman shows herself at once a thief and an honest friend of
the clever, progressive, democratic people. A Wehrhahn in the audience
might feel himself justified – Sad parallelism of the four acts. In the
first act there is stealing, in the second act is the judgement, the same
in the third and fourth acts.

Der Schneider als Gemeinderat at the Jews. Without the Tschissiks
but with two new, terrible people, the Liebgold couple. Bad play by
Richter. The beginning like Molière, the purse-proud alderman hung
with watches. The Liebgold woman can't read, her husband has to
rehearse with her.

It is almost a custom for a comedian to marry a serious actress and
a serious actor a comedienne, and in general to take along with them
only married women or relatives. The way once, at midnight, the
piano player, probably a bachelor, slipped out of the door with his
music.

Brahms concert by the Singing Society. The essence of my un-
musicalness consists in my inability to enjoy music connectedly, it only
now and then has an effect on me, and how seldom it is a musical one.
The natural effect of music on me is to circumscribe me with a wall,
and its only constant influence on me is that, confined in this way, I
am different from what I am when free.

There is, among the public, no such reverence for literature as there
is for music. The singing girls. It was only the melody that held open
the mouths of many of them. The throat and head of one with a clumsy
body quivered when she sang.

Three clerics in a box. The middle one, wearing a red skull-cap,
listens with calm and dignity, unmoved and heavy, but not stiff; the
one on the right is sunken into himself, with a pointed, rigid, wrinkled
face; the one on the left, stout, holds his face propped at an angle on
his half-opened fist.

Played: *Tragic Overture*. (I hear only slow, solemn beats, now here,
now there. It is instructive to watch the music pass from one group of
players to another and to follow it with the ear. The dishevelled hair
of the conductor.) 'Beherzigung' by Goethe, 'Nänie' by Schiller,
'Gesang der Parzen', 'Triumphlied'.

The singing women who stood up on the low balustrade as though
on a piece of early Italian architecture.

Despite the fact that for a considerable time I have been standing
deep in literature and it has often broken over me, it is certain that for
the past three days, aside from a general desire to be happy, I have felt
no genuine desire for literature. In the same way I considered Löwy
my indispensable friend last week, and now I have easily dispensed
with him for three days.

When I begin to write after a rather long interval, I draw the words
as if out of the empty air. If I capture one, then I have just this one
alone and all the toil must begin anew.

14 December. My father reproached me at noon because I don't
bother with the factory. I explained that I had accepted a share because
I expected profit but that I cannot take an active part so long as I am

in the office. Father quarrelled on, I stood silently at the window. This evening, however, I caught myself thinking, as a result of that noon-time discussion, that I could put up with my present situation very contentedly, and that I only had to be careful not to have all my time free for literature. I had scarcely exposed this thought to a closer inspection when it became no longer astonishing and already appeared accustomed. I disputed my ability to devote all my time to literature. This conviction arose, of course, only from the momentary situation, but was stronger than it. I also thought of Max as of a stranger despite the fact that today he has an exciting evening of reading and acting in Berlin; it occurs to me now that I thought of him only when I approached Miss Taussig's house on my evening walk.

Walk with Löwy down by the river. The one pillar of the vault rising out of the Elizabeth Bridge, lit on the inside by an electric light, looked – a dark mass between light streaming from the sides – like a factory chimney, and the dark wedge of shadow stretching over it to the sky was like ascending smoke. The sharply outlined green areas of light at the side of the bridge.

The way, during the reading of *Beethoven und das Liebespaar* by W. Schäfer, various thoughts (about dinner, about Löwy, who was waiting) unconnected with what I was reading passed through my mind with great distinctness without disturbing my reading, which just today was very pure.

16 December. Sunday, 12 noon. Idled away the morning with sleeping and reading newspapers. Afraid to finish a review for the *Prager Tagblatt*. Such fear of writing always expresses itself by my occasionally making up, away from my desk, initial sentences for what I am to write, which immediately prove unusable, dry, broken off long before their end, and pointing with their towering fragments to a sad future.

The old tricks at the Christmas Fair. Two cockatoos on a crossbar pull fortunes. Mistakes: a girl has a lady-love predicted. A man offers artificial flowers for sale in rhyme: *To jest ruže udělená z kuže* [This is a rose, made of leather].

Young Pipes when singing. As sole gesture, he rolls his right forearm back and forth at the joint, he opens his hands a little and then draws them together again. Sweat covers his face, especially his upper lip, as though with splinters of glass. A buttonless dickey has been hurriedly tucked into the vest under his straight black coat.

The warm shadow in the soft red of Mrs Klug's mouth when she sings.

Jewish streets in Paris, rue Rosier, side-street of rue de Rivoli.

If a disorganized education having only that minimum coherence indispensable for the merest uncertain existence is suddenly challenged to a task limited in time, therefore necessarily arduous, to self-development, to articulate speech, then the response can only be a bitterness in which are mingled arrogance over achievements which could be attained only by calling upon all one's untrained powers, a last glance at the knowledge that escapes in surprise and that is so very fluctuating because it was suspected rather than certain, and, finally, hate and admiration for the environment.

Before falling asleep yesterday I had an image of a drawing in which a group of people were isolated like a mountain in the air. The technique of the drawing seemed to me completely new and, once discovered, easily executed.

A company was assembled around a table, the earth extended somewhat beyond the circle of people, but of all these people, at the moment, I saw with a powerful glance only one young man in ancient dress. His left arm was propped on the table, the hand hung loosely over his face, which was playfully turned up towards someone who was solicitously or questioningly bent over him. His body, especially the right leg, was stretched out in careless youthfulness, he lay rather than sat. The two distinct pairs of lines that outlined his legs crossed and softly merged with the lines outlining his body. His pale, coloured clothes lay heaped up between these lines with feeble corporeality. In astonishment at this beautiful drawing, which begot in my head an excitement that I was convinced was that same and indeed permanent excitement which would guide the pencil in my hand when I wished, I forced myself out of my twilight condition in order better to be able to think the drawing through. Then it soon turned out, of course, that I had imagined nothing but a small, grey-white porcelain group.

In periods of transition such as the past week has been for me and as this moment at least still is, a sad but calm astonishment at my lack of feeling often grips me. I am divided from all things by a hollow space and I don't even push myself to the limits of it.

Now, in the evening, when my thoughts begin to move more freely and I would perhaps be capable of something, I must go to the National Theatre to the first night of *Hippodamie* by Vrchlicky.

It is certain that Sunday can never be of more use to me than a week-day because its special organization throws all my habits into confusion and I need the additional free time to adjust myself half-way to this special day.

The moment I were set free from the office I would yield at once to my desire to write an autobiography. I would have to have some such decisive change before me as a preliminary goal when I began to write in order to be able to give direction to the mass of events. But I cannot imagine any other inspiriting change than this, which is itself so terribly improbable. Then, however, the writing of the autobiography would be a great joy because it would move along as easily as the writing down of dreams, yet it would have an entirely different effect, a great one, which would always influence me and would be accessible as well to the understanding and feeling of everyone else.

18 December. Day before yesterday *Hippodamie*. Bad play. A rambling about in Greek mythology without rhyme or reason. Kvapil's essay in the programme which expresses between the lines the view apparent throughout the whole performance, that a good production (which here, however, was nothing but an imitation of Reinhardt) can make a bad play into a great theatrical work. All this must be sad for a Czech who knows even a little of the world.

The Lieutenant-Governor, who during the intermission snatched air from the corridor through the open door of his box.

The appearance of the dead Axiocha, called up in the shape of a phantom, who soon disappears because, having died only a short time ago, she relives her old human sorrows too keenly at the sight of the world.

I hate Werfel, not because I envy him, but I envy him too. He is healthy, young and rich, everything that I am not. Besides, gifted with a sense of music, he has done very good work early and easily, he has the happiest life behind him and before him, I work with weights I cannot get rid of, and I am entirely shut off from music.

I am not punctual because I do not feel the pains of waiting. I wait like an ox. For if I feel a purpose in my momentary existence, even a very uncertain one, I am so vain in my weakness that I would gladly bear anything for the sake of this purpose once it is before me. If I were in love, what couldn't I do then. How long I waited, years ago, under the arcades of the Ring until M. came by, even to see her walk with her lover. I have been late for appointments partly out of carelessness, partly out of ignorance of the pains of waiting, but also partly in order to attain new, complicated purposes through a renewed, uncertain search for the people with whom I had made the appointments, and so to achieve the possibility of long, uncertain waiting. From the fact that as a child I had a great nervous fear of waiting one could conclude that I was destined for something better and that I foresaw my future.

My good periods do not have time or opportunity to live themselves out naturally; my bad ones, on the other hand, have more than they need. As I see from the diary, I have now been suffering from such a state since the 9th, for almost ten days. Yesterday I once again went to bed with my head on fire, and was ready to rejoice that the bad time was over and ready to fear that I would sleep badly. It passed, however, I slept fairly well and feel badly when I'm awake.

19 December. Yesterday *Davids Geige* by Lateiner. The disinherited son, a good violinist, returns home a rich man, as I used to dream of doing in my early days at the Gymnasium. But first, disguised

as a beggar, his feet bound in rags like a snow-shoveller, he tests his relatives who have never left home: his poor, honest daughter, his rich brother who will not give his son in marriage to his poor cousin and who despite his age himself wants to marry a young woman. He reveals himself later on by tearing open a Prince Albert under which, on a diagonal sash, hang decorations from all the princes of Europe. By violin playing and singing he turns all the relatives and their hangers-on into good people and straightens out their affairs.

Mrs Tschissik acted again. Yesterday her body was more beautiful than her face, which seemed narrower than usual so that the forehead, which is thrown into wrinkles at her first word, was too striking. The beautifully founded, moderately strong, large body did not belong with her face yesterday, and she reminded me vaguely of hybrid beings like mermaids, sirens, centaurs. When she stood before me then, with her face distorted, her complexion spoiled by make-up, a stain on her dark-blue short-sleeved blouse, I felt as though I were speaking to a statue in a circle of pitiless onlookers.

Mrs Klug stood near her and watched me. Miss Weltsch watched me from the left. I said as many stupid things as possible. I did not stop asking Mrs Tschissik why she had gone to Dresden, although I knew that she had quarrelled with the others and for that reason had gone away, and that this subject was embarrassing to her. In the end it was even more embarrassing to me, but nothing else occurred to me. When Mrs Tschissik joined us while I was speaking to Mrs Klug, I turned to Mrs Tschissik, saying 'Pardon!' to Mrs Klug as though I intended to spend the rest of my life with Mrs Tschissik. Then while I was speaking with Mrs Tschissik I observed that my love had not really grasped her, but only flitted about her, now nearer, now farther. Indeed, it can find no peace.

Mrs Liebgold acted a young man in a costume that tightly embraced her pregnant body. As she does not obey her father (Löwy), he presses the upper part of her body down on a chair and beats her over her very tightly trousered behind. Löwy said that he touched her with the same repugnance that he would a mouse. Seen from the front, however, she is pretty, it is only in profile that her nose slants down too long, too pointed and too cruel.

I first arrived at ten, took a walk and tasted to the full the slight nervousness of having a seat in the theatre and going for a walk during the performance, that is, while the soloists were trying to sing me into my seat. I missed Mrs Klug too. Listening to her always lively singing does nothing less than prove the solidity of the world, which is what I need, after all.

Today at breakfast I spoke with my mother by chance about children and marriage, only a few words, but for the first time saw clearly how untrue and childish is the conception of me that my mother builds up for herself. She considers me a healthy young man who suffers a little from the notion that he is ill. This notion will disappear by itself with time; marriage, of course, and having children would put an end to it best of all. Then my interest in literature would also be reduced to the degree that is perhaps necessary for an educated man. A matter-of-fact, undisturbed interest in my profession or in the factory or in whatever may come to hand will appear. Hence there is not the slightest, not the trace of a reason for permanent despair about my future. There is occasion for temporary despair, which is not very deep, however, whenever I think my stomach is upset, or when I can't sleep because I write too much. There are thousands of possible solutions. The most probable is that I shall suddenly fall in love with a girl and will never again want to do without her. Then I shall see how good their intentions towards me are and how little they will interfere with me. But if I remain a bachelor like my uncle in Madrid, that too will be no misfortune because with my cleverness I shall know how to make adjustments.

23 December. Saturday. When I look at my whole way of life going in a direction that is foreign and false to all my relatives and acquaintances, the apprehension arises, and my father expresses it, that I shall become a second Uncle Rudolf, the fool of the new generation of the family, the fool somewhat altered to meet the needs of a different period; but from now on I'll be able to feel how my mother (whose opposition to this opinion grows continually weaker in the course of the years) sums up and enforces everything that speaks for me and against

Uncle Rudolf, and that enters like a wedge between the conceptions entertained about the two of us.

Day before yesterday in the factory. In the evening at Max's where the artist, Novak, was just then displaying the lithographs of Max. I could not express myself in their presence, could not say yes or no. Max voiced several opinions which he had already formed, whereupon my thinking revolved about them without result. Finally I became accustomed to the individual lithographs, overcame at least the surprise of my unaccustomed eye, found a chin round, a face compressed, a chest armourlike, or rather he looked as though he were wearing a giant dress shirt under his street clothes. The artist replied to this with something which was not to be understood either at the first or second attempt, weakening its significance only by saying it to us of all people who thus, if his opinions were proved to be genuinely correct, were in the position of having spoken the cheapest nonsense.

He asserted that it is the felt and even conscious task of the artist to assimilate his subject to his own art form. To achieve this he had first prepared a portrait sketch in colour, which also lay before us and which in dark colours showed a really too sharp, dry likeness (this too-great-sharpness I can acknowledge only now), and was declared by Max to be the best portrait, as, aside from its likeness about the eyes and mouth, it showed nobly composed features brought out in the right degree by the dark colours. If one were asked about it, one couldn't deny it. From this sketch the artist now worked at home on his lithographs, endeavouring in lithograph after lithograph to get farther and farther away from the natural phenomenon but at the same time not only not to violate his own art form but rather to come closer to it stroke by stroke. So, for instance, the ear lost its human convolutions, and its clearly defined edge and became a sudden semicircular whorl around a small, dark opening. Max's bony chin, starting from the ear itself, lost its simple boundary, indispensable as it seems, and a new one was as little created for the observer as a new truth is created by the removal of the old. The hair flowed in sure, understandable outlines and remained human hair no matter how the artist denied it.

After having demanded from us understanding of these transformations, the artist indicated only hastily, but with pride, that everything on these sheets had significance and that even the accidental was necessary because its effect influenced everything that followed. Thus, alongside one head a narrow, pale coffee stain extended almost the entire length of the picture, it was part of the whole, so intended, and not to be removed without damage to all the proportions. There was in the left corner of another sheet a thinly stippled, scarcely noticeable, large blue stain; this stain had even been placed there intentionally, for the sake of the slight illumination that passed from it across the picture, and which the artist had taken advantage of when he continued his work. His next objective was now chiefly the mouth on which something, but not enough, had already been done, and then he intended to transform the nose too. In response to Max's complaint that in this way the lithograph would move farther and farther away from the beautiful colour sketch, he observed that it wasn't at all impossible that it should again approach it.

One certainly could not overlook the sureness with which the artist relied throughout the discussion on the unexpected in his inspiration, and that only this reliance gave his work its best title to being almost a scientific one. – Bought two lithographs, 'Apple Seller', and 'Walk'.

One advantage in keeping a diary is that you become aware with reassuring clarity of the changes which you constantly suffer and which in a general way are naturally believed, surmised, and admitted by you, but which you'll unconsciously deny when it comes to the point of gaining hope or peace from such an admission. In the diary you find proof that in situations which today would seem unbearable, you lived, looked around and wrote down observations, that this right hand moved then as it does today, when we may be wiser because we are able to look back upon our former condition, and for that very reason have got to admit the courage of our earlier striving in which we persisted even in sheer ignorance.

All yesterday morning my head was as if filled with mist from Werfel's poems. For a moment I feared the enthusiasm would carry me along straight into nonsense.

Tormenting discussion with Weltsch[37] evening before last. My startled gaze ran up and down his face and throat for an hour. Once, in the midst of a facial distortion caused by excitement, weakness, and bewilderment, I was not sure that I would get out of the room without permanent damage to our relationship. Outside, in the rainy weather intended for silent walking, I drew a deep breath of relief and then for an hour waited contentedly for M. in front of the Orient. I find this sort of waiting, glancing slowly at the clock and walking indifferently up and down, almost as pleasant as lying on the sofa with legs stretched out and hands in my trouser pockets. (Half asleep, one then thinks one's hands are no longer in the trouser pockets at all, but are lying clenched on top of one's thighs.)

24 December. Sunday. Yesterday it was gay at Baum's. I was there with Weltsch. Max is in Breslau. I felt myself free, could carry every moment to its conclusion, I answered and listened properly, made the most noise, and if I occasionally said something stupid it did not loom large but blew over at once. The walk home in the rain with Weltsch was the same; despite puddles, wind, and cold it passed as quickly for us as though we had ridden. And we were both sorry to say goodbye.

As a child I was anxious, and if not anxious then uneasy, when my father spoke – as he often did, since he was a businessman – of the last day of the month (called the 'ultimo'). Since I wasn't curious, and since I wasn't able – even if I sometimes did ask about it – to digest the answer quickly enough with my slow thinking, and since a weakly stirring curiosity once risen to the surface is often already satisfied by a question and an answer without requiring that it understand as well, the expression 'the last day of the month' remained a disquieting mystery for me, to be joined later (the result of having listened more attentively) by the expression 'ultimo', even if the latter expression did not have the same great significance. It was bad too that the last day, dreaded so long in advance, could never be completely done away with. Sometimes, when it passed with no special sign, indeed with no special attention (I realized only much later that it always came after about thirty days), and when the first had happily arrived, one again began to speak of the last day, not with special dread, to be sure, but it was still something that I put without examination beside the rest of the incomprehensible.

When I arrived at W.'s yesterday noon I heard the voice of his sister greeting me, but I did not see her herself until her fragile figure detached itself from the rocking-chair standing in front of me.

This morning my nephew's circumcision. A short, bow-legged man, Austerlitz, who already has 2,800 circumcisions behind him, carried the thing out very skilfully. It is an operation made more difficult by the fact that the boy, instead of lying on a table, lies on his grandfather's lap, and by the fact that the person performing the operation, instead of paying close attention, must whisper prayers. First the boy is prevented from moving by wrappings which leave only his member free, then the surface to be operated on is defined precisely by putting on a perforated metal disc, then the operation is performed with what is almost an ordinary knife, a sort of fish knife. One sees blood and raw flesh, the *moule* [38] bustles about briefly with his long-nailed, trembling fingers and pulls skin from some place or other over the wound like the finger of a glove. At once everything is all right, the child has scarcely cried. Now there remains only a short prayer during which the *moule* drinks some wine and with his fingers, not yet entirely unbloody, carries some wine to the child's lips. Those present pray: 'As he has now achieved the covenant, so may he achieve knowledge of the Torah, a happy marriage, and the performance of good deeds.'

Today when I heard the *moule*'s assistant say the grace after meals and those present, aside from the two grandfathers, spent the time in dreams or boredom with a complete lack of understanding of the prayer, I saw Western European Judaism before me in a transition whose end is clearly unpredictable and about which those most closely affected are not concerned, but, like all people truly in transition, bear what is imposed upon them. It is so indisputable that these religious forms which have reached their final end have merely a historical character, even as they are practised today, that only a short time was needed this very morning to interest the people present in the obsolete

147

custom of circumcision and its half-sung prayers by describing it to them as something out of history.

Löwy, whom I keep waiting half an hour almost every evening, said to me yesterday: For several days I have been looking up at your window while waiting. First I see a light there; if I have come early, as I usually do, I assume that you are still working. Then the light is put out, in the next room the light stays on, you are therefore having dinner; then the light goes on again in your room, you are therefore brushing your teeth; then the light is put out, you are therefore already on the stairs, but then the light is put on again.

25 December. What I understand of contemporary Jewish literature in Warsaw through Löwy, and of contemporary Czech literature partly through my own insight, points to the fact that many of the benefits of literature – the stirring of minds, the coherence of national consciousness, often unrealized in public life and always tending to disintegrate, the pride which a nation gains from a literature of its own and the support it is afforded in the face of a hostile surrounding world, this keeping of a diary by a nation which is something entirely different from historiography and results in a more rapid (and yet always closely scrutinized) development, the spiritualization of the broad area of public life, the assimilation of dissatisfied elements that are immediately put to use precisely in this sphere where only stagnation can do harm, the constant integration of a people with respect to its whole that the incessant bustle of the magazines creates, the narrowing down of the attention of a nation upon itself and the accepting of what is foreign only in reflection, the birth of a respect for those active in literature, the transitory awakening in the younger generation of higher aspirations, which nevertheless leaves its permanent mark, the acknowledgement of literary events as objects of political solicitude, the dignification of the antithesis between fathers and sons and the possibility of discussing this, the presentation of national faults in a manner that is very painful, to be sure, but also liberating and deserving of forgiveness, the beginning of a lively and therefore self-respecting book trade and the eagerness or books – all these effects can be produced even by a literature whose development is not in actual fact unusually broad in

scope, but seems to be, because it lacks outstanding talents. The liveliness of such a literature exceeds even that of one rich in talent, for, as it has no writer whose great gifts could silence at least the majority of cavillers, literary competition on the greatest scale has a real justification.

A literature not penetrated by a great talent has no gap through which the irrelevant might force its way. Its claim to attention thereby becomes more compelling. The independence of the individual writer, naturally only within the national boundaries, is better preserved. The lack of irresistible national models keeps the completely untalented away from literature. But even mediocre talent would not suffice for a writer to be influenced by the unstriking qualities of the fashionable writers of the moment, or to introduce the works of foreign literatures, or to imitate the foreign literature that has already been introduced; this is plain, for example, in a literature rich in great talents, such as the German is, where the worst writers limit their imitation to what they find at home. The creative and beneficent force exerted in these directions by a literature poor in its component parts proves especially effective when it begins to create a literary history out of the records of its dead writers. These writers' undeniable influence, past and present, becomes so matter-of-fact that it can take the place of their writings. One speaks of the latter and means the former, indeed, one even reads the latter and sees only the former. But since that effect cannot be forgotten, and since the writings themselves do not act independently upon the memory, there is no forgetting and no remembering again. Literary history offers an unchangeable, dependable whole that is hardly affected by the taste of the day.

A small nation's memory is not smaller than the memory of a large one and so can digest the existing material more thoroughly. There are, to be sure, fewer experts in literary history employed, but literature is less a concern of literary history than of the people, and thus, if not purely, it is at least reliably preserved. For the claim that the national consciousness of a small people makes on the individual is such that everyone must always be prepared to know that part of the literature which has come down to him, to support it, to defend it – to defend it even if he does not know it and support it.

The old writings acquire a multiplicity of interpretations; despite the mediocre material, this goes on with an energy that is restrained only by the fear that one may too easily exhaust them, and by the reverence they are accorded by common consent. Everything is done very honestly, only within a bias that is never resolved, that refuses to countenance any weariness, and is spread for miles around when a skilful hand is lifted up. But in the end bias interferes not only with a broad view but with a close insight as well – so that all these observations are cancelled out.

Since people lack a sense of context, their literary activities are out of context too. They depreciate something in order to be able to look down upon it from above, or they praise it to the skies in order to have a place up there beside it. (Wrong.) Even though something is often thought through calmly, one still does not reach the boundary where it connects up with similar things, one reaches this boundary soonest in politics, indeed, one even strives to see it before it is there, and often sees this limiting boundary everywhere. The narrowness of the field, the concern too for simplicity and uniformity, and, finally, the consideration that the inner independence of the literature makes the external connexion with politics harmless, result in the dissemination of literature without a country on the basis of political slogans.

There is universal delight in the literary treatment of petty themes whose scope is not permitted to exceed the capacity of small enthusiasms and which are sustained by their polemical possibilities. Insults, intended as literature, roll back and forth. What in great literature goes on down below, constituting a not indispensable cellar of the structure, here takes place in the full light of day, what is there a matter of passing interest for a few, here absorbs everyone no less than as a matter of life and death.

A character sketch of the literature of small peoples.
Good results in both cases.
Here the results in individual instances are even better.

1. Liveliness:
   a. Conflict.
   b. Schools.
   c. Magazines.

150

2. Less constraint:
   a. Absence of principles.
   b. Minor themes.
   c. Easy formation of symbols.
   d. Throwing off of the untalented.

3. Popularity:
   a. Connexion with politics.
   b. Literary history.
   c. Faith in literature, can make up their own laws.

It is difficult to readjust when one has felt this useful, happy life in all one's being.

Circumcision in Russia. Throughout the house, wherever there is a door, tablets the size of a hand printed with Kabbalistic symbols are hung up to protect the mother from evil spirits during the time between the birth and the circumcision. The evil spirits are especially dangerous to her and the child at this time, perhaps because her body is so very open and therefore offers an easy entrance to everything evil and because the child, too, so long as it has not been accepted into the covenant, can offer no resistance to evil. That is also the reason why a female attendant is taken in, so that the mother may not remain alone for a moment. For seven days after the birth, except on Friday, also in order to ward off evil spirits, ten to fifteen children, always different ones, led by the *belfer* (assistant teacher), are admitted to the bedside of the mother, there repeat the *Shema Israel*, and are then given candy. These innocent, five- to eight-year-old children are supposed to be especially effective in driving back the evil spirits, who press forward most strongly towards evening. On Friday a special celebration is held, just as in general one banquet follows another during this week. Before the day of the circumcision the evil ones are wildest, and so the last night is a night of wakefulness and until morning someone watches beside the mother. The circumcision follows, often in the presence of more than a hundred relatives and friends. The most distinguished person present is permitted to carry the child. The circumciser, who performs his office without payment, is usually a drinker – busy as he is, he has no time for the various holiday foods and so simply pours down some brandy. Thus they all have red noses and reeking breaths. It is therefore not very pleasant when, after the operation has been performed, they suck the bloody member with this mouth, in the prescribed manner. The member is then sprinkled with sawdust and heals in about three days.

A close-knit family life does not seem to be so very common among and characteristic of the Jews, especially those in Russia. Family life is also found among Christians, after all, and the fact that women are excluded from the study of the Talmud is really destructive of Jewish family life; when the man wants to discuss learned talmudic matters – the very core of his life – with guests, the women withdraw to the next room even if they need not do so – so it is even more characteristic of the Jews that they come together at every possible opportunity, whether to pray or to study or to discuss divine matters or to eat holiday meals whose basis is usually a religious one and at which alcohol is drunk only very moderately. They flee to one another, so to speak.

Goethe probably retards the development of the German language by the force of his writing. Even though prose style has often travelled away from him in the interim, still, in the end, as at present, it returns to him with strengthened yearning and even adopts obsolete idioms found in Goethe but otherwise without any particular connexion with him, in order to rejoice in the completeness of its unlimited dependence.

In Hebrew my name is Amschel, like my mother's maternal grandfather, whom my mother, who was six years old when he died, can remember as a very pious and learned man with a long, white beard. She remembers how she had to take hold of the toes of the corpse and ask forgiveness for any offence she may have committed against her grandfather. She also remembers her grandfather's many books which lined the walls. He bathed in the river every day, even in winter, when he chopped a hole in the ice for his bath. My mother's mother died of typhus at an early age. From the time of this death her grandmother became melancholy, refused to eat, spoke with no one, once, a year after the death of her daughter, she went for a walk and did not return, her body was found in the Elbe. An even more learned man than her grandfather was my mother's great-grandfather, Christians and Jews held him in equal honour; during a fire a miracle took place as a result of his piety, the flames jumped over and spared his house while the houses around it burned down. He had four sons, one was converted to Christianity and became a doctor. All but my mother's grandfather died young. He had one son, whom my mother knew as crazy Uncle Nathan, and one daughter, my mother's mother.

To run against the window and, weak after exerting all one's strength, to step over the window sill through the splintered wood and glass.

26 December. Slept badly again, the third night now. So the three holidays during which I had hoped to write things which were to have helped me through the whole year, I spent in a state requiring help. On Christmas Eve, walk with Löwy in the direction of Stern. Yesterday *Blümale oder die Perle von Warschau*. For her steadfast love and loyalty Blümale is distinguished by the author with the honorific title, 'Pearl of Warsaw', in the name of the play. Only the exposed, long, delicate throat of Mrs Tschissik explains the shape of her face. The glint of tears in Mrs Klug's eyes when singing a monotonously rhythmic melody into which the audience lets their heads hang, seemed to me by far to surpass in significance the song, the theatre, the cares of all the audience, indeed my imagination. View through the back curtain into the dressing-room, directly to Mrs Klug, who is standing there in a white petticoat and a short-sleeved shirt. My uncertainty about the feelings of the audience and therefore my strenuous inner spurring on of its enthusiasm. The skilful, amiable manner in which I spoke to Miss T. and her escort yesterday. It was part of the freedom of the good spirits which I felt yesterday and even as early as Saturday, that, although it was definitely not necessary, because of a certain complaisance toward the world and a reckless modesty I made use of a few seemingly embarrassed words and gestures. I was alone with my mother, and that too I took easily and well; looked at everyone with steadiness.

List of things which today are easy to imagine as ancient: the crippled beggars on the way to promenades and picnic places, the unilluminated atmosphere at night, the crossed girders of the bridge.

A list of those passages in *Dichtung und Wahrheit* that, by a peculiarity on which one cannot place one's finger, give an unusually strong impression of liveliness not essentially consistent with what is actually described; for instance, call up the image of the boy Goethe, how – curious, richly dressed, loved and lively – he makes his way into the homes of all his acquaintances so that he may see and hear everything that is to be seen and heard. Now, when I leaf through the book, I cannot find any such passages, they all seem clear to me and have a liveliness that cannot be heightened by any accident. I must wait until some time when I am reading innocently along and then stop at the right passages.

It is unpleasant to listen to Father talk with incessant insinuations about the good fortune of people today and especially of his children, about the sufferings he had to endure in his youth. No one denies that for years, as a result of insufficient winter clothing, he had open sores on his legs, that he often went hungry, that when he was only ten he had to push a cart through the villages, even in winter and very early in the morning – but, and this is something he will not understand, these facts, taken together with the further fact that I have not gone through all this, by no means lead to the conclusion that I have been happier than he, that he may pride himself on these sores on his legs, which is something he assumes and asserts from the very beginning, that I cannot appreciate his past sufferings, and that, finally, just because I have not gone through the same sufferings I must be endlessly grateful to him. How gladly I would listen if he would talk on about his youth and parents, but to hear all this in a boastful and quarrelsome tone is torment. Over and over again he claps his hands together: 'Who can understand that today! What do the children know! No one has gone through that! Does a child understand that today!' He spoke again in the same way today to Aunt Julie, who was visiting us. She too has the huge face of all Father's relatives. There is something wrong and somewhat disturbing about the set or colour of her eyes. At the age of ten she was hired out as a cook. In a skimpy wet skirt, in the severe cold, she had to run out for something, the skin of her legs cracked, the skimpy skirt froze and it was only that evening, in bed, that it dried.

27 December. An unfortunate man, one who is condemned to have no children, is terribly imprisoned in his misfortune. Nowhere a hope for revival, for help from luckier stars. He must live his life, afflicted by his misfortune, and when its circle is ended must resign himself to it and not start out again to see whether, on a longer path, under other circumstances of body and time, the misfortune which he has suffered could disappear or even produce something good.

My feeling when I write something that is wrong might be depicted as follows: In front of two holes in the ground a man is waiting for something to appear that can rise up only out of the hole on his right. But while this hole remains covered over by a dimly visible lid, one thing after another rises up out of the hole on his left, keeps trying to attract his attention, and in the end succeeds in doing this without any difficulty because of its swelling size, which, much as the man may try to prevent it, finally covers up even the right hole. But the man – he does not want to leave this place, and indeed refuses to at any price – has nothing but these appearances, and although – fleeting as they are, their strength is used up by their merely appearing – they cannot satisfy him, he still strives, whenever out of weakness they are arrested in their rising up, to drive them up and scatter them into the air if only he can thus bring up others; for the permanent sight of one is unbearable, and moreover he continues to hope that after the false appearances have been exhausted, the true will finally appear.

How weak this picture is. An incoherent assumption is thrust like a board between the actual feeling and the metaphor of the description.

28 December. The torment that the factory causes me. Why didn't I object when they made me promise to work there in the afternoons. No one used force to make me do it, but my father compels me by his reproaches, Karl by his silence, and I by my consciousness of guilt. I know nothing about the factory, and this morning, when the committee

made an inspection, I stood around uselessly with my tail between my legs. I deny that it is possible for me to fathom all the details of the operation of the factory. And if I should succeed in doing it by endlessly questioning and pestering all those concerned, what would I have achieved? I would be able to do nothing practical with this knowledge, I am fit only for spectacular performances to which the sound common sense of my boss adds the salt that makes it look like a really good job. But through this empty effort spent on the factory I would, on the other hand, rob myself of the use of the few afternoon hours that belong to me, which would of necessity lead to the complete destruction of my existence, which, even apart from this, becomes more and more hedged in.

This afternoon, while taking a walk, for the duration of a few steps I saw coming towards me or crossing my path entirely imaginary members of the committee that caused me such anxiety this morning.

29 December. Those lively passages in Goethe. Page 265, 'I therefore led my friend into the woods.'
Goethe: 307. 'Now I heard during these hours no other conversation save what concerned medicine or natural history, and my imagination was drawn in quite another direction.'

The difficulties of bringing to an end even a short essay lie not in the fact that we feel the end of the piece demands a fire which the actual content up to that point has not been able to produce out of itself, they arise rather from the fact that even the shortest essay demands of the author a degree of self-satisfaction and of being lost in himself out of which it is difficult to step into the everyday air without great determination and an external incentive, so that, before the essay is rounded to a close and one might quietly slip away, one bolts, driven by unrest, and then the end must be completed from the outside with hands which must not only do the work but hold on as well.

30 December. My urge to imitate has nothing of the actor in it, its chief lack is unity. The whole range of those characteristics which are

rough and striking, I cannot imitate at all, I have always failed when I attempted it, it is contrary to my nature. On the other hand, I have a decided urge to imitate them in their details, the way certain people manipulate walking-sticks, the way they hold their hands, the movements of their fingers, and I can do it without any effort. But this very effortlessness, this thirst for imitation, sets me apart from the actor, because this effortlessness reflects itself in the fact that no one is aware that I am imitating. Only my own satisfied, or more often reluctant, appreciation shows me that I have been successful. Far beyond this external imitation, however, goes the inner, which is often so striking and strong that there is no room at all within me to observe and verify it, and it first confronts me in my memory. But here the imitation is so complete and replaces my own self with so immediate a suddenness that, even assuming it could be made visible at all, it would be unbearable on the stage. The spectator cannot be asked to endure what passes beyond the bounds of play-acting. If an actor who is supposed to thrash another according to the plot really does thrash him, out of excitement, out of an excess of emotion, and the other actor screams in pain, then the spectator must become a man and intervene. But what seldom happens in this way happens countless times in lesser ways. The essence of the bad actor consists not in the fact that he imitates too little, but rather in the fact that as a result of gaps in his education, experience, and talent he imitates the wrong models. But his most essential fault is still that he does not observe the limits of the play and imitates too much. His hazy notion of the demands of the stage drives him to this, and even if the spectator thinks one actor or another is bad because he stands around stiffly, toys with his fingers at the edge of his pocket, puts his hands on his hips improperly, listens for the prompter, in spite of the fact that things have changed completely maintains an anxious solemnity regardless, still, even this actor who suddenly dropped from nowhere on the stage is bad only because he imitates too much, even if he does so only in his mind. (31 December.) For the very reason that his abilities are so limited, he is afraid to give less than all he has. Even though his ability may not be so small that it cannot be divided up, he does not want to betray the fact that under certain circumstances, by the exercise of his own will, he can dispose of less than all his art.

In the morning I felt so fresh for writing, but now the idea that I am to read to Max in the afternoon blocks me completely. This shows too how unfit I am for friendship, assuming that friendship in this sense is even possible. For since a friendship without interruption of one's daily life is unthinkable, a great many of its manifestations are blown away time and again, even if its core remains undamaged. From the undamaged core they are formed anew, but as every such formation requires time, and not everything that is expected succeeds, one can never, even aside from the change in one's personal moods, pick up again where one left off last time. Out of this, in friendships that have a deep foundation, an uneasiness must arise before every fresh meeting which need not be so great that it is felt as such, but which can disturb one's conversation and behaviour to such a degree that one is consciously astonished, especially as one is not aware of, or cannot believe, the reason for it. So how am I to read to M. or even think, while writing down what follows, that I shall read it to him.

Besides, I am disturbed by my having leafed through the diary this morning to see what I could read to M. In this examination I have found neither that what I have written so far is especially valuable nor that it must simply be thrown away. My opinion lies between the two and closer to the first, yet it is not of such a nature that, judging by the value of what I have written, I must, in spite of my weakness, regard myself as exhausted. Despite that, the sight of the mass of what I had written diverted me almost irrecoverably from the fountainhead of my writing for the next hour, because my attention was to a certain extent lost downstream, as it were, in the same channel.

While I sometimes think that all through the time I was at the Gymnasium and before that, as well, I was able to think unusually clearly, and only the later weakening of my memory prevents me from judging it correctly today, I still recognize at other times that my poor memory is only trying to flatter me and that I was mentally inert, at least in things themselves insignificant but having serious consequences. So I remember that when I was at the Gymnasium I often – even if not very thoroughly, I probably tired easily even then – argued the existence of God with Bergmann in a talmudic style either my own or imitated from him. At the time I liked to begin with a theme I had found in a Christian magazine (I believe it was *Die Christliche Welt*) in which a watch and the world and the watchmaker and God were compared to one another, and the existence of the watchmaker was supposed to prove that of God. In my opinion I was able to refute this very well as far as Bergmann was concerned, even though this refutation was not firmly grounded in me and I had to piece it together for myself like a jigsaw puzzle before using it. Such a refutation once took place while we were walking around the Rathaus tower. I remember this clearly because once, years ago, we reminded each other of it.

But while I thought I was distinguishing myself – I had no other motive than the desire to distinguish myself and my joy in making an impression and in the impression itself – it was only as a result of giving it insufficient thought that I endured always having to go around dressed in the wretched clothes which my parents had made for me by one customer after another, longest by a tailor in Nusle. I naturally noticed – it was obvious – that I was unusually badly dressed, and even had an eye for others who were well dressed, but for years on end my mind did not succeed in recognizing in my clothes the cause of my miserable appearance. Since even at that time, more in tendency than in fact, I was on the way to underestimating myself, I was convinced that it was only on me that clothes assumed this appearance, first looking as stiff as a board, then hanging in wrinkles. I did not want new clothes at all, for if I was going to look ugly in any case, I wanted at least to be comfortable and also to avoid exhibiting the ugliness of the new clothes to the world that had grown accustomed to the old ones. These always long-drawn-out refusals on the frequent occasions when my mother (who with the eyes of an adult was still able to find differences between these new clothes and the old ones) wanted to have new clothes of this sort made for me, had this effect upon me that, with my parents concurring, I had to conclude that I was not at all concerned about my appearance.

꒰ ꒰ ꒰

2 January. As a result I let the awful clothes affect even my posture, walked around with my back bowed, my shoulders drooping, my hands and arms at awkward angles, was afraid of mirrors because they showed

in me an ugliness which in my opinion was inevitable, which more-over could not have been an entirely truthful reflection, for had I actually looked like that, I certainly would have attracted even more attention, suffered gentle pokes in the back from my mother on Sunday walks and admonitions and prophecies which were much too abstract for me to be able to relate them to the worries I then had. In general I lacked principally the ability to provide even in the slightest detail for the real future. I thought only of things in the present and their present condition, not because of thoroughness or any special, strong interest, but rather, to the extent that weakness in thinking was not the cause, because of sorrow and fear – sorrow, because the present was so sad for me that I thought I could not leave it before it resolved itself into happiness; fear, because, like my fear of the slightest action in the present, I also considered myself, in view of my contemptible, childish appearance, unworthy of forming a serious, responsible opinion of the great, manly future which usually seemed so impossible to me that every short step forward appeared to me to be counterfeit and the next step unattainable.

I admitted the possibility of miracles more readily than that of real progress, but was too detached not to keep the sphere of miracles and that of real progress sharply divided. I was therefore able to spend a good deal of time before falling asleep in imagining that some day, a rich man in a coach and four, I would drive into the Jewish quarter, with a magic word set free a beautiful maiden who was being beaten unjustly, and carry her off in my coach; but untouched by this silly make-believe, which probably fed only on an already unhealthy sexuality, I remained convinced that I would not pass my final exam-inations that year, and if I did, I would not get on in the next class, and if by some swindle I could avoid even that, then I would certainly fail decisively in my graduation examination, convinced also that I would all at once – the precise moment did not matter – reveal some unheard-of inability and very definitely surprise my parents as well as the rest of the world, who had been lulled to sleep by my outwardly regular progress. Since I always looked only to my inability as my guide into the future – only seldom to my feeble literary work – con-sidering the future never did me any good; it was only a spinning out of my present grief. If I chose to, I could of course walk erect, but it made me tired, nor could I see how a crooked back would hurt me in the future. If I should have a future, then, I felt, everything will straighten itself out of its own accord. I did not choose such a principle because it involved a confidence in a future in whose existence I did not believe, its purpose was only to make living easier for me, to walk, to dress, to wash, to read, above all to coop myself up at home in a way that took the least effort and required the least spirit. If I went beyond that I could think only of ridiculous solutions.

Once it seemed impossible to get along without a black dress suit, especially as I also had to decide whether I would join a dancing class. The tailor in Nusle was sent for and the cut of the suit discussed. I was undecided, as I always was in such cases, they made me afraid that by a definite statement I would be swept away not only into an immediate unpleasantness, but beyond that into something even worse. So at first I didn't want a dress suit, but when they shamed me before the stranger by pointing out that I had no dress suit, I put up with having a tail-coat discussed; but since I regarded a tail-coat as a fearful revolution one could forever talk about but on which one could never decide, we agreed on a tuxedo, which, because of its similarity to the usual sack coat, seemed to me at least bearable. But when I heard that the vest of the tuxedo had to be cut low and I would therefore have to wear a stiff shirt as well, my determination almost exceeded my strength, since something like this had to be averted. I did not want such a tuxedo, rather, if I had to have one, a tuxedo lined and trimmed with silk indeed, but one that could be buttoned high. The tailor had never heard of such a tuxedo, but he remarked that no matter what I intended to do with such a jacket, it couldn't be worn for dancing. Good, then it couldn't be worn for dancing, I didn't want to dance anyhow, that hadn't been decided on yet in any case, on the contrary, I wanted the jacket made for me as I had described it. The tailor's stubbornness was increased by the fact that until now I had always submitted with shamed haste to being measured for new clothes and to having them tried on, without expressing any opinions or wishes. So there was nothing else for me to do, and also since my mother insisted on it, but to go with him, painful as it was, across the Altstädster Ring to a second-hand clothing store in the window of which I had for quite some time seen displayed a simple tuxedo and had recognized it as suitable for me. But unfortunately it had already been removed from the window, I could not see it inside the store even by looking my hardest, I did not dare to go into the store just to look at the tuxedo, so we returned, disagreeing as before. I felt as though the future tuxedo was already cursed by the uselessness of this errand, at least I used my annoyance with the pros and cons of the argument as an excuse to send the tailor away with some small order or other and an indefinite promise about the tuxedo while I, under the reproaches of my mother, remained wearily behind, barred forever – everything happened to me forever – from girls, an elegant appearance, and dances. The instantaneous cheerfulness that this induced in me made me miserable, and besides, I was afraid that I had made myself ridiculous before the tailor as none of his customers ever had before.

3 January. Read a good deal in *Die Neue Rundschau*. Beginning of the novel *Der Nackte Mann*.[39] The clarity of the whole a little too thin, sureness in the details. *Gabriel Schillings Flucht* by Hauptmann. Education of people. Instructive in the bad and the good.

New Year's Eve I had planned to read to Max from the diaries in the afternoon, I looked forward to it, and it did not come off. We were not in tune, I felt a calculating pettiness and haste in him that afternoon, he was almost not my friend but nevertheless still dominated me to the extent that through his eyes I saw myself uselessly leafing through the notebooks over and over again, and found this leafing back and forth, which continually showed the same pages flying by, disgusting. It was naturally impossible to work together in this mutual tension, and the one page of *Richard and Samuel* that we finished amidst mutual resistance is simply proof of Max's energy, but otherwise bad. New Year's Eve at Čada's. Not so bad, because Weltsch, Kisch, and someone else added new blood so that finally, although only within the limits of that group, I again found my way back to Max. I then pressed his hand on the crowded Graben, though without looking at him, and with my three notebooks pressed to me, as I remember, proudly went straight home.

The fern-shaped flames blazing up from a melting-pot on the street in front of a building under construction.

It is easy to recognize a concentration in me of all my forces on writing. When it became clear in my organism that writing was the most productive direction for my being to take, everything rushed in that direction and left empty all those abilities which were directed towards the joys of sex, eating, drinking, philosophical reflection, and above all music. I atrophied in all these directions. This was necessary because the totality of my strengths was so slight that only collectively could they even half-way serve the purpose of my writing. Naturally, I did not find this purpose independently and consciously, it found itself, and is now interfered with only by the office, but that interferes with it completely. In any case I shouldn't complain that I can't put up with a sweetheart, that I understand almost exactly as much of love as I do of music and have to resign myself to the most superficial efforts I may pick up, that on New Year's Eve I dined on parsnips and spinach, washed down with a glass of Ceres, and that on Sunday I was unable to take part in Max's lecture on his philosophical work – the compensation for all this is clear as day. My development is now complete and, so far as I can see, there is nothing left to sacrifice; I need only throw my work in the office out of this complex in order to begin my real life in which, with the progress of my work, my face will finally be able to age in a natural way.

The sudden turn a conversation takes when in the discussion, which at first has dealt in detail with worries of the inner existence, the question is raised (not really breaking the conversation off, but naturally not growing out of it, either) of when and where one will meet the next time and the circumstances that must be considered in deciding this. And if the conversation also ends with a shaking of hands, then one takes one's leave with momentary faith in the pure, firm structure of our life and with respect for it.

In an autobiography one cannot avoid writing 'often' where truth would require that 'once' be written. For one always remains conscious that the word 'once' explodes that darkness on which the memory draws; and though it is not altogether spared by the word 'often', either, it is at least preserved in the opinion of the writer, and he is carried across parts which perhaps never existed at all in his life but serve him as a substitute for those which his memory can no longer guess at.

4 January. It is only because of my vanity that I like so much to read to my sisters (so that today, for instance, it is already too late to write). Not that I am convinced that I shall achieve something significant in the reading, it is only that I am dominated by the passion to get so close to the good works I read that I merge with them, not through my own merit, indeed, but only through the attentiveness of my listening sisters, which has been excited by what is being read and is unresponsive to inessentials; and therefore too, under the concealment my vanity affords me, I can share as creator in the effect which the work alone has exercised. That is why I really read admirably to my sisters and stress the accents with extreme exactness just as I feel them, because later I am abundantly rewarded not only by myself but also by my sisters.

But if I read to Brod or Baum or others, just because of my pretensions my reading must appear horribly bad to everyone, even if they know nothing of the usual quality of my reading; for here I know that the listener is fully aware of the separation between me and what is being read, here I cannot merge completely with what I read without becoming ridiculous in my own opinion, an opinion which can expect no support from the listener; with my voice I flutter around what is being read, try to force my way in here and there because they don't expect that much from me at all; but what they really want me to do, to read without vanity, calmly and distantly, and to become passionate only when a genuine passion demands it, that I cannot do; but although I believe that I have resigned myself to reading badly to everyone except my sisters, my vanity, which this time has no justification, still shows itself: I feel offended if anyone finds fault with my reading, I become flushed and want to read on quickly, just as I usually strive, once I have begun, to read on endlessly, out of an unconscious yearning that during the course of the long reading there may be produced, at least in me, that vain, false feeling of integration with what I read which makes me forget that I shall never be strong enough at any one moment to impose my feelings on the clear vision of the listener and that at home it is always my sisters who initiate this longed-for substitution.

5 January. For two days I have noticed, whenever I choose to, an inner coolness and indifference. Yesterday evening, during my walk, every little street sound, every eye turned towards me, every picture in a showcase, was more important to me than myself.

Uniformity. History.

When it looks as if you had made up your mind finally to stay at home for the evening, when you have put on your house jacket and sat down after supper with a light on the table to the piece of work or the game that usually precedes your going to bed, when the weather outside is unpleasant so that staying indoors seems natural, and when you have already been sitting quietly at the table for so long that your departure must occasion not only paternal anger but surprise to everyone, when besides, the stairs are in darkness and the front door locked and in spite of all that you have started up in a sudden fit of restlessness, changed your jacket, abruptly dressed yourself for the street, explained that you must go out and with a few curt words of leave-taking actually gone out, banging the flat door more or less hastily according to the degree of displeasure you think you have left behind you and so cut off the general discussion of your departure, and when you find yourself once more in the street with limbs swinging extra freely in answer to the unexpected liberty you have procured for them, when as a result of this decisive action you feel aroused within yourself all the potentialities of decisive action, when you recognize with more than usual significance that your strength is greater than your need to accomplish effortlessly the swiftest of changes, that left alone you grow in understanding and calm, and in the enjoyment of them – then for that evening you have so completely got away from your family that the most distant journey could not take you farther and you have lived through what is for Europe so extreme an experience of solitude that one can only call it Russian. All this is still heightened if at such a late hour in the evening you look up a friend to see how he is getting on.[40]

Invited Weltsch to come to Mrs Klug's benefit. Löwy, with his severe headaches that probably indicate a serious head ailment, leaned against a wall down in the street where he was waiting for me, his right hand pressed in despair against his forehead. I pointed him out to

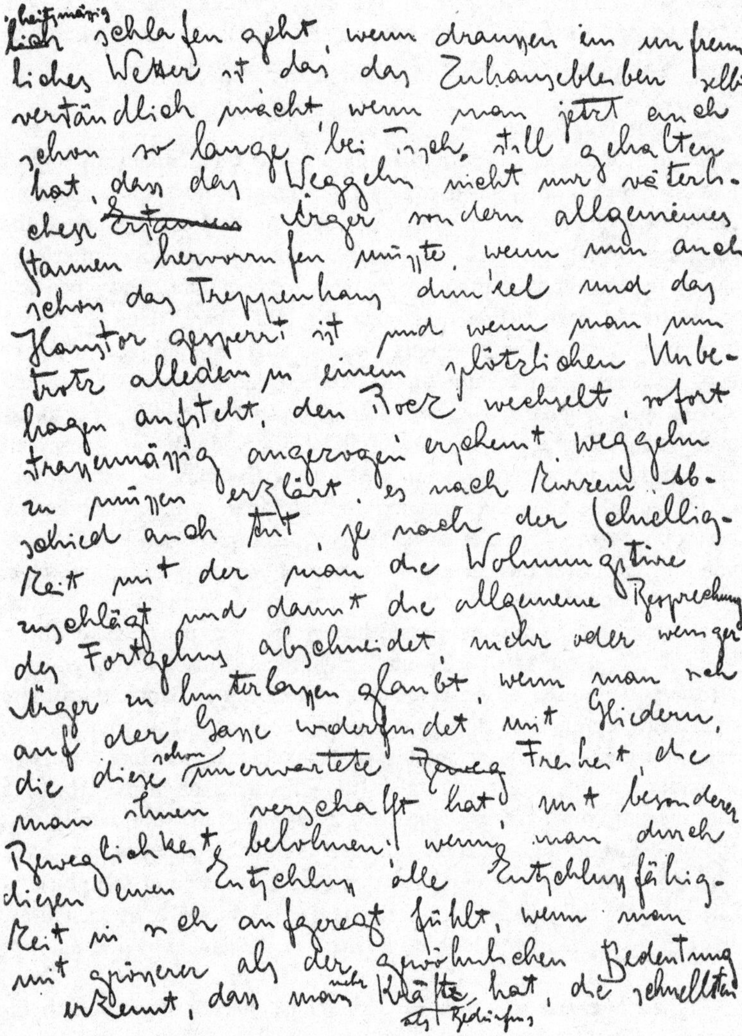
gewohnheitsmässig schlafen geht, wenn draussen ein unfreund-
liches Wetter ist, das das Zuhausebleiben selbst-
verständlich macht, wenn man jetzt auch
schon so lange bei Tisch still gehalten
hat, dass das Weggehn nicht nur väterli-
chen Ärger sondern allgemeines
Staunen hervorrufen müsste, wenn nun auch
schon das Treppenhaus dunkel und das
Haustor gesperrt ist und wenn man nun
trotz alledem in einem plötzlichen Unbe-
hagen aufsteht, den Rock wechselt, sofort
strassenmässig angezogen erscheint, weggehn
zu müssen erklärt, es nach kurzem Abschied auch tut, je nach der Schnellig-
keit mit der man die Wohnungstüre
zuschlägt und damit die allgemeine Besprechung
des Fortgehns abschneidet, mehr oder weniger
Ärger zu hinterlassen glaubt, wenn man sich
auf der Gasse wiederfindet mit Gliedern,
die diese schon unerwartete Freiheit, die
man ihnen verschafft hat, mit besonderer
Beweglichkeit belohnen, wenn man durch
diesen einen Entschluss alle Entschlussfähig-
keit in sich aufgeregt fühlt, wenn man
mit grösserer als der gewöhnlichen Bedeutung
erkennt, dass man mehr Kräfte als Bedürfnis hat, die schnellste

A Manuscript page of the *Diaries* (see page 165).

Weltsch who, from his sofa, leaned out of the window. I thought it was the first time in my life that I had so easily observed from the window an incident down in the street that concerned me so closely. In and of itself, this kind of observation is familiar to me from Sherlock Holmes.

6 January. Yesterday *Vizekönig* by Feimann. My receptivity to the Jewishness in these plays deserts me because they are too monotonous and degenerate into a wailing that prides itself on isolated, violent outbreaks. When I saw the first plays it was possible for me to think that I had come upon a Judaism on which the beginnings of my own rested, a Judaism that was developing in my direction and so would enlighten and carry me farther along in my own clumsy Judaism, instead, it moves farther away from me the more I hear of it. The people remain, of course, and I hold fast to them.

Mrs Klug was giving a benefit and therefore sang several new songs and made a few new jokes. But only her opening song held me wholly under her influence, after that I had the strongest reaction to every detail of her appearance, to her arms, stretched out when she sings, and her snapping fingers, to the tightly twisted curls at her temples, to her thin shirt, flat and innocent under her vest, to her lower lip that she pursed once while she savoured the effect of a joke ('Look, I speak every language, but in Yiddish'), to her fat little feet in their thick white stockings. But when she sang new songs yesterday she spoiled the main effect she had on me, which lay in the fact that here was a person exhibiting herself who had discovered a few jokes and songs that revealed her temperament and all its strong points to the utmost perfection. When this display is a success, everything is a success, and if we like to let this person affect us often, we will naturally – and in this, perhaps, all the audience agrees with me – not let ourselves be misled by the constant repetition of the songs, which are always the same, we will rather approve of it as an aid to concentration, like the darkening of the hall, for example, and, as far as the woman is concerned, recognize in her that fearlessness and self-awareness which are exactly what we are seeking. So when the new songs came along, songs that could reveal nothing new in Mrs Klug since the old ones had done their duty so completely, and when these songs, without any justification at all, claimed one's attention purely as songs, and when they in this way distracted one's attention from Mrs Klug but at the same time showed that she herself was not at ease in them either, part of the time making a failure of them and part of the time exaggerating her grimaces and gestures, one had to become annoyed and was consoled only by the fact that the memory of her perfect performances in the past, resulting from her unshakeable integrity, was too firm to be disturbed by the present sight.

7 January. Unfortunately Mrs Tschissik always has parts which show only the essence of her character, she always plays women and girls who all at once are unhappy, despised, dishonoured, wronged, but who are not allowed time to develop their characters in a natural sequence. The explosive, natural strength with which she plays these roles makes them climactic only when she acts them, in the play as it is written, because of the wealth of acting they require, these roles are only suggestions, but this shows what she would be capable of. One of her important gestures begins as a shudder in her trembling hips, which she holds somewhat stiffly. Her little daughter seems to have one hip completely stiff. When the actors embrace, they hold each other's wigs in place.

Recently, when I went up to Löwy's room with him so that he could read me the letter he had written to the Warsaw writer, Nomberg, we met the Tschissik couple on the landing. They were carrying their costumes for *Kol Nidre*, wrapped in tissue paper like matzos, up to their room. We stopped for a little while. The railing supported my hands and the intonations of my sentences. Her large mouth, so close in front of me, assumed surprising but natural shapes. It was my fault that the conversation threatened to end hopelessly, for in my effort hurriedly to express all my love and devotion I only remarked that the affairs of the troupe were going wretchedly, that their repertoire was exhausted, that they could therefore not remain much longer and that the lack of interest that the Prague Jews took in them was incomprehensible. Monday I must – she asked me – come to see *Sedernacht*, although I already know the play. Then I shall hear her sing the song ('Hear, O Israel') which, she remembers from a remark I once made, I love especially.

'Yeshivahs' are talmudic colleges supported by many communities in

Poland and Russia. The cost is not very great because these schools are usually housed in old, unusable buildings in which, besides the rooms where the students study and sleep, is found the apartment of the Rosh Yeshivah, who also performs other services in the community, and of his assistant. The students pay no tuition and take their meals in turn with the various members of the community. Although these schools are based on the most severely orthodox principles, it is precisely in them that apostate progress has its source: since young people from distant places come together here, precisely the poor, the energetic and those who want to get away from their homes; since the supervision is not very strict and the young people are entirely thrown upon one another, and since the most essential part of the instruction is common study and mutual explanation of difficult passages; since the orthodoxy in the various home towns of the students is always the same and therefore not much of a topic for conversation, while the suppressed progressive tendencies take the most varied forms, differing in strength according to the varying circumstances of the towns, so that there is always a lot to talk about; since, furthermore, one person always lays hands on only one or another copy of the forbidden progressive literature, while in the Yeshivah many such copies are brought together from everywhere and exercise a particularly telling effect because every possessor of a copy propagates not only the text but also his own zeal – because of all these reasons and their immediate consequences, in the recent past all the progressive writers, politicians, journalists, and scholars have come out of these schools. The reputation of these schools among the orthodox has therefore deteriorated very much, while on the other hand young people of advanced inclinations stream to them more than ever.

One famous Yeshivah is in Ostro, a small place eight hours by train from Warsaw. All Ostro is really only a bracket around a short stretch of the highway. Löwy insists it's no longer than his stick. Once, when a count stopped in Ostro with his four-horse travelling carriage, the two lead horses stood outside one end of the place and the rear of the carriage outside the other.

Löwy decided, about the age of fourteen when the constraint of life at home became unbearable for him, to go to Ostro. His father had just slapped him on the shoulder as he was leaving the *klaus* towards evening and had casually told him to see him later, he had something to discuss with him. Because he could obviously expect nothing but the usual reproaches, Löwy went directly from the *klaus* to the railway station, with no baggage, wearing a somewhat better caftan than usual because it was Saturday evening, and carrying all his money, which he always had with him. He took the ten o'clock train to Ostro where he arrived at seven the next morning. He went straight to the Yeshivah where he made no special stir, anyone can enter a Yeshivah, there are no special entrance requirements. The only striking thing was his entering at this time – it was summer – which was not customary, and the good caftan he was wearing. But all this was soon settled too, because very young people such as these were, bound to each other by their Jewishness in a degree unknown to us, get to know each other easily. He distinguished himself in his studies, for he had acquired a good deal of knowledge at home. He liked talking to the strange boys, especially as, when they found out about his money, they all crowded around him offering to sell him things. One, who wanted to sell him 'days', astonished him especially. Free board was called 'days'. They were a saleable commodity because the members of the community, who wanted to perform a deed pleasing to God by providing free board for no matter what student, did not care who sat at their tables. If a student was unusually clever, it was possible for him to provide himself with two sets of free meals for one day. He could bear up under these double meals so much the better because they were not very ample, after the first meal, one could still swallow down the second with great pleasure, and because it might also happen that one day was doubly provided for while other days were empty. Nevertheless, everyone was happy, naturally, if he found an opportunity to sell such an additional set of free meals advantageously. Now if someone arrived in summer, as Löwy did, at a time when the free board had long since been distributed, the only possible way to get any was to buy it, as the additional sets of free meals which had been available at first had all been reserved by speculators.

The night in the Yeshivah was unbearable. Of course, all the windows were open since it was warm, but the stench and the heat would not stir out of the rooms, the students, who had no real beds, lay down to sleep without undressing, in their sweaty clothes, wherever they happened to be sitting last. Everything was full of fleas. In the morning everyone hurriedly wet his hands and face with water and resumed his studies. Most of the time they studied together, usually two from one book. Debates would often draw a number into a circle. The Rosh Yeshivah explained only the most difficult passages here and there. Although Löwy later – he stayed in Ostro ten days, but slept and ate at the inn – found two like-minded friends (they didn't find one another so easily, because they always first had carefully to test the opinions and reliability of the other person), he nevertheless was very glad to return home because he was accustomed to an orderly life and couldn't stand the homesickness.

In the large room there was the clamour of card playing and later the usual conversation which Father carries on when he is well, as he is today, loudly if not coherently. The words represented only small shapes in a formless clamour. Little Felix slept in the girls' room, the door of which was wide open. I slept across the way, in my own room. The door of this room, in consideration of my age, was closed. Besides, the open door indicated that they still wanted to lure Felix into the family while I was already excluded.

Yesterday at Baum's. Strobl was supposed to be there, but was at the theatre. Baum read a column, 'On the Folksong'; bad. Then a chapter from *Des Schicksals Spiele und Ernst*; very good. I was indifferent, in a bad mood, got no clear impression of the whole. On the way home in the rain Max told me the present plan of 'Irma Polak'. I could not admit my mood, as Max never gives it proper recognition. I therefore had to be insincere, which finally spoiled everything for me. I was so sorry for myself that I preferred to speak to Max when his face was in the dark, although mine, in the light, could then betray itself more easily. But then the mysterious end of the novel gripped me in spite of all the obstacles. On the way home, after saying good night, regret because of my falsity and pain because of its inevitability. Plan to start a special notebook on my relationship with Max. What is not written down swims before one's eyes and optical accidents determine the total impression.

171

When I lay on the sofa the loud talking in the room on either side of me, by the women on the left, by the men on the right, gave me the impression that they were coarse, savage beings who could not be appeased, who did not know what they were saying and spoke only in order to set the air in motion, who lifted their faces while speaking and followed the spoken words with their eyes.

So passes my rainy, quiet Sunday, I sit in my bedroom and am at peace, but instead of making up my mind to do some writing, into which I could have poured my whole being the day before yesterday, I have been staring at my fingers for quite a while. This week I think I have been completely influenced by Goethe, have really exhausted the strength of this influence and have therefore become useless.

From a poem by Rosenfeld describing a storm at sea: 'The souls flutter, the bodies tremble.' When he recites, Löwy clenches the skin on his forehead and the bridge of his nose the way one would think only hands could be clenched. At the most gripping passages, which he wants to bring home to the listener, he himself comes close to us, or rather he enlarges himself by making his appearance more distinct. He steps forward only a little, opens his eyes wide, plucks at his straight black coat with his absent-minded left hand and holds the right out to us, open and large. And we are supposed, even if we are not gripped, to acknowledge that he is gripped and to explain to him how the misfortune which has been described was possible.

I am supposed to pose in the nude for the artist Ascher, as a model for a St Sebastian.

If I should now, in the evening, return to my relatives, I shall, since I have written nothing that I could enjoy, not appear stranger, more despicable, more useless to them than I do to myself. All this, naturally, only in my feelings (which cannot be deceived even by the most precise observation), for actually they all respect me and love me, too.

24 January. Wednesday. For the following reasons have not written for so long: I was angry with my boss and cleared it up only by means

of a good letter; was in the factory several times; read, and indeed greedily, Pines's *L'Histoire da la littérature Judéo-Allemande*, 500 pages, with such thoroughness, haste, and joy as I have never yet shown in the case of similar books; now I am reading Fromer, *Organismus des Judentums*; finally I spent a lot of time with the Jewish actors, wrote letters for them, prevailed on the Zionist society to inquire of the Zionist societies of Bohemia whether they would like to have guest appearances of the troupe; I wrote the circular that was required and had it reproduced; saw *Sulamith* once more and Richter's *Herzele Mejiches* for the first time, was at the folksong evening of the Bar Kokhba Society, and day before yesterday saw *Graf von Gleichen* by Schmidtbonn.

Folksong evening: Dr Nathan Birnbaum is the lecturer. Jewish habit of inserting 'my dear ladies and gentlemen' or just 'my dear' at every pause in the talk. Was repeated at the beginning of Birnbaum's talk to the point of being ridiculous. But from what I know of Löwy I think that these recurrent expressions, which are frequently found in ordinary Yiddish conversations too, such as '*Weh ist mir!*' or '*S'ist nischt*', or '*S'ist viel zu reden*', are not intended to cover up embarrassment but are rather intended, like ever-fresh springs, to stir up the sluggish stream of speech that is never fluent enough for the Jewish temperament.

26 January. The back of Mr Weltsch and the silence of the entire hall while listening to the bad poems. Birnbaum: his hair, worn somewhat longish, is cut off abruptly at his neck, which is very erect either in itself or because of its sudden nudity. Large, crooked nose, not too narrow and yet with broad sides, which looks handsome chiefly because it is in proper proportion to his large beard – Gollanin, the singer. Peaceful, sweetish, beatific patronizing face turned to the side and down, prolonged smile somewhat sharpened by his wrinkled nose, which may be only part of his breathing technique.

Pines: *Histoire de la littérature Judéo-Allemande*. Paris 1911.
Soldiers' song: They cut off our beards and earlocks. And they forbid us to keep the Sabbath and holy days.

Or: At the age of five I entered the 'Heder' and now I must ride a horse.

Wos mir seinen, seinen mir
Ober jüden seinen mir.
[What we are, we are,
But Jews we are.]

Haskalah movement introduced by Mendelssohn at the beginning of the nineteenth century, adherents are called Maskilim, are opposed to the popular Yiddish, tend towards Hebrew and the European sciences. Before the pogroms of 1881 it was not nationalist, later strongly Zionist. Principle formulated by Gordon: 'Be a man on the street and a Jew at home.' To spread its ideas the Haskalah must use Yiddish and, much as it hates the latter, lays the foundation of its literature.

Other aims are *'la lutte contre le chassidisme, l'exaltation de l'instruction et des travaux manuels.'*

Badchan, the sad folk and wedding minstrel (Eliakum Zunser), talmudic trend of thought.

Le Roman populaire: Eisik Meir Dick (1808–94) instructive, haskalic. Schomer, still worse, title, for example, *Der podriatechik (l'entrepreneur), ein höchst interessanter Roman. Ein richtiger fach fun leben,* or *Die eiserne Frau oder das verkaufte Kind. Ein wunderschöner Roman.* Further, in America serial novels, *Zwischen Menschenfressern,* twenty-six volumes.

S. J. Abramowitsch (Mendele Mocher Sforim), lyric, subdued gaiety, confused arrangement. *Fishke der Krummer,* Jewish habit of biting the lips.

End of Haskalah 1881. New nationalism and democracy. Flourishing of Yiddish literature.

S. Frug, lyric writer, life in the country by all means. *Délicieux est le sommeil du seigneur dans sa chambre. Sur des oreillers doux, blancs comme la neige. Mais plus délicieux encore est le repos dans le champ sur du foin frais à l'heure du soir, après le travail.*

Talmud: He who interrupts his study to say, 'How beautiful is this tree,' deserves death.

Lamentations at the west wall of the Temple Poem: 'La Fille du Shammes'. The beloved rabbi is on his deathbed. The burial of a shroud the size of the rabbi and other mystical measures are of no avail. Therefore at night the elders of the congregation go from house to house with a list and collect from the members of the congregation renunciations of days or weeks of their lives in favour of the rabbi. Deborah, *la Fille du Shammes*, gives 'the rest of her life'. She dies, the rabbi recovers. At night, when he is studying alone in the synagogue, he hears the voice of Deborah's whole aborted life. The singing at her wedding, her screams in childbed, her lullabies, the voice of her son studying the Torah, the music at her daughter's wedding. While the songs of lamentation sound over her corpse the rabbi, too, dies.

Peretz: bad Heine lyrics and social poems. Né 1851. Rosenfeld: The poor Yiddish public took up a collection to assure him of a livelihood.

S. Rabinowitz (Sholom Aleichem), né 1859. Custom of great jubilee celebrations in Yiddish literature. Kasrilevke, Menachem Mendel, who emigrated and took his entire fortune with him; although previously he had only studied Talmud, he begins to speculate in the stock market in the big city, comes to a new decision every day and always reports it to his wife with great self-satisfaction; until finally he must beg for travelling expenses.

Peretz: The figure of the *batlan* frequent in the ghettos, lazy and grown clever through idling, lives in the circle of the pious and learned. Many marks of misfortune on them, as they are young people who, although they enjoy idleness, also waste away in it, live in dreams, under the domination of the unrestrained force of unappeased desires.

Mitat neshika, death by a kiss: reserved only for the most pious.

Baal Shem: Before he became a rabbi in Miedzyboz he lived in the Carpathians as a vegetable gardener, later he was his brother-in-law's coachman. His visions came to him on lonely walks. Zohar, 'Bible of the Kabbalists.'

Jewish theatre. Frankfort Purim play, 1708. *Ein schön neu Achashverosh-spiel*, Abraham and Goldfaden, 1876–7 Russo-Turkish War, Russian and Galician army contractors had gathered in Bucharest, Goldfaden had also come there in search of a living, heard the crowds in the stores singing Yiddish songs and was encouraged to found a theatre. He was not yet able to put women on the stage. Yiddish

175

performances were forbidden in Russia 1883. They began in London and New York 1884.

J. Gordin 1897 in a jubilee publication of the Jewish theatre in New York: 'The Yiddish theatre has an audience of hundreds of thousands, but it cannot expect to see a writer of great talent emerge as long as the majority of its authors are people like me who have become dramatic authors only by chance, who write plays only by force of circumstance, and remain isolated and see about them only ignorance, envy, enmity, and spite.'

31 January. Wrote nothing. Weltsch brings me books about Goethe that provoke in me a distracted excitement that can be put to no use. Plan for an essay, 'Goethe's Frightening Nature', fear of the two hours' walk which I have now begun to take in the evening.

4 February. Three days ago Wedekind: *Erdgeist*. Wedekind and his wife, Tilly, act in it. Clear, precise voice of the woman. Narrow, crescent-shaped face. The lower part of the leg branching off to the left when she stood quietly. The play clear even in retrospect, so that one goes home peaceful and aware of oneself. Contradictory impression of what is thoroughly well established and yet remains strange.

On my way to the theatre I felt well. I savoured my innermost being as though it were honey. Drank it in an uninterrupted draught. In the theatre this passed away at once. *Orpheus in the Underworld* with Pallenberg. The performance was so bad, applause and laughter around me in the standing-room so great, that I could think of no way out but to run away after the second act and so silence it all.

Day before yesterday wrote a good letter to Trautenau about a guest appearance for Löwy. Each fresh reading of the letter calmed and strengthened me, there was in it so much unspoken indication of everything good in me.

The zeal, permeating every part of me, with which I read about Goethe (Goethe's conversations, student days, hours with Goethe, a visit of Goethe's to Frankfort) and which keeps me from all writing.

S., merchant, thirty-five years old, member of no religious community, educated in philosophy, interested in literature for the most part only to the extent that it pertains to his writing. Round head, black eyes, small, energetic moustache, firm flesh on his cheeks, thick-set body. For years has been studying from nine to one o'clock at night. Born in Stanislau, knows Hebrew and Yiddish. Married to a woman who gives the impression of being limited only because of the quite round shape of her face.

For two days coolness towards Löwy. He asks me about it. I deny it.

Quiet, restrained conversation with Miss T. in the balcony between the acts of *Erdgeist*. In order to achieve a good conversation one must, as it were, push one's hand more deeply, more lightly, more drowsily under the subject to be dealt with, then it can be lifted up astonishingly. Otherwise one breaks one's fingers and thinks of nothing but one's pains.

Story: The evening walks, discovery of quick walking. Introduction, a beautiful, dark room.

Miss T. told me about a scene in her new story where a girl with a bad reputation enters the sewing school. The impression on the other girls. I say that they, who feel clearly in themselves the capacity and desire to earn a bad reputation and who at the same time are able to see for themselves at first hand the kind of misfortune into which one hurls oneself by it, will pity her.

A week ago a lecture in the banquet room of the Jewish Town Hall by Dr Theilhaber on the decline of the German Jews. It is unavoidable, for (1) if the Jews collect in the cities, the Jewish communities in the country disappear. The pursuit of profit devours them. Marriages are made only with regard to the bride's settlement. Two-child system. (2) Mixed marriages. (3) Conversion.

Amusing scene when Prof. Ehrenfels,[41] who grows more and more handsome and who – with his bald head sharply outlined against the light in a curve that is puffed out at the top, his hands pressed together, with his full voice, which he modulates like a musical instrument, and a confident smile at the meeting – declares himself in favour of mixed races.

5 February. Monday. Weary even of reading *Dichtung und Wahrheit*. I am hard on the outside, cold on the inside. Today, when I came to Dr F., although we approached each other slowly and deliberately, it was as though we had collided like balls that drive one another back and, themselves out of control, get lost. I asked him whether he was tired. He was not tired, why did I ask? I am tired, I replied, and sat down.

To lift yourself out of such a mood, even if you have to do it by strength of will, should be easy. I force myself out of my chair, circle the table in long strides, exercise my head and neck, make my eyes sparkle, tighten the muscles around them. Defy my own feelings, welcome Löwy enthusiastically supposing he comes to see me, amiably tolerate my sister in the room while I write, swallow all that is said at Max's, whatever pain and trouble it may cost me, in long draughts. Yet even if I managed fairly well in some of this, one obvious slip, and slips cannot be avoided, will stop the whole process, the easy and the difficult alike, and I will have to turn backwards in the circle. So the best resource is to meet everything as calmly as possible, to make yourself an inert mass, and, if you feel that you are carried away, not to let yourself be lured into taking a single unnecessary step, to stare at others with the eyes of an animal, to feel no compunction, to yield to the non-conscious that you believe far away while it is precisely what is burning you, with your own hand to throttle down whatever ghostly life remains in you, that is, to enlarge the final peace of the graveyard and let nothing survive save that. A characteristic movement in such a condition is to run your little finger along your eyebrows.[42]

Short spell of faintness yesterday in the Café City with Löwy. How I bent down over a newspaper to hide it.

Goethe's beautiful silhouette. Simultaneous impression of repugnance when looking at this perfect human body, since to surpass this degree of perfection is unimaginable and yet it looks only as though it had been put together by accident. The erect posture, the dangling arms, the slender throat, the bend in the knees.

My impatience and grief because of my exhaustion are nourished especially on the prospect of the future that is thus prepared for me and which is never out of my sight. What evenings, walks, despair in bed and on the sofa (7 February) are still before me, worse than those I have already endured!

Yesterday in the factory. The girls, in their unbearably dirty and untidy clothes, their hair dishevelled as though they had just got up, the expressions on their faces fixed by the incessant noise of the transmission belts and by the individual machines, automatic ones, of course, but unpredictably breaking down, they aren't people, you don't greet them, you don't apologize when you bump into them, if you call them over to do something, they do it but return to their machine at once, with a nod of the head you show them what to do, they stand there in petticoats, they are at the mercy of the pettiest power and haven't enough calm understanding to recognize this power and placate it by a glance, a bow. But when six o'clock comes and they call it out to one another, when they untie the kerchiefs from around their throats and their hair, dust themselves with a brush that passes around and is constantly called for by the impatient, when they pull their skirts on over their heads and clean their hands as well as they can – then at last they are women again, despite pallor and bad teeth they can smile, shake their stiff bodies, you can no longer bump into them, stare at them, or overlook them, you move back against the greasy crates to make room for them, hold your hat in your hand when they say good evening, and do not know how to behave when one of them holds your winter coat for you to put on.

8 February. Goethe: 'My delight in creating was infinite.'

I have become more nervous, weaker, and have lost a large part of the calm on which I prided myself years ago. Today, when I received the card from Baum in which he writes that he cannot give the talk at the evening for the Eastern Jews after all, and when I was therefore compelled to think that I should have to take it over, I was overpowered by uncontrollable twitchings, the pulsing of my arteries sprang along my body like little flames; if I sat down, my knees trembled under the table and I had to press my hands together. I shall, of course, give a good lecture, that is certain, besides, the restlessness itself, heightened to an extreme on that evening, will pull me together in such a way that there will not be room for restlessness and the talk will come straight out of me as though out of a gun barrel. But it is possible that I shall collapse after it, in any event I shall not be able to get over it for a long time. So little physical strength! Even these few words are written under the influence of weakness.

Yesterday evening with Löwy at Baum's. My liveliness. Recently Löwy translated a bad Hebrew story, 'The Eye', at Baum's.

13 February. I am beginning to write the lecture for Löwy's performance. It is on Sunday, the 18th. I shall not have much time to prepare and am really striking up a kind of recitative here as though in an opera. The reason is only that an incessant excitement has been oppressing me for days and that, somewhat hesitant in the face of the actual beginning of the lecture, I want to write down a few words only for myself; in that way, given a little momentum, I shall be able to stand up before the audience. Cold and heat alternate in me with the successive words of the sentence, I dream melodic rises and falls, I read sentences of Goethe's as though my whole body were running down the stresses.

25 February. Hold fast to the diary from today on! Write regularly! Don't surrender! Even if no salvation should come, I want to be worthy of it at every moment. I spent this evening at the family table in complete indifference, my right hand on the arm of the chair in which my sister sat playing cards, my left hand weak in my lap. From time to time I tried to realize my unhappiness, I barely succeeded.

I have written nothing for so long because of having arranged an evening for Löwy in the banquet room of the Jewish Town Hall on 18 February, at which I delivered a little introductory lecture on Yiddish. For two weeks I worried for fear that I could not produce the lecture. On the evening before the lecture I suddenly succeeded.

Preparations for the lecture: Conferences with the Bar Kokhba Society, getting up the programme, tickets, hall, numbering the seats, key to the piano (Toynbee Hall), setting up the stage, pianist, costumes, selling tickets, newspaper notices, censorship by the police and the religious community.

Places in which I was and people with whom I spoke or to whom I wrote. In general: with Max, with Schmerler, who visited me, with Baum, who at first assumed the responsibility for the lecture but then refused it, whose mind I changed again in the course of an evening devoted to that purpose and who the next day again notified me of his refusal by special delivery, with Dr Hugo Hermann and Leo Hermann in the Café Arco, often with Robert Weltsch at his home; about selling tickets with Dr Bl. (in vain), Dr H., Dr Fl., visit to Miss T., lecture at Afike Jehuda (by Rabb. Ehrentreu on Jeremiah and his time, during the social part of the evening that followed, a short, abortive talk about Löwy), at the teacher W.'s place (then in the Café, then for a walk, from twelve to one he stood in front of my door as large as life and would not let me go in). About the hall, at Dr Karl B.'s, twice at L.'s house on Heuwagsplatz, several times at Otto Pick's, in the bank; about the key to the piano for the Toynbee lecture, with Mr R. and the teacher S., then to the latter's home to get the key and to return it; about the stage, with the custodian and the porter of the town hall; about payment, in the town hall office (twice); about the sale, with Mrs Fr. at the exposition, 'The Set Table'. Wrote to Miss T., to one Otto Kl. (in vain), for the *Tagblatt* (in vain), to Löwy ('I won't be able to give the talk, save me!').

Excitements: About the lecture, one night twisted up in bed, hot and sleepless, hatred of Dr B., fear of Weltsch (he will not be able to sell anything), Afike Jehuda, the notices are not published in the papers the way in which they were expected to be, distraction in the office, the stage does not come, not enough tickets are sold, the colour of the tickets upsets me, the lecture has to be interrupted because the pianist forgot his music at home in Košíř, a great deal of indifference towards Löwy, almost disgust.

Benefits: Joy in Löwy and confidence in him, proud, unearthly consciousness during my lecture (coolness in the presence of the audience, only the lack of practice kept me from using enthusiastic gestures freely), strong voice, effortless memory, recognition, but above all the power with which I loudly, decisively, determinedly, faultlessly, irresistibly, with clear eyes, almost casually, put down the impudence of the three town hall porters and gave them, instead of the twelve kronen they demanded, only six kronen, and even these with a grand air. In all this are revealed powers to which I would gladly entrust myself if they would remain. (My parents were not there.)

Also: Academy of the Herder Association on the Sophien Island. Bie shoves his hand in his trouser pocket at the beginning of the lecture. This face, satisfied despite all disappointment, of people who work as they please. Hofmannsthal reads with a false ring in his voice. A close-knit figure, beginning with the ears pressed close to his head. Wiesenthal. The beautiful parts of the dance, for example, when in sinking to the ground the natural heaviness of the body is revealed.

Impression of Toynbee Hall.

Zionist meeting. Blumenfeld. Secretary of the World Zionist Organization.

A new stabilizing force has recently appeared in my deliberations about myself which I can recognize now for the first time and only now, since during the last week I have been literally disintegrating because of sadness and uselessness.

Changing emotions among the young people in the Café Arco.

26 February. Better consciousness of myself. The beating of my heart more as I would wish it. The hissing of the gaslight above me.

I opened the front door to see whether the weather would tempt me to take a walk. The blue sky could not be denied, but large grey clouds through which the blue shimmered, with flap-shaped, curved edges, hovered low, one could see them against the near-by wooded hills. Nevertheless the street was full of people out for a walk. Baby carriages were guided by the firm hands of mothers. Here and there in the crowd a vehicle came to a stop until the people made way for the prancing horses. Meanwhile the driver, quietly holding the quivering reins, looked ahead, missed no details, examined everything several times and at the right moment set the carriage in motion. Children were able to run about, little room as there was. Girls in light clothes with hats as emphatically coloured as postage stamps walked arm in arm with young men, and a song, suppressed in their throats, revealed itself in their dancing pace. Families stayed close together, and even if sometimes they were shaken out into a single file, there were still arms stretched back, hands waving, pet names called, to join together those who had strayed. Men who had no part in this tried to shut themselves off even more by sticking their hands in their pockets. That was petty nonsense. First I stood in the doorway, then I leaned against the doorpost in order to look on more comfortably. Clothes brushed against me, once I seized a ribbon that ornamented the back of a girl's skirt and let her draw it out of my hand as she walked away; once, when I stroked the shoulder of a girl, just to flatter her, the passer-by behind her struck me over the fingers. But I pulled him behind the bolted half of the door, I reproached him with raised hands, with looks out of the corners of my eyes, a step towards him, a step away from him, he was happy when I let go of him with a shove. From then on, naturally, I often called people to me, a crook of my finger was enough, or a quick, unhesitating glance.

How sleepily and without effort I wrote this useless, unfinished thing.

Today I am writing to Löwy. I am copying down the letters to him here because I hope to do something with them:
Dear friend –
27 February. I have no time to write letters in duplicate.

Yesterday evening, at ten o'clock, I was walking at my sad pace down the Zeltnergasse. Near the Hess hat store a young man stops three steps in front of me, so forces me to stop too, removes his hat, and then runs at me. In my first fright I step back, think at first that someone wants to know how to get to the station, but why in this way? – then think, since he approaches me confidentially and looks up into my face because I am taller: Perhaps he wants money, or something worse. My confused attention and his confused speech mingle.

'You're a lawyer, aren't you? A doctor? Please, couldn't you give me some advice? I have a case here for which I need a lawyer.'

Because of caution, general suspicion, and fear that I might make a fool of myself, I deny that I am a lawyer, but am ready to advise him, what is it? He begins to talk, it interests me; to increase my confidence I ask him to talk while we walk, he wants to go my way, no, I would rather go with him, I have no place in particular to go.

He is a good reciter, he was not nearly as good in the past as he is now, now he can already imitate Kainz so that no one can tell the difference. People may say he only imitates him, but he puts in a lot of his own too. He is short, to be sure, but he has mimicry, memory, presence, everything, everything. During his military service out there in Milowitz, in camp, he recited, a comrade sang, they really had a very good time. It was a beautiful time. He prefers to recite Dehmel most of all, the passionate, frivolous poems, for instance, about the bride who pictures her bridal night to herself, when he recites that it makes a huge impression, especially on the girls. Well, that is really obvious. He has Dehmel very beautifully bound in red leather. (He describes it with dropping gestures of his hands.) But the binding really doesn't matter. Aside from this he likes very much to recite Rideamus. No, they don't clash with one another at all, he sees to it that there's a transition, talks between them, whatever occurs to him, makes a fool of the public. Then 'Prometheus' is on his programme too. There he isn't afraid of anyone, not even of Moissi, Moissi drinks, he doesn't. Finally, he likes very much to read from Swet Marten; he's a new Scandinavian writer. Very good. It's sort of epigrams and short sayings. Those about Napoleon, especially, are excellent, but so are all the others about other great men. No, he can't recite any of this yet, he hasn't learned it yet, not even read it all, but his aunt read it to him recently and he liked it so much.

So he wanted to appear in public with this programme and therefore offered himself to the Women's Progress for an evening's appearance. Really, at first he wanted to present *Eine Gutsgeschichte* by Lagerlöf, and had even lent this story to the chairwoman of the Women's Progress, Mrs Durège-Wodnanski, to look over. She said the story was beautiful, of course, but too long to be read. He saw that, it was really too long, especially as, according to the plan of the evening, his brother was supposed to play the piano too. This brother, twenty-one years old, a very lovely boy, is a virtuoso, he was at the music college in Berlin for two years (four years ago, now). But came home quite spoiled. Not really spoiled, but the woman with whom he boarded fell in love with him. Later he said that he was often too tired to play because he had to keep riding around on this boarding-bag.

So, since the *Gutsgeschichte* wouldn't do, they agreed on the other programme: Dehmel, Rideamus, 'Prometheus', and Swet Marten. But now, in order to show Mrs Durège in advance the sort of person he really was, he brought her the manuscript of an essay, 'The Joy of Life', which he had written this summer. He wrote it in a summer resort, wrote it in shorthand during the day, in the evening made a clean copy, polished, crossed out, but really it wasn't much work because it came off at once. He'll lend it to me if I like, it's written in a popular style, of course, on purpose, but there are good ideas in it and it is *betamt*, as they say. (Pointed laughter with chin raised.) I may leaf through it here under the electric light. (It is an appeal to youth not to be sad, for after all there is nature, freedom, Goethe, Schiller, Shakespeare, flowers, insects, etc.) The Durège woman said she really didn't have time to read it just then, but he could lend it to her, she would return it in a few days. He suspected something even then and didn't want to leave it there, evaded, said, for instance, 'Look, Mrs Durège, why should I leave it here, it's really just ordinary, it's well written, of course, but . . .' None of it did any good, he had to leave it there. This was on Friday.

(28 February.) Sunday morning, while washing, it occurs to me that he hadn't seen the *Tagblatt* yet. He opens it by chance just at the first page of the magazine section. The title of the first essay, 'The Child as Creator', strikes him. He reads the first few lines – and begins to cry with joy. It is his essay, word for word his essay. So for the first time he is in print, he runs to his mother and tells her. What joy! The old woman, she has diabetes and is divorced from his father, who, by the way, is in the right, is so proud. One son is already a virtuoso, now the other is becoming an author!

After the first excitement he thinks the matter over. How did the essay get into the paper? Without his consent? Without the name of the author? Without his being paid a fee? This is really a breach of faith, a fraud. This Mrs Durège is really a devil. And women have no souls, says Mohammed (often repeated). It's really easy to see how the plagiarism came about. Here was a beautiful essay, it's not easy to come across one like it. So Mrs D. therefore went to the *Tagblatt*, sat down with one of the editors, both of them overjoyed, and now they begin to rewrite it. Of course, it had to be rewritten, for in the first place the plagiarism should not be obvious at first sight and in the second place the thirty-two-page essay was too long for the paper.

In reply to my question whether he would not show me passages which correspond, because that would interest me especially and because only then could I advise him what to do, he begins to read his essay, turns to another passage, leafs through it without finding anything, and finally says that everything was copied. Here, for instance, the paper says: The soul of the child is an unwritten page, and 'unwritten page' occurs in his essay too. Or the expression 'surnamed' is copied too, because how else could they hit upon 'surnamed'. But he can't compare individual passages. Of course, everything was copied, but in a disguised way, in a different sequence, abridged, and with small, foreign interpolations.

I read aloud a few of the more striking passages from the paper. Is that in the essay? No. This? No. This? No. Yes, but these are just the interpolated passages. In its spirit, the whole thing, the whole thing, is copied. But proving it, I am afraid, will be difficult. He'll prove it, all right, with the help of a clever lawyer, that's what lawyers are for, after all. (He looks forward to this proof as an entirely new task, completely separate from this affair, and is proud of his confidence that he will be able to accomplish it.)

That it is his essay, moreover, can be seen from the very fact that it was printed within two days. Usually it takes six weeks at the very least before a piece that is accepted is printed. But here speed was necessary, of course, so that he would not be able to interfere. That's why two days were enough.

Besides, the newspaper essay is called 'The Child as Creator'. That clearly refers to him, and besides, it is sarcasm. By 'child' they really mean him, because he used to be regarded as a 'child', as 'dumb' (he really was so only during his military service, he served a year and a half), and they now mean to say with this title that he, a child, had accomplished something as good as this essay, that he had therefore proved himself as a creator, but at the same time remained dumb and a child in that he let himself be cheated like this. The child who is referred to in the original essay is a cousin from the country who is at present living with his mother.

But the plagiarism is proved especially convincingly by a circumstance which he hit upon only after a considerable amount of deliberation: 'The Child's Creator' is on the first page of the magazine section, but on the third there is a little story by a certain 'Feldstein' woman. The name is obviously a pseudonym. Now one needn't read all of this story, a glance at the first few lines is enough to show one immediately that this is an unashamed imitation of Lagerlöf. The whole story makes it even clearer. What does this mean? This means that this Feldstein, or whatever her name is, is the Durège woman's tool, that she read the *Gutsgeschichte*, brought by him to the Durège woman, at her house, that in writing this story she made use of what she had read, and that therefore both women are exploiting him, one on the first page of the magazine section, the other on the third page. Naturally anyone can read and imitate Lagerlöf on his own initiative, but in this case, after all, his influence is too apparent. (He keeps waving the page back and forth.)

Monday noon, right after the bank closed, he naturally went to see Mrs Durège. She opens her door only a crack, she is very nervous: 'But, Mr Reichmann, why have you come at noon? My husband is asleep. I can't let you in now' – 'Mrs Durège, you must let me in by all means. It's about an important matter.' She sees I am in earnest and lets me come in. Her husband, of course, was definitely not at home. In the next room I see my manuscript on the table and this immediately starts me thinking. 'Mrs Durege, what have you done with my manuscript. Without my consent you gave it to the *Tagblatt*. How much did they pay you?' She trembles, she knows nothing, has no idea how it could have got into the paper. '*J'accuse*, Mrs Durège,' I said, half jokingly, but still in such a way that she sees what I really mean, and I keep repeating this '*J'accuse*, Mrs Durège' all the time I am there so that she can take note of it, and when I go I even say it several times at the door. Indeed, I understand her nervousness well. If

I make it public or sue her, her position would really be impossible, she
would have to leave the Women's Progress, etc.

From her house I go straight to the office of the *Tagblatt* and have
the editor, Löw, fetched. He comes out quite pale, naturally, is hardly
able to walk. Nevertheless I do not want to begin with my business at
once and I want to test him first too. So I ask him: 'Mr Löw, are you
a Zionist?' (For I know he used to be a Zionist.) 'No,' he says. I know
enough, he must be acting a part in front of me. Now I ask about the
essay. Once more incoherent talk. He knows nothing, has nothing to
do with the magazine section, will, if I wish, get the editor who is in
charge of it. 'Mr Wittmann, come here,' he calls, and is happy that he
can leave. Wittmann comes, also very pale. I ask: 'Are you the editor of
the magazine section?' He: 'Yes.' I just say, '*J'accuse*,' and leave.

In the bank I immediately telephone *Bohemia*. I want to give them
the story for publication. But I can't get a good connexion. Do you
know why? The office of the *Tagblatt* is pretty close to the telephone
exchange, so from the *Tagblatt* it's easy for them to control the connexions as they please, to hold them up or put them through. And as
a matter of fact, I keep hearing indistinct whispering voices on the
telephone, obviously the editors of the *Tagblatt*. They have, of course,
a good deal of interest in not letting this call go through. Then I hear
(naturally very indistinctly) some of them persuading the operator not
to put the call through, while others are already connected with
Bohemia and are trying to keep them from listening to my story.
'Operator,' I shout into the telephone, 'if you don't put this call
through at once, I'll complain to the management.' My colleagues all
around me in the bank laugh when they hear me talking to the telephone operator so violently. Finally I get my party. 'Let me talk to
Editor Kisch. I have an extremely important piece of news for
Bohemia. If you don't take it, I'll give it to another paper at once. It's
high time.' But since Kisch is not there I hang up without revealing
anything.

In the evening I go to the office of *Bohemia* and get the editor,
Kisch, called out. I tell him the story but he doesn't want to publish
it. *Bohemia*, he says, can't do anything like that, it would cause a
scandal and we can't risk it because we're dependent. Hand it over to a
lawyer, that would be best.

188

On my way from the *Bohemia* office I met you and so I am asking your advice.

'I advise you to settle the matter in a friendly way.'

'Indeed, I was thinking myself that would be best. She's a woman, after all. Women have no souls, says Mohammed, with good reason. To forgive would be more humane, too, more Goethe-like.'

'Certainly. And then you wouldn't have to give up the recitation evening, either, which would otherwise be lost, after all.'

'But what should I do now?'

'Go to them tomorrow and say that this one time you are willing to assume it was unconscious influence.'

'That's very good. That's just what I'll do.'

'But because of this you needn't give up your revenge, either. Simply have the essay published somewhere else and then send it to Mrs Durège with a nice dedication.'

'That will be the best punishment. I'll have it published in the *Deutsches Abendblatt*. They'll take it; I'm not worried about that. I'll just not ask for any payment.'

Then we speak about his talent as an actor, I am of the opinion that he should really have training. 'Yes, you're right about that. But where? Do you perhaps know where it can be studied?' I say: 'That's difficult. I really don't know.' He: 'That doesn't really matter. I'll ask Kisch. He's a journalist and has a lot of connexions. He'll be able to give me good advice. I'll just telephone him, spare him and myself the trip, and get all the information.'

'And about Mrs Durège, you'll do what I advised you to?'

'Yes, but I forgot; what did you advise me to do?' I repeat my advice.

'Good, that's what I'll do.' He turns into the Café Corso, I go home, having experienced how refreshing it is to speak with a perfect fool. I hardly laughed, but was just thoroughly awakened.

The melancholy 'formerly', used only on business plaques.

2 March. Who is to confirm for me the truth or probability of this, that it is only because of my literary mission that I am uninterested in all other things and therefore heartless.

3 March. 28 February to hear Moissi. Unnatural spectacle. He sits in apparent calm, whenever possible keeps his folded hands between his knees, his eyes on the book lying before him, and lets his voice pass over us with the breath of a runner.

The hall's good acoustics. Not a word is lost, nor is there the whisper of an echo, instead everything grows gradually larger, as though the voice, already occupied with something else, continued to exercise a direct after-effect, it grows stronger after the initial impetus and swallows us up. The possibilities one sees here for one's own voice. Just as the hall works to the advantage of Moissi's voice, his voice works to the advantage of ours. Unashamed tricks and surprises at which one must look down at the floor and which one would never use oneself: singing individual verses at the very beginning, for instance, 'Sleep, Miriam, my child';[43] wandering around of the voice in the melody; rapid utterance of the May song, it seems as if only the tip of the tongue were stuck between the words; dividing the phrase 'November wind' in order to push the 'wind' down and then let it whistle upwards. If one looks up at the ceiling of the hall, one is drawn upward by the verses.

Goethe's poems unattainable for the reciter, but one cannot for that reason find fault with this recitation, for each poem moves towards the goal. Great effect later, when in reciting the encore, Shakespeare's 'Rain Song', he stood erect, was free of the text, pulled at his handkerchief and then crushed it in his hands, and his eyes sparkled. Round cheeks and yet an angular face. Soft hair, stroked over and over again with soft movements of his hand. The enthusiastic reviews that one has read are a help to him, in our opinion, only until the first hearing, then he becomes entangled in them and cannot produce a pure impression.

This sort of reciting from a chair, with the book before one, reminds one a little of ventriloquism. The artist, seemingly not participating, sits there like us, in his bowed face we see only the mouth move from time to time, and instead of reading the verses himself, he lets them be read over his head. Despite the fact that so many melodies were to be heard, that the voice seemed as controlled as a light boat in the water, the melody of the verses could really not be heard. Many words were dissolved by the voice, they were taken hold of so gently that they shot up into the air and had nothing more to do with the human voice until, out of sheer necessity, the voice spoke some sharp consonant or other, brought the word back to earth, and completed it.

Later, a walk with Ottla, Miss Taussig, the Baum couple, and Pick; the Elizabeth Bridge, the Quai, the Kleinseite, the Radetzky Café, the Stone Bridge, Karlsgasse. I still saw the prospect of a good mood, so that really there was not much fault to find with me.

5 March. These revolting doctors! Businesslike, determined and so ignorant of healing that, if this businesslike determination were to leave them, they would stand at sick-beds like schoolboys. I wished I had the strength to found a nature-cure society. By scratching around in my sister's ear Dr K. turns an inflammation of the eardrum into an inflammation of the inner ear; the maid collapses while fixing the fire; with the quick diagnosis which is his custom in the case of maids, the doctor declares it to be an upset stomach and a resulting congestion of blood. The next day she takes to her bed again, has a high fever; the doctor turns her from side to side, affirms it is angina, and runs away so that the next moment will not refute him. Even dares to speak of the 'vulgarly violent reaction of this girl', which is true to this extent, that he is used to people whose physical condition is worthy of his curative power and is produced by it, and he feels insulted, more than he is aware, by the strong nature of this country girl.

Yesterday at Baum's. Read *Der Dämon*. Total impression unfriendly. Good, precise mood on the way up to Baum's, died down immediately I got up there, embarrassment in the presence of the child.

Sunday: In the Continental, at the card-players'. *Journalisten* with Kramer first, one and a half acts. A good deal of forced merriment can be seen in Bolz, which produces, indeed, a little that is really delicate. Met Miss Taussig in front of the theatre in the intermission after the second act. Ran to the cloakroom, returned with cloak flying, and escorted her home.

8 March. Day before yesterday was blamed because of the factory. Then for an hour on the sofa thought about jumping-out-of-the-window.

Yesterday, Harden lecture on 'The Theatre'. Apparently entirely impromptu; I was in a fairly good mood and therefore did not find it as empty as did the others. Began well: 'At this hour in which we have met together here to discuss the theatre, the curtain is rising in every theatre of Europe and the other continents to reveal the stage to the audience.' With an electric light attached to a stand in front of him at the level of his breast so that it can be moved about, he lights up the front of his shirt as though it were on display, and during the course of the lecture he changes the lighting by moving the light. Toe-dancing to make himself taller, as well as to tighten up his talent for improvisation. Trousers tight even around the groin. A short tail-coat like that tacked on to a doll. Almost strained, serious face, sometimes like an old lady's, sometimes like Napoleon's. Fading colour of his forehead as of a wig. Probably corseted.

Read through some old notebooks. It takes all my strength to last it out. The unhappiness one must suffer when one interrupts oneself in a task that can never succeed except all at once, and this is what has always happened to me until now; in rereading one must re-experience this unhappiness in a more concentrated way though not as strongly as before.

Today, while bathing, I thought I felt old powers, as though they had been untouched by the long interval.

10 March. Sunday. He seduced a girl in a small place in the Iser mountains where he spent a summer to restore his delicate lungs. After a brief effort to persuade her, incomprehensibly, the way lung cases sometimes act, he threw the girl – his landlord's daughter, who liked to walk with him in the evening after work – down in the grass on the river bank and took her as she lay there unconscious with fright. Later he had to carry water from the river in his cupped hands and pour it over the girl's face to restore her. 'Julie, but Julie,' he said countless times, bending over her. He was ready to accept complete responsibility for his offence and was only making an effort to make himself realize how serious his situation was. Without thinking about it he could not have realized it. The simple girl who lay before him, now breathing regularly again, her eyes still closed because of fear and embarrass-

ment, could make no difficulty for him; with the tip of his toe, he, the great, strong person, could push the girl aside. She was weak and plain, could what had happened to her have any significance that would last even until tomorrow? Would not anyone who compared the two of them have to come to this conclusion? The river stretched calmly between the meadows and fields to the distant hills. There was still sunshine only on the slope of the opposite shore. The last clouds were drifting out of that clear evening sky.

Nothing, nothing. This is the way I raise up ghosts before me. I was involved, even if only superficially, only in the passage, 'Later he had. . . .' mostly in the 'pour'. For a moment I thought I saw something real in the description of the landscape.

So deserted by myself, by everything. Noise in the next room.

11 March. Yesterday unendurable. Why doesn't everyone join in the evening meal? That would really be so beautiful.

The reciter, Reichmann, landed in the lunatic asylum the day after our conversation.

Today burned many old, disgusting papers.

W., Baron von Biedermann, *Gespräche mit Goethe*. The way the daughters of the Leipzig copperplate-engraver, Stock, comb his hair, 1767.
The way, in 1772, Kestner found him lying in the grass in Garbenheim and the way he 'was conversing with several people who were standing around, an Epicurean philosopher (v. Goné, a great genius), a Stoic philosopher (v. Kielmansegg) and a cross between the two (Dr König), and he really enjoyed himself'.
With Seidel [Goethe's valet] in 1783: 'Once he rang in the middle of the night, and when I came into his room he had rolled his iron trundle bed from the farthest end of the room up to the window and was watching the sky. "Haven't you seen anything in the sky?" he asked me, and when I denied this, "Then just run to the guardroom and ask the sentry whether he saw anything." I ran there; but the sentry

had seen nothing, which I reported to my master, who was still lying in the same position fixedly regarding the sky. "Listen," he then said to me, "this is an important moment. Either we are having an earthquake at this very instant or we shall have one." And now I had to sit down on his bed and he showed me what signs had led him to this conclusion.' (Messina earthquake.)

A geological walk with von Trebra (September 1783) through underbrush and rocks. Goethe in front.

To Herder's wife in 1788. Among other things he said also that before he left Rome he cried like a child every day for fourteen days. The way Herder's wife watched him in order to report everything to her husband in Italy. Goethe shows great concern for Herder in the presence of his wife.

14 September, 1794, from eleven-thirty, when Schiller got dressed, until eleven o'clock, Goethe spent the time without interruption in literary consultation with Schiller, and often so.

David Veit, 19 October, 1794, Jewish kind of observation, therefore so easy to understand, as though it had happened yesterday.

In the evening in Weimar, *Der Diener zweier Herrn* was acted quite nicely, to my surprise. Goethe was also in the theatre, and indeed, as always, in the section reserved for the nobility. In the middle of the play he leaves this section – which he is supposed to do very seldom – sits down, as long as he could not speak to me, behind me (so the ladies beside me said) and as soon as the act is over comes forward, bows to me with extreme courtesy, and begins in a quite intimate tone ... brief remarks and replies about the play. ... Thereupon he falls silent for a moment; meanwhile I forget that he is the director of the theatre and say, 'They're acting it quite nicely too.' He still keeps looking straight ahead, and so in my stupidity – but really in a frame of mind which I cannot analyse – I say once more, 'They are acting quite nicely.' At that moment he bows to me, but really as courteously as the first time, and he is gone! Have I insulted him or not? ... You really won't believe how distressed I still am, regardless of the fact that I already have the assurance from Humboldt, who now knows him well, that he often leaves in this sudden manner, and Humboldt has undertaken to speak to him about me once again.

Another time they were speaking about Maimon: 'I kept interrupting a good deal and often came to his assistance; for usually there are many words he cannot recall and he keeps making faces.'

1796. Goethe recites Hermann's conversations with his mother at the pear tree in first half of September.[44] He wept. 'Thus one melts over one's own coals,' he said, while drying his tears.

'The wide wooden parapet of the old gentleman's box.' Goethe sometimes liked to have a supply of cold food and wine ready in his box, more for the other people – residents and friends of importance – whom he not infrequently received there.

Performance of Schlegel's *Alarcos* in 1802. 'In the middle of the orchestra Goethe, serious and solemn, throning in his tall arm-chair.' The audience becomes restless, finally at one passage a roar of laughter, the whole house shakes. 'But only for a moment, in a trice Goethe jumped up, with thunderous voice and threatening gestures shouted, Silence, Silence, and it worked like a charm. In an instant the tumult subsided and the unhappy *Alarcos* went on to the end with no further disturbance, but also without the slightest sign of applause.'

Staël: What the French apparently take for wit in foreigners is often only ignorance of French. Goethe called an idea of Schiller's *neuve et courageuse*, that was wonderful, but it turned out that he had intended to say *hardie*.

Was lockst Du meine Brut . . . herauf in Todesglut.[45] Staël translated *air brûlant*. Goethe said he meant the glow of coals. She found that extremely *maussade* and tasteless and said that the fine sense for the seemly is lacking in German poets.

1804. Love for Heinrich Voss – Goethe reads *Luise* together with the Sunday company.

To Goethe fell the passage about the marriage, which he read with the deepest emotion. But his voice grew dejected, he wept and gave the book to his neighbour. A holy passage, he cried out with a degree of fervour which shook us all to the depths.

We were sitting at lunch and had just consumed the last bit of food when Goethe ordered a bone 'because Voss still looks so hungry'.

But never is he pleasanter and more lovable than in the evening in his room when he is undressed or is sitting on the sofa.

When I came to him I found everything quite comfortable there. He had lit a fire, had undressed down to a short woollen jacket, in which the man looks really splendid.

Books: Stilling, *Goethe Yearbook, Briefwechsel zwischen Rahel und David Veit.*

12 March. In the tram-car rapidly passing by there sat in a corner, his cheek against the window, his left arm stretched along the back of the seat, a young man with an unbuttoned overcoat billowing around him, looking down the long, empty bench. Today he had become engaged and he could think of nothing else. His being engaged made him feel comfortable and with this feeling he sometimes looked casually up at the ceiling of the tram. When the conductor came to sell him his ticket, after some jingling, he easily found the right coin, with a single motion put it into the conductor's hand, and seized the ticket between two fingers held open like a pair of scissors. There was no real connexion between him and the tram-car and it would not have been surprising if, without using the platform or steps, he had appeared on the street and gone his way on foot with the same look.

Only the billowing overcoat remains, everything else is made up.

16 March. Saturday. Again encouragement. Again I catch hold of myself, as one catches hold of a ball in its fall. Tomorrow, today, I'll begin an extensive work which, without being forced, will shape itself according to my abilities. I will not give it up as long as I can hold out at all. Rather be sleepless than live on in this way.

Cabaret Lucerna. Several young people each sing a song. Such a performance, if we are fresh and listen closely, more strongly impresses upon us the conclusions which the text offers for our own life than is possible by the performance of experienced artistes. For the singer cannot increase the force of the poetry, it always retains an independent forcefulness which tyrannizes us through the singer, who doesn't even wear patent-leather shoes, whose hand sometimes will not leave his knee, and, if it must, still shows its reluctance, who throws himself quickly down on the bench in order to conceal as much as possible how many small, awkward movements he had needed.

Love scene in spring, the sort one finds on picture postcards. Devotion, a portrayal which touches and shames the public – Fatinitza. Viennese singer. Sweet, significant laugh. Reminds me of Hansi. A face with meaningless details, mostly too sharp, held together and smoothed down by laughter. Ineffective superiority over the audience which one must grant her when she stands on the stage and laughs out into the indifferent audience – The Degen's stupid dance, with flying will-o'-wisps, twigs, butterflies, death's head.

Four 'Rocking Girls'. One very pretty. The programme does not give her name. She was on the audience's extreme right. How busily she threw her arms about, in what unusually palpable, silent movement were her thin long legs and delicately playing little joints, the way she didn't keep time, but didn't let herself be frightened out of her business, what a soft smile she had in contrast to the distorted ones of the others, how almost voluptuous her face and hair were in comparison with the sparseness of her body, the way she called 'slowly' to the musicians, for her sisters as well as for herself. Their dancing master, a young, strikingly dressed, thin person, stood behind the musicians and waved one hand in rhythm, regarded neither by the musicians nor by the dancers and with his own eyes on the audience.

Warnebold, fiery nervousness of a powerful person. In his movements there is sometimes a joke whose strength lifts one up. How he hurries to the piano with long steps after the number is announced.

Read *Aus dem Leben eines Schlachtenmalers*. Read Flaubert aloud with satisfaction.

The necessity of speaking of dancers with exclamation marks. Because in that way one imitates their motion, because one remains in the rhythm and the thought does not then interfere with the enjoyment, because then the action always comes at the end of the sentence and prolongs its effect better.

17 March. During these days read *Morgenrot* by Stössl.[46]

Max's concert Sunday. My almost unconscious listening. From now on I can no longer be bored by music. I no longer seek, as I did in vain in the past, to penetrate this impenetrable circle which immediately forms about me together with the music, I am also careful not to jump over it, which I probably could do, but instead I remain calmly in my thoughts that develop and subside in this narrowed space without it being possible for disturbing self-observations to step into their slow swarm. The beautiful 'magic circle' (by Max) that seems here and there to open the breast of the singer.

Goethe, 'Trost in Tränen.' *Alles geben die Götter, die unendlichen,/ Ihren Lieblingen ganz:/ Alle Freuden, die unendlichen,/ Alle Schmerzen, die unendlichen, ganz.*

My incompetence in the presence of my mother, in the presence of Miss T., and in the presence of all those in the Continental at that time and later on the street.

Mam'zelle Nitouche on Monday. The good effect of a French word in a dreary German performance. Boarding-school girls in bright dresses, with their arms outstretched, run into the garden behind a fence. Barracks-yard of the dragoon regiment at night. Some officers in a barracks in the background are having a farewell celebration in a hall that is reached by going up a few steps. Mam'zelle Nitouche enters and is persuaded by love and recklessness to take part in the celebration. The sort of thing that can happen to a girl! In the morning at the convent, in the evening a substitute for an operetta singer who couldn't come, and at night in the dragoons' barracks.

Today, painfully tired, spent the afternoon on the sofa.

18 March. I was wise, if you like, because I was prepared for death at any moment, but not because I had taken care of everything that was given to me to do, rather because I had done none of it and could not even hope ever to do any of it.

22 March. (The last few days I have been writing down the wrong dates.) Baum's lecture in the lecture hall. G. F., nineteen years old, getting married next week. Dark, faultless, slender face. Distended

nostrils. For years she has been wearing hats and clothes styled like a hunter's. The same dark-green gleam on her face. The strands of hair running along the cheeks, just as in general a slight down seems to cover all her face which she has bowed down into the darkness. Points of her elbows resting lightly on the arms of her chair. Then on the Wenzelsplatz a brisk bow, completed with little energy, a turn, and a drawing erect of the poorly dressed, slender body. I looked at her much less often than I wanted to.

24 March. Sunday, yesterday. *Die Sternenbraut* by Christian von Ehrenfels – Lost in watching. The sick officer in the play. The sick body in the tight uniform that made health and decisiveness a duty.

In the morning in the bright sun at Max's for half an hour.

In the next room my mother is entertaining the L. couple. They are talking about vermin and corns. (Mrs L. has six corns on each toe.) It is easy to see that there is no real progress made in conversations of this sort. It is information that will be forgotten again by both and that even now proceeds along in self-forgetfulness without any sense of responsibility. But for the very reason that such conversations are unthinkable without absent-mindedness, they reveal empty spaces which, if one insists, can be filled only by thinking, or, better yet, by dreams.

25 March. The broom sweeping the rug in the next room sounds like the train of a dress moving in jerks.

26 March. Only not to overestimate what I have written, for in that way I make what is to be written unattainable.

27 March. Monday, on the street. The boy who, with several others, threw a large ball at a servant girl walking defencelessly in front of them; just as the ball was flying at the girl's behind I grabbed him by the throat, choked him in fury, thrust him aside, and swore. Then walked on and didn't even look at the girl. One quite forgets one's earthly existence because one is so entirely full of fury and is permitted

to believe that, given the opportunity, one would in the same way fill oneself with even more beautiful emotions.

28 March. From Mrs Fanta's lecture, 'Impressions of Berlin': Grillparzer once didn't want to go to a party because he knew that Hebbel, with whom he was friendly, would also be there. 'He will question me again about my opinion on God, and when I don't know what to say, he will become rude' – My awkward behaviour.

29 March. Delighted with the bathroom. Gradual understanding. The afternoons I spent on my hair.

1 April. For the first time in a week an almost complete failure in writing. Why? Last week too I lived through various moods and kept their influence away from my writing; but I am afraid to write about it.

3 April. This is how a day passes – in the morning, the office, in the afternoon, the factory, now in the evening, shouting to the right and left of me at home, later brought my sister home from *Hamlet* – and I haven't been able to make use of a single moment.

8 April. Saturday before Easter. Complete knowledge of oneself. To be able to seize the whole of one's abilities like a little ball. To accept the greatest decline as something familiar and so still remain elastic in it.

Desire for a deeper sleep that dissolves more. The metaphysical urge is only the urge toward death.

How affectedly I spoke today in Haas's [47] presence because he praised Max's and my travel report, so that in this way, at least, I might make myself worthy of the praise that the report does not warrant, or so that I might continue by fraud the fraudulent or lying effect of the travel report, or in the spirit of Haas's amiable lie, which I tried to make easier for him.

6 May. 11 o'clock. For the first time in a considerable while a complete failure in writing. The feeling of a tried man.

Dreamed recently:

I was riding with my father through Berlin in a tram-car. The big-city quality was represented by countless striped toll bars standing upright, finished off bluntly at the ends. Apart from that everything was almost empty, but there was a great forest of these toll bars. We came to a gate, got out without any sense of getting out, stepped through the gate. On the other side of the gate a sheer wall rose up, which my father ascended almost in a dance, his legs flew out as he climbed, so easy was it for him. There was certainly also some inconsiderateness in the fact that he did not help me one bit, for I got to the top only with the utmost effort, on all fours, often sliding back again, as though the wall had become steeper under me. At the same time it was also distressing that [the wall] was covered with human excrement so that flakes of it clung to me, chiefly to my breast. I looked down at the flakes with bowed head and ran my hand over them.

When at last I reached the top, my father, who by this time was already coming out of a building, immediately fell on my neck and kissed and embraced me. He was wearing an old-fashioned, short Prince Albert, padded on the inside like a sofa, which I remembered well. 'This Dr von Leyden! He is an excellent man,' he exclaimed over and over again. But he had by no means visited him in his capacity as doctor, but rather only as a man worth knowing. I was a little afraid that I should have to go in to see him too, but this wasn't required of me. Behind me to the left I saw, sitting in a room literally surrounded by glass walls, a man who turned his back on me. It turned out that this man was the professor's secretary, that my father had in fact spoken only with him and not with the professor himself, but that somehow or other, through the secretary, he had recognized the excellences of the professor in the flesh, so that in every respect he was as much entitled to an opinion on the professor as if he had spoken to him in person.

Lessing Theatre: *Die Ratten*.

Letter to Pick because I haven't written to him. Card to Max in joy over *Arnold Beer*.

9 May. Yesterday evening in the coffee-house with Pick. How I

hold fast to my novel[48] against all restlessness, like a figure on a monument that looks into the distance and holds fast to its pedestal.

Hopeless evening with the family today. My brother-in-law needs money for the factory, my father is upset because of my sister, because of the business, and because of his heart, my unhappy second sister, my mother unhappy about all of them, and I with my scribblings.

22 May. Yesterday a wonderfully beautiful evening with Max. If I love myself, I love him more. Cabaret Lucerna. *Madame la mort* by Rachilde. *Dream of a Spring Morning*. The gay, fat girl in the box. The wild one with the coarse nose, her face smudged with soot, her shoulders squeezed up out of her dress (which wasn't décolleté, however) and her back twisted to and fro, her simple, blue blouse with white polka dots, her fencer's glove, which was always visible since most of the time her right hand was either resting flat, or on its fingertips, on the right thigh of her lively mother seated beside her. Her braids twisted over her ears, a not-too-clean light-blue ribbon on the back of her head, the hair in front encircles her forehead in a thin but compact tuft that projects far out in front. Her warm, wrinkled, light cloak carelessly falling in folds when she was negotiating at the box office.

23 May. Yesterday, behind us, out of boredom, a man fell from his chair – Comparison by Rachilde: Those who rejoice in the sun and demand that others rejoice are like drunkards coming from a wedding at night who force those they meet to drink the health of the unknown bride.

Letter to Weltsch, proposed that we use 'Du' to one another. Yesterday a good letter to Uncle Alfred about the factory. Day before yesterday letter to Löwy.

Now, in the evening, out of boredom, washed my hands in the bathroom three times in succession.

The child with the two little braids, bare head, loose little red dress with white dots, bare legs and feet, who, with a little basket in one hand, a little box in the other, hesitatingly walked across the street near the National Theatre.

How the actors in the play, *Madame la mort*, turn their backs to the audience, on the principle that the back of an amateur is, other things being equal, as beautiful as the back of a professional actor. The conscientiousness of people!

A few days ago an excellent lecture by Davis Trietsch on colonization in Palestine.

25 May. Weak tempo, little blood.

27 May. Yesterday Whit Sunday, cold weather, a not very nice excursion with Max and Weltsch. In the evening, coffee-house, Werfel gives me *Besuch aus dem Elysium*.

Part of Niklasstrasse and all the bridge turns around to look sentimentally at a dog who, loudly barking, is chasing an ambulance. Until suddenly the dog stops, turns away and proves to be an ordinary, strange dog who meant nothing in particular by his pursuit of the vehicle.

1 June. Wrote nothing.

2 June. Wrote almost nothing.
Yesterday lecture on America by Dr Soukup. (The Czechs in Nebraska, all officials in America are elected, everyone must belong to one of the three parties – Republican, Democratic, Socialist – Roosevelt's election meeting, with his glass he threatened a farmer who had made an objection, street speakers who carry a small box with them to serve as a platform.) Then spring festival, met Paul Kisch who talked about his dissertation, 'Hebrew and the Czechs'.

6 June. Thursday. Corpus Christi. Two horses in a race, how one lowers its head out of the race and shakes its mane vigorously, then

raises its head and only now, apparently feeling better, resumes the race which it has never really interrupted.

I have just read in Flaubert's letters: 'My novel is the cliff on which I am hanging, and I know nothing of what is going on in the world' – Like what I noted down about myself on 9 May.

Without weight, without bones, without body, walked through the streets for two hours considering what I overcame this afternoon while writing.

7 June. Bad. Wrote nothing today. Tomorrow no time.

6 July. Monday. Began a little. Am a little sleepy. Also lost among these entirely strange people.[49]

9 July. Nothing written for so long. Begin tomorrow. Otherwise I shall again get into a prolonged, irresistible dissatisfaction; I am really in it already. The nervous states are beginning. But if I can do something, then I can do it without superstitious precautions.

The invention of the devil. If we are possessed by the devil, it cannot be by one, for then we should live, at least here on earth, quietly, as with God, in unity, without contradiction, without reflection, always sure of the man behind us. His face would not frighten us, for as diabolical beings we would, if somewhat sensitive to the sight, be clever enough to prefer to sacrifice a hand in order to keep his face covered with it. If we were possessed by only a single devil, one who had a calm, untroubled view of our whole nature, and freedom to dispose of us at any moment, then that devil would also have enough power to hold us for the length of a human life high above the spirit of God in us, and even to swing us to and fro, so that we should never get to see a glimmer of it and therefore should not be troubled from that quarter. Only a crowd of devils could account for our earthly misfortunes. Why don't they exterminate one another until only a single one is left, or why don't they subordinate themselves to one great devil? Either way would be in accord with the diabolical principle of deceiving us as completely as possible. With unity lacking, of what use is the scrupulous attention all the devils pay us? It simply goes without saying that the falling of a human hair must matter more to the devil than to God, since the devil really loses that hair and God does not. But we still do not arrive at any state of well-being so long as the many devils are within us.

7 August. Long torment. Finally wrote to Max that I cannot clear up the little pieces that still remain, do not want to force myself to it, and therefore will not publish the book.[50]

8 August. Completed 'Confidence Trickster' more or less satisfactorily. With the last strength of a normal state of mind. Twelve o'clock, how will I be able to sleep?

9 August. The upset night. Yesterday the maid who said to the little boy on the steps, 'Hold on to my skirt!'
My inspired reading aloud of *Der arme Spielmann*. The perception in this story of what is manly in Grillparzer. The way he can risk everything and risks nothing, because there is nothing but truth in him already, a truth that even in the face of the contradictory impressions of the moment will justify itself as such when the crucial time arrives. The calm self-possession. The slow pace that neglects nothing. The immediate readiness, when it is needed, not sooner, for long in advance he sees everything that is coming.

10 August. Wrote nothing. Was in the factory and breathed gas in the engine-room for two hours. The energy of the foreman and the stoker before the engine, which for some undiscoverable reason will not start. Miserable factory.

11 August. Nothing, nothing. How much time the publishing of the little book takes from me and how much harmful, ridiculous pride comes from reading old things with an eye to publication. Only that keeps me from writing. And yet in reality I have achieved nothing, the disturbance is the best proof of it. In any event, now, after the publication of the book, I will have to stay away from magazines and reviews even more than before, if I do not wish to be content with just sticking the tips of my fingers into the truth. How immovable I have

become! Formerly, if I said only one word that opposed the direction of the moment, I at once flew over to the other side, now I simply look at myself and remain as I am.

14 August. Letter to Rowohlt.

Dear Mr Rowohlt,

I am enclosing the little prose pieces you wanted to see; they will probably be enough to make up a small book. While I was putting them together towards this end, I sometimes had to choose between satisfying my sense of responsibility and an eagerness to have a book among your beautiful books. Certainly I did not in each instance make an entirely clear-cut decision. But now I should naturally be happy if the things pleased you sufficiently to print them. After all, even with the greatest skill and the greatest understanding the bad in them is not discernible at first sight. Isn't what is most universally individual in writers the fact that each conceals his bad qualities in an entirely different way?

Faithfully –

15 August. Wasted day. Spent sleeping and lying down. Feast of St Mary on the Altstädter Ring. The man with a voice that seemed to come from a hole in the ground. Thought much of – what embarrassment before writing down names – F. B.[51] O. has just been reciting poems by Goethe. She chooses them with right feeling. 'Trost in Tränen'. 'An Lotte'. 'An Werther'. 'An den Mond'.

Again read old diaries instead of keeping away from them. I live as irrationally as is at all possible. And the publication of the thirty-one pages is to blame for everything. Even more to blame, of course, is my weakness, which permits a thing of this sort to influence me. Instead of shaking myself, I sit here and consider how I could express all this as insultingly as possible. But my horrible calm interferes with my inventiveness. I am curious as to how I shall find a way out of this state. I don't permit others to push me, nor do I know which is 'the right path'. So what will happen? Have I finally run aground, a great mass in shallow water? In that case, however, I should at least be able to turn my head. That's what I do, however.

16 August. Nothing, either in the office or at home. Wrote a few pages in the Weimar diary.

This evening the whimpering of my poor mother because I don't eat.

20 August. Outside my window, across the university building site partly overgrown with weeds, the little boys, both in blue blouses, one in light blue, the other, smaller one in darker blue, are each carrying a bundle of dry hay that fills their arms. They struggle up a slope with it. Charm of it all for the eyes.

This morning the empty open wagon and the large, emaciated horse pulling it. Both, making a final effort to get up a slope, stretched out to an unusual length. Seen at an angle by the spectator. The horse, front legs raised a little, his neck stretched sideways and upwards. Over him the whip of the driver.

If Rowohlt would send it back and I could lock it up again as if it had all never happened, so that I should be only as unhappy as I was before.

Miss F. B. When I arrived at Brod's on 13 August, she was sitting at the table. I was not at all curious about who she was, but rather took her for granted at once. Bony, empty face that wore its emptiness openly. Bare throat. A blouse thrown on. Looked very domestic in her dress although, as it later turned out, she by no means was. (I alienate myself from her a little by inspecting her so closely. What a state I'm in now, indeed, alienated in general from the whole of everything good, and don't even believe it yet. If the literary talk at Max's doesn't distract me too much, I'll try to write the story about Blenkelt today. It needn't be long, but I must hit it off right.) Almost broken nose. Blonde, somewhat straight, unattractive hair, strong chin. As I was taking my seat I looked at her closely for the first time, by the time I was seated I already had an unshakeable opinion.

21 August. Read Lenz incessantly and – such is my state – he restored me to my senses.

The picture of dissatisfaction presented by a street, where everyone is perpetually lifting his feet to escape from the place on which he stands.

30 August. All this time did nothing. The visit of my uncle from Spain. Last Saturday in the Arco Werfel recited his 'Lebenslieder' and 'Opfer'. A monster! But I looked him in the eye and held it all evening.

It will be hard to rouse me, and yet I am restless. When I lay in bed this afternoon and someone quickly turned a key in the lock, for a moment I had locks all over my body, as though at a fancy-dress ball, and at short intervals a lock was opened or shut here and there.

Questionnaire by the magazine *Miroir*, about love in the present and the way love has changed since the days of our grandparents. An actress answered: Never did they love as well as today.

How shaken and exalted I was after hearing Werfel! How I behaved afterwards at L.'s party, wild, almost, and without a fault.

This month, which, because of the absence of the boss, could have been put to exceptionally good use, I have wasted and slept away without much excuse (sending the book off to Rowohlt, abscesses, my uncle's visit). Even this afternoon I stretched out on the bed for three hours with dreamy excuses.

4 September. My uncle from Spain. The cut of his coat. The effect of his nearness. The details of his personality. His floating through the ante-room into the toilet, in the course of which he makes no reply to what is said to him. Becomes milder from day to day, if one judges not in terms of a gradual change but by the moments which stand out.

5 September. I ask him: How is one to reconcile the fact that you are generally dissatisfied, as you recently said, and that nevertheless you are at home everywhere, as can be seen time and again (and which is revealed in the rudeness always characteristic of this sort of being-at-home, I thought). He answers, as I remember it: 'In individual things I am dissatisfied, this doesn't extend to the whole. I often dine in a little French pension that is very exclusive and expensive. For example, a room for a couple, with meals, costs fifty francs a day. So I sit there between the secretary of the French legation, for example, and a Spanish general of artillery. Opposite me sit a high official of the navy ministry and some count or other. I know them all well by now, sit down in my

place, greeting them on all sides, because I am in a peculiar mood I say not another word until the good-bye with which I take my leave. Then I am alone on the street and really can't see what purpose this evening served. I go home and regret that I didn't marry. Naturally this mood passes away again, whether because I have thought it through to the end, whether because the thoughts have dispersed. But on occasion it comes back again.'

8 September. Sunday morning. Yesterday a letter to Dr Schiller.
Afternoon. The way my mother, together with a crowd of women, with a very loud voice, is playing with some small children near by and drives me out of the house. Don't cry! Don't cry! etc. That's his! That's his! etc. Two big people! etc. He doesn't want to! . . . But! But! . . . How did you like Vienna, Dolphi? Was it nice there? . . . I ask you, just look at his hands!

11 September. The evening of the day before yesterday with Utitz.

A dream: I found myself on a jetty of square-cut stones built far out into the sea. Someone, or even several people, were with me, but my awareness of myself was so strong that I hardly knew more about them than that I was speaking to them. I can remember only the raised knees of someone sitting near me. At first I did not really know where I was, only when once I accidentally stood up did I see on my left and behind me on my right the distant, clearly outlined sea with many battleships lined up in rows and at anchor. On the right New York could be seen, we were in New York Harbour. The sky was grey, but of a constant brightness. I moved back and forth in my seat, freely exposed to the air on all sides, in order to be able to see everything. In the direction of New York my glance slanted downwards a little, in the direction of the sea it slanted upwards. I now noticed the water rise up near us in high waves on which was borne a great cosmopolitan traffic. I can remember only that instead of the rafts we have, there were long timbers lashed together into gigantic bundles the cut ends of which kept popping out of the water during the voyage, higher or lower, according to the height of the waves, and at the same time kept turning end over end in the water. I sat down, drew up my feet, quivered with pleasure, virtually dug myself into the ground in delight, and said: Really, this is even more interesting than the traffic on á Paris boulevard.

12 September. This evening Dr L. at our house. Another emigrant to Palestine. Is taking his bar examination a year before the end of his clerkship and is leaving (in two weeks) for Palestine with 1,200 K. Will try to get a position with the Palestine Office. All these emigrants to Palestine (Dr B., Dr K.) have downcast eyes, feel blinded by their listeners, fumble around on the table with the tips of their extended fingers, their voices quiver, they smile weakly and prop up these smiles with a little irony. Dr K. told us that his students are chauvinists, have the Maccabees forever in their mouths and want to take after them.

I became aware that I wrote so eagerly and well to Dr Schiller only because Miss B. stopped in Breslau, and I have been thinking about sending flowers to her through Dr Schiller, and although all this was two weeks ago, a trace of it is still in the air.

15 September. Engagement of my sister Valli.

Aus dem Grunde	From the pit
der Ermattung	of exhaustion
steigen wir	we ascend
mit neuen Kräften,	with renewed strength –
Dunkle Herren,	Dark lords,
welche warten	who wait
bis die Kinder	until the children
sich entkräften.	exhaust themselves.

Love between brother and sister – the repeating of the love between mother and father.

The hollow which the work of genius has burned into our surroundings is a good place into which to put one's little light. Therefore the inspiration that emanates from genius, the universal inspiration that doesn't only drive one to imitation.

18 September. H.'s stories yesterday in the office. The stone breaker on the highway who begged a frog from him, held it by the feet, and with three bites swallowed down first the little head, then the rump, and finally the feet – The best way to kill cats, who cling stubbornly to life: Squeeze their throats in a closed door and pull their tails – His horror of vermin. In the army one night he had an itch under his nose, he slapped it in his sleep and crushed something. But the something was a bedbug and he carried the stench of it around with him for days.

Four people ate a well-prepared roast cat, but only three knew what they were eating. After the meal the three began to meow, but the fourth refused to believe it, only when they showed him the bloody skin did he believe it, could not run out fast enough to vomit everything up again, and was very sick for two weeks.

This stone breaker ate nothing but bread and whatever else in the way of fruit or living flesh that he accidentally came upon, and drank nothing but brandy. Slept in the shed of a brickyard. Once H. met him at twilight in the fields. 'Stand still,' the man said, 'or . . .' For the sport of it, H. stopped. 'Give me your cigarette,' the man went on. H. gave it to him. 'Give me another one!' – 'So you want another one?' H. asked him, held his gnarled stick in his left hand in case of trouble, and struck him in the face with his right so that he dropped the cigarette. The man ran away at once, cowardly and weak, the way such brandy drinkers are.

Yesterday at B.'s with Dr L. Song about Reb Dovidl, Reb Dovidl of Vassilko is going to Talne today. In a city between Vassilko and Talne they sing it indifferently, in Vassilko weepingly, in Talne happily.

19 September. Comptroller P. tells about the trip which he took in the company of a schoolmate at the age of thirteen with seventy kreuzers in his pocket. How one evening they came to an inn where a huge drinking bout was going on in honour of the mayor who had returned from his military service. More than fifty empty beer bottles were standing on the floor. The whole place was full of pipe smoke. The stench of the beer dregs. The two little boys against the wall. The drunken mayor who, remembering his military service, wants to maintain discipline everywhere, comes up to them and threatens to have

them sent home under arrest as deserters, what he takes them for in spite of all their explanations. The boys tremble, show their Gymnasium identity cards, decline 'mensa'; a half-drunk teacher looks on without helping them. Without being given any definite decision about their fate they are compelled to join in the drinking, are very pleased to get for nothing so much good beer which, with their limited means, they would never have dared to allow themselves. They drink themselves full and then, late at night, after the last guests have departed, go to sleep on thinly spread straw in this room which had not been aired, and sleep like lords. But at four o'clock a gigantic maid with a broom arrives, says she has no time, and would have swept them out into the morning mist if they had not themselves run away. When the room was cleaned up a little, two large coffee-pots, filled to the brim, were placed on the table for them. But when they stirred their coffee with their spoons, something large, dark, round kept coming to the surface from time to time. They thought it would be explained in time and drank with appetite until, in view of the half-emptied pots and the dark object, they became really worried and asked the maid's advice. Then it turned out that the black object was old, congealed goose blood which had been left in the pots from yesterday's feast and on to which the coffee had simply been poured in the stupor of the morning after. At once the boys ran out and vomited everything to the last little drop. Later they were called before the parson who, after a short examination in religion, established that they were honest boys, the cook told to serve them some soup, and then sent them on their way with his spiritual blessing. As pupils in a clerical Gymnasium they had this soup and this blessing given to them in almost every parsonage they came to.

20 September. Letters to Löwy and Miss Taussig yesterday, to Miss B. and Max today.

23 September.[52] This story, 'The Judgement', I wrote at one sitting during the night of the 22nd–23rd, from ten o'clock at night to six o'clock in the morning. I was hardly able to pull my legs out from under the desk, they had got so stiff from sitting. The fearful strain and joy, how the story developed before me, as if I were advancing over water. Several times during this night I heaved my own weight on

my back. How everything can be said, how for everything, for the strangest fancies, there waits a great fire in which they perish and rise up again. How it turned blue outside the window. A wagon rolled by. Two men walked across the bridge. At two I looked at the clock for the last time. As the maid walked through the ante-room for the first time I wrote the last sentence. Turning out the light and the light of day. The slight pains around my heart. The weariness that disappeared in the middle of the night. The trembling entrance into my sisters' room. Reading aloud. Before that, stretching in the presence of the maid and saying, 'I've been writing until now.' The appearance of the undisturbed bed, as though it had just been brought in. The conviction verified that with my novel-writing I am in the shameful lowlands of writing. Only *in this way* can writing be done, only with such coherence, with such a complete opening out of the body and the soul. Morning in bed. The always clear eyes. Many emotions carried along in the writing, joy, for example, that I shall have something beautiful for Max's *Arkadia*, thoughts about Freud, of course; in one passage, of *Arnold Beer*; in another, of Wassermann; in one, of Werfel's giantess; of course, also of my 'The Urban World'.

I, only I, am the spectator in the orchestra.

Gustav Blenkelt was a simple man with regular habits. He didn't like any unnecessary display and had a definite opinion about people who went in for such display. Although he was a bachelor, he felt he had an absolute right to say a few deciding words in the marital affairs of his acquaintances and anyone who would even have questioned such a right would have fared badly with him. He used to speak his mind freely and did not in any way seek to detain those listeners whom his opinions happened not to suit. As there are everywhere, there were people who admired him, people who honoured him, people who put up with him, and, finally, those who wanted to have nothing to do with him. Indeed, every person, even the emptiest, is, if one will only look carefully, the centre of a tight circle that forms about him here and there, how could it be otherwise in the case of Gustav Blenkelt, at bottom an exceptionally social person?

In his thirty-fifth year, the last year of his life, he spent an unusual amount of time with a young couple named Strong. It is certain that for Mr Strong, who had opened a furniture store with his wife's money, the acquaintance with Blenkelt had numerous advantages, since the largest part of the latter's acquaintances consisted of young, marriageable people who sooner or later had to think of providing new furniture for themselves and who, out of old habit, were usually accustomed not to neglect Blenkelt's advice in this matter, either. 'I keep them on a tight rein,' Blenkelt used to say.

24 September. My sister said: The house (in the story) is very like ours. I said: How? In that case, then, Father would have to be living in the toilet.

25 September. By force kept myself from writing. Tossed in bed. The congestion of blood in my head and the useless drifting by of things. What harmfulness! – Yesterday read at Baum's, to the Baum family, my sisters, Marta, Dr Block's wife, and her two sons (one of them a one-year volunteer in the army). Towards the end my hand was moving uncontrollably about and actually before my face. There were tears in my eyes. The indubitability of the story was confirmed – This evening tore myself away from my writing. Films in the National Theatre. Miss O., whom a clergyman once pursued. She came home soaked in cold sweat. Danzig. Life of Körner. The horses. The white horse. The smoke of powder. '*Lützows wilde Jagd.*'[53]

∞ ∞ ∞

11 February. While I read the proofs of 'The Judgement', I'll write down all the relationships which have become clear to me in the story as far as I now remember them. This is necessary because the story came out of me like a real birth, covered with filth and slime, and only I have the hand that can reach to the body itself and the strength of desire to do so:

The friend is the link between father and son, he is their strongest common bond. Sitting alone at his window, Georg rummages voluptuously in this consciousness of what they have in common, believes he has his father within him, and would be at peace with everything if it

were not for a fleeting, sad thoughtfulness. In the course of the story
the father, with the strengthened position that the other, lesser things
they share in common give him – love, devotion to the mother, loyalty
to her memory, the clientele that he (the father) had been the first to
acquire for the business – uses the common bond of the friend to set
himself up as Georg's antagonist. Georg is left with nothing; the bride,
who lives in the story only in relation to the friend, that is, to what
father and son have in common, is easily driven away by the father
since no marriage has yet taken place, and so she cannot penetrate the
circle of blood relationship that is drawn around father and son. What
they have in common is built up entirely around the father, Georg can
feel it only as something foreign, something that has become independent, that he has never given enough protection, that is exposed
to Russian revolutions, and only because he himself has lost everything except his awareness of the father does the judgement, which
closes off his father from him completely, have so strong an effect on
him.

Georg has the same number of letters as Franz. In Bendemann,
'mann' is a strengthening of 'Bende' to provide for all the as yet un-
foreseen possibilities in the story. But Bende has exactly the same
number of letters as Kafka, and the vowel *e* occurs in the same places
as does the vowel *a* in Kafka.

Frieda has as many letters as F. and the same initial, Brandenfeld
has the same initial as B., and in the word 'Feld' a certain connexion in
meaning, as well. Perhaps even the thought of Berlin was not without
influence and the recollection of the Mark Brandenburg perhaps had
some influence.

12 February. In describing the friend I kept thinking of Steuer. Now
when I happened to meet him about three months after I had written
the story, he told me that he had become engaged about three months
ago.

After I read the story at Weltsch's yesterday, old Mr Weltsch went
out and, when he returned after a short time, praised especially the
graphic descriptions in the story. With his arm extended he said, 'I
see this father before me,' all the time looking directly at the empty
chair in which he had been sitting while I was reading.

My sister said, 'It is our house.' I was astonished at how mistaken she was in the setting and said, 'In that case, then, Father would have to be living in the toilet.'

28 February. Ernst Liman arrived in Constantinople on a business trip one rainy autumn morning and, as was his custom – this was the tenth time he was making this trip – without paying attention to anything else, drove through the otherwise empty streets to the hotel at which he always stopped and which he found suited him. It was almost cool, and drizzling rain blew into the carriage, and, annoyed by the bad weather which had been pursuing him all through his business trip this year, he put up the carriage window and leaned back in a corner to sleep away the fifteen minutes or so of the drive that was before him. But since the driver took him straight through the business district, he could get no rest, and the shouts of the street vendors, the rolling of the heavy wagons, as well as other noises, meaningless on the surface, such as a crowd clapping its hands, disturbed his usually sound sleep.

At the end of his drive an unpleasant surprise awaited him. During the last great fire in Stambul, about which Liman had probably read during his trip, the Hotel Kingston, at which it was his habit to stop, had been burned almost to the ground, but the driver, who of course knew this, had nevertheless carried out his passenger's instructions with complete indifference, and without a word had brought him to the site of the hotel which had burned down. Now he calmly got down from the box and would even have unloaded Liman's luggage if the latter had not seized him by the shoulder and shaken him, whereupon the driver then let go of the luggage, to be sure, but as slowly and sleepily as if not Liman but his own change of mind had diverted him from it.

Part of the ground floor of the hotel was still intact and had been made fairly habitable by being boarded over at the top and sides. A notice in Turkish and French indicated that the hotel would be rebuilt in a short time as a more beautiful and more modern structure. Yet the only sign of this was the work of three day labourers, who with shovels and rakes were heaping up the rubble at one side and loading it into a small handbarrow.

As it turned out, part of the hotel staff, unemployed because of the fire, was living in these ruins. A gentleman in a black frock-coat and a bright red tie at once came running out when Liman's carriage stopped, told Liman, who sulkily listened to him, the story of the fire, meanwhile twisting the ends of his long, thin beard around his finger and interrupting this only to point out to Liman where the fire started, how it spread, and how finally everything collapsed. Liman, who had hardly raised his eyes from the ground throughout this whole story and had not let go the handle of the carriage door, was just about to call out to the driver the name of another hotel to which he could drive him when the man in the frock-coat, with arms raised, implored him not to go to any other hotel, but to remain loyal to this hotel, where, after all, he had always received satisfactión. Despite the fact that this was only meaningless talk and no one could remember Liman, just as Liman recognized hardly a single one of the male and female employees he saw in the door and windows, he still asked, as a man to whom his habits were dear, how, then, at the moment, he was to remain loyal to the burned-down hotel. Now he learned – and involuntarily had to smile at the idea – that beautiful rooms in private homes were available for former guests of this hotel, but only for them, Liman need but say the word and he would be taken to one at once, it was quite near, there would be no time lost and the rate – they wished to oblige and the room was of course only a substitute – was unusually low, even though the food, Viennese cooking, was, if possible, even better and the service even more attentive than in the former Hotel Kingston, which had really been inadequate in some respects.

'Thank you,' said Liman, and got into the carriage. 'I shall be in Constantinople only five days, I really can't set myself up in a private home for this short space of time, no, I'm going to a hotel. Next year, however, when I return and your hotel has been rebuilt, I'll certainly stop only with you. Excuse me!' And Liman tried to close the carriage door, the handle of which the representative of the hotel was now holding. 'Sir,' the latter said pleadingly, and looked up at Liman.

'Let go!' shouted Liman, shook the door and directed the driver: 'To the Hotel Royal.' But whether it was because the driver did not understand him, whether it was because he was waiting for the door to be closed, in any event he sat on his box like a statue. In no case, however, did the representative of the hotel let go of the door, he even beckoned eagerly to a colleague to rouse himself and come to his aid. There was some girl he particularly hoped could do something, and he kept calling, 'Fini! Hey, Fini! Where's Fini?' The people at the windows and the door had turned towards the inside of the house, they shouted in confusion, one saw them running past the windows, everyone was looking for Fini.

The man who was keeping Liman from driving off and whom obviously only hunger gave the courage to behave like this, could have been easily pushed away from the door. He realized this and did not dare even to look at Liman; but Liman had already had too many unfortunate experiences on his travels not to know how important it is in a foreign country to avoid doing anything that attracts attention, no matter how very much in the right one might be. He therefore quietly got out of the carriage again, for the time being paid no attention to the man who was holding the door in a convulsive grip, went up to the driver, repeated his instructions, expressly added that he was to drive away from here as fast as he could, then walked up to the man at the door of the carriage, took hold of his hand with an apparently ordinary grip, but secretly squeezed the knuckles so hard that the man almost jumped and was forced to remove his hand from the door handle, shrieking 'Fini!' which was at once a command and an outburst of pain.

'Here she comes! Here she comes!' shouts now came from all the windows, and a laughing girl, her hands still held to her hair, which had just been dressed, her head half bowed, came running out of the house towards the carriage. 'Quick! Into the carriage! It's pouring,' she cried, grasping Liman by the shoulders and holding her face very close to his. 'I am Fini,' she then said softly, and let her hands move caressingly along his shoulders.

They really don't mean so badly by me, Liman said to himself, smiling at the girl, too bad that I'm no longer a young fellow and don't permit myself risky adventures.

'There must be some mistake, Miss,' he said, and turned towards his carriage; 'I neither asked them to call you nor do I intend to drive off with you.' From inside the carriage he added, 'Don't trouble yourself any further.'

But Fini had already set one foot on the step and said, her arms crossed over her breast, 'Now why won't you let me recommend a place for you to stay?'

Tired of the annoyances to which he had already been subjected, Liman leaned out to her and said, 'Please don't delay me any longer with useless questions! I am going to a hotel and that's all. Take your foot off the step, otherwise you may be hurt. Go ahead, driver!'

'Stop!' the girl shouted, however, and now in earnest tried to swing herself into the carriage. Liman, shaking his head, stood up and blocked all of the door with his stout body. The girl tried to push him away, using her head and knees in the attempt, the carriage began to rock on its wretched springs, Liman had no real grip.

'And why won't you take me with you? And why won't you take me with you?' the girl kept repeating.

Certainly Liman would have been able to push away the girl without exerting any special force, even though she was strong, if the man in the frock-coat, who had remained silent until now as though he had been relieved by Fini, had not now, when he saw Fini waver, hurried over with a bound, supported Fini from behind and tried to push the girl into the carriage by exerting all his strength against Liman's still restrained efforts at defence. Sensing that he was holding back, she actually forced her way into the carriage, pulled at the door which at the same time was slammed shut from the outside, said, as though to herself, 'Well, now,' first hastily straightened her blouse and then, more deliberately, her hair. 'This is unheard of,' said Liman, who had fallen back into his seat, to the girl who was sitting opposite him.

2 May. It has become very necessary to keep a diary again. The uncertainty of my thoughts, F., the ruin in the office, the physical impossibility of writing and the inner need for it.

Valli walks out through our door behind my brother-in-law who to-morrow will leave for Czortkov for manoeuvres. Remarkable, how much is implied in this following-after of a recognition of marriage as an institution which one has become thoroughly used to.

The story of the gardener's daughter who interrupted my work the day before yesterday. I, who want to cure my neurasthenia through my work, am obliged to hear that the young lady's brother, his name was

Jan and he was the actual gardener and presumed successor of old Dvorsky, already even the owner of the flower garden, had poisoned himself because of melancholia two months ago at the age of twenty-eight. During the summer he felt relatively well despite his solitary nature, since at least he had to have contact with the customers, but during the winter he was entirely withdrawn. His sweetheart was a clerk – *uřednice* – a girl as melancholy as he. They often went to the cemetery together.

The gigantic Menasse at the Yiddish performance. Something magical that seized hold of me at his movements in harmony with the music. I have forgotten what.

My stupid laughter today when I told my mother that I am going to Berlin[54] at Whitsuntide. 'Why are you laughing?' said my mother (among several other remarks, one of which was, 'Look before you leap,' all of which, however, I warded off with remarks like, 'It's nothing,' etc.). 'Because of embarrassment,' I said, and was happy for once to have said something true in this matter.

Yesterday met B.[55] Her calmness, contentedness, clarity, and lack of embarrassment, even though in the last two years she has become an old woman, her plumpness – even at that time a burden to her – that will soon have reached the extreme of sterile fatness, her walk has become a sort of rolling or shuffle with the belly thrust, or rather carried, to the fore, and on her chin – at a quick glance only on her chin – hairs now curling out of what used to be down.

3 May. The terrible uncertainty of my inner existence.

How I unbutton my vest to show Mr B. my rash. How I beckon him into another room.

The leper and his wife. The way her behind – she is lying in bed on her belly – keeps rising up with all its ulcers again and again although a guest is present. The way her husband keeps shouting at her to keep covered.

The husband has been struck from behind by a stake – no one knows where it came from – knocked down and pierced. Lying on the ground with his head raised and his arms stretched out, he laments. Later he is able to stand up unsteadily for a moment. He can talk about nothing except how he was struck, and points to the approximate direction from which in his opinion the stake came. This talk, always the same, is by now tiresome to the wife, particularly since the man is always pointing in another direction.

4 May. Always the image of a pork butcher's broad knife that quickly and with mechanical regularity chops into me from the side and cuts off very thin slices which fly off almost like shavings because of the speed of the action.

Early one morning, the streets were still empty up and down their length and breadth, a man, he was in his bare feet and wore only a nightshirt and trousers, opened the door of a large tenement on the main street. He seized the two sections of the door and took a deep breath. 'Misery, oh, damned misery,' he said and looked, apparently calmly, first along the street and then at some houses.

Despair from this direction too. Nowhere a welcome.

1. Digestion. 2. Neurasthenia. 3. Rash. 4. Inner insecurity.

24 May. Walk with Pick.[56] In high spirits because I consider 'The Stoker' so good. This evening I read it to my parents, there is no better critic than I when I read to my father, who listens with the most extreme reluctance. Many shallow passages followed by unfathomable depths.

5 June. The inner advantages that mediocre literary works derive from the fact that their authors are still alive and present behind them. The real sense of growing old.

Löwy, story about crossing the frontier.

21 June. The anxiety I suffer from all sides. The examination by the doctor, the way he presses forward against me, I virtually empty myself

out and he makes his empty speeches into me, despised and unrefuted.

The tremendous world I have in my head. But how free myself and free it without being torn to pieces. And a thousand times rather be torn to pieces than retain it in me or bury it. That, indeed, is why I am here, that is quite clear to me.

On a cold spring morning about five o'clock a tall man in a cloak that reached to his feet knocked with his fist against the door of a small hut which stood in a bare, hilly region. The moon was still white and bright in the sky. After each blow of his fist he listened, within the hut there was silence.

1 July. The wish for an unthinking, reckless solitude. To be face to face only with myself. Perhaps I shall have it in Riva.

Day before yesterday with Weiss,[57] author of *Die Galeere*. Jewish physician, Jew of the kind that is closest to the type of the Western European Jew and to whom one therefore immediately feels close. The tremendous advantage of Christians who always have and enjoy such feelings of closeness in general intercourse, for instance a Christian Czech among Christian Czechs.

The honeymoon couple that came out of the Hotel de Saxe. In the afternoon. Dropping the card in the mailbox. Wrinkled clothing, lazy pace, dreary, tepid afternoon. Faces scarcely individualized at first sight.

The picture of the celebration of the Romanov tercentenary in Yaroslavl on the Volga. The Tsar, the annoyed princesses standing in the sun, only one – delicate, elderly, indolent, leaning on her parasol – is looking straight ahead. The heir to the throne on the arm of the huge, bareheaded Cossack. In another picture, men who had long since passed by are saluting in the distance.

The millionaire in the motion picture *Slaves of Gold*. Mustn't forget him. The calmness, the slow movement, conscious of its goal, a faster step when necessary, a shrug of the shoulder. Rich, spoiled, lulled to sleep, but how he springs up like a servant and searches the room into which he was locked in the forest tavern.

2 July. Wept over the report of the trial of twenty-three-year-old Marie Abraham who, because of poverty and hunger, strangled her not quite nine-month-old child, Barbara, with a man's tie that she used as a garter. Very routine story.

The fire with which, in the bathroom, I described to my sister a funny motion picture. Why can I never do that in the presence of strangers?

I would never have married a girl with whom I had lived in the same city for a year.

3 July. The broadening and heightening of existence through marriage. Sermon text. But I almost sense it.

When I say something it immediately and finally loses its importance, when I write it down it loses it too, but sometimes gains a new one.

A band of little golden beads around a tanned throat.

19 July. Out of a house there stepped four armed men. Each held a halberd upright before him. Now and then one of them looked to the rear to see whether he was coming on whose account they were standing here. It was early in the morning, the street was entirely empty.

So what do you want? Come! – We do not want to. Leave us!–

All the inner effort just for this! That is why the music from the coffee-house rings so in one's ear. The stone's throw about which Elsa B. spoke becomes visible.

[*A woman is sitting at the distaff. A man pushes the door open with a sword which is sheathed in its scabbard (he is holding it loosely in his hand).*]
MAN: He was here!

WOMAN: Who? What do you want?

MAN: The horse thief. He is hiding here. Don't lie!

[*He brandishes the sword.*]

WOMAN [*raising the distaff to protect herself*]: No one was here. Let me alone!

20 July. Down on the river lay several boats, fishermen had cast their lines, it was a dreary day. Some youths, their legs crossed, were leaning against the railing of the dock.

When they rose to toast her departure, lifting up their champagne glasses, the dawn had already broken. Her parents and several wedding guests escorted her to the carriage.

21 July. Don't despair, not even over the fact that you don't despair. Just when everything seems over with, new forces come marching up, and precisely that means that you are alive. And if they don't then everything is over with here, once and for all.

I cannot sleep. Only dreams, no sleep. Today, in my dream, I invented a new kind of vehicle for a park slope. You take a branch, it needn't be very strong, prop it up on the ground at a slight angle, hold one end in your hand, sit down on it side-saddle, then the whole branch naturally rushes down the slope, since you are sitting on the bough you are carried along at full speed, rocking comfortably on the elastic wood. It is also possible to use the branch to ride up again. The chief advantage, aside from the simplicity of the whole device, lies in the fact that the branch, thin and flexible as it is, can be lowered or raised as necessary and gets through anywhere, even where a person by himself would get through only with difficulty.

To be pulled in through the ground-floor window of a house by a rope tied around one's neck and to be yanked up, bloody and ragged, through all the ceilings, furniture, walls, and attics, without consideration, as if by a person who is paying no attention, until the empty noose, dropping the last fragments of me when it breaks through the roof tiles, is seen on the roof.

Special methods of thinking. Permeated with emotion. Everything feels itself to be a thought, even the vaguest feelings (Dostoyevsky).

This block and tackle of the inner being. A small lever is somewhere secretly released, one is hardly aware of it at first, and at once the whole apparatus is in motion. Subject to an incomprehensible power, as the watch seems subject to time, it creaks here and there, and all the chains clank down their prescribed path one after the other.

Summary of all the arguments for and against my marriage:

1. Inability to endure life alone, which does not imply inability to live, quite the contrary, it is even improbable that I know how to live with anyone, but I am incapable, alone, of bearing the assault of my own life, the demands of my own person, the attacks of time and old age, the vague pressure of the desire to write, sleeplessness, the nearness of insanity – I cannot bear all this alone. I naturally add a 'perhaps' to this. The connexion with F. will give my existence more strength to resist.

2. Everything immediately gives me pause. Every joke in the comic paper, what I remember about Flaubert and Grillparzer, the sight of the nightshirts on my parents' beds, laid out for the night, Max's marriage. Yesterday my sister said, 'All the married people (that we know) are happy, I don't understand it,' this remark too gave me pause, I became afraid again.

3. I must be alone a great deal. What I accomplished was only the result of being alone.

4. I hate everything that does not relate to literature, conversations bore me (even if they relate to literature), to visit people bores me, the sorrows and joys of my relatives bore me to my soul. Conversations take the importance, the seriousness, the truth of everything I think.

5. The fear of the connexion, of passing into the other. Then I'll never be alone again.

6. In the past, especially, the person I am in the company of my sisters has been entirely different from the person I am in the company of other people. Fearless, powerful, surprising, moved as I otherwise am only when I write. If through the intermediation of my wife I

could be like that in the presence of everyone! But then would it not be at the expense of my writing? Not that, not that!

7. Alone, I could perhaps some day really give up my job. Married, it will never be possible.

In our class, the fifth class of the Amalia Gymnasium, there was a boy named Friedrich Guss whom we all hated very much. If we came into the classroom early and saw him sitting in his place near the stove we could hardly understand how he could have pulled himself together to come to school again. But I'm not telling it right. We didn't hate only him, we hated everyone. We were a terrible confederacy. Once, when the District School Inspector was present at a lesson – it was a geography lesson and the professor, his eyes turned to the blackboard or the window like all our professors, was describing the Morea Peninsula –

It was the first day of school, evening was already approaching. The professors of the Obergymnasium were still sitting in the staff-room, studying the lists of pupils, preparing new roll books, talking about their vacation trips.

Miserable creature that I am!

Just whip the horse properly! Dig the spurs into him slowly, then pull them out with a jerk, but now let them bite into the flesh with all your strength.

What an extremity!

Were we crazy? We ran through the park at night swinging branches.

I sailed a boat into a small, natural bay.

While I was at the Gymnasium, now and then I used to visit a certain Josef Mack, a friend of my dead father. When, after graduation from the Gymnasium, I –

While he was at the Gymnasium Hugo Seifert now and then used to pay a visit to a certain Josef Kiemann, an old bachelor who had been

226

a friend of Hugo's dead father. The visits suddenly ceased when Hugo, who received the offer of a job abroad which he had to accept at once, left his home town for several years. When he returned he intended to visit the old man, but he found no opportunity, perhaps such a visit would not have suited his changed views, and although he often went through the street where Kiemann lived and several times even saw him leaning out of the window and was probably noticed by him too, he neglected to pay the visit.

Nothing, nothing, nothing. Weakness, self-destruction, tip of a flame of hell piercing the floor.

23 July. With Felix in Rostock. The bursting sexuality of the women. Their natural impurity. The flirtation, senseless for me, with little Lena. The sight of a stout woman hunched up in a basket chair, one foot curiously pushed backwards, who was sewing something and talking to an old woman, probably an old spinster, whose teeth appeared unusually large on one side of her mouth. The full-bloodedness and wisdom of the pregnant woman. Her behind almost faceted by evenly divided planes. The life on the small terrace. How I coldly took the little girl on my lap, not at all unhappy about the coolness.

How childishly a tinker, seen through the open door of his shop, sits at his work and keeps striking with his hammer.

Roskoff, *History of the Devil*: Among the present-day Caribs, 'he who works at night' is regarded as the creator of the world.

13 August. Perhaps everything is now ended and the letter I wrote yesterday was the last one. That would certainly be the best. What I shall suffer, what she will suffer – that cannot be compared with the common suffering that would result. I shall gradually pull myself to-gether, she will marry, that is the only way out among the living. We cannot beat a path into the rock for the two of us, it is enough that we wept and tortured ourselves for a year. She will realize this from my last letters. If not, then I will certainly marry her, for I am too weak

to resist her opinion about our common fortune and am unable not to carry out, as far as I can, something she considers possible.

Yesterday evening on the Belvedere under the stars.

14 August. The opposite has happened. There were three letters. The last letter I could not resist. I love her as far as I am capable of it, but the love lies buried to the point of suffocation under fear and self-reproaches.

Conclusion for my case from 'The Judgement'. I am indirectly in her debt for the story. But Georg goes to pieces because of his fiancée.

Coitus as punishment for the happiness of being together. Live as ascetically as possible, more ascetically than a bachelor, that is the only possible way for me to endure marriage. But she?

And despite all this, if we, I and F., had equal rights, if we had the same prospects and possibilities, I would not marry. But this blind alley into which I have slowly pushed her life makes it an unavoidable duty for me, although its consequences are by no means unpredictable. Some secret law of human relationship is at work here.

I had great difficulty writing the letter to her parents, especially because a first draft, written under particularly unfavourable circumstances, for a long time resisted every change. Today, nevertheless, I have just about succeeded, at least there is no untruth in it, and after all it is still something that parents can read and understand.

15 August. Agonies in bed towards morning. Saw only solution in jumping out of the window. My mother came to my bedside and asked whether I had sent off the letter and whether it was my original text. I said it was the original text, but made even sharper. She said she does not understand me. I answered, she most certainly does not understand me, and by no means only in this matter. Later she asked me if I were going to write to Uncle Alfred, he deserved it. I asked why he deserved it. He has telegraphed, he has written, he has your welfare so much at heart. 'These are simply formalities,' I said, 'he is a complete stranger to me, he misunderstands me entirely, he does not know what I want and need, I have nothing in common with him.'

'So no one understands you,' my mother said, 'I suppose I am a stranger to you too, and your father as well. So we all want only what is bad for you.'

'Certainly, you are all strangers to me, we are related only by blood, but that never shows itself. Of course you don't want what is bad for me.'

Through this and several other observations of myself I have come to believe that there are possibilities in my ever-increasing inner decisiveness and conviction which may enable me to pass the test of marriage in spite of everything, and even to steer it in a direction favourable to my development. Of course, to a certain extent this is a belief that I grasp at when I am already on the window sill.

I'll shut myself off from everyone to the point of insensibility. Make an enemy of everyone, speak to no one.

The man with the dark, stern eyes who was carrying the pile of old coats on his shoulder.

LEOPOLD S. [*a tall, strong man, clumsy, jerky movements, loosely hanging, wrinkled, checked clothes, enters hurriedly through the door on the right into the large room, claps his hands, and shouts*]: Felice! Felice! [*Without pausing an instant for a reply to his shout he hurries to the middle door which he opens, again shouting*] Felice!

FELICE S. [*enters through the door at the left, stops at the door, a forty-year-old woman in a kitchen apron*]: Here I am, Leo. How nervous you have become recently! What is it you want?

LEOPOLD [*turns with a jerk, then stops and bites his lips*]: Well, then, come over here! [*He walks over to the sofa.*]

FELICE [*does not move*]: Quick! What do you want? I really have to go back to the kitchen.

LEOPOLD [*from the sofa*]: Forget the kitchen! Come here! I want to tell you something important. It will make up for it. All right, come on!

FELICE [*walks towards him slowly, raising the shoulder straps of*

her apron]: Well, what is it that's so important? If you're making a
fool of me I'll be angry, seriously. [*Stops in front of him.*]
LEOPOLD: Well, sit down, then.
FELICE: And suppose I don't want to?
LEOPOLD: Then I can't tell it to you. I must have you close to me.
FELICE: All right, now I am sitting.

21 August. Today I got Kierkegaard's *Buch des Richters*.[58] As I
suspected, his case, despite essential differences, is very similar to
mine, at least he is on the same side of the world. He bears me out like
a friend. I drafted the following letter to her father, which, if I have
the strength, I will send off tomorrow.

You hesitate to answer my request, that is quite understandable, every
father would do the same in the case of any suitor. Hence your hesitation
is not the reason for this letter, at most it increases my hope for a calm
and correct judgement of it. I am writing this letter because I fear that
your hesitation or your considerations are caused by more general
reflections, rather than by that single passage in my first letter which
indeed makes them necessary and which might have given me away. That
is the passage concerning the unbearableness of my job.

You will perhaps pass over what I say, but you shouldn't, you should
rather inquire into it very carefully, in which case I should carefully and
briefly have to answer you as follows. My job is unbearable to me because
it conflicts with my only desire and my only calling, which is literature.
Since I am nothing but literature and can and want to be nothing else,
my job will never take possession of me, it may, however, shatter me
completely, and this is by no means a remote possibility. Nervous states
of the worst sort control me without pause, and this year of worry and
torment about my and your daughter's future has revealed to the full my
inability to resist. You might ask why I do not give up this job and – I
have no money – do not try to support myself by literary work. To this
I can make only the miserable reply that I don't have the strength for it,
and that, as far as I can see, I shall instead be destroyed by this job, and
destroyed quickly.

And now compare me to your daughter, this healthy, gay, natural,
strong girl. As often as I have repeated it to her in perhaps five hundred
letters, and as often as she has calmed me with a 'no' that to be sure
has no very convincing basis – it nevertheless remains true that she must
be unhappy with me, so far as I can see. I am, not only because of my

external circumstances but even much more because of my essential nature, a reserved, silent, unsocial, dissatisfied person, but without being able to call this my misfortune, for it is only the reflection of my goal. Conclusions can at least be drawn from the sort of life I lead at home. Well, I live in my family, among the best and most lovable people, more strange than a stranger. I have not spoken an average of twenty words a day to my mother these last years, hardly ever said more than hello to my father. I do not speak at all to my married sisters and my brothers-in-law, and not because I have anything against them. The reason for it is simply this, that I have not the slightest thing to talk to them about. Everything that is not literature bores me and I hate it, for it disturbs me or delays me, if only because I think it does. I lack all aptitude for family life except, at best, as an observer. I have no family feeling and visitors make me almost feel as though I were maliciously being attacked.

A marriage could not change me, just as my job cannot change me.

30 August. Where am I to find salvation? How many untruths I no longer even knew about will be brought to the surface. If they are going to pervade our marriage as they pervaded the good-bye, then I have certainly done the right thing. In me, by myself, without human relationship, there are no visible lies. The limited circle is pure.[59]

14 October. The little street began with the wall of a graveyard on the one side and a low house with a balcony on the other. In the house lived the pensioned official, Friedrich Munch, and his sister, Elizabeth.

A herd of horses broke out of the enclosure.

Two friends went for a morning ride.

'Devils, save me from this benightedness!' shouted an old merchant who had wearily lain down on the sofa in the evening and now, in the night, got up with difficulty only by calling upon all his strength. There was a hollow knock at the door. 'Come in, come in, everything that is outside!' he shouted.

15 October. Perhaps I have caught hold of myself again, perhaps I secretly took the shorter way again, and now I, who already despair in loneliness, have pulled myself up again. But the headaches, the sleeplessness! Well, it is worth the struggle, or rather, I have no choice.

The stay in Riva was very important to me. For the first time I understood a Christian girl and lived almost entirely within the sphere of her influence. I am incapable of writing down the important things that I need to remember. This weakness of mine makes my dull head clear and empty only in order to preserve itself, but only insofar as the confusion lets itself be crowded off to the periphery. But I almost prefer this condition to the merely dull and indefinite pressure the uncertain release from which first would require a hammer to crush me.

Unsuccessful attempt to write to E. Weiss. And yesterday, in bed, the letter was boiling in my head.

To sit in the corner of a tram, your coat wrapped around you.

Prof. G. on the trip from Riva. His German-Bohemian nose reminding one of death, swollen, flushed, pimpled cheeks set on the bloodless leanness of his face, the blond, full beard around it. Possessed by a voracious appetite and thirst. The gulping down of the hot soup, the biting into and at the same time the licking of the unskinned heel of salami, the solemn gulps of the beer grown warm, the sweat breaking out around his nose. A loathsomeness that cannot be savoured to the full even by the greediest staring and sniffing.

The house was already locked up. There was light in two windows on the second floor, and in one window on the fourth floor as well. A carriage stopped before the house. A young man stepped to the lighted window on the fourth floor, opened it, and looked down into the street. In the moonlight.

It was already late in the evening. The student had lost all desire to continue working. Nor was it at all necessary, he had really made great progress the last few weeks, he could probably relax a little and reduce the amount of work he did at night. He closed his books and notebooks, arranged everything on his little table, and was about to undress and go to sleep. By accident, however, he looked towards the window, and when he saw the bright full moon it occurred to him that he might still take a short walk in the beautiful autumn night and somewhere or other, perhaps, refresh himself with a cup of black coffee. He turned out the lamp, took his hat, and opened the door to the kitchen. Usually it did not matter to him at all that he always had to go through the kitchen, this inconvenience also considerably reduced the rent of his room, but now and then, when there was an unusual amount of noise in the kitchen, or when, as today, he wanted to go out late in the evening, it was annoying.

In despair. Today, in the half-asleep during the afternoon: In the end the pain will really burst my head. And at the temples. What I saw when I pictured this to myself was really a gunshot wound, but around the hole the jagged edges were bent straight back, as in the case of a tin can violently torn open.

Don't forget Kropotkin![60]

20 October. The unimaginable sadness in the morning. In the evening read Jacobsohn's *Der Fall Jacobsohn*. This strength to live, to make decisions, joyfully to set one's foot in the right place. He sits in himself the way a practised rower sits in his boat and would sit in any boat. I wanted to write to him.

Instead of which I went for a walk, erased all the emotion I had absorbed in a conversation with Haas, whom I had run into, women excited me, I am now reading 'The Metamorphosis' at home and find it bad. Perhaps I am really lost, the sadness of this morning will return again, I shall not be able to resist it for long, it deprives me of all hope. I don't even have the desire to keep a diary, perhaps because there is already too much lacking in it, perhaps because I should perpetually have to describe incomplete – by all appearances *necessarily* incomplete – actions, perhaps because writing itself adds to my sadness.

I would gladly write fairy tales (why do I hate the word so?) that could please W. and that she might sometimes keep under the table at meals, read between courses, and blush fearfully when she noticed that the sanatorium doctor has been standing behind her for a little while now and watching her. Her excitement sometimes – or really all of the time – when she hears stories.

I notice that I am afraid of the almost physical strain of the effort to remember, afraid of the pain beneath which the floor of the thoughtless vacuum of the mind slowly opens up, or even merely heaves up a little in preparation. All things resist being written down. If I knew that her commandment not to mention her were at work here (I have kept it faithfully, almost without effort), then I should be satisfied, but it is nothing but inability. Besides, what am I to think of the fact that this evening, for a long while, I was pondering what the acquaintance with W. had cost me in pleasures with the Russian woman, who at night perhaps (this is by no means impossible) might have let me into her room, which was diagonally across from mine. While my evening's intercourse with W. was carried on in a language of knocks whose meaning we never definitely agreed upon. I knocked on the ceiling of my room below hers, received her answer, leaned out of the window, greeted her, once let myself be blessed by her, once snatched at a ribbon she let down, sat on the window sill for hours, heard every one of her steps above, mistakenly regarded every chance knock to be the sign of an understanding, heard her coughing, her singing before she fell asleep.

21 October. Lost day. Visit to the Ringhoffer factory, Ehrenfels's seminar, at Weltsch's, dinner, walk, now here at ten o'clock. I keep thinking of the black beetle,[61] but will not write.

In the small harbour of a fishing village a barque was being fitted out for a voyage. A young man in wide sailor-trousers was supervising the work. Two old sailors were carrying sacks and chests to a gangplank where a tall man, his legs spread wide, took everything and handed it over into hands that stretched towards him from the dark interior of the barque. On the large, square-hewn stones enclosing a corner of the dock, half reclining, sat five men, they blew the smoke of their pipes in all directions. From time to time the man in the wide sailor-trousers went up to them, made a little speech, and slapped them on the knees. Usually a wine jug was brought out from behind a stone in whose shade it was kept, and a glass of opaque red wine passed from man to man.

22 October. Too late. The sweetness of sorrow and of love. To be

234

smiled at by her in the boat. That was most beautiful of all. Always only the desire to die and the not-yet-yielding; this alone is love.

Yesterday's observation. The most appropriate situation for me: To listen to a conversation between two people who are discussing a matter that concerns them closely while I have only a very remote interest in it which is in addition completely selfless.

26 October. The family sat at dinner. Through the uncurtained windows one could look out into the tropic night.

'Who am I, then?' I rebuked myself. I got up from the sofa upon which I had been lying with my knees drawn up, and sat erect. The door, which led straight from the stairway into my room, opened and a young man with a bowed head and searching eyes entered. He walked, as far as this was possible in the narrow room, in a curve around the sofa and stopped in the darkness of the corner near the window. I wanted to see what kind of apparition this was, went over, and grasped the man by the arm. He was a living person. He looked up – a little shorter than I – at me with a smile, the very carelessness with which he nodded and said 'Just try me' should have convinced me. Despite that, I seized him in front by the waistcoat and at the back by the jacket and shook him. His beautiful, strong, gold watch-chain attracted my attention, I grabbed it and pulled down on it so that the buttonhole to which it was fastened tore. He put up with this, simply looked down at the damage, tried in vain to keep the waistcoat button in the torn buttonhole. 'What are you doing?' he said finally, and showed me the waistcoat. 'Just be quiet!' I said threateningly.

I began to run round the room, from a walk I passed into a trot, from a trot into a gallop, every time I passed the man I raised my fist to him. He did not even look at me but worked on his vest. I felt very free, even my breathing was extraordinary, my breast felt that only my clothes prevented it from heaving gigantically.

For many months Wilhelm Menz, a book-keeper, had been intending to accost a girl whom he used regularly to meet on the way to the office in the morning on a very long street, sometimes at one point, sometimes at another. He had already become reconciled to the fact that this would remain an intention – he was not very bold in the presence of women and, besides, the morning was not a propitious time to speak to a girl who was in a hurry – when it happened that one evening, about Christmas time, he saw the girl walking right in front of him. 'Miss,' he said. She turned, recognized the man whom she always encountered in the morning, without stopping let her eye rest on him for a moment, and since Menz said nothing further, turned away again. They were in a brightly lit street in the midst of a great crowd of people and Menz was able, without attracting attention, to step up quite close to her. In this moment of decision Menz could think of nothing to say, but he was resolved to remain a stranger to the girl no longer, for he definitely intended to carry farther something begun so seriously, and so he made bold enough to tug at the bottom of the girl's jacket. The girl suffered it as though nothing had happened.

6 November. Whence the sudden confidence? If it would only remain! If I could go in and out of every door in this way, a passably erect person. Only I don't know whether I want that.

We didn't want to tell our parents anything about it, but every evening after nine o'clock we met, I and two cousins, near the cemetery fence at a place where a little rise in the ground provided a good view.

The iron fence of the cemetery leaves a large, grass-grown place free on the left.

17 November. Dream: On a rising way, beginning at the left when seen from below, there lay, about at the middle of the slope and mostly in the road, a pile of rubbish or solidly packed clay that had crumbled lower and lower on the right while on the left it stood up as tall as the palings of a fence. I walked on the right where the way was almost clear and saw a man on a tricycle coming towards me from below and apparently riding straight at the obstacle. He was a man who seemed to have no eyes, at least his eyes looked like holes that had been effaced. The tricycle was rickety and went along in an uncertain and shaky fashion, but nevertheless without a sound, with almost exaggerated

quietness and ease. I seized the man at the last moment, held him as though he were the handle-bars of his vehicle, and guided the latter into the gap through which I had come. Then he fell towards me, I was as large as a giant now and yet had an awkward hold on him, besides, the vehicle, as though out of control, began to move backwards, even if slowly, and pulled me after it. We went past an open van on which a number of people were standing crowded together, all dressed in dark clothes, among them a Boy Scout wearing a light-grey hat with the brim turned up. I expected this boy, whom I had already recognized at some distance, to help me, but he turned away and squeezed himself in among the people. Then, behind this open van – the tricycle kept rolling on and I, bent low, with legs astraddle, had to follow – there came towards me someone who brought me help, but whom I cannot remember. I only know that he was a trustworthy person who is now concealing himself as though behind a black cloth curtain and whose concealment I should respect.

18 November. I will write again, but how many doubts have I meanwhile had about my writing? At bottom I am an incapable, ignorant person who, if he had not been compelled – without any effort on his own part and scarcely aware of the compulsion – to go to school, would be fit only to crouch in a kennel, to leap out when food is offered him, and to leap back when he has swallowed it.

Two dogs in a yard into which the sun shone hotly ran towards each other from opposite directions.

Worried and slaved over the beginning of a letter to Miss Bl.

19 November. The reading of the diary moves me. Is it because I no longer have the slightest confidence now? Everything appears to me to be an artificial construction of the mind. Every mark by someone else, every chance look throws everything in me over on the other side, even what has been forgotten, even what is entirely insignificant. I am more uncertain than I ever was, I feel only the power of life. And I am senselessly empty. I am really like a lost sheep in the night and in the mountains, or like a sheep which is running after this sheep. To be so lost and not have the strength to regret it.

I intentionally walk through the streets where there are whores. Walking past them excites me, the remote but nevertheless existent possibility of going with one. Is that grossness? But I know no better, and doing this seems basically innocent to me and causes me almost no regret. I want only the stout, older ones, with outmoded clothes that have, however, a certain luxuriousness because of various adornments. One woman probably knows me by now. I met her this afternoon, she was not yet in her working clothes, her hair was still flat against her head, she was wearing no hat, a work blouse like a cook's, and was carrying a bundle of some sort, perhaps to the laundress. No one would have found anything exciting in her, only me. We looked at each other fleetingly. Now, in the evening, it had meanwhile grown cold, I saw her, wearing a tight-fitting, yellowish-brown coat, on the other side of the narrow street that branches off from Zeltnerstrasse, where she has her beat. I looked back at her twice, she caught the glance too, but then I really ran away from her.

This uncertainty is surely the result of thinking about F.

20 November. Was at the cinema. *Lolotte*. The good minister. The little bicycle. The reconciliation of the parents. Was tremendously entertained. Before it, a sad film, *The Accident on the Dock*, after it, the gay *Alone at Last*. Am entirely empty and insensible, the passing tram has more living feeling.

21 November. Dream: The French cabinet, four men, is sitting around a table. A conference is taking place. I remember the man sitting on the long right side of the table, with his face flattened out in profile, yellowish-coloured skin, his very straight nose jutting far forward (jutting so far forward because of the flatness of his face) and an oily, black, heavy moustache arching over his mouth.

Miserable observation which again is certainly the result of something artificially constructed whose lower end is swinging in emptiness somewhere: When I picked up the inkwell from the desk to carry it into the living-room I felt a sort of firmness in me, just as, for instance, the corner of a tall building appears in the mist and at once disappears again. I did not feel lost, something waited in me that was independent of people, even of F. What would happen if I were to run away, as one sometimes runs through the fields?

These predictions, this imitating of models, this fear of something definite, is ridiculous. These are constructions that even in the imagination, where they are alone sovereign, only approach the living surface but then are always suddenly driven under. Who has the magic hand to thrust into the machinery without its being torn to pieces and scattered by a thousand knives?

I am on the hunt for constructions. I come into a room and find them whitely merging in a corner.

24 November. Evening before last at Max's. He is becoming more and more a stranger, he has often been one to me, now I am becoming one to him too. Yesterday evening simply went to bed.

A dream towards morning: I am sitting in the garden of a sanatorium at a long table, at the very head, and in the dream I actually see my back. It is a gloomy day, I must have gone on a trip and am in a motor-car that arrived a short time ago, driving up in a curve to the front of the platform. They are just about to bring in the food when I see one of the waitresses, a young, delicate girl wearing a dress the colour of autumn leaves, approaching with a very light or unsteady step through the pillared hall that served as the porch of the sanatorium, and going down into the garden. I don't yet know what she wants but nevertheless point questioningly at myself to learn whether she wants me. And in fact she brings me a letter. I think, this can't be the letter I'm expecting, it is a very thin letter and a strange, thin, unsure handwriting. But I open it and a great number of thin sheets covered in writing come out, all of them in the strange handwriting. I begin to read, leaf through the pages, and recognize that it must be a very important letter and apparently from F.'s youngest sister. I eagerly begin to read, then my neighbour on the right, I don't know whether man or woman, probably a child, looks down over my arm at the letter. I scream, 'No!' The round table of nervous people begins to tremble. I have probably caused a disaster. I attempt to apologize with a few hasty words in order to be able to go on with the reading. I bend over my letter again, only to wake up without resistance, as if awakened by my own scream. With complete awareness I force myself to fall asleep again, the scene reappears, in fact I quickly read two or three more misty lines of the letter, nothing of which I remember, and lose the dream in further sleep.

The old merchant, a huge man, his knees giving way beneath him, mounted the stairs to his room, not holding the banister but rather pressing against it with his hand. He was about to take his keys out of his trouser pocket, as he always did, in front of the door to the room, a latticed glass door, when he noticed in a dark corner a young man who now bowed.

'Who are you? What do you want?' asked the merchant, still groaning from the exertion of the climb.

'Are you the merchant Messner?' the young man asked.

'Yes,' said the merchant.

'Then I have some information for you. Who I am is really beside the point here, for I myself have no part at all in the matter, am only delivering the message. Nevertheless I will introduce myself, my name is Kette and I am a student.'

'So,' said Messner, considering this for a moment. 'Well, and the message?' he then said.

'We can discuss that better in your room,' said the student. 'It is something that can't be disposed of on the stairs.'

'I didn't know that I was to receive any such message,' said Messner, and looked out of the corner of his eye at the floor.

'That may be,' said the student.

'Besides,' said Messner, 'it is past eleven o'clock now, no one will overhear us here.'

'No,' the student replied, 'it is impossible for me to say it here.'

'And I,' said Messner, 'do not receive guests at night,' and he stuck the key into the lock so violently that the other keys in the bunch continued to jingle for a while.

'Now look, I've been waiting here since eight o'clock, three hours,' said the student.

'That only proves that the message is important to you. But I don't want to receive any messages. Every message that I am spared is a gain, I am not curious, only go, go.' He took the student by his thin overcoat and pushed him away a little. Then he partly opened the door and tremendous heat flowed from the room into the cold hall. 'Besides, is it a business message?' he asked further, when he was already standing in the open doorway.

'That too I cannot say here,' said the student.

'Then I wish you good night,' said Messner, went into his room, locked the door with the key, turned on the light of the electric bed-lamp, filled a small glass at a little wall cabinet in which were several bottles of liquor, emptied it with a smack of his lips, and began to undress. Leaning back against the high pillows, he was on the point of beginning to read a newspaper when it seemed to him that someone was knocking softly on the door. He laid the newspaper back on the bed cover, crossed his arms, and listened. And in fact the knock was repeated, very softly and as though down very low on the door. 'A really impertinent puppy,' laughed Messner. When the knocking stopped, he again picked up the newspaper. But now the knocking came more strongly, there was a real banging on the door. The knocking came the way children at play scatter their knocks over the whole door, now down low, dull against the wood, now up high, clear against the glass. 'I shall have to get up,' Messner thought, shaking his head. 'I can't telephone the housekeeper because the instrument is over there in the ante-room and I should have to wake the landlady to get to it. There's nothing else I can do except to throw the boy down the stairs myself.' He pulled a felt cap over his head, threw back the cover, pulled himself to the edge of the bed with his weight on his hands, slowly put his feet on the floor, and pulled on high, quilted slippers. 'Well now,' he thought, and, chewing his upper lip, stared at the door; 'now it is quiet again. But I must have peace once and for all,' he then said to himself, pulled a stick with a horn knob out of a stand, held it by the middle, and went to the door.

'Is anyone still out there?' he asked through the closed door.

'Yes,' came the answer. 'Please open the door for me.'

'I'll open it,' said Messner, opened the door and stepped out holding the stick.

'Don't hit me,' said the student threateningly, and took a step back-ward.

241

'Then go!' said Messner, and pointed his index finger in the direction of the stairs.

'But I can't,' said the student, and ran up to Messner so surprisingly –

27 November. I must stop without actually being shaken off. Nor do I feel any danger that I might get lost, still, I feel helpless and an outsider. The firmness, however, which the most insignificant writing brings about in me is beyond doubt and wonderful. The comprehensive view I had of everything on my walk yesterday!

The child of the housekeeper who opened the gate. Bundled up in a woman's old shawl, pale, numb, fleshy little face. At night is carried to the gate like that by the housekeeper.

The housekeeper's poodle that sits downstairs on a step and listens when I begin tramping down from the fourth floor, looks at me when I pass by. Pleasant feeling of intimacy, since he is not frightened by me and includes me in the familiar house and its noise.

Picture: Baptism of the cabin boys when crossing the equator. The sailors lounging around. The ship, clambered over in every direction and at every level, everywhere provides them with places to sit. The tall sailors hanging on the ship's ladders, one foot in front of the other, pressing their powerful, round shoulders against the side of the ship and looking down on the play.

[*A small room.* ELSA *and* GERTRUD *are sitting at the window with their needlework. It is beginning to get dark.*]

E: Someone is ringing. [*Both listen.*]

G: Was there really a ring? I didn't hear anything, I keep hearing less all the time.

E: It was just very low. [*Goes into the ante-room to open the door. A few words are exchanged. Then the voice.*]

E: Please step in here. Be careful not to stumble. Please walk ahead, there's only my sister in the room.

Recently the cattle-dealer Morsin told us the following story. He was still excited when he told it, despite the fact that the matter is several months old now:

'I very often have business in the city, on the average it certainly comes to ten days a month. Since I must usually spend the night there too, and have always tried, whenever it is at all possible, to avoid stopping at a hotel, I rented a private room that simply –'

4 December. Viewed from the outside it is terrible for a young but mature person to die, or worse, to kill himself. Hopelessly to depart in a complete confusion that would make sense only within a further development, or with the sole hope that in the great account this appearance in life will be considered as not having taken place. Such would be my plight now. To die would mean nothing else than to surrender a nothing to the nothing, but that would be impossible to conceive, for how could a person, even only as a nothing, consciously surrender himself to the nothing, and not merely to an empty nothing but rather to a roaring nothing whose nothingness consists only in its incomprehensibility.

A group of men, masters and servants. Rough-hewn faces shining with living colours. The master sits down and the servant brings him food on a tray. Between the two there is no greater difference, no difference of another category than, for instance, that between a man who as a result of countless circumstances is an Englishman and lives in London, and another who is a Laplander and at the very same instant is sailing on the sea, alone in his boat during a storm. Certainly the servant can – and this only under certain conditions – become a master, but this question, no matter how it may be answered, does not change anything here, for this is a matter that concerns the present evaluation of a present situation.

The unity of mankind, now and then doubted, even if only emotionally, by everyone, even by the most approachable and adaptable person, on the other hand also reveals itself to everyone, or seems to reveal itself, in the complete harmony, discernible time and again, between the development of mankind as a whole and of the individual man. Even in the most secret emotions of the individual.

The fear of folly. To see folly in every emotion that strives straight ahead and makes one forget everything else. What, then, is non-folly? Non-folly is to stand like a beggar before the threshold, to one side of the entrance, to rot and collapse. But P. and O. are really disgusting fools. There must be follies greater than those who perpetrate them. What is disgusting, perhaps, is this puffing-themselves-up of the little fools in their great folly. But did not Christ appear in the same light to the Pharisees?

Wonderful, entirely self-contradictory idea that someone who died at 3 a.m., for instance, immediately thereafter, about dawn, enters into a higher life. What incompatibility there is between the visibly human and everything else! How out of one mystery there always comes a greater one! In the first moment the breath leaves the human calculator. Really one should be afraid to step out of one's house.

5 December. How furious I am with my mother! I need only begin to talk to her and I am irritated, almost scream.

O. is really suffering and I do not believe that she is suffering, that she is capable of suffering, do not believe it in the face of my knowing better, do not believe it in order not to have to stand by her, which I could not do, for she irritates me too.

Externally I see only little details of F., at least sometimes, so few they may be counted. By these her picture is made clear, pure, original, distinct, and lofty, all at once.

8 December. Artificial constructions in Weiss's novel. The strength to abolish them, the duty to do so. I almost deny experience. I want peace, step by step or running, but not calculated leaps by grasshoppers.

9 December. Weiss's *Galeere*. Weakening of the effect when the end of the story begins. The world is conquered and we have watched it with open eyes. We can therefore quietly turn away and live on.

Hatred of active introspection. Explanations of one's soul, such as: Yesterday I was so, and for this reason; today I am so, and for this reason. It is not true, not for this reason and not for that reason, and therefore also not so and so. To put up with oneself calmly, without being precipitate, to live as one must, not to chase one's tail like a dog.

I fell asleep in the underbush. A noise awakened me. I found in my hands a book in which I had previously been reading. I threw it away and sprang up. It was shortly after midday; in front of the hill on which I stood there lay spread out a great lowland with villages and ponds and uniformly shaped, tall, reed-like hedges between them. I put my hands on my hips, examined everything with my eyes, and at the same time listened to the noise.

10 December. Discoveries have forced themselves on people.

The laughing, boyish, sly, revealing face of the chief inspector, a face that I have never before seen him wear and noticed only today at the moment when I was reading him a report by the director and happened to glance up from it. At the same time he also stuck his right hand into his trouser pocket with a shrug of his shoulder as though he were another person.

It is never possible to take note of and evaluate all the circumstances that influence the mood of the moment, are even at work within it, and finally are at work in the evaluation, hence it is false to say that I felt resolute yesterday, that I am in despair today. Such differentiations only prove that one desires to influence oneself, and, as far removed from oneself as possible, hidden behind prejudices and fantasies, temporarily to create an artificial life, as sometimes someone in the corner of a tavern, sufficiently concealed behind a small glass of whisky, entirely alone with himself, entertains himself with nothing but false, unprovable imaginings and dreams.

Towards midnight a young man in a tight, pale-grey, checked overcoat sprinkled with snow came down the stairs into the little music hall. He paid his admission at the cashier's desk behind which a dozing young lady started up and looked straight at him with large, black eyes, and then he stopped for a moment to survey the hall lying three steps below him.

Almost every evening I go to the railway station; today, because it was raining, I walked up and down the hall there for half an hour. The boy who kept eating candy from the slot machine. His reaching into his pocket, out of which he pulls a pile of change, the careless dropping of a coin into the slot, reading the labels while he eats, the dropping of some pieces which he picks up from the dirty floor and sticks right into his mouth. The man, calmly chewing, who is speaking confidentially at the window with a woman, a relative.

11 December. In Toynbee Hall read the beginning of *Michael Kohlhaas*. Complete and utter fiasco. Badly chosen, badly presented, finally swam senselessly around in the text. Model audience. Very small boys in the front row. One of them tries to overcome his innocent boredom by carefully throwing his cap on the floor and then carefully picking it up, and then again, over and over. Since he is too small to accomplish this from his seat, he has to keep sliding off the chair a little. Read wildly and badly and carelessly and unintelligibly. And in the afternoon I was already trembling with eagerness to read, could hardly keep my mouth shut.

No push is really needed, only a withdrawal of the last force placed at my disposal, and I fall into a despair that rips me to pieces. Today, when I imagined that I would certainly be calm during the lecture, I asked myself what sort of calm this would be, on what it would be based, and I could only say that it would merely be a calm for its own sake, an incomprehensible grace, nothing else.

12 December. And in the morning I got up relatively quite fresh.

Yesterday, on my way home, the little boy bundled in grey who was running along beside a group of boys, hitting himself on the thigh, catching hold of another boy with his other hand, and shouting – rather absentmindedly, which I must not forget – '*Dnes to bylo docela hezky*' ['Very nicely done today'].[62]

The freshness with which, after a somewhat altered division of the day, I walked along the street about six o'clock today. Ridiculous observation, when will I get rid of this habit.

I looked closely at myself in the mirror a while ago – though only by artificial light and with the light coming from behind me, so that actually only the down at the edges of my ears was illuminated – and my face, even after fairly close examination, appeared to me better than I know it to be. A clear, well-shaped, almost beautifully outlined face. The black of the hair, the brows and the eye sockets stand livingly forth from the rest of the passive mass. The glance is by no means haggard, there is no trace of that, but neither is it childish, rather unbelievably energetic, but perhaps only because it was observing me, since I was just then observing myself and wanted to frighten myself.

12 December. Yesterday did not fall asleep for a long time. F. B. Finally decided – and with that I fell uncertainly asleep – to ask Weiss to go to her office with a letter, and to write nothing else in this letter other than that I must have news from her or about her and have therefore sent Weiss there so that he might write to me about her. Meanwhile Weiss is sitting beside her desk, waits until she has finished reading the letter, bows, and – since he has no further instructions and it is highly unlikely that he will receive an answer – leaves.

Discussion evening at the officials' club. I presided. Funny, what sources of self-respect one can draw upon. My introductory sentence: 'I must begin the discussion this evening with a regret that it is taking place.' For I was not advised in time and therefore not prepared.

14 December. Lecture by Beerman. Nothing, but presented with a self-satisfaction that is here and there contagious. Girlish face with a goitre. Before almost every sentence the same contraction of muscles in his face as in sneezing. A verse from the Christmas Fair in his newspaper column today.

> Sir, buy it for your little lad
> So he'll laugh and not be sad.

Quoted Shaw: 'I am a sedentary, faint-hearted civilian.'

Wrote a letter to F. in the office.

The fright this morning on the way to the office when I met the girl from the seminar who resembles F., for the moment did not know who it was and simply saw that she resembled F., was not F., but had some sort of further relationship to F. beyond that, namely this, that in the seminar, at the sight of her, I thought of F. a great deal.

Now read in Dostoyevsky the passage that reminds me so of my 'being unhappy'.

When I put my left hand inside my trousers while I was reading and felt the lukewarm upper part of my thigh.

15 December. Letters to Dr Weiss and Uncle Alfred. No telegram came.

Read *Wir Jungen von 1870–1*. Again read with suppressed sobs of the victories and scenes of enthusiasm. To be a father and speak calmly to one's son. For this, however, one shouldn't have a little toy hammer in place of a heart.

'Have you written to your uncle yet?' my mother asked me, as I had maliciously been expecting for some time. She had long been watching me with concern, for various reasons did not dare in the first place to ask me, and in the second place to ask me in front of my father, and at last, in her concern when she saw that I was about to leave, asked me nevertheless. When I passed behind her chair she looked up from her cards, turned her face to me with a long-vanished, tender motion somehow revived for the moment, and asked me, looking up only furtively, smiling shyly, and already humbled in the asking of the question, before any answer had been received.

16 December. 'The thundering scream of the seraphim's delight.'

I sat in the rocking-chair at Weltsch's, we spoke of the disorder of our lives, he always with a certain confidence ('One must want the impossible'), I without it, eyeing my fingers with the feeling that I was the representative of my inner emptiness, an emptiness that replaces everything else and is not even very great.

17 December. Letter to W. commissioning him 'to overflow and yet be only a pot on the cold hearth'.

Lecture by Bergmann, 'Moses and the Present'. Pure impression – In any event I have nothing to do with it. The truly terrible paths between freedom and slavery cross each other with no guide to the way ahead and accompanied by an immediate obliterating of those paths already traversed. There are a countless number of such paths, or only one, it cannot be determined, for there is no vantage ground from which to observe. There am I. I cannot leave. I have nothing to complain about. I do not suffer excessively, for I do not suffer consistently, it does not pile up, at least I do not feel it for the time being, and the degree of my suffering is far less than the suffering that is perhaps my due.

The silhouette of a man who, his arms half raised at different levels, confronts the thick mist in order to enter it.

The good, strong way in which Judaism separates things. There is room there for a person. One sees oneself better, one judges oneself better.

18 December. I am going to sleep, I am tired. Perhaps it has already been decided there. Many dreams about it.

19 December. Letter from F. Beautiful morning, warmth in my blood.

20 December. No letter.

The effect of a peaceful face, calm speech, especially when exercised by a strange person one hasn't seen through yet. The voice of God out of a human mouth.

An old man walked through the streets in the mist one winter evening. It was icy cold. The streets were empty. No one passed near him, only now and then he saw in the distance, half concealed by the mist, a tall policeman or a woman in furs or shawls. Nothing troubled him, he merely intended to visit a friend at whose house he had not been for a long time and who had just now sent a servant girl to ask him to come.

It was long past midnight when there came a soft knock on the door of the room of the merchant Messner. It wasn't necessary to wake him, he fell asleep only towards morning, and until that time he used to lie awake in bed on his belly, his face pressed into the pillow, his arms extended, and his hands clasped over his head. He had heard the knocking immediately. 'Who is it?' he asked. An indistinct murmur, softer than the knocking, replied. 'The door is open,' he said, and turned on the electric light. A small, delicate woman in a large grey shawl entered.

❧ ❧ ❧

2 January. A lot of time well spent with Dr Weiss.

4 January. We had scooped out a hollow in the sand, where we felt quite comfortable. At night we rolled up together inside the hollow, Father covered it over with trunks of trees, scattering underbrush on top, and we were as well protected as we could be from storms and wild beasts. 'Father,' we would often call out in fright when it had already grown dark under the tree trunks and Father had still not appeared. But then we would see his feet through a crack, he would slide in beside us, would give each of us a little pat, for it calmed us to feel his hand, and then we would all fall asleep as it were together. In addition to our parents we were five boys and three girls; the hollow was too small for us, but we should have felt afraid if we had not been so close to one another at night.

5 January. Afternoon. Goethe's father was senile when he died. At the time of his father's last illness Goethe was working on *Iphigenie.*

'Take that woman home, she's drunk,' some court official said to Goethe about Christiane.

August, a drunkard like his mother, vulgarly ran around with common women. Ottilie, whom he did not love but was made to marry by his father for social reasons.

250

Wolf, the diplomat and writer.

Walter, the musician, couldn't pass his examinations. Withdrew into the Gartenhaus for months; when the Tsarina wanted to see him: 'Tell the Tsarina that I am not a wild animal.' 'My conscience is more lead than iron.'

Wolf's petty, ineffectual literary efforts.

The old people in the garret rooms. Eighty-year-old Ottilie, fifty-year-old Wolf, and their old acquaintances.

Only in such extremes does one become aware of how every person is lost in himself beyond hope of rescue, and one's sole consolation in this is to observe other people and the law governing them and everything. How, outwardly, Wolf can be guided, moved here or there, cheered up, encouraged, induced to work systematically – and how, inwardly, he is held fast and immovable.

Why don't the Tchuktchis simply leave their awful country; considering their present life and wants they would be better off anywhere else. But they cannot; all things possible do happen, only what happens is possible.

A wine cellar had been set up in the small town of F. by a wine dealer from the larger city near by. He had rented a small vaulted cellar in a house on the Ringplatz, painted oriental decorations on the wall, and had put in old plush furniture almost past its usefulness.

6 January. Dilthey: *Das Erlebnis und die Dichtung:* Love for humanity, the highest respect for all the forms it has taken; stands back quietly in the best post from which he can observe. On Luther's early writings: 'the mighty shades, attracted by murder and blood, that step from an invisible world into the visible one' – Pascal.

Letter for A. to his mother-in-law. Liesl kissed the teacher.

8 January. Fantl recited *Tête d'or*:[63] 'He hurls the enemy about like a barrel.'

Uncertainty, aridity, peace – all things will resolve themselves into these and pass away.

What have I in common with Jews? I have hardly anything in common with myself and should stand very quietly in a corner, content that I can breathe.

Description of inexplicable emotions. A.: Since that happened, the sight of women has been painful to me, it is neither sexual excitement nor pure sorrow, it is simply pain. That's the way it was too before I felt sure of Liesl.

12 January. Yesterday: Ottilie's love affairs, the young Englishman – Tolstoy's engagement; I have a clear impression of a young, sensitive, and violent person, restraining himself, full of forebodings. Well dressed, dark, and dark blue.

The girl in the coffee-house. Her tight skirt, her white, loose, fur-trimmed silk blouse, bare throat, close-fitting grey hat. Her full, laughing, eternally pulsating face; friendly eyes, though a little affected. My face flushes whenever I think of F.

Clear night on the way home; distinctly aware of what in me is mere dull apathy, so far removed from a great clarity expanding without hindrance.

Nikolai *Literaturbriefe*.
There are possibilities for me, certainly; but under what stone do they lie?

Carried forward on the horse –

Youth's meaninglessness. Fear of youth, fear of meaninglessness, of the meaningless rise of an inhuman life.

Tellheim: 'He has – what only the creations of true poets possess – that spontaneous flexibility of the inner life which, as circumstances alter, continually surprises us by revealing entirely new facets of itself.'[64]

19 January. Anxiety alternating with self-assurance at the office. Otherwise more confident. Great antipathy to 'Metamorphosis'. Unreadable ending. Imperfect almost to its very marrow. It would have turned out much better if I had not been interrupted at the time by the business trip.

23 January. B., the chief auditor, tells the story of a friend of his, a half-pay colonel who likes to sleep beside an open window: 'During the night it is very pleasant; but in the morning, when I have to shovel the snow off the ottoman near the window and then start shaving, it is unpleasant.'

Memoirs of Countess Thürheim: 'Her gentle nature made her especially fond of Racine. I have often heard her praying God that He might grant him eternal peace.'

There is no doubt that at the great dinners given in his honour at Vienna by the Russian ambassador Count Rasumovsky, he (Suvorov) ate like a glutton the food served upon the table without pausing for a soul. When he was full he would get up and leave the guests to themselves.

To judge by an engraving, a frail, determined, pedantic old man.

'It wasn't your fate,' my mother's lame consolation. The bad part of it is, that at the moment it is almost all the consolation that I need. There is my weak point and will remain my weak point; otherwise the regular, hardly varying, semi-active life I have led these last days (worked at the office on a description of our bureau's activities; A.'s worries about his bride; Ottla's Zionism; the girls' enjoyment of the Salten-Schildkraut lecture; reading the memoirs of Thürheim; letters to Weiss and Löwy; proof-reading 'Metamorphosis') has really pulled me together and instilled some resolution and hope in me.

24 January. Napoleonic era: the festivities came hard upon each other, everyone was in a hurry 'to taste to the full the joys of the brief interlude of peace'. 'On the other hand, the women exercised an influence as if in passing, they had really no time to lose. In those days love

expressed itself in an intensified enthusiasm and a greater abandonment.' 'In our time there is no longer any excuse for passing an empty hour.'

Incapable of writing a few lines to Miss Bl., two letters already remain unanswered, today the third came. I grasp nothing correctly and at the same time I feel quite hale, though hollow. Recently, when I got out of the elevator at my usual hour, it occurred to me that my life, whose days more and more repeat themselves down to the smallest detail, resembles that punishment in which each pupil must according to his offence write down the same meaningless (in repetition, at least) sentence ten times, a hundred times or even oftener; except that in my case the punishment is given me with only this limitation: 'as many times as you can stand it'.

A. cannot calm himself. In spite of the confidence he has in me and in spite of the fact that he wants my advice, I always learn the worst details only incidentally in the course of the conversation, whereupon I have always to suppress my sudden astonishment as much as I can – not without a feeling that my indifference in face of the dreadful news either must strike him as coldness, or on the contrary must greatly console him. And in fact so I mean it. I learn the story of the kiss in the following stages, some of them weeks apart: A teacher kissed her; she was in his room; he kissed her several times; she went to his room regularly because she was doing some needlework for A.'s mother and the teacher had a good lamp; she let herself be kissed without resistance; he had already made her a declaration of his love; she still goes for walks with him in spite of everything, wanted to give him a Christmas present; once she wrote, Something unpleasant has happened to me but nothing came of it.

A. questioned her in the following way: How did it happen? I want to know all the details. Did he only kiss you? How often? Where? Didn't he lie on you? Did he touch you? Did he want to take off your clothes?

Answer: I was sitting on the sofa with my sewing, he on the other side of the table. Then he came over, sat down beside me, and kissed me; I moved away from him towards the arm of the sofa and was pressed down with my head against the arm. Except for the kiss, nothing happened.

During the questioning she once said: 'What are you thinking of? I *am* a virgin.'

Now that I think of it, my letter to Dr Weiss was written in such a way that it could all be shown to F. Suppose he did that today and for that reason put off his answer?

26 January. Unable to read Thürheim, though she has been my delight these past few days. Letter to Miss Bl. now sent on its way. How it has hold of me and presses against my brow. Father and Mother playing cards at the same table.

The parents and their grown children, a son and a daughter, were seated at table Sunday noon. The mother had just stood up and was dipping the ladle into the round-bellied tureen to serve the soup, when suddenly the whole table lifted up, the tablecloth fluttered, the hands lying on the table slid off, the soup with its tumbling bacon balls spilled into the father's lap.

The way I almost insulted my mother just now because she had lent Elli[65] *Die böse Unschuld*, which I had myself intended to offer her only yesterday. 'Leave me my books! I have nothing else.' Speeches of this kind in a real rage.

The death of Thürheim's father: 'The doctors who came in soon thereafter found his pulse very weak and gave the invalid only a few more hours to live. My God, it was my father they were speaking of! A few hours only, and then dead.'

28 January. Lecture on the miracles of Lourdes. Free-thinking doctor; bares his strong and energetic teeth, takes great delight in rolling his words. 'It is time that German thoroughness and probity stand up to Latin charlatanism.' Newsboys of the *Messager de Lourdes*: '*Superbe guérison de ce soir!*' '*Guérison affirmée!*' – Discussion: 'I am a simple postal official, nothing more.' 'Hôtel de l'Univers.' –

Infinite sadness as I left, thinking of F. Am gradually calmed by my reflections.

Sent letter and Weiss's *Galeere* to Bl.

Quite some time ago A.'s sister was told by a fortune-teller that her eldest brother was engaged and that his fiancée was deceiving him. At that time he rejected all such stories in a rage. I: 'Why only at that time? It is as false today as it was then. She hasn't deceived you, has she?' He: 'It's true that she hasn't, isn't it?'

2 February. A.: A girl friend's lewd letter to his fiancée. 'If we were to take everything as seriously as when we were under the domination of the confessional sermons.' 'Why were you so backward in Prague, better to have one's fling on a small scale than a large.' I interpret the letter according to my own opinion, in favour of his fiancée, with several good arguments occurring to me.

Yesterday A. was in Schluckenau. Sat in the room with her all day holding the bundle of letters (his only baggage) in his hand and didn't stop questioning her. Learned nothing new; an hour before leaving he asked her: 'Was the light out during the kissing?' and learned the news, which makes him inconsolable, that the second time W. kissed her he switched off the light. W. sat sketching on one side of the table, L. sat on the other (in W.'s room, at 11 p.m.) and read *Asmus Semper* aloud. Then W. got up, went to the chest to get something (a compass, L. thinks, A. thinks a contraceptive), then suddenly switched off the light, overwhelmed her with kisses; she sank down on the sofa, he held her arms, her shoulders, and kept saying, 'Kiss me!'

L. on another occasion: 'W. is very clumsy.' Another time: 'I didn't kiss him.' Another time: 'I felt as if I were lying in your arms.'

A. 'I must find out the truth, mustn't I?' (he is thinking of having her examined by a doctor). 'Only suppose I learn on the wedding night that she has been lying. Perhaps she's so calm only because he used a contraceptive.'

Lourdes: Attack on faith in miracles, also attack on the church. With equal justification he could argue against the churches, processions, confessions, the unhygienic practices everywhere, since it can't be proved that prayer does any good. Karlsbad is a greater swindle than Lourdes; Lourdes has the advantage that people go there out of deepest conviction. What about the crackpot notions people have concerning operations, serum therapy, vaccination, medicines?

On the other hand: The huge hospitals for the pilgrimaging invalids; the filthy piscinas; the brancards waiting for the special trains; the medical commission; the great incandescent crosses on the mountains; the Pope receives three million a year. The priest with the monstrance passes by, a woman screams from her stretcher, 'I am cured!' Her tuberculosis of the bone continues unchanged.

The door opened a crack. A revolver appeared and an outstretched arm.

Thürheim, II, 35, 28, 37: nothing sweeter than love, nothing pleasanter than flirtation; 45, 48: Jews.

10 February. Eleven o'clock, after a walk. Fresher than usual. Why?
1. Max said I was calm.
2. Felix is going to be married (was angry with him).
3. I remain alone, unless F. will still have me after all.
4. Mrs X.'s invitation; I think how I shall introduce myself to her.

By chance I walked in the direction opposite to my usual one, that is, Kettensteg, Hradčany, Karlsbrücke. Ordinarily I nearly collapse on this road; today, coming from the opposite direction, I felt somewhat lifted up.

11 February. Hastily read through Dilthey's *Goethe*; tumultuous impression, carries one along, why couldn't one set oneself afire and be destroyed in the flames? Or obey, even if one hears no command? Or sit on a chair in the middle of one's empty room and look at the floor? Or shout 'Forward!' in a mountain defile and hear answering shouts and see people emerge from all the bypaths in the cliffs.

13 February. Yesterday at Mrs X.'s. Calm and energetic, an energy that is perfect, triumphant, penetrating, that finds its way into everything with eyes, hands, and feet. Her frankness, a frank gaze. I keep

remembering the ugly, huge, ceremonious Renaissance hats with ostrich feathers that she used to wear; she repelled me so long as I didn't know her personally. How her muff, when she hurries towards the point of her story, is pressed against her body and yet twitches. Her children, A. and B.

Reminds one a good deal of W. in her looks, in her self-forgetfulness in the story, in her complete absorption, in her small, lively body, even in her hard, hollow voice, in her talk of fine clothes and hats at the same time that she herself wears nothing of the sort.

View from the window of the river. At many points in the conversation, in spite of the fact that she never allows it to flag, my complete failure, vacant gaze, incomprehension of what she is saying; I mechanically drop the silliest remarks at the same time that I am forced to see how closely she attends to them; I stupidly pet her little child.

Dreams: In Berlin, through the streets to her house, calm and happy in the knowledge that, though I haven't arrived at her house yet, a slight possibility of doing so exists; I shall certainly arrive there. I see the streets, on a white house a sign, something like 'The Splendours of the North' (saw it in the paper yesterday); in my dream 'Berlin W' has been added to it. Ask the way of an affable, red-nosed old policeman who in this instance is stuffed into a sort of butler's livery. Am given excessively detailed directions, he even points out the railing of a small park in the distance which I must keep hold of for safety's sake when I go past. Then advice about the tram-car, the U-Bahn, etc. I can't follow him any longer and ask in a fright, knowing full well that I am underestimating the distance: 'That's about half an hour away?' But the old man answers, 'I can make it in six minutes.' What joy! Some man, a shadow, a companion, is always at my side, I don't know who it is. Really have no time to turn around, to turn sideways.

Live in Berlin in some pension or other apparently filled with young Polish Jews; very small rooms. I spill a bottle of water. One of them is tapping incessantly on a small typewriter, barely turns his head when he is asked for something. Impossible to lay hands on a map of Berlin. In the hand of one of them I continually notice a book that looks like a map. But it always proves to be something entirely different, a list of the Berlin schools, tax statistics, or something of the sort.

I don't want to believe it, but, smiling, they prove it to me beyond any doubt.

14 February. There will certainly be no one to blame if I should kill myself, even if the immediate cause should for instance appear to be F.'s behaviour. Once, half asleep, I pictured the scene that would ensue if, in anticipation of the end, the letter of farewell in my pocket, I should come to her house, should be rejected as a suitor, lay the letter on the table, go to the balcony, break away from all those who run up to hold me back, and, forcing one hand after another to let go its grip, jump over the ledge. The letter, however, would say that I was jumping off because of F., but that even if my proposal had been accepted nothing essential would have been changed for me. My place is down below, I can find no other solution, F. simply happens to be the one through whom my fate is made manifest; I can't live without her and must jump, yet – and this F. suspects – I couldn't live with her either. Why not use tonight for the purpose, I can already see before me the people talking at the parents' gathering this evening, talking of life and the conditions that have to be created for it – but I cling to abstractions, I live completely entangled in life, I won't do it, I am cold, am sad that a shirt collar is pinching my neck, am damned, gasp for breath in the mist.

15 February. How long this Saturday and Sunday seem in retrospect. Yesterday afternoon I had my hair cut, then wrote the letter to Bl., then was over at Max's new place for a moment, then the parents' gathering, sat next to L.W., then Baum (met Kr. in the tram), then on the way home Max's complaints about my silence, then my longing for suicide, then my sister returned from the parents' gathering unable to report the least thing. In bed until ten, sleepless, sorrow after sorrow. No letter, not here, not in the office, mailed a letter to Bl. at the Franz-Josef station, saw G. in the afternoon, walked along the Moldau, read aloud at his house; his queer mother who ate sandwiches and played solitaire; walked around alone for two hours; decided to leave Berlin Friday, met Kohl,[66] at home with my brothers-in-law and sisters, then the discussion of his engagement at Weltsch's (J. K.'s putting out the candles), then at home attempted by my silence to elicit aid and sympathy from my

mother; now my sister tells me about her meeting, the clock strikes a quarter to twelve.

At Weltsch's, in order to comfort his mother who was upset, I said: 'I too am losing Felix by this marriage. A friend who is married is none.' Felix said nothing, naturally couldn't say anything, but he didn't even want to.

The notebook begins with F., who on 2 May 1913 made me feel uncertain; this same beginning can serve as conclusion too, if in place of 'uncertain' I use a worse word.[67]

16 February. Wasted day. My only joy was the hope that last night has given me of sleeping better.

I was going home in my usual fashion in the evening after work, when, as though I had been watched for, they excitedly waved to me from all three windows of the Genzmer house to come up.

22 February. In spite of my drowsy head, whose upper left side is near aching with restlessness, perhaps I am still able quietly to build up some greater whole wherein I might forget everything and be conscious only of the good in one.

Director at his table. Servant brings in a card.
DIRECTOR: Witte again, this is a nuisance, the man is a nuisance.

23 February. I am on my way. Letter from Musil.[68] Pleases me and depresses me, for I have nothing.

A young man on a beautiful horse rides out of the gate of a villa.

8 March. A prince can wed the Sleeping Beauty, or someone even harder to win too, but the Sleeping Beauty can be no prince.

It happened that when Grandmother died only the nurse was with her. She said that just before Grandmother died she lifted herself up a little from the pillow so that she seemed to be looking for someone, and then peacefully lay back again and died.

There is no doubt that I am hemmed in all around, though by something that has certainly not yet fixed itself in my flesh, that I occasionally feel slackening, and that could be burst asunder. There are two remedies, marriage or Berlin; the second is surer, the first more immediately attractive.

I dived down and soon everything felt fine. A small shoal floated by in an upwards-mounting chain and disappeared in the green. Bells borne back and forth by the drifting of the tide – wrong.

9 March. Rense walked a few steps down the dim passageway, opened the little papered door of the dining-room, and said to the noisy company, almost without regarding them: 'Please be a little more quiet. I have a guest. Have some consideration.'

As he was returning to his room and heard the noise continuing unabated, he halted a moment, was on the verge of going back again, but thought better of it and returned to his room.

A boy of eighteen was standing at the window, looking down into the yard. 'It is quieter now,' he said when Rense entered, and lifted his long nose and deep-set eyes to him.

'It isn't quieter at all,' said Rense, taking a swallow from the bottle of beer standing on the table. 'It's impossible ever to have any quiet here. You'll have to get used to that, boy.'

I am too tired, I must try to rest and sleep, otherwise I am lost in every respect. What an effort to keep alive! Erecting a monument does not require the expenditure of so much strength.

The general argument: I am completely lost in F.

Rense, a student, sat studying in his small back room. The maid came in and announced that a young man wished to speak to him. 'What is his name?' Rense asked. The maid did not know.

I shall never forget F. in this place, therefore shan't marry. Is that definite?

Yes, that much I can judge of: I am almost thirty-one years old, have known F. for almost two years, must therefore have some perspective by now. Besides, my way of life here is such that I can't forget, even if F. didn't have such significance for me. The uniformity, regularity, comfort, and dependence of my way of life keep me unresistingly fixed wherever I happen to be. Moreover, I have a more than ordinary inclination toward a comfortable and dependent life, and so even strengthen everything that is pernicious to me. Finally, I am getting older, any change becomes more and more difficult. But in all this I foresee a great misfortune for myself, one without end and without hope; I should be dragging through the years up the ladder of my job, growing ever sadder and more alone as long as I could endure it at all.

But you wanted that sort of life for yourself, didn't you?

An official's life could benefit me if I were married. It would in every way be a support to me against society, against my wife, against writing, without demanding too many sacrifices, and without on the other hand degenerating into indolence and dependence, for as a married man I should not have to fear that. But I cannot live out such a life as a bachelor.

But you could have married, couldn't you?

I couldn't marry then; everything in me revolted against it, much as I always loved F. It was chiefly concern over my literary work that prevented me, for I thought marriage would jeopardize it. I may have been right, but in any case it is destroyed by my present bachelor's life. I have written nothing for a year, nor shall I be able to write anything in the future; in my head there is and remains the one single thought, and I am devoured by it. I wasn't able to consider it all at the time. Moreover, as a result of my dependence, which is at least encouraged by this way of life, I approach everything hesitantly and complete nothing at the first stroke. That was what happened here too.

Why do you give up all hope eventually of having F.?

I have already tried every kind of self-humiliation. In the Tiergarten I once said: 'Say "yes"; even if you consider your feeling for me insufficient to warrant marriage, my love for you is great enough to make up the insufficiency, and strong enough in general to take everything on itself.' In the course of a long correspondence I had alarmed F. by my peculiarities, and these now seemed to make her uneasy. I said: 'I love you enough to rid myself of anything that might trouble you. I will become another person.' Now, when everything must be cleared up, I can confess that even at the time when our relationship was at its most affectionate, I often had forebodings and fears, founded on trifling occurrences, that F. did not love me very much, not with all the force of the love she was capable of. F. has now realized this too, though not without my assistance. I am almost afraid that after my last two visits F. even feels a certain disgust for me, despite the fact that outwardly we are friendly, call each other 'Du', walk arm in arm together. The last thing I remember of her is the quite hostile grimace she made in the entrance hall of her house when I was not satisfied to kiss her glove but pulled it open and kissed her hand. Added to this there is the fact that, despite her promise to be punctual in the future in her correspondence, she hasn't answered two of my letters, merely telegraphed to promise letters but hasn't kept her promise; indeed, she hasn't even so much as answered my mother. There can be no doubt of the hopelessness in all this.

One should really never say that. Didn't your previous behaviour likewise seem hopeless from F.'s point of view?

That was something else. I always freely confessed my love for her, even during what appeared to be our final farewell in the summer; I was never so cruelly silent; I had reasons for my behaviour which, if they could not be approved, could yet be discussed. F.'s only reason is the complete insufficiency of her love. Nevertheless, it is true that I could wait. But I cannot wait in double hopelessness: I cannot see F. more and more slipping from my grasp, and myself more and more unable to escape. It would be the greatest gamble I could take with myself, although – or because – it would best suit all the overpowering evil forces within me. 'You never know what will happen' is no argument against the intolerableness of an existing state of affairs.

Then what do you want to do?

Leave Prague. Counter the greatest personal injury that has ever befallen me with the strongest antidote at my disposal.

Leave your job?

In light of the above, my job is only a part of the general intolerableness. I should be losing only what is intolerable in any case. The security, the lifelong provision, the good salary, the fact that it doesn't demand all my strength – after all, so long as I am a bachelor all these things mean nothing to me and are transformed into torments.

Then what do you want to do?

I could answer all such questions at once by saying: I have nothing to lose; every day, each tiniest success, is a gift; whatever I do is all to the good. But I can also give a more precise answer: as an Austrian lawyer, which, speaking seriously, I of course am not, I have no prospects; the best thing I might achieve for myself in this direction I already possess in my present post, and it is of no use to me. Moreover, in the quite impossible event I should want to make some money out of my legal training, there are only two cities that could be considered: Prague, which I must leave, and Vienna, which I hate and where I should inevitably grow unhappy because I should go there with the deepest conviction of that inevitability. I therefore have to leave Austria and – since I have no talent for languages and would do poorly at physical labour or at a business job – go to Germany, at least at first, and in Germany to Berlin, where the chances of earning a living are best. Also, there, in journalism, I can make best and directest use of my ability to write, and so find a means of livelihood at least partially suited to me. Whether in addition I shall be capable of inspired work, that I cannot say at present with any degree of certainty. But I think I know definitely that from the independence and freedom I should have in Berlin (however miserable I otherwise would be) I should derive the only feeling of happiness I am still able to experience.

But you are spoiled.

No, I need a room and a vegetarian diet, almost nothing more.

Aren't you going there because of F.?

No, I choose Berlin only for the above reasons, although I love it and perhaps I love it because of F. and because of the aura of thoughts that surrounds F.; but that I can't help. It is also probable that I shall meet F. in Berlin. If our being together will help me to get F. out of my blood, so much the better, it is an additional advantage Berlin has.

Are you healthy?

No – heart, sleep, digestion.

[*A small furnished room. Dawn. Disorder. The student is in bed asleep, his face to the wall. There is a knock at the door. Silence. A louder knock. The student sits up in fright, looks at the door.*]

STUDENT: Come in.

MAID [*a frail girl*]: Good morning.

STUDENT: What do you want? It's still night.

MAID: Excuse me, but a gentleman is asking for you.

STUDENT: *For me?* [*Hesitates.*] Nonsense! Where is he?

MAID: He is waiting in the kitchen.

STUDENT: What does he look like?

MAID [*smiling*]: Well, he's still a boy, he's not very handsome; I think he's a Yid.

STUDENT: And that wants to see me in the middle of the night? But I don't need your opinion of my guests, do you hear? Send him in. Be quick about it.

[*The student fills the small pipe lying on the chair beside his bed and smokes it.*

KLEIPE *stands at the door and looks at the student, who calmly smokes on with his eyes turned towards the ceiling. Short, erect, a large, long, somewhat crooked, pointed nose, dark complexion, deep-set eyes, long arms.*]

STUDENT: How much longer? Come over here to the bed and say what you want. Who are you? What do you want? Quick! Quick!

KLEIPE [*walks very slowly towards the bed and at the same time attempts to gesture something in explanation. He stretches his neck and raises and lowers his eyebrows to assist his speech*]: What I mean to say is, I am from Wulfenshausen too.

STUDENT: Really? That's nice, that's very nice. Then why didn't you stay there?

KLEIPE: Only think! It is the home town of both of us, a beautiful place, but still a miserable hole.

It was Sunday afternoon, they lay in bed in one another's arms. It was winter, the room was unheated, they lay beneath a heavy feather quilt.

15 March. The students wanted to carry Dostoyevsky's chains behind

his coffin. He died in the workers' quarter, on the fifth floor of a tenement house.

Once, during the winter, at about five o'clock in the morning, the half-clothed maid announced a visitor to the student. 'What's that? What did you say?' the student, still half asleep, was asking, when a young man entered, carrying a lighted candle that he had borrowed from the maid. He raised the candle in one hand the better to see the student and lowered his hat in his other hand almost to the floor, so long was his arm.

Only this everlasting waiting, eternal helplessness.

17 March. Sat in the room with my parents, leafed through magazines for two hours, on and off simply stared before me; in general simply waited for ten o'clock to arrive and for me to be able to go to bed.

27 March. On the whole passed in much the same way.

Hass hurried to get aboard the ship, ran across the gangplank, climbed up on deck, sat down in a corner, pressed his hands to his face and from then on no longer concerned himself with anyone. The ship's bell sounded, people were running along, far off, as though at the other end of the ship someone were singing with full voice.

They were just about to pull in the gangplank when a small black carriage came along, the coachman shouted from the distance, he had to exert all his strength to hold back the rearing horse; a young man sprang out of the carriage, kissed an old, white-bearded gentleman bending forward under the roof of the carriage, and with a small valise in his hand ran aboard the ship, which at once pushed off from the shore.

It was about three o'clock in the morning, but in the summer, and already half light. Herr von Irmenhof's five horses Famos, Grasaffe, Tournemento, Rosina and Brabant – rose up in the stable. Because of the sultry night the stable door had been left ajar; the two grooms slept on their backs in the straw, flies hovered up and down above their open mouths, there was nothing to hinder them. Grasaffe stood up so that he straddled the two men under him, and, watching their faces, was ready to strike down at them with his hoofs at their slightest sign of awakening. Meanwhile the four others sprang out of the stable in two easy leaps, one behind the other; Grasaffe followed them.

Through the glass door Anna saw the lodger's room was dark; she went in and turned on the electric light to make the bed ready for the night. But the student was sitting half reclined upon the sofa, smiling at her. She excused herself and turned to leave. But the student asked her to stay and to pay no attention to him. She did stay, in fact, and did her work, casting an occasional sidelong glance at the student.

5 April. If only it were possible to go to Berlin, to become independent, to live from one day to the next, even to go hungry, but to let all one's strength pour forth instead of husbanding it here, or rather – instead of one's turning aside into nothingness! If only F. wanted it, would help me!

8 April. Yesterday incapable of writing even one word. Today no better. Who will save me? And the turmoil in me, deep down, scarcely visible; I am like a living lattice-work, a lattice that is solidly planted and would like to tumble down.

Today in the coffee-house with Werfel. How he looked from the distance, seated at the coffee-house table. Stooped, half reclining even in the wooden chair, the beautiful profile of his face pressed against his chest, his face almost wheezing in its fullness (not really fat); entirely indifferent to the surroundings, impudent, and without flaw. His dangling glasses by contrast make it easier to trace the delicate outlines of his face.

6 May. My parents seem to have found a beautiful apartment for F. and me; I ran around for nothing one entire beautiful afternoon. I wonder whether they will lay me in my grave too, after a life made happy by their solicitude.

A nobleman, Herr von Griesenau by name, had a coachman, Joseph, whom no other employer would have put up with. He lived in a ground-floor room near the gate-keeper's lodge, for he was too fat and short of breath to climb stairs. All he had to do was drive a coach, but even for this he was employed only on special occasions, to honour a visitor perhaps; otherwise, for days on end, for weeks on end, he lay on a couch near the window, with remarkable rapidity blinking his small eyes deep-sunken in fat as he looked out of the window at the trees which --

Joseph the coachman lay on his couch, sat up only in order to take a slice of bread and butter and herring from a little table, then sank back again and stared vacantly around as he chewed. He laboriously sucked in the air through his large round nostrils; sometimes, in order to breathe in enough air, he had to stop chewing and open his mouth; his large belly trembled without stop under the many folds of his thin, dark blue suit.

The window was open, an acacia tree and an empty square were visible through it. It was a low ground-floor window. Joseph saw everything from his couch and everybody on the outside could see him. It was annoying, but he hadn't been able to climb stairs for the last six months at least, ever since he had got so fat, and thus was obliged to live on a lower storey. When he had first been given this room near the park-keeper's lodge, he had pressed and kissed the hands of his employer, Herr von Griesenau, with tears in his eyes, but now he knew its disadvantages: the eternal observation he was subjected to, the proximity of the unpleasant gate-keeper, all the commotion at the entrance gate and on the square, the great distance from the rest of the servants and the consequent estrangement and neglect that he suffered -- he was now thoroughly acquainted with all these disadvantages and in fact intended to petition the Master to permit him to move back to his old room. What after all were all these newly hired fellows standing uselessly around for, especially since the Master's engagement? Let them simply carry him up and down the stairs, rare and deserving man that he was.

An engagement was being celebrated. The banquet was at an end, the company got up from the table; all the windows were open, it was a warm and beautiful evening in June. The fiancée stood in a circle of friends and acquaintances, the others were gathered in small groups; now and then there was an outburst of laughter. The man to whom she was engaged stood apart, leaning in the doorway to the balcony and looking out.

After some time the mother of the fiancée noticed him, went over to him and said: 'Why are you standing here all alone? Aren't you joining Olga? Have you quarrelled?'

'No,' he answered, 'we haven't quarrelled.'

'Very well,' the mother said, 'then join your fiancée! Your behaviour is beginning to attract attention.'

The horror in the merely schematic.

The landlady of the rooming house, a decrepit widow dressed in black and wearing a straight skirt, stood in the middle room of her empty house. It was still perfectly quiet, the bell did not stir. The street, too, was quiet; the woman had purposely chosen so quiet a street because she wanted good roomers, and those who insist on quiet are the best.

27 May. Mother and sister in Berlin. I shall be alone with my father in the evening. I think he is afraid to come up. Should I play cards [*Karten*] with him? (I find the letter *K* offensive, almost disgusting, and yet I use it; it must be very characteristic of me.) How Father acted when I touched F.

The first appearance of the white horse was on an autumn afternoon, in a large but not very busy street in the city of A. It passed through the entrance-way of a house in whose yard a trucking company had extensive storerooms; thus it would often happen that teams of horses, now and then a single horse as well, had to be led out through the entrance-way, and for this reason the white horse attracted little attention. It was not, however, one of the horses belonging to the trucking company. A workman tightening the cords around a bale of goods in front of the gate noticed the horse, looked up from his work, and then into the yard to see whether the coachman was following after. No one came. The horse had hardly stepped into the road when it reared up mightily, struck several sparks from the pavement, for a moment was on the point of falling, but at once regained its balance, and then trotted neither rapidly nor slowly up the street, which was almost deserted at this twilight hour. The workman cursed what he thought had been the carelessness of the coachmen, shouted several names into the yard; some men came out in response, but when they immediately perceived that the horse was not one of theirs, simply stopped short together in the entrance-way, somewhat astonished. A short interval elapsed before some of them thought what to do; they ran after the horse for a distance, but, failing to catch sight of it again, soon returned.

In the meantime the horse had already reached the outermost streets of the suburbs without being halted. It accommodated itself to the life of the streets better than horses running alone usually do. Its slow pace could frighten no one, it never strayed out of the roadway or from its own side of the street; when it was obliged to stop for a vehicle coming out of a cross-street, it stopped; had the most careful driver been leading it by the halter it could not have behaved more perfectly. Still, of course, it was a conspicuous sight; here and there someone stopped and looked after it with a smile, a coachman in a passing beer wagon jokingly struck down at the horse with his whip; it was frightened, of course, and reared, but did not quicken its pace.

It was just this incident, however, that a policeman saw; he went over to the horse, who at the very last moment had tried to turn off in another direction, took hold of the reins (despite its light frame it wore the harness of a dray horse) and said, though in a friendly way: 'Whoa! Now where do you think you are running off to?' He held on to it for some time in the middle of the road, thinking that the animal's owner would soon be along after the runaway.

It has meaning but is weak; its blood flows thin, too far from the heart. There are still some pretty scenes in my head but I will stop regardless. Yesterday the white horse appeared to me for the first time before I fell asleep; I have an impression of its first stepping out of my head, which was turned to the wall, jumping across me and down from the bed, and then disappearing. The last is unfortunately not refuted by the fact of my having begun the story.

270

If I am not very much mistaken, I am coming closer. It is as though the spiritual battle were taking place in a clearing somewhere in the woods. I make my way into the woods, find nothing, and out of weakness immediately hasten out again; often as I leave the woods I hear, or I think I hear, the clashing weapons of that battle. Perhaps the eyes of the warriors are seeking me through the darkness of the woods, but I know so little of them, and that little is deceptive.

A heavy downpour. Stand and face the rain, let its iron rays pierce you; drift with the water that wants to sweep you away but yet stand fast, and upright in this way abide the sudden and endless shining of the sun.

The landlady dropped her skirts and hurried through the rooms. A cold, haughty woman. Her projecting lower jaw frightened roomers away. They ran down the steps, and when she looked after them through the window they covered their faces as they ran. Once a gentleman came for a room, a solid, thickset young man who constantly kept his hands in his coat pockets. It was a habit, perhaps, but it was also possible that he wanted to conceal the trembling of his hands.

'Young man,' said the woman, and her lower jaw jutted forward, 'you want to live here?'

'Yes,' the young man said, tossing his head upward.

'You will like it here,' the woman said, leading him to a chair on which she sat him down. In doing this she noticed a stain on his trousers, kneeled down beside him and began to scrape at the stain with her fingernails.

'You're a dirty fellow,' she said.

'It's an old stain.'

'Then you are an old dirty fellow.'

'Take your hand away,' he said suddenly, and actually pushed her away. 'What horrible hands you have.' He caught her hand and turned it over. 'All black on top, whitish below, but still black enough and' – he ran his fingers inside her wide sleeve – 'there is even some hair on your arm.'

'You're tickling me,' she said.

'Because I like you. I don't understand how they can say that you are ugly. Because they did say it. But now I see that it isn't true at all.'

And he stood up and walked up and down the room. She remained on her knees and looked at her hand.

For some reason this made him furious; he sprang to her side and caught her hand again.

'You're quite a woman,' he then said, and clapped her long thin cheek. 'It would really add to my comfort to live here. But it would have to be cheap. And you would not be allowed to take in other roomers. And you would have to be faithful to me. I am really much younger than you and can after all insist on faithfulness. And you would have to cook well. I am used to good food and never intend to disaccustom myself.'

Dance on, you pigs; what concern is it of mine?

But it has more reality than anything I have written this past year. Perhaps after all it is a matter of loosening the joint. I shall once more be able to write.

Every evening for the past week my neighbour in the adjoining room has come to wrestle with me. He was a stranger to me, even now I haven't yet spoken to him. We merely shout a few exclamations at one another, you can't call that 'speaking'. With a 'well then' the struggle is begun; 'scoundrel!' one of us sometimes groans under the grip of the other; 'there' accompanies a surprise thrust; 'stop!' means the end, yet the struggle always goes on a little while longer. As a rule, even when he is already at the door he leaps back again and gives me a push that sends me to the ground. From his room he then calls good night to me through the wall. If I wanted to give up this acquaintance once and for all I should have to give up my room, for bolting the door is of no avail. Once I had the door bolted because I wanted to read, but my neighbour hacked the door in two with an axe, and, since he can part with something only with the greatest difficulty once he has taken hold of it, I was even in danger of the axe.

I know how to accommodate myself to circumstances. Since he always comes to me at a certain hour, I take up some easy work beforehand which I can interrupt at once, should it be necessary. I straighten out a chest, for example, or copy something, or read some unimportant book. I have to arrange matters in this way – no sooner has he appeared in the door than I must drop everything, slam the chest to at once, drop the penholder, throw the book away, for it is only fighting that he wants, nothing else. If I feel particularly strong I tease him a little by first attempting to elude him. I crawl under the table, throw chairs under his feet, wink at him from the distance, though it is of course in bad taste to joke in this very one-sided way with a stranger. But usually our bodies close in battle at once. Apparently he is a student, studies all day, and wants some hasty exercise in the evening before he goes to bed. Well, in me he has a good opponent; accidents aside, I perhaps am the stronger and more skilful of the two. He, however, has more endurance.

28 May. Day after tomorrow I leave for Berlin. In spite of insomnia, headaches, and worries, perhaps in a better state than ever before.

Once he brought a girl along. While I say hello to her, not watching him, he springs upon me and jerks me into the air. 'I protest,' I cried, and raised my hand.

'Keep quiet,' he whispered in my ear. I saw that he was determined to win at all costs, even by resorting to unfair holds, so that he might shine before the girl.

'He said "Keep quiet" to me,' I cried, turning my head to the girl.

'Wretch!' the man gasped in a low voice, exerting all his strength against me. In spite of everything he was able to drag me to the sofa, put me down on it, knelt on my back, paused to regain his breath, and said: 'Well, there he lies.'

'Just let him try it again,' I intended to say, but after the very first word he pressed my face so hard into the upholstery that I was forced to be silent.

'Well then,' said the girl, who had sat down at my table and was reading a half-finished letter lying there, 'shouldn't we leave now? He has just begun to write a letter.'

'He won't go on with it if we leave. Come over here, will you? Touch him, here on his thigh, for instance; he's trembling just like a sick animal.'

'I say leave him alone and come along.' Very reluctantly the man crawled off me. I could have thrashed him soundly then, for I was rested while all his muscles had been tensed in the effort to hold me down. He was the one who had been trembling and had thought that it was me. I was still trembling even now. But I let him alone because the girl was present.

'You will probably have drawn your own conclusions as to this battle,' I said to the girl, walked by him with a bow and sat down at the table to go on with the letter. 'And who is trembling?' I asked, before beginning to write, and held the penholder rigid in the air in proof that it was not me. I was already in the midst of my writing when I called out a short adieu to them in the distance, but kicked out my foot a little to indicate, at least to myself, the farewell that they both probably deserved.

29 May. Tomorrow to Berlin. Is it a nervous or a real, trustworthy security that I feel? How is that possible? Is it true that if one once acquires a confidence in one's ability to write, nothing can miscarry, nothing is wholly lost, while at the same time only seldom will something rise up to a more than ordinary height? Is this because of my approaching marriage to F.? Strange condition, though not entirely unknown to me when I think back.

Stood a long time before the gate with Pick. Thought only of how I might quickly make my escape, for my supper of strawberries was ready for me upstairs. Everything that I shall now note down about him is simply a piece of shabbiness on my part, for I won't let him see any of it, or am content that he won't see it. But I am really an accessory to his behaviour so long as I go about in his company, and therefore what I say of him applies as well to me, even if one discounts the pretended subtlety that lies in such a remark.

I make plans. I stare rigidly ahead lest my eyes lose the imaginary peepholes of the imaginary kaleidoscope into which I am looking. I mix noble and selfish intentions in confusion; the colour of the noble ones is washed away, in recompense passing off on to the merely selfish ones. I invite heaven and earth to take part in my schemes, at the same time

I am careful not to forget the insignificant little people one can draw out of every side-street and who for the time being are more useful to my schemes. It is of course only the beginning, always only the beginning. But as I stand here in my misery, already the huge wagon of my schemes comes driving up behind me, I feel underfoot the first small step up, naked girls, like those on the carnival floats of happier countries, lead me backwards up the steps; I float because the girls float, and raise my hand to command silence. Rose bushes stand at my side, incense burns, laurel wreaths are let down, flowers are strewn before and over me; two trumpeters, as if hewn out of stone, blow fanfares, throngs of little people come running up, in ranks behind leaders; the bright, empty, open squares become dark, tempestuous, and crowded; I feel myself at the farthest edge of human endeavour, and, high up where I am, with suddenly acquired skill spontaneously execute a trick I had admired in a contortionist years ago – I bend slowly backwards (at that very moment the heavens strain to open to disclose a vision of me, but then stop), draw my head and trunk through my legs, and gradually stand erect again. Was this the ultimate given to mankind? It would seem so, for already I see the small horned devils leaping out of all the gates of the land, which lies broad and deep beneath me, overrunning the countryside; everything gives way in the centre under their feet, their little tails expunge everything, fifty devils' tails are already scouring my face; the ground begins to yield, first one of my feet sinks in and then the other; the screams of the girls pursue me into the depths into which I plummet, down a shaft precisely the width of my body but infinitely deep. This infinity tempts one to no extraordinary accomplishments, anything that I should do would be insignificant; I fall insensibly and that is best.

Dostoyevsky's letter to his brother on life in prison.

6 June. Back from Berlin. Was tied hand and foot like a criminal. Had they sat me down in a corner bound in real chains, placed policemen in front of me, and let me look on simply like that, it could not have been worse. And that was my engagement; everybody made an effort to bring me to life, and when they couldn't, to put up with me as I was. F. least of all, of course, with complete justification, for she

suffered the most. What was merely a passing occurrence to the others, to her was a threat.

We couldn't bear it at home even a moment. We knew that they would look for us. But despite its being evening we ran away. Hills encircled our city; we clambered up them. We set all the trees to shaking as we swung down the slope from one end to the other.

The posture of the clerks in the store shortly before closing time in the evening: hands in trouser pockets, a trifle stooped, looking from the vaulted interior past the open door on to the square. Their tired movements behind the counters. Weakly tie up a package, distractedly dust a few boxes, pile up used wrapping paper.

An acquaintance comes and speaks to me. He makes the following statement: Some say this, but I say exactly the opposite. He cites the reasons for his opinion. I wonder. My hands lie in my trouser pockets as if they had been dropped there, and yet as relaxed as if I had only to turn my pockets inside out and they would quickly drop out again.

I had closed the store, employees and customers departed carrying their hats in hand. It was a June evening, eight o'clock already but still light. I had no desire to take a walk, I never feel an inclination to go walking; but neither did I want to go home. When my last apprentice had turned the corner I sat down on the ground in front of the closed store.

An acquaintance and his young wife came by and saw me sitting on the ground. 'Why, look who is sitting here,' he said. They stopped, and the man shook me a little, despite the fact that I had been calmly regarding him from the very first.

'My God, why are you sitting here like this?' his young wife asked.

'I am going to give up my store,' I said. 'It isn't going too badly, and I can meet all my obligations, even if only just about. But I can't stand the worries, I can't control the clerks, I can't talk to the customers. From tomorrow on I won't even open the store. I've thought it all over carefully.' I saw how the man sought to calm his wife by taking her hand between both of his.

'Fine,' he said, 'you want to give up your store; you aren't the first to do it. We too' – he looked across at his wife – 'as soon as we have enough to take care of ourselves (may it be soon), won't hesitate to give up our store any more than you have done. Business is as little a pleasure to us as it is to you, believe me. But why do you sit on the ground?'

'Where shall I go?' I said. Of course, I knew why they were questioning me. It was sympathy and astonishment as well as embarrassment that they felt, but I was in no position whatsoever to help them too.

'Don't you want to join us?' I was recently asked by an acquaintance when he ran across me alone after midnight in a coffee-house that was already almost deserted. 'No, I don't,' I said.

It was already past midnight. I sat in my room writing a letter on which a lot depended for me, for with the letter I hoped to secure an excellent post abroad. I sought to remind the acquaintance to whom I was writing – by chance, after a ten-year interval, I had been put in touch with him again by a common friend – of past times, and at the same time make him understand that all my circumstances pressed me to leave the country and that in the absence of good and far-reaching connexions of my own, I was placing my greatest hopes in him.

It was getting on towards nine o'clock in the evening before Bruder, a city official, came home from his office. It was already quite dark. His wife was waiting for him in front of the gate, clutching her little girl to her. 'How is it going?' she asked.

'Very badly,' said Bruder. 'Come into the house and I'll tell you everything.' The moment they set foot in the house, Bruder locked the front door. 'Where is the maid?' he asked.

'In the kitchen,' his wife replied.

'Good; come!'

The table lamp was lit in the large, low living-room, they all sat down, and Bruder said: 'Well, this is how things stand. Our men are in full retreat. As I understand it from unimpeachable reports that have been received at City Hall, the fighting at Rumdorf has gone entirely against us. Moreover, the greater part of the troops have already withdrawn from the city. They are still keeping it secret so as not to add enormously to the panic in the city; I don't consider that altogether wise, it would be better to tell the truth frankly. However, my duty demands that I be silent. But of course there is no one to prevent me from telling you the truth. Besides, everybody suspects the real situation, you can see that everywhere. Everybody is shutting up his house, hiding whatever can be hidden.'[69]

It was about ten o'clock in the evening before Bruder, a city official, came home from his office; nevertheless he at once knocked on the door that separated his room from Rumford's, the furniture dealer, from whom he rented the room. Though he could hear only an indistinct response, he went in. Rumford was seated at the table with a newspaper; his fat was troubling him this hot July evening, he had thrown his coat and vest on the sofa; his shirt –

Several city officials were standing by the stone ledge of a window in City Hall, looking down into the square. The last of the rearguard was waiting below for the command to retreat. They were young, tall, red-cheeked fellows who held their quivering horses tightly reined. Two officers rode slowly back and forth in front of them. They were apparently waiting for a report. They sent out numerous riders who disappeared at a gallop up a steeply ascending side-street opening off the square. None had yet returned.

The city official Bruder, still a young man but wearing a full beard, had joined the group at the window. Since he enjoyed higher rank and was held in particular esteem because of his abilities, they all bowed courteously and made way for him at the window ledge. 'This must be the end,' he said, looking down on the square. 'It is only too apparent.'

'Then it is your opinion, Councillor,' said an arrogant young man who in spite of Bruder's approach had not stirred from his place and now stood close to him in such a way that it was impossible for them to look at each other; 'then it is your opinion that the battle has been lost?'

'Certainly. There can be no doubt of it. Speaking in confidence, our leadership is bad. We must pay for all sorts of old sins. This of course is not the time to talk of it, everybody must look out for himself now.

We are indeed face to face with final collapse. Our visitors may be here by this evening. It may be that they won't even wait until evening but will arrive here in half an hour.'

I step out of the house for a short stroll. The weather is beautiful but the street is startlingly empty, except for a municipal employee in the distance who is holding a hose and playing a huge arc of water along the street. 'Unheard of,' I say, and test the tension of the arc. 'An insignificant municipal employee,' I say, and again look at the man in the distance.

At the corner of the next intersection two men are fighting; they collide, fly far apart, guardedly approach one another and are at once locked together in struggle again. 'Stop fighting, gentlemen,' I say.

The student Kosel was studying at his table. He was so deeply engrossed in his work that he failed to notice it getting dark; in spite of the brightness of the May day, dusk began to descend at about four o'clock in the afternoon in this ill-situated back room. He read with pursed lips, his eyes, without his being aware of it, bent close to the book. Occasionally he paused in his reading, wrote short excerpts from what he had read into a little notebook, and then, closing his eyes, whispered from memory what he had written down. Across from his window, not five yards away, was a kitchen and in it a girl ironing clothes who would often look across at Karl.

Suddenly Kosel put his pencil down and listened. Someone was pacing back and forth in the room above, apparently barefooted, making one round after another. At every step there was a loud splashing noise, of the kind one makes when one steps into water. Kosel shook his head. These walks which he had had to endure for perhaps a week now, ever since a new roomer had moved in, meant the end, not only of his studying for today, but of his studying altogether, unless he did something in his own defence.

There are certain relationships which I can feel distinctly but which I am unable to perceive. It would be sufficient to plunge down a little deeper; but just at this point the upward pressure is so strong that I should think myself at the very bottom if I did not feel the currents moving below me. In any event, I look upward to the surface whence the thousand-times-refracted brilliance of the light falls upon me. I float up and splash around on the surface, in spite of the fact that I loathe everything up there and –

'Herr Direktor, a new actor has arrived,' the servant was heard distinctly to announce, for the door to the ante-room was wide open. 'I merely wish to *become* an actor,' said Karl in an undertone, and in this way corrected the servant's announcement. 'Where is he?' the director asked, craning his neck.

The old bachelor with the altered cut to his beard.

The woman dressed in white in the centre of the Kinsky Palace courtyard. Distinct shadow under the high arch of her bosom in spite of the distance. Stiffly seated.

11 June.

TEMPTATION IN THE VILLAGE[70]

One summer, towards evening, I arrived in a village where I had never been before. It struck me how broad and open were the paths. Everywhere one saw tall old trees in front of the farmhouses. It had been raining, the air was fresh, everything pleased me. I tried to indicate this by the manner in which I greeted the people standing in front of the gates; their replies were friendly even if somewhat aloof. I thought it would be nice to spend the night here if I could find an inn.

I was just walking past the high ivy-covered wall of a farm when a small door opened in the wall, three faces peered out, vanished, and the door closed again. 'Strange,' I said aloud, turning to one side as if I had someone with me. And, as if to embarrass me, there in fact stood a tall man next to me with neither hat nor coat, wearing a black knitted vest and smoking a pipe. I quickly recovered myself and said, as though I had already known that he was there: 'The door! Did you see the way that little door opened?'

'Yes,' the man said, 'but what's strange in that? It was the tenant farmer's children. They heard your footsteps and looked out to see who was walking by here so late in the evening.'

'The explanation is a simple one, of course,' I said with a smile. 'It's easy for things to seem queer to a stranger. Thank you.' And I went on.

But the man followed me. I wasn't really surprised by that, the man could be going the same way; yet there was no reason for us to walk one behind the other and not side by side. I turned and said, 'Is this the right way to the inn?'

The man stopped and said, 'We don't have an inn, or rather we have one but it can't be lived in. It belongs to the community and, years ago now, after no one had applied for the management of it, it was turned over to an old cripple whom the community already had to provide for. With his wife he now manages the inn, but in such a way that you can hardly pass by the door, the smell coming out of it is so strong. The floor of the parlour is slippery with dirt. A wretched way of doing things, a disgrace to the village, a disgrace to the community.'

I wanted to contradict the man; his appearance provoked me to it, this thin face with yellowish, leathery, bony cheeks and black wrinkles spreading over all of it at every movement of his jaws. 'Well,' I said, expressing no further surprise at this state of affairs, and then went on: 'I'll stop there anyway, since I have made up my mind to spend the night here.'

'Very well,' the man quickly said, 'but this is the path you must take to reach the inn,' and he pointed in the direction I had come from. 'Walk to the next corner and then turn right. You'll see the inn sign at once. That's it.'

I thanked him for the information and now walked past him again while he regarded me very closely. I had no way of guarding against the possibility that he had given me wrong directions, but was determined not to be put out of countenance either by his forcing me to march past him now, or by the fact that he had with such remarkable abruptness abandoned his attempts to warn me against the inn. Somebody else could direct me to the inn as well, and if it were dirty, why then for once I would simply sleep in dirt, if only to satisfy my stubbornness. Moreover, I did not have much of a choice; it was already dark, the roads were muddy from the rain, and it was a long way to the next village.

By now the man was behind me and I intended not to trouble myself with him any further when I heard a woman's voice speak to him. I turned. Out of the darkness under a group of plane trees stepped a tall, erect woman. Her skirts shone a yellowish-brown colour, over her head and shoulders was a black coarse-knit shawl. 'Come home now, won't you?' she said to the man; 'why aren't you coming?'

'I'm coming,' he said; 'only wait a little while. I want to see what that man is going to do. He's a stranger. He's hanging around here for no reason at all. Look at him.'

He spoke of me as if I were deaf or did not understand his language. Now to be sure it did not much matter to me what he said, but it would naturally be unpleasant for me were he to spread false reports about me in the village, no matter of what kind. For this reason I said to the woman: 'I'm looking for the inn, that's all. Your husband has no right to speak of me that way and perhaps give you a wrong impression of me.'

But the woman hardly looked at me and went over to her husband (I had been correct in thinking him her husband; there was such a direct, self-evident relationship between the two), and put her hand on his shoulder: 'If there is anything you want, speak to my husband, not to me.'

'But I don't want anything,' I said, irritated by the manner in which I was being treated; 'I mind my business, you mind yours. That's all I ask.' The woman tossed her head; that much I was able to make out in the dark, but not the expression in her eyes. Apparently she wanted to say something in reply, but her husband said, 'Keep still!' and she was silent.

Our encounter now seemed definitely at an end; I turned, about to go on, when someone called out, 'Sir!' It was probably addressed to me. For a moment I could not tell where the voice came from, but then I saw a young man sitting above me on the farmyard wall, his legs dangling down and knees bumping together, who insolently said to me: 'I have just heard that you want to spend the night in the village. You won't find liveable quarters anywhere except here on this farm.'

'On this farm?' I asked, and involuntarily – I was furious about it later – cast a questioning glance at the man and wife, who still stood there pressed against each other watching me.

'That's right,' he said, with the same arrogance in his reply that there was in all his behaviour.

'Are there beds to be had here?' I asked again, to make sure and to force the man back into his role of landlord.

'Yes,' he said, already averting his glance from me a little, 'beds for the night are furnished here, not to everyone, but only to those to whom they are offered.'

'I accept,' I said, 'but will naturally pay for the bed, just as I would at the inn.'

'Please,' said the man, who had already been looking over my head for a long time, 'we shall not take advantage of you.'

He sat above like a master, I stood down below like a petty servant; I had a great desire to stir him up a little by throwing a stone up at him. Instead I said, 'Then please open the door for me.'

'It's not locked,' he said.

'It's not locked,' I grumbled in reply, almost without knowing it, opened the door, and walked in. I happened to look up at the top of the wall immediately afterwards; the man was no longer there, in spite of its height he had apparently jumped down from the wall and was perhaps discussing something with the man and wife. Let them discuss it, what could happen to me, a young man with barely three gulden in cash and the rest of whose property consisted of not much more than a clean shirt in his rucksack and a revolver in his trouser pocket. Besides, the people did not look at all as if they would rob anyone. But what else could they want of me?

It was the usual sort of neglected garden found on large farms, though the solid stone wall would have led one to expect more. In the tall grass, at regular intervals, stood cherry trees with fallen blossoms. In the distance one could see the farmhouse, a one-storey rambling structure. It was already growing quite dark; I was a late guest; if the man on the wall had lied to me in any way, I might find myself in an unpleasant situation. On my way to the house I met no one, but when a few steps away from the house I saw, in the room into which the open door gave, two tall old people side by side, a man and wife, their faces towards the door, eating some sort of porridge out of a bowl. I could not make anything out very clearly in the darkness but now and then something on the man's coat sparkled like gold, it was probably his buttons or perhaps his watch-chain.

I greeted them and then said, not crossing the threshold for the moment: 'I happened to be looking in the village for a place to spend the night when a young man sitting on your garden wall told me it was possible to rent a room for the night here on the farm.' The two old people had put their spoons into the porridge, leaned back on their bench, and looked at me in silence. There was none too great hospitality in their demeanour. I therefore added, 'I hope the information given me was correct and that I haven't needlessly disturbed you.' I said this very loudly, for they might perhaps have been hard of hearing.

'Come nearer,' said the man after a little pause.

I obeyed him only because he was so old, otherwise I should naturally have had to insist that he give a direct answer to my direct question. At any rate, as I entered I said, 'If putting me up causes you even the slightest difficulty, feel free to tell me so; I don't absolutely insist on it. I can go to the inn, it wouldn't matter to me at all.'

'He talks so much,' the woman said in a low voice.

It could only have been intended as an insult, thus it was with insults that they met my courtesy; yet she was an old woman, I could not say anything in my defence. And my very defencelessness was perhaps the reason why this remark to which I dared not retort had so much greater an effect on me than it deserved. I felt there was some justification for a reproach of some sort, not because I had talked too much, for as a matter of fact I had said only what was absolutely necessary, but because of other reasons that touched my existence very closely. I said nothing further, insisted on no reply, saw a bench in a dark corner near by, walked over, and sat down.

The old couple resumed their eating, a girl came in from the next room and placed a lighted candle on the table. Now one saw even less than before, everything merged in the darkness, only the tiny flame flickered above the slightly bowed heads of the two old people. Several children came running in from the garden, one fell headlong and cried, the others stopped running and now stood dispersed about the room; the old man said, 'Go to sleep, children.'

They gathered in a group at once, the one who had been crying was only sobbing now, one boy near me plucked at my coat as if he meant that I was to come along; since I wanted to go to sleep too, I got up and, adult though I was, went silently from the room in the midst of the children as they loudly chorused good night. The friendly little boy took me by the hand and made it easier for me to find my way in the dark. Very soon we came to a ladder, climbed up it, and were in the attic. Through a small open skylight in the roof one could just then see the thin crescent of the moon; it was delightful to step under the skylight – my head almost reached up to it – and to breathe the mild yet cool air. Straw was piled on the floor against one wall; there was enough room for me to sleep too. The children – there were two boys and three girls – kept laughing while they undressed; I had thrown myself down in my clothes on the straw, I was among strangers, after all, and they were under no obligation to take me in. For a little while, propped up on my elbows, I watched the half-naked children playing in a corner. But then I felt so tired that I put my head on my rucksack, stretched out my arms, let my eyes travel along the roof beams a while longer, and fell asleep. In my first sleep I thought I could still hear one boy shout, 'Watch out, he's coming!' whereupon the noise of the hurried tripping of the children running to their beds penetrated my already receding consciousness.

I had surely slept only a very short time, for when I awoke the moonlight still fell almost unchanged through the window on the same part of the floor. I did not know why I had awakened – my sleep had been dreamless and deep. Then near me, at about the height of my ear, I saw a very small bushy dog, one of those repulsive little lap dogs with disproportionately large heads encircled by curly hair, whose eyes and muzzle are loosely set into their heads like ornaments made out of some kind of lifeless horny substance. What was a city dog like this doing in the village! What was it that made it roam the house at night? Why did it stand next to my ear? I hissed at it to make it go away; perhaps it was the children's pet and had simply strayed to my side. It was frightened by my hissing but did not run away, only turned around, then stood there on its crooked little legs and I could see its stunted (especially by contrast with its large head) little body.

Since it continued to stand there quietly, I tried to go back to sleep, but could not; over and over again in the space immediately before my closed eyes I could see the dog rocking back and forth with its protruding eyes. It was unbearable, I could not stand the animal near me; I rose and picked it up in my arms to carry it outside. But though it had been apathetic until then, it now began to defend itself and tried to

seize me with its claws. Thus I was forced to hold its little paws fast too
– an easy matter, of course; I was able to hold all four in one hand. 'So,
my pet,' I said to the excited little head with its trembling curls, and
went into the dark with it, looking for the door.

Only now did it strike me how silent the little dog was, it neither
barked nor squeaked, though I could feel its blood pounding wildly
through its arteries. After a few steps – the dog had claimed all my
attention and made me careless – greatly to my annoyance, I stumbled
over one of the sleeping children. It was now very dark in the attic,
only a little light still came through the skylight. The child sighed, I
stood still for a moment, dared not move even my toe away lest any
change waken the child still more. It was too late; suddenly, all around
me, I saw the children rising up in their white shifts as though by agreement, as though on command. It was not my fault; I had made only
one child wake up, though it had not really been an awakening at all,
only a slight disturbance that a child should have easily slept through.
But now they were awake. 'What do you want, children?' I asked. 'Go
back to sleep.'

'You're carrying something,' one of the boys said, and all five children
searched my person.

'Yes,' I said; I had nothing to hide, if the children wanted to take the
dog out, so much the better. 'I'm taking this dog outside. It was keeping
me from sleeping. Do you know whose it is?'

'Mrs Cruster's,' at least that's what I thought I made of their confused, indistinct drowsy shouts which were intended not for me but only
for each other.

'Who is Mrs Cruster?' I asked, but got no further answer from the
excited children. One of them took the dog, which had now become
entirely still, from my arm and hurried away with it; the rest followed.

I did not want to remain here alone, also my sleepiness had left me by
now; for a moment I hesitated, it seemed to me that I was meddling too
much in the affairs of this house where no one had shown any great
confidence in me; but finally I ran after the children. I heard the patter-
ing of their feet a short distance ahead of me, but often stumbled in the
pitch darkness on the unfamiliar way and once even bumped my head
painfully against the wall. We came into the room in which I had first

met the old people; it was empty, through the door that was still standing open one could see the moonlit garden.

'Go outside,' I said to myself, 'the night is warm and bright, you can continue your journey or even spend the night in the open. After all, it is so ridiculous to run about after the children here.' But I ran nevertheless; I still had a hat, stick, and rucksack up in the attic. But how the children ran! With their shifts flying they leaped through the moonlit room in two bounds, as I distinctly saw. It occurred to me that I was giving adequate thanks for the lack of hospitality shown me in this house by frightening the children, causing a race through the house and myself making a great din instead of sleeping (the sound of the children's bare feet could hardly be heard above the tread of my heavy boots) – and I had not the faintest notion of what would come of all this.

Suddenly a bright light appeared. In front of us, in a room with several windows opened wide, a delicate-looking woman sat at a table writing by the light of a tall, splendid table lamp. 'Children!' she called out in astonishment; she hadn't seen me yet, I stayed back in the shadow outside the door. The children put the dog on the table; they obviously loved the woman very much, kept trying to look into her eyes, one girl seized her hand and caressed it; she made no objection, was scarcely aware of it. The dog stood before her on the sheet of letter paper on which she had just been writing and stretched out its quivering little tongue toward her, the tongue could be plainly seen a short distance in front of the lampshade. The children now begged to be allowed to remain and tried to wheedle the woman's consent. The woman was undecided, got up, stretched her arms, and pointed to the single bed and the hard floor. The children refused to give it any importance and lay down on the floor wherever they happened to be, to try it; for a while everything was quiet. Her hands folded in her lap, the woman looked down with a smile at the children. Now and then one raised its head, but when it saw the others still lying down, lay back again.

One evening I returned home to my room from the office somewhat later than usual – an acquaintance had detained me below at the house entrance for a long time – opened the door (my thoughts were still engrossed by our conversation, which had consisted chiefly of gossip about people's social standing), hung my overcoat on the hook, and was about to cross over to the washstand when I heard a strange, spasmodic breathing. I looked up and, on top of the stove that stood deep in the gloom of a corner, saw something alive. Yellowish glittering eyes stared at me; large round woman's breasts rested on the shelf of the stove, on either side beneath the unrecognizable face; the creature seemed to consist entirely of a mass of soft white flesh; a thick yellowish tail hung down beside the stove, its tip ceaselessly passing back and forth over the cracks of the tiles.

The first thing I did was to cross over with long strides and sunken head – nonsense! I kept repeating like a prayer – to the door that led to my landlady's rooms. Only later I realized that I had entered without knocking. Miss Hefter –

It was about midnight. Five men held me, behind them a sixth had his hand raised to grab me. 'Let go,' I cried, and whirled in a circle, making them all fall back. I felt some sort of law at work, had known that this last effort of mine would be successful, saw all the men reeling back with raised arms, realized that in a moment they would all throw themselves on me together, turned towards the house entrance – I was standing only a short distance from it – lifted the latch (it sprang open of itself, as it were, with extraordinary rapidity), and escaped up the dark stairs.

On the top floor stood my old mother in the open doorway of our apartment, a candle in her hand. 'Look out! look out!' I cried while still on the floor below, 'they are coming after me!'

'Who? Who?' my mother asked. 'Who could be coming after you, son?' my mother asked.

'Six men,' I said breathlessly.

'Do you know them?' my mother asked.

'No, strangers,' I said.

'What do they look like?'

'I barely caught a glimpse of them. One has a black full beard, one a large ring on his finger, one has a red belt, one has his trousers torn at the knee, one has only one eye open, and the last bares his teeth.'

'Don't think about it any more,' my mother said. 'Go to your room, go to sleep, I've made the bed.'

My mother! This old woman already proof against the assaults of life, with a crafty wrinkle round her mouth, mouth that unwittingly repeated eighty-year-old follies.

'Sleep now?' I cried –

12 June. Kubin. Yellowish face, sparse hair lying flat on his skull, from time to time a heightened sparkle in his eyes.

W., half blind, detached retina; has to be careful not to fall or be pushed, for the lens might fall out and then it would be all over with. Has to hold the book close to his eyes when he reads and try to catch the letters through the corners of his eyes. Was in India with Melchior Lechter, fell ill with dysentery; eats everything, every piece of fruit he finds lying in the dust of the street.

P. sawed a silver chastity belt off a skeleton; pushed aside the workers who had dug it up somewhere in Roumania, reassured them by saying that he saw in the belt a valuable trifle which he wanted as a souvenir, sawed it open and pulled it off. If he finds a valuable Bible or picture or page that he wants in a village church, he tears what he wants out of the book, off the wall, from the altar, puts a two-heller piece down as compensation, and his conscience is clear – Loves fat women. Every woman he has had has been photographed. The bundle of photographs that he shows every visitor. Sits at one end of the sofa, his visitor, at a considerable distance from him, at the other. P. hardly looks across and yet always knows which picture is on top and supplies the necessary explanations: This was an old widow; these were the two Hungarian maids; etc. – Of Kubin: 'Yes, Master Kubin, you are indeed on the way up; in ten or twenty years, if this keeps on, you may come to occupy a position like that of Bayros.'[71]

Dostoyevsky's letter to a woman painter.

The life of society moves in a circle. Only those burdened with a common affliction understand each other. Thanks to their affliction they constitute a circle and provide each other mutual support. They glide along the inner borders of their circle, make way for or jostle one another gently in the crowd. Each encourages the other in the hope that it will react upon himself, or – and then it is done passionately – in the immediate enjoyment of this reaction. Each has only that experience which his affliction grants him; nevertheless one hears such comrades exchanging immensely varying experiences. 'This is how you are,' one says to the other; 'instead of complaining, thank God that this is how you are, for if this were not how you are, you would have this or that misfortune, this or that shame.' How does this man know that? After all, he belongs – his statement betrays it – to the same circle as does the one to whom he spoke; he stands in the same need of comfort. In the same circle, however, one knows only the same things. There exists not the shadow of a thought to give the comforter an advantage over the comforted. Thus their conversations consist only of a coming-together of their imaginations, outpourings of wishes from one upon the other. One will look down at the ground and the other up at a bird; it is in such differences that their intercourse is realized. Sometimes they will unite in faith and, their heads together, look up into the unending reaches of the sky. Recognition of their situation shows itself, however, only when they bow down their heads in common and the common hammer descends upon them.

14 June. How I calmly walk along while my head twitches and a branch feebly rustles overhead, causing me the worst discomfort. I have in me the same calm, the same assurance as other people, but somehow or other inverted.

19 June. The excitement of the last few days. The calm that is transferred from Dr W. to me. The worries he takes upon himself for me. How they moved back into me early this morning when I awoke about four after a deep sleep. Pištekovo Divadlo.[72] Löwenstein. Now the crude, exciting novel by Soyka. Anxiety. Convinced that I need F.

How the two of us, Ottla and I, explode in rage against every kind of human relationship.

The parents' grave, in which the son (Pollak, a graduate of a commercial school) is also buried.[73]

25 June. I paced up and down my room from early morning until twilight. The window was open, it was a warm day. The noises of the

narrow street beat in uninterruptedly. By now I knew every trifle in the room from having looked at it in the course of my pacing up and down. My eyes had travelled over every wall. I had pursued the pattern of the rug to its last convolution, noted every mark of age it bore. My fingers had spanned the table across the middle many times. I had already bared my teeth repeatedly at the picture of the landlady's dead husband.

Towards evening I walked over to the window and sat down on the low sill. Then, for the first time not moving restlessly about, I happened calmly to glance into the interior of the room and at the ceiling. And finally, finally, unless I were mistaken, this room which I had so violently upset began to stir. The tremor began at the edges of the thinly plastered white ceiling. Little pieces of plaster broke off and with a distinct thud fell here and there, as if at random, to the floor. I held out my hand and some plaster fell into it too; in my excitement I threw it over my head into the street without troubling to turn around. The cracks in the ceiling made no pattern yet, but it was already possible somehow to imagine one. But I put these games aside when a bluish violet began to mix with the white; it spread straight out from the centre of the ceiling, which itself remained white, even radiantly white, where the shabby electric lamp was stuck. Wave after wave of the colour – or was it a light? – spread out towards the now darkening edges. One no longer paid any attention to the plaster that was falling away as if under the pressure of a skilfully applied tool. Yellow and golden-yellow colours now penetrated the violet from the side. But the ceiling did not really take on these different hues; the colours merely made it somewhat transparent; things striving to break through seemed to be hovering above it, already one could almost see the outlines of a movement there, an arm was thrust out, a silver sword swung to and fro. It was meant for me, there was no doubt of that; a vision intended for my liberation was being prepared.

I sprang up on the table to make everything ready, tore out the electric light together with its brass fixture and hurled it to the floor, then jumped down and pushed the table from the middle of the room to the wall. That which was striving to appear could drop down unhindered on the carpet and announce to me whatever it had to announce. I had barely finished when the ceiling did in fact break open. In the dim light, still at a great height, I had judged it badly, an angel in bluish-violet robes girt with gold cords sank slowly down on great white silken-shining wings, the sword in its raised arm thrust out horizontally. 'An angel, then!' I thought; 'it has been flying towards me all the day and in my disbelief I did not know it. Now it will speak to me.' I lowered my eyes. When I raised them again the angel was still there, it is true, hanging rather far off under the ceiling (which had closed again), but it was no living angel, only a painted wooden figurehead off the prow of some ship, one of the kind that hangs from the ceiling in sailors' taverns, nothing more.

The hilt of the sword was made in such a way as to hold candles and catch the dripping tallow. I had pulled the electric light down; I didn't want to remain in the dark, there was still one candle left, so I got up on a chair, stuck the candle into the hilt of the sword, lit it, and then sat late into the night under the angel's faint flame.

30 June. Hellerau to Leipzig with Pick. I behaved terribly. Couldn't ask a question, answer one, or move; was barely able to look him in the eye. The Navy League agitator, the fat, sausage-eating Thomas couple in whose house we lived, Prescher, who took us there; Mrs Thomas, Hegner, Fantl and Mrs Adler, the woman and the child, Anneliese, Mrs K., Miss P., Mrs Fantl's sister, K., Mendelssohn (the brother's child; Alpinum, cockchafer larvae, pineneedle bath); tavern in the forest called Natura, Wolff, Haas; reading *Narciss* aloud in the Adler garden, sightseeing in the Dalcroze house, evening in the tavern in the forest, Bugra – terror after terror.

Failures: didn't find the Natura, ran up and down Struvestrasse; wrong tram to Hellerau; no room in the tavern in the forest; forgot that I was supposed to get a telephone call from E.[74] there, hence went back; Fantl had left; Dalcroze in Geneva; next morning got to the tavern in the forest too late (F. had telephoned for nothing); decided to go not to Berlin but Leipzig; pointless trip; by mistake, a local train; Wolff was just going to Berlin; Lasker-Schüler appropriated Werfel; pointless visit to the exhibition; finally, to cap it all, quite pointlessly dunned Pick for an old debt in the Arco.

1 July. Too tired.

5 July. To have to bear and to be the cause of such suffering!

23 July. The tribunal in the hotel. Trip in the cab. F.'s face. She patted her hair with her hand, wiped her nose, yawned. Suddenly she gathered herself together and said very studied, hostile things she had long been saving up. The trip back with Miss Bl.[75] The room in the hotel; heat reflected from the wall across the street. Afternoon sun, in addition. Energetic waiter, almost an Eastern Jew in his manner. The courtyard noisy as a boiler factory. Bad smells. Bedbug. Crushing is a difficult decision. Chambermaid astonished: There are no bedbugs anywhere; once only did a guest find one in the corridor.

At her parents'. Her mother's occasional tears. I recited my lesson. Her father understood the thing from every side. Made a special trip from Malmö to meet me, travelled all night; sat there in his shirt sleeves. They agreed that I was right, there was nothing, or not much, that could be said against me. Devilish in my innocence. Miss Bl.'s apparent guilt.

Evening alone on a bench on Unter den Linden. Stomach-ache. Sad-looking ticket-seller. Stood in front of people, shuffled the tickets in his hands, and you could only get rid of him by buying one. Did his job properly in spite of all his apparent clumsiness – on a full-time job of this kind you can't keep jumping around; he must also try to remember people's faces. When I see people of this kind I always think: How did he get into this job, how much does he make, where will he be tomorrow, what awaits him in his old age, where does he live, in what corner does he stretch out his arms before going to sleep, could I do his job, how should I feel about it? All this together with my stomach-ache. Suffered through a horrible night. And yet almost no recollection of it.

In the Restaurant Belvedere on the Strahlau Brücke with E. She still hopes it will end well, or acts as if she does. Drank wine. Tears in her eyes. Ships leave for Grünau, for Schwertau. A lot of people. Music. E. consoled me, though I wasn't sad; that is, my sadness has to do only with myself, but as such it is inconsolable. Gave me *The Gothic Rooms*. Talked a lot (I knew nothing). Especially about how she got her way in her job against a venomous white-haired old woman who worked in the same place. She would like to leave Berlin, to have her own business. She loves quiet. When she was in Sebnitz she often slept all day on Sunday. Can be gay too.

Why did her parents and aunt wave after me? Why did F. sit in the hotel and not stir in spite of the fact that everything was already settled? Why did she telegraph me: 'Expecting you, but must leave on business Tuesday?' Was I expected to do something? Nothing could have been more natural. From nothing (interrupted by Dr Weiss, who walks over to the window) –

27 July. The next day didn't visit her parents again. Merely sent a messenger with a letter of farewell. Letter dishonest and coquettish. 'Don't think badly of me.' Speech from the gallows.

Went twice to the swimming-pool on the Strahlauer Ufer. Lots of Jews. Bluish faces, strong bodies, wild running. Evening in the garden of the Askanischer Hof. Ate rice à la Trautmannsdorf and a peach. A man drinking wine watched my attempts to cut the unripe little peach with my knife. I couldn't. Stricken with shame under the old man's eyes, I let the peach go completely and ten times leafed through *Die Fliegenden Blätter*. I waited to see if he wouldn't at last turn away. Finally I collected all my strength and in defiance of him bit into the completely juiceless and expensive peach. A tall man in the booth near me occupied with nothing but the roast he was painstakingly selecting and the wine in the ice bucket. Finally he lit a long cigar; I watched him over my *Fliegende Blätter*.

Left from the Lehrter railway station.[76] Swede in shirt sleeves. Strong-looking girl with all the silver bracelets. Changing trains in Buchen during the night. Lübeck. Hotel Schützenhaus dreadful. Cluttered walls, dirty clothes under the sheet, neglected building; a bus boy was the only servant. Afraid of the room, I went into the garden and sat down over a bottle of mineral water. Opposite me a hunchback drinking beer and a thin, anaemic young man who was smoking. Slept nevertheless, but was awakened early in the morning by the sun shining through the large window straight into my face. The window looked out on the railway tracks; incessant noise of the trains. Relief and happiness after moving to the Hotel Kaiserhof on the Trave.

Trip to Travemünde. Mixed bathing. View of the beach. Afternoon on the sand. My bare feet struck people as indecent. Near me a man who was apparently an American. Instead of eating lunch walked past all the pensions and restaurants. Sat among the trees in front of the Kurhaus and listened to the dinner music.

In Lübeck a walk on the Wall. Sad, forlorn-looking man on a bench. Bustle on the Sportplatz. Quiet square, people on stairs and stones in front of every door. Morning from the window. Unloading timber from a sailing-boat. Dr Weiss at the railway station. Unfailing resemblance to Löwy. Unable to make up my mind on Gleschendorf. Meal in the Hansa dairy. 'The Blushing Virgin'. Shopping for dinner. Telephone conversation with Gleschendorf. Trip to Marienlyst. Ferry. Mysterious disappearance of a young man wearing a raincoat and hat and his mysterious reappearance in the carriage on the trip from Vaggerloese to Marienlyst.

28 July. Despairing first impression of the barrenness, the miserable house, the bad food with neither fruit nor vegetables, the quarrels between W. and H. Decided to leave the next day. Gave notice. Stayed nevertheless. A reading from *Überfall*; I was unable to listen, to enjoy it with them, to judge. W.'s improvised speeches. Beyond me. The man writing in the middle of the garden; fat face, black eyes, pomaded long hair brushed straight back. Rigid stare, looked right and left out of the corners of his eyes. *The children, uninterested, sat around his table like flies – I am more and more unable to think, to observe, to determine the truth of things, to remember, to speak, to share an experience; I am turning to stone, this is the truth.* I am more and more unable even in the office. If I can't take refuge in some work, I am lost. Is my knowledge of this as clear as the thing itself? I shun people not because I want to live quietly, but rather because I want to die quietly. I think of the walk we, E. and I, took from the tram to the Lehrter railway station. Neither of us spoke, I thought nothing but that each step taken was that much of a gain for me. And E. is nice to me, believes in me for some incomprehensible reason, in spite of having seen me before the tribunal; now and then I even feel the effect of this faith in me, without, however, fully believing in the feeling.

The first time in many months that I felt any life stir in me in the presence of other people was in the compartment on the return trip from Berlin, opposite the Swiss woman. She reminded me of G.W.

Once she even exclaimed: Children! She had headaches, her blood gave her so much trouble. Ugly, neglected little body; bad, cheap dress from a Paris department store. Freckles on her face. But small feet; a body completely under control because of its diminutive size, and despite its clumsiness, round, firm cheeks, sparkling, inextinguishable eyes.

The Jewish couple who lived next to me. Young people, shy and unassuming; her large hooked nose and slender body; he had a slight squint, was pale, short, and stout; at night he coughed a little. They often walked one behind the other. Sight of the tumbled bed in their room.

Danish couple. The man often very proper in a dinner jacket, the woman tanned, a weak yet coarse-featured face. Were silent a good deal; sometimes sat side by side, their heads inclined towards one another as on a cameo.

The impudent, good-looking youngster. Always smoking cigarettes. Looked at H. impudently, challengingly, admiringly, scornfully, and contemptuously, all in one glance. Sometimes he paid her no attention at all. Silently demanded a cigarette from her. Soon thereafter, from the distance, offered her one. Wore torn trousers. If anyone is going to spank him, it will have to be done this summer; by next summer he will be doing the spanking. Strokes the arms of almost all the chambermaids; not humbly, however, not with embarrassment but rather like some lieutenant whose still childish face permitted him liberties that would later be denied him. How he makes as if to chop off the head of a doll with his knife at the dinner table.

Lancers. Four couples. By lamplight and to gramophone music in the main hall. After each figure a dancer hurried to the gramophone and put on a new record. A decorous, graceful, and earnestly executed dance, especially on the part of the men. Cheerful, red-cheeked fellow, a man of the world, whose inflated stiff shirt made his broad, high chest seem even higher; the pale nonchalant fellow with a superior air, joking with everyone; beginning of a paunch; loud, ill-fitting clothes; many languages; read *Die Zukunft*; the gigantic father of the goitrous, wheezing family; you were able to recognize them by their laboured breathing and infantile bellies; he and his wife (with whom he danced very gallantly) demonstratively sat at the children's table, where indeed his offspring were most heavily represented.

The proper, neat, trustworthy gentleman with a face looking almost sulky in its utter solemnity; modesty and manliness. Played the piano. The gigantic German with duelling scars on his square face whose puffed lips came together so placidly when he spoke. His wife, a hard and friendly Nordic face, accentuated, beautiful walk, accentuated freedom of her swaying hips. Woman from Lübeck with shining eyes. Three children, including Georg who, thoughtless as a butterfly, alighted beside complete strangers. Then in childish talkativeness asked some meaningless question. For example, we were sitting and correcting the 'Kampf'.[77] Suddenly he appeared and in a matter-of-fact, trustful, and loud voice asked where the other children had run off to.

The stiff old gentleman who was a demonstration of what the noble Nordic wise-heads look like in old age. Decayed and unrecognizable; yet beautiful young wise-heads were also running around there.

29 July. The two friends, one of them blond, resembling Richard Strauss, smiling, reserved, clever; the other dark, correctly dressed, mild-mannered yet firm, too dainty, lisped; both of them gourmets, kept drinking wine, coffee, beer, brandy, smoked incessantly, one poured for the other; their room across from mine full of French books; wrote a great deal in the stuffy writing-room when the weather was mild.

Joseph K., the son of a rich merchant, one evening after a violent quarrel with his father—his father had reproached him for his dissipated life and demanded that he put an immediate stop to it – went, with no definite purpose but only because he was tired and completely at a loss, to the house of the corporation of merchants which stood all by itself near the harbour. The doorkeeper made a deep bow, Joseph looked casually at him without a word of greeting. 'These silent underlings do everything one supposes them to be doing,' he thought. 'If I imagine that he is looking at me insolently, then he really is.' And he once more turned to the doorkeeper, again without a word of greeting; the latter turned towards the street and looked up at the overcast sky.

I was in great perplexity. Only a moment ago I had known what to do. With his arm held out before him the boss had pushed me to the door of the store. Behind the two counters stood my fellow clerks, supposedly my friends, their grey faces lowered in the darkness to conceal their expressions.

'Get out!' the boss shouted. 'Thief! Get out! Get out, I say!'

'It's not true,' I shouted for the hundredth time; 'I didn't steal! It's a mistake or a slander! Don't you touch me! I'll sue you! There are still courts here! I won't go! For five years I slaved for you like a son and now you treat me like a thief. I didn't steal; for God's sake, listen to me, I didn't steal.'

'Not another word,' said the boss, 'you're fired!'

We were already at the glass door, an apprentice darted out in front of us and quickly opened it; the din coming in from what was indeed an out-of-the-way street brought me back to reality; I halted in the door-way, arms akimbo, and, as calmly as I could despite my breathlessness, merely said, 'I want my hat.'

'You'll get it,' the boss said, walked back a few steps, took the hat from Grassmann, one of the clerks, who had jumped over the counter, tried to throw it to me but missed his aim, and anyway threw it too hard, so that the hat flew past me into the street.

'You can keep the hat now,' I said, and went out into the street. And now I was in a quandary. I had stolen, had slipped a five-gulden bill out of the till to take Sophie to the theatre that evening. But she didn't even want to go to the theatre; payday was three days off, at that time I should have had my own money; besides, I had committed the theft stupidly, in broad daylight, near the glass window of the office in which the boss sat looking at me. 'Thief!' he shouted, and sprang out of the office. 'I didn't steal,' was the first thing I said, but the five-gulden bill was in my hand and the till open.

Made jottings on the trip in another notebook. Began things that went wrong. But I will not give up in spite of insomnia, headaches, a general incapacity. I've summoned up my last resources to this end. I made the remark that 'I don't avoid people in order to live quietly, but rather in order to be able to die quietly'. But now I will defend myself. For a month, during the absence of my boss, I'll have the time.

30 July. Tired of working in other people's stores, I had opened up a little stationery store of my own. Since my means were limited and I had to pay cash for almost everything –

I sought advice, I wasn't stubborn. It was not stubbornness when I silently laughed with contorted face and feverishly shining cheeks at someone who had unwittingly proffered me advice. It was suspense, a readiness on my part to be instructed, an unhealthy lack of stubbornness.

The director of the Progress Insurance Company was always greatly dissatisfied with his employees. Now every director is dissatisfied with his employees; the difference between employees and directors is too vast to be bridged by means of mere commands on the part of the director and mere obedience on the part of the employees. Only mutual hatred can bridge the gap and give the whole enterprise its perfection.

Bauz, the director of the Progress Insurance Company, looked doubtfully at the man standing in front of his desk applying for a job as attendant with the company. Now and then he also glanced at the man's papers lying before him on the desk.
'You're tall enough,' he said, 'I can see that; but what can you do? Our attendants must be able to do more than lick stamps; in fact, that's the one thing they don't have to be able to do, because we have machines to do that kind of thing. Our attendants are part officials, they have responsible work to do; do you feel you are qualified for that? Your head is shaped peculiarly. Your forehead recedes so. Remarkable. Now, what was your last position? What? You haven't worked for a year? Why was that? You had pneumonia? Really? Well, that isn't much of a recommendation, is it? Naturally, we can employ only people who are in good health. Before you are taken on you will have to be examined by the doctor. You are quite well now? Really? Of course, that could be. Speak up a little! Your whispering makes me nervous. I see here that you're also married, have four children. And you haven't worked for a year! Really, man! Your wife takes in washing? I see. Well, all right. As long as you're already here, get the doctor to examine you

now; the attendant will show you the way. But that doesn't mean that you will be hired, even if the doctor's opinion is favourable. By no means. In any event, you'll receive our decision in writing. To be frank, I may as well tell you at once: I'm not at all impressed with you. We need an entirely different kind of attendant. But have yourself examined in any case. And now go, go. Trembling like that won't do you any good. I have no authority to hand out favours. You're willing to do any kind of work? Certainly. Everyone is. That's no special distinction. It merely indicates the low opinion you have of yourself. And now I'm telling you for the last time: Go along and don't take up any more of my time. This is really enough.'

Bauz had to strike the desk with his hand before the man let himself be led out of the director's office by the attendant.

I mounted my horse and settled myself firmly in the saddle. The maid came running to me from the gate and announced that my wife still wanted to speak to me on an urgent matter; would I wait just a moment, she hadn't quite finished dressing yet. I nodded and sat quietly on my horse, who now and then gently raised his forelegs and reared a little. We lived on the outskirts of the village; before me, in the sun, the highway mounted a slope whose opposite side a small wagon had just ascended, which now came driving down into the village at a rapid pace. The driver brandished his whip, a woman in a provincial yellow dress sat in the dark and dusty interior of the wagon.

I was not at all surprised that the wagon stopped in front of my house.

31 July. I have no time.[78] General mobilization. K. and P. have been called up. Now I receive the reward for living alone. But it is hardly a reward; living alone ends only with punishment. Still, as a consequence, I am little affected by all the misery and am firmer in my resolve than ever. I shall have to spend my afternoons in the factory; I won't live at home, for Elli and the two children are moving in with us. But I will write in spite of everything, absolutely; it is my struggle for self-preservation.

1 August. Went to the train to see K. off. Relatives everywhere in the office. Would like to go to Valli's.

2 August. Germany has declared war on Russia – Swimming in the afternoon.

3 August. Alone in my sister's apartment. It is lower down than my room, it is also on a side street, hence the neighbours' loud talking below, in front of their doors. Whistling too. Otherwise complete solitude. No longed-for wife to open the door. In one month I was to have been married. The saying hurts: You've made your bed, now lie in it. You find yourself painfully pushed against the wall, apprehensively lower your eyes to see whose hand it is that pushes you, and, with a new pain in which the old is forgotten, recognize your own contorted hand holding you with a strength it never had for good work. You raise your head, again feel the first pain, again lower your gaze; this up-and-down motion of your head goes on without pause.

4 August. When I rented the place for myself I probably signed something for the landlord by which I bound myself to a two- or even six-year lease. Now he is basing his demand on this agreement. My stupidity, or rather, my general and utter helplessness. Drop quietly into the river. Dropping probably seems so desirable to me because it reminds me of 'being pushed'.

5 August. The business almost settled, by the expenditure of the last of my strength. Was there twice with Malek as witness, at Felix's to draft the lease, at the lawyers' (6 kr), and all of it unnecessary; I could and should have done it all myself.

6 August. The artillery that marched across the Graben. Flowers, shouts of hurrah! and *nazdar!*[79] The rigidly silent, astonished, attentive black face with black eyes.

I am more broken down than recovered. An empty vessel, still intact yet already in the dust among the broken fragments; or already in fragments yet still ranged among those that are intact. Full of lies, hate, and envy. Full of incompetence, stupidity, thickheadedness. Full of laziness, weakness, and helplessness. Thirty-one years old. I saw the two agriculturists in Ottla's picture. Young, fresh people possessed of some knowledge and strong enough to put it to use among people who in the nature of things resist their efforts somewhat. One of them leading beautiful horses; the other lies in the grass, the tip of his tongue playing between his lips in his otherwise unmoving and absolutely trustworthy face.

I discover in myself nothing but pettiness, indecision, envy, and hatred against those who are fighting and whom I passionately wish everything evil.

What will be my fate as a writer is very simple. My talent for portraying my dreamlike inner life has thrust all other matters into the background; my life has dwindled dreadfully, nor will it cease to dwindle. Nothing else will ever satisfy me. But the strength I can muster for that portrayal is not to be counted upon: perhaps it has already vanished forever, perhaps it will come back to me again, although the circumstances of my life don't favour its return. Thus I waver, continually fly to the summit of the mountain, but then fall back in a moment. Others waver too, but in lower regions, with greater strength; if they are in danger of falling, they are caught up by the kinsman who walks beside them for that very purpose. But I waver on the heights; it is not death, alas, but the eternal torments of dying.

Patriotic parade. Speech by the mayor. Disappears, then reappears, and a shout in German: 'Long live our beloved monarch, hurrah!' I stand there with my malignant look. These parades are one of the most disgusting accompaniments of the war. Originated by Jewish businessmen who are German one day, Czech the next; admit this to themselves, it is true, but were never permitted to shout it out as loudly as they do now. Naturally they carry many others along with them. It was well organized. It is supposed to be repeated every evening, twice tomorrow and Sunday.

7 August. Even if you have not the slightest sensitivity to individual differences, you still treat everyone in his own way. L. of Binz, in order to attract attention, poked his stick at me and frightened me.

Yesterday and today wrote four pages, trivialities difficult to surpass. Strindberg is tremendous. This rage, these pages won by fist-fighting. Chorus from the tavern across the way. I just went to the window.

Sleep seems impossible. The song is coming through the open door of
the tavern. A girl's voice is leading them. They are singing simple love
songs. I hope a policeman comes along. There he comes. He stops in
front of the door for a moment and listens. Then calls out: 'Landlord!'
The girl's voice: 'Vojtíšku.'[80] A man in trousers and shirt jumps forward out of a corner. 'Close the door! You're making too much noise.'
'Oh sorry, sorry,' says the landlord, and with delicate and obliging
gestures, as if he were dealing with a lady, first closes the door behind
him, then opens it to slip out, and closes it again. The policeman (whose
behaviour, especially his anger, is incomprehensible, for the singing
can't disturb him but must rather sweeten his monotonous round)
marches off; the singers have lost all desire to sing.

11 August. I imagine that I have remained in Paris, walk through it
arm in arm with my uncle, pressed close to his side.

12 August. Didn't sleep at all. Lay three hours in the afternoon on
the sofa, sleepless and apathetic; the same at night. But it mustn't
thwart me.

15 August. I have been writing these past few days, may it continue.
Today I am not so completely protected by and enclosed in my work
as I was two years ago,[81] nevertheless have the feeling that my monotonous, empty, mad bachelor's life has some justification. I can once
more carry on a conversation with myself, and don't stare so into complete emptiness. Only in this way is there any possibility of improvement for me.

MEMOIRS OF THE KALDA RAILWAY

During one period of my life – it is many years ago now – I had a
post with a small railway in the interior of Russia. I have never been so
forsaken as I was there. For various reasons that do not matter now, I
had been looking for just such a place at the time; the more solitude
ringing in my ears the better I liked it, and I don't mean now to make
any complaint. At first I had only missed a little activity. The little
railway may originally have been built with some commercial purpose

Kafka Sketch

in view, but the capital had been insufficient, construction came to a halt, and instead of terminating at Kalda, the nearest village of any size, a five-days journey from us by wagon, the railway came to an end at a small settlement right in the wilderness, still a full day's journey from Kalda.

Now even if the railway had extended to Kalda it would perforce have remained an unprofitable venture for an indefinite period, for the whole notion' of it was wrong; the country needed roads, not railways, nor could the railway manage at all in its present state; the two trains running daily carried freight a light wagon could have hauled, and its only passengers were a few farm hands during the summer. But still they did not want to shut down the railway altogether, for they went on hoping that if it were kept in operation they could attract the necessary capital for furthering the construction work. Even this hope was, in my opinion, not so much hope as despair and laziness. They kept the railway in operation so long as there were still supplies of coal available, the wages of their few workers they paid irregularly and not in full, as though they were gifts of charity; as for the rest, they waited for the whole thing to collapse.

It was by this railway, then, that I was employed, living in a wooden shed left standing from the time of the railway's construction, and now serving at the same time as a station. There was only one room, in which a bunk had been set up for me – and a desk for any writing I might have to do. Above it was installed the telegraphic apparatus. In the spring, when I arrived, one train would pass the station very early in the day – later this was changed – and it sometimes happened that a passenger would alight at the station while I was still asleep. In that case, of course – the nights there were very cool until midsummer – he did not remain outside in the open but knocked, I would unbolt the door, and then we would often pass hours in chatting. I lay on my bunk, my guest squatted on the floor or, following my instructions, brewed tea which we then drank together sociably. All these village people were distinguished by a great sociability. Moreover, I perceived that I was not particularly suited to stand a condition of utter solitude, admit as I had to that my self-imposed solitude had already, after a short time, begun to dissipate my past sorrows. I have in general found that it is extremely difficult for a misfortune to dominate a solitary person for any length of time. Solitude is powerful beyond everything else, and drives one back to people. Naturally, you then attempt to find new ways, ways seemingly less painful but in reality simply not yet known.

I became more attached to the people there than I should have thought possible. It was naturally not a regular contact with them that I had. All the five villages with which I had to do were several hours distant from the station as well as from each other. I dared not venture too far from the station, lest I lose my job. And under no circumstances did I want that, at least not in the beginning. For this reason I could not go to the villages themselves, and had to depend on the passengers or on people not deterred by the long journey that had to be made to visit me. During the very first month such people dropped in; but no matter how friendly they were, it was easy to see that they came only on the chance of transacting some business with me, nor did they make any attempt to conceal their purpose. They brought butter, meat, corn, all sorts of things; at first, so long as I had any money, I habitually bought everything almost sight unseen, so welcome were these people to me, some of them especially. Later, though, I limited my purchases, among other reasons because I thought I noticed a certain contempt on their part for the manner in which I bought things. Besides, the train also brought me food, food, however, that was very bad and even more expensive than that which the peasants brought.

Originally I had intended to plant a small vegetable garden, to buy a cow, and in this way make myself as self-sufficient as I could. I had even brought along gardening tools and seed; there was a great deal of uncultivated ground around my hut stretching away on one level without the slightest rise as far as the eye could see. But I was too weak to conquer the soil. A stubborn soil that was frozen solid until spring and that even resisted the sharp edge of my new pick. Whatever seed one sowed in it was lost. I had attacks of despair during this labour. I lay in my bunk for days, not coming out even when the trains arrived. I would simply put my head through the window, which was right above my bunk, and report that I was sick. Then the train crew, which consisted of three men, came in to get warm, though they found very little warmth – whenever possible I avoided using the old iron stove that so easily blew up. I preferred to lie there wrapped in an old warm coat and covered by the various skins I had bought from the peasants over a period of time. 'You're often sick,' they said to me. 'You're a sickly person. You won't leave this place alive.' They did not say this to depress me, but rather strove straightforwardly to speak the truth whenever possible. Their eyes usually goggled peculiarly at such times.

Once a month, but always on a different day of the month, an inspector came to examine my record book, to collect the money I had taken in and – but not always – to pay me my salary. I was always warned of his arrival a day in advance by the people who had dropped him at the last station. They considered this warning the greatest favour they could do me in spite of the fact that I naturally always had everything in good order. Nor was the slightest effort needed for this. And the inspector too always came into the station with an air as if to say, this time I shall unquestionably uncover the evidence of your mismanagement. He always opened the door of the hut with a push of his knee, giving me a look at the same time. Hardly had he opened my book when he found a mistake. It took me a long time to prove to him, by recomputing it before his eyes, that the mistake had been made not by me but by him. He was always dissatisfied with the amount I had taken in, then clapped his hand on the book and gave me a sharp look again. 'We'll have to shut down the railway,' he would say each time. 'It will come to that,' I usually replied.

After the inspection had been concluded, our relationship would change. I always had brandy ready and, whenever possible, some sort of delicacy. We drank to each other; he sang in a tolerable voice, but always the same two songs. One was sad and began: 'Where are you going, O child in the forest?' The other was gay and began like this: 'Merry comrades, I am yours!' – It depended on the mood I was able to put him in, how large an instalment I got on my salary. But it was only at the beginning of these entertainments that I watched him with any purpose in mind; later we were quite at one, cursed the company shamelessly, he whispered secret promises into my ear about the career he would help me to achieve, and finally we fell together on the bunk in an embrace that often lasted ten hours unbroken. The next morning he went on his way, again my superior. I stood beside the train and saluted; often as not he turned to me while getting aboard and said, 'Well, my little friend, we'll meet again in a month. You know what you have at stake.' I can still see the bloated face he turned to me with an effort, every feature in his face stood prominently forth, cheeks, nose, lips.

This was the one great diversion during the month when I let myself go; if inadvertently some brandy had been left over, I guzzled it down immediately after the inspector left. I could generally hear the parting whistle of the train while it gurgled into me. The thirst that followed a night of this sort was terrible; it was as if another person were within me, sticking his head and throat out of my mouth and screaming for something to drink. The inspector was provided for, he always carried a large supply of liquor on his train; but I had to depend on whatever was left over.

But then the whole month thereafter I did not drink, did not smoke either; I did my work and wanted nothing more. There was, as I have said, not very much to do, but what there was I did thoroughly. It was my duty every day, for instance, to clean and inspect the track a kilo-metre on either side of the station. But I did not limit myself to what was required and often went much farther, so far that I was barely able to make out the station. In clear weather the station could be seen at a distance of perhaps five kilometres, for the country was quite flat. And then, if I had gone so far off that the hut in the distance only glimmered before my eyes, I sometimes saw – it was an optical illusion – many black dots moving towards the hut. There were whole com-panies, whole troops. But sometimes someone really came; then, swing-ing my pick, I ran all the long way back.

I finished my work towards evening and finally could retreat into my hut. Generally no visitors came at this hour, for the journey back to the villages was not entirely safe at night. All sorts of shiftless fellows drifted about in the neighbourhood; they were not natives, however, and others would take their place from time to time, but then the original ones would come back again. I got to see most of them, they were attracted by the lonely station; they were not really dangerous, but you had to deal firmly with them.

They were the only ones who disturbed me during the long twilight hours. Otherwise I lay on my bunk, gave no thought to the past, no thought to the railway, the next train did not come through till between ten and eleven at night; in short, I gave no thought to anything. Now and then I read an old newspaper thrown to me from the train; it contained the gossip of Kalda, which would have interested me but which I could not understand from disconnected issues. Moreover, in every issue there was an instalment of a novel called *The Commander's Revenge*. I once dreamed of this commander, who always wore a dagger at his side, on one particular occasion even held it between his teeth. Besides, I could not read much, for it got dark early and paraffin or a tallow candle was prohibitively expensive. Every month the railway gave me only half a litre of paraffin, which I used up long before the end of the month merely in keeping the signal light lit half an hour for the train every evening. But this light wasn't at all necessary, and later on, at least on moonlit nights, I would neglect to light it. I correctly foresaw that with the passing of summer I should stand in great need of paraffin. I therefore dug a hole in one corner of the hut, put an old tarred beer keg in it, and every month poured in the paraffin I had saved. It was covered with straw and could attract no attention. The more the hut stank of paraffin, the happier I was; the smell got so strong because the old and rotten staves of the keg had soaked up the paraffin. Later, as a precaution, I buried the keg outside the hut; for once the inspector had boasted to me of a box of wax matches, and when I had asked to see them, threw them one after the other blazing into the air. Both of us, and especially the paraffin, were in real danger; I saved everything by throttling him until he dropped all the matches.

In my leisure hours I often considered how I might prepare for winter. If I was freezing even now, during the warm part of the year – and they said it was warmer than it had been for many years – it would fare very badly with me during the winter. That I was hoarding paraffin was only a whim; if I had been acting sensibly, I should have had to lay up many things for the winter; there was little doubt that the company would not be especially solicitous of my welfare; but I was too heedless, or rather, I was not heedless but I cared too little about myself to want to make much of an effort. Now, during the warm season, things were going tolerably, I left it at that and did nothing further.

One of the attractions that had drawn me to this station had been the prospect of hunting. I had been told that the country was extraordinarily rich in game, and I had already put down a deposit on a gun I wanted sent to me when I had saved up a little money. Now it turned out that there was no trace of game animals here, only wolves and bears were reported, though during the first few months I had failed to see any; otherwise there were only unusually large rats which I had immediately caught sight of running in packs across the steppe as if driven by the wind. But the game I had been looking forward to was not to be found. The people hadn't misinformed me; a region rich in game did exist, but it was a three-days journey away – I had not considered that directions for reaching a place in this country, with its hundreds of kilometres of uninhabited areas, must necessarily be uncertain. In any event, for the time being I had no need of the gun and could use the money for other purposes; still, I had to provide myself with a gun for the winter and I regularly laid money aside for that purpose. As for the rats that sometimes attacked my provisions, my long knife sufficed to deal with them.

During the first days, when I was still eagerly taking in everything, I spitted one of these rats on the point of my knife and held it before me at eye level against the wall. You can see small animals clearly only if you hold them before you at eye level; if you stoop down to them on the ground and look at them there, you acquire a false, imperfect notion of them. The most striking feature of these rats was their claws – large, somewhat hollow, and yet pointed at the ends, they were well suited to dig with. Hanging against the wall in front of me in its final agony, it rigidly stretched out its claws in what seemed to be an unnatural way; they were like small hands reaching out to you.

In general these animals bothered me little, only sometimes woke me up at night when they hurried by the hut in a patter of running feet on the hard ground. If I then sat up and perhaps lit a small wax candle, I could see a rat's claws sticking in from the outside and working feverishly at some hole it was digging under the boards. This work was all in vain, for to dig a hole big enough for itself it would have had to work days on end, and yet it fled with the first brightening of the day; despite this it laboured on like a workman who knew what he was doing. And it did good work; the particles it threw up as it dug were imperceptible indeed, on the other hand its claw was probably never used without result. At night I often watched this at length, until the calm and regularity of it put me to sleep. Then I would no longer have the energy to put out the little candle, and for a short while it would shine down for the rat at its work.

Once, on a warm night, when I had again heard these claws at work,
I cautiously went outside without lighting a candle in order to see the
animal itself. Its head, with its sharp snout, was bowed very low, pushed
down almost between its forelegs in the effort to crowd as close as
possible to the wood and dig its claws as deep as possible under it. You
might have thought there was someone inside the hut holding it by the
claws and trying bodily to pull the animal in, so taut was every muscle.
And yet everything was ended with one kick, by which I killed the
beast. Once fully awake, I could not tolerate any attack on my only
possession, the hut.

To safeguard the hut against these rats I stopped all the holes with
straw and tow and every morning examined the floor all around. I also
intended to cover the hard-packed earthen floor of the hut with planks;
such a flooring would also be useful for the winter. A peasant from the
next village, Jekoz by name, long ago had promised to bring me some
well-seasoned planks for this purpose, and I had often entertained him
hospitably in return for this promise, nor did he stay very long away
from me but came every fortnight, occasionally bringing shipments to
send by the railway; but he never brought the planks. He had all sorts
of excuses for this, usually that he himself was too old to carry such a
load, and his son, who would be the one to bring the planks, was just
then hard at work in the fields. Now according to his own account,
which seemed correct enough, Jekoz was considerably more than seventy
years old; but he was a tall man and still very strong. Besides, his excuses varied, and on another occasion he spoke of the difficulties of
obtaining planks as long as those I needed. I did not press him, had no
urgent need for the planks, it was Jekoz himself who had given me the
idea of a plank flooring in the first place; perhaps a flooring would do
no good at all; in short, I was able to listen calmly to the old man's
lies. My customary greeting was: 'The planks, Jekoz!' At once the
apologies began in a half-stammer, I was called inspector or captain or
even just telegrapher, which had a particular meaning for him; he
promised me not only to bring the planks very shortly, but also, with
the help of his son and several neighbours, to tear down my whole hut
and build me a solid house in its stead. I listened until I grew tired, then
pushed him out. While yet in the doorway, in apology he raised his supposedly feeble arms, with which he could in reality have throttled a

grown man to death. I knew why he did not bring the planks; he sup-posed that when the winter was closer at hand I should have a more pressing need for them and would pay a better price; besides, as long as the boards were not delivered he himself would be more important to me. Now he was of course not stupid and knew that I was aware of what was in the back of his mind, but in the fact that I did not exploit this knowledge he saw his advantage, and this he preserved.

But all the preparations I had been making to secure the hut against the animals and protect myself against the winter had to be interrupted when (the first three months of my service were coming to an end) I became seriously ill. For years I had been spared any illness, even the slightest indisposition, but now I became indisputably sick. It began with a heavy cough. About two hours up-country from the station there was a little brook, where I used to go to fetch my supply of water in a barrel on a wheelbarrow. I often bathed there too, and this cough was the result. The fits of coughing were so severe that I had to double up when I coughed, I imagined I should not be able to survive the cough-ing unless I doubled up and so gathered together all my strength. I thought my coughing would terrify the train crew, but they knew all about it, called it the wolf's cough. After that I began to hear the howl in the cough. I sat on the little bench in front of the hut and greeted the train with a howl, with a howl I accompanied it on its way when it departed. At night, instead of lying down, I knelt on the bunk and pressed my face into the skins at least to spare myself hearing my howls. I waited tensely until the bursting of some vital blood vessel should put an end to everything. But nothing of the kind happened and the cough-ing even abated after a few days. There is a tea that cures it, and one of the locomotive engineers promised to bring me some, but explained that it must be drunk only on the eighth day after the coughing began, otherwise it was of no use. On the eighth day he did in fact bring it, and I remember how not only the train crew but the passengers as well, two young peasants, came into my hut, for it was accounted lucky to hear the first cough after the drinking of the tea. I drank, coughed the first mouthful into the faces of my guests, but then immediately felt a real relief, though indeed the coughing had already been easier during the last two days. But a fever remained and did not go down.

This fever tired me a great deal, I lost all my resistance; sometimes, quite unexpectedly, sweat would break out on my forehead, my whole body would tremble, and regardless of where I was I had to lie down and wait until I came to my senses again. I clearly perceived that I was not getting better, but worse, and that it was essential that I go to Kalda and stay there a few days until my condition improved.

21 August. Began with such hope and was then repulsed by all three stories; today more so than ever. It may be true that the Russian story ought to be worked on only after *The Trial*. In this ridiculous hope, which apparently has only some mechanical notion behind it of how things work, I start *The Trial* again – The effort wasn't entirely without result.

29 August. The end of one chapter a failure; another chapter, which began beautifully, I shall hardly – or rather certainly not – be able to continue as beautifully, while at the time, during the night, I should certainly have succeeded with it. But I must not forsake myself, I am entirely alone.

30 August. Cold and empty. I feel only too strongly the limits of my abilities, narrow limits, doubtless, unless I am completely inspired. And I believe that even in the grip of inspiration I am swept along only within these narrow limits, which, however, I then no longer feel because I am being swept along. Nevertheless, within these limits there is room to live, and for this reason I shall probably exploit them to a despicable degree.

A quarter to two at night. Across the street a child is crying. Suddenly a man in the same room, as near to me as if he were just outside the window, speaks. 'I'd rather jump out of the window than listen to any more of that.' He nervously growls something else, his wife, silent except for her shushing, tries to put the child to sleep again.

1 September. In complete helplessness barely wrote two pages. I fell back a great deal today, though I slept well. Yet if I wish to transcend the initial pangs of writing (as well as the inhibiting effect of my way of life) and rise up into the freedom that perhaps awaits me, I know

that I must not yield. My old apathy hasn't completely deserted me yet, as I can see, and my coldness of heart perhaps never. That I recoil from no ignominy can as well indicate hopelessness as give hope.

13 September. Again barely two pages. At first I thought my sorrow over the Austrian defeats and my anxiety for the future (anxiety that appears ridiculous to me at bottom, and base too) would prevent me from doing any writing. But that wasn't it, it was only an apathy that forever comes back and forever has to be put down again. There is time enough for sorrow when I am not writing. The thoughts provoked in me by the war resemble my old worries over F. in the tormenting way in which they devour me from every direction. I can't endure worry, and perhaps have been created expressly in order to die of it. When I shall have grown weak enough – it won't take very long – the most trifling worry will perhaps suffice to rout me. In this prospect I can also see a possibility of postponing the disaster as long as possible. It is true that, with the greatest effort on the part of a nature then comparatively unweakened, there was little I was able to do against my worries over F.; but I had had the great support of my writing in the first days of that period; henceforth I will never allow it to be taken from me.

7 October. I have taken a week's vacation to push the novel on. Until today – it is Wednesday night, my vacation ends Monday – it has been a failure. I have written little and feebly. Even last week I was on the decline, but could not foresee that it would prove so bad. Are these three days enough to warrant the conclusion that I am unworthy of living without the office?

15 October. Two weeks of good work; full insight into my situation occasionally. Today, Thursday (Monday my holiday is over, I have taken an additional week), a letter from Miss Bl. I don't know what to do about it, I know it is certain that I shall live on alone (if I live at all – which is *not* certain), I also don't know whether I love F. (I remember the aversion I felt at the sight of her dancing with her severe eyes lowered, or when she ran her hand over her nose and hair in the Askanischer Hof shortly before she left, and the numberless moments

of complete estrangement); but in spite of everything the enormous temptation returns again. I played with the letter all through the evening; I don't work though I could (even if I've had excruciating headaches this whole past week). I'm noting down from memory the letter I wrote to Miss Bl.:

What a strange coincidence, Grete, that it was just today I received your letter. I will not say with what it coincided, that concerns only me and the things that were troubling me tonight as I went to bed, about three. (Suicide; letter full of instructions to Max.)

Your letter was a great surprise to me. Not because you wrote to me. Why shouldn't you write to me? Though you do say that I hate you; but it isn't true. Were the whole world to hate you, I still shouldn't, and not only because I have no right to do so. You sat as a judge over me in the Askanischer Hof – it was awful for you, for me, for everyone – but it only *seemed* so; in reality all the time I was sitting in your place and sit there to this day.

You are completely mistaken about F. I don't say this to worm details from you. I can think of no detail – and my imagination has so often gone back and forth across this ground that I can trust it – I say I can think of no detail that could persuade me you are not mistaken. What you suggest is completely impossible; it makes me unhappy to think that F. should perhaps be deceiving herself for some undiscoverable reason. But that is also impossible.

I have always believed your interest to be honest and free from any personal consideration. Nor was your last letter an easy one to write. I warmly thank you for it.

What did this accomplish? The letter sounds unyielding, but only because I was ashamed, because I considered it irresponsible, because I was afraid to be yielding; by no means because I did not want to yield. That was the only thing I did want. It would be best for all of us if she would not answer, but she will answer and I shall wait for her answer.

. . .[82] I have now lived calmly for two months without any real contact with F. (except through the correspondence with E.), have dreamed of F. as though of someone who was dead and could never live again, and now, when I am offered a chance to come near her, she is at once the centre of everything again. She is probably also interfering with my work. How very much a stranger she has sometimes seemed to me these latter days when I would think of her, of all the people I had ever met the most remote; though at the same time I told myself that this was simply because F. had been closer to me than any other person, or at least had been thrust so close to me by other people.

Leafed through the diary a little. Got a kind of inkling of the way a life like this is constituted.

21 October. For four days almost no work at all, only an hour or so all the time and only a few lines, but slept better; as a result almost got rid of my headaches. No reply from Bl.; tomorrow is the last possible day.

25 October. My work almost completely at a standstill. What I write seems to lack independence, seems only the pale reflection of earlier work. Reply from Bl. arrived; I am completely undecided as to how to answer it. Thoughts so base that I cannot even write them down. Yesterday's sadness . . .

1 November. Yesterday, after a long time, made a great deal of progress; today again virtually nothing; the two weeks since my holiday have been almost a complete loss – Part of the day – it's Sunday – has been beautiful. In Chotek Park read Dostoyevsky's pamphlet in his own defence. The guard at the castle and the corps headquarters. The fountain in the Thun palace – Much self-satisfaction all day. And now I completely balk at any work. Yet it isn't balking; I see the task and the way to it, I simply have to push past small obstacles but cannot do it – Toying with thoughts of F.

3 November. In the afternoon a letter to E., looked through a story by Pick, 'Der blinde Gast', and made some corrections, read a little Strindberg, then didn't sleep, home at half past eight, back at ten in fear of headaches which had already begun; and because I had slept very little during the night, did not work any more, partly too because I was afraid to spoil a fair passage I had written yesterday. Since August, the fourth day on which I have written nothing. The letters are the cause of it; I'll try to write none at all or only very short ones. How

embarrassed I now am, and how it agitates me. Yesterday evening my excessive happiness after having read several lines by Jammes, whom otherwise I don't care for, but whose French (it is a description of a visit to a poet who was a friend of his) had so strong an effect on me.

4 November. P. back.[83] Shouting excited past all bounds. Story about the mole burrowing under him in the trenches which he looked upon as a warning from heaven to leave that spot. He had just got away when a bullet struck a soldier crawling after him at the moment he was over the mole – His captain. They distinctly saw him taken prisoner. But the next day found him naked in the woods, pierced through by bayonets. He probably had had money on him, they wanted to search him and rob him of it, but he – 'the way officers are' – wouldn't voluntarily submit to being touched – P. almost wept with rage and excitement when he met his boss (whom in the past he had admired ridiculously, out of all measure) on the train, elegantly dressed, perfumed, his opera glass dangling from his neck, on his way to the theatre. (A month later he himself did the same with a ticket given him by this boss. He went to see *Der ungetreue Eckehart*, a comedy.)[84] Slept one night in the castle of Princess Sapieha; one night, while his unit was in reserve, right in front of the Austrian batteries; one night in a peasant cottage, where two women were sleeping in each of the two beds standing right and left against each wall, a girl behind the stove, and eight soldiers on the floor – Punishment given soldiers. Stand bound to a tree until they turn blue.

12 November. Parents who expect gratitude from their children (there are even some who insist on it) are like usurers who gladly risk their capital if only they receive interest.

24 November. Yesterday on Tuchmachergasse, where they distribute old clothing to the refugees from Galicia. Max, his mother, Mr Chaim Nagel. The intelligence, the patience, the friendliness, the industry, the affability, the wit, the dependability of Mr Nagel. People who, within their sphere, do their work so thoroughly that you believe they could succeed in anything on earth – yet it is part of their perfection too that they don't reach out for anything beyond their sphere.

The clever, lively, proud, and unassuming Mrs Kannegiesser from

Tarnow, who wanted only two blankets, but nice ones, and who nevertheless, in spite of Max's influence, got only old, dirty ones, while the new blankets were put aside for the better people in another room, together with all the best things. Then, they didn't want to give her good ones because she needed them for only two days until her linen arrived from Vienna; they aren't permitted to take back used articles because of the danger of cholera.

Mrs Lustig, with a lot of children of every size and her fresh, self-assured, sprightly little sister. She spent so much time looking for a dress for a little girl that Mrs Brod shouted at her: 'Now you take this or you won't get anything.' But then Mrs Lustig answered in an even louder shout, ending with a wide, violent sweep of her arm: 'The *mitzveh* [good deed] is worth more than all these *shmattes* [rags].'

25 November. Utter despair, impossible to pull myself together; only when I have become satisfied with my sufferings can I stop.

30 November. I can't write any more. I've come up against the last boundary, before which I shall in all likelihood again sit down for years, and then in all likelihood begin another story all over again that will again remain unfinished. This fate pursues me. And I have become cold again, and insensible; nothing is left but a senile love for unbroken calm. And like some kind of beast at the farthest pole from man, I shift my neck from side to side again and for the time being should like to try again to have F. back. I'll really try it, if the nausea I feel for myself doesn't prevent me.

2 December. Afternoon at Werfel's with Max and Pick. Read 'In the Penal Colony' aloud; am not entirely dissatisfied, except for its glaring and ineradicable faults. Werfel read some poems and two acts of *Esther, Kaiserin von Persien.* The acts carry one away. But I am easily carried away. The criticisms and comparisons put forward by Max, who was not entirely satisfied with the piece, disturb me, and I am no longer so sure of my impression of the play as a whole as I was while listening to it, when it overwhelmed me. I remember the Yiddish actors. W.'s handsome sisters. The elder one leaned against the chair, often looked at the mirror out of the corner of her eye, and then – as if she

were not already devoured by my eyes – gently pointed a finger to a brooch pinned to her blouse. It was a low-cut dark blue blouse, her throat was covered with a tulle scarf. Repeated account of something that happened at the theatre: some officers kept saying to each other in a loud voice during *Kabale und Liebe*: 'Speckbacher is cutting a figure,' by which they meant an officer leaning against the side of a box.

The day's conclusion, even before meeting Werfel: Go on working regardless of everything; a pity I can't work today, for I am tired and have a headache, already had preliminary twinges in the office this morning. I'll go on working regardless of everything, it must be possible in spite of the office or the lack of sleep.

Dreamed tonight. With Kaiser Wilhelm. In the castle. The beautiful view. A room similar to that in the Tabakskollegium.[85] Meeting with Matilde Serav. Unfortunately forgot everything.

From *Esther*: God's masterpieces fart at one another in the bath.

5 December. A letter from E. on the situation in her family. My relation to her family has a consistent meaning only if I conceive of myself as its ruin. This is the only natural explanation there is to make plausible everything that is astonishing in the relation. It is also the only connexion I have at the moment with her family; otherwise I am completely divorced from it emotionally, although not more effectually, perhaps, than I am from the whole world. (A picture of my existence apropos of this would portray a useless stake covered with snow and frost, fixed loosely and slantwise into the ground in a deeply ploughed field on the edge of a great plain on a dark winter's night.) Only ruin has effect. I have made F. unhappy, weakened the resistance of all those who need her so much now, contributed to the death of her father, come between F. and E., and in the end made E. unhappy too, an unhappiness that gives every indication of growing worse. I am in the harness and it is my fate to pull the load. The last letter to her that I tortured out of myself she considers calm; it 'breathes so much calmness', as she puts it. It is of course not impossible that she puts it this way out of delicacy, out of forbearance, out of concern for me. I am indeed sufficiently punished in general, even my position in my own

family is punishment enough; I have also suffered so much that I shall never recover from it (my sleep, my memory, my ability to think, my resistance to the tiniest worries have been weakened past all cure – strangely enough, the consequences of a long period of imprisonment are about the same); for the moment, however, my relationship to them causes me little suffering, at least less than F. or E. There is of course something tormenting in the fact that I am now supposed to take a Christmas trip with E., while F. will remain in Berlin.

8 December. Yesterday for the first time in ever so long an indisputable ability to do good work. And yet wrote only the first page of the 'mother' chapter,[86] for I had barely slept at all two nights, in the morning already had had indications of a headache, and had been too anxious about the next day. Again I realized that everything written down bit by bit rather than all at once in the course of the larger part (or even the whole) of one night is inferior, and that the circumstances of my life condemn me to this inferiority.

9 December. Together with E. K. of Chicago. He is almost touching. Description of his placid life. From eight to half past five in the mail-order house. Checking the shipments in the textile department. Fifteen dollars a week. Two weeks' holiday, one week with pay; after five years both weeks with pay. For a while, when there wasn't much to do in the textile department, he helped out in the bicycle department. Three hundred bicycles are sold a day. A wholesale business with ten thousand employees. They get all their customers by sending out catalogues. The Americans like to change their jobs, they don't particularly like to work in summer; but he doesn't like to change, doesn't see the point of it, you lose time and money by it. So far he has had two jobs, each for five years, and when he returns – he has an indefinite leave – he will go back to the same job, they can always use him, but can always do without him too. Evenings he generally stays at home, plays cards with friends; sometimes, for diversion, an hour at the cinema, in summer a walk, Sunday a boat-ride on the lake. He is wary of marriage, even though he is already thirty-four years old, since American women often marry only in order to get divorced, a simple matter for them, but very expensive for the man.

13 December. Instead of working – I have written only one page (exegesis of the 'Legend'[87]) – looked through the finished chapters and found parts of them good. Always conscious that every feeling of satisfaction and happiness that I have, such, for example, as the 'Legend' in particular inspires in me, must be paid for, and must be paid for moreover at some future time, in order to deny me all possibility of recovery in the present.

Recently at Felix's. On the way home told Max that I shall lie very contentedly on my deathbed, provided the pain isn't too great. I forgot – and later purposely omitted – to add that the best things I have written have their basis in this capacity of mine to meet death with contentment. All these fine and very convincing passages always deal with the fact that someone is dying, that it is hard for him to do, that it seems unjust to him, or at least harsh, and the reader is moved by this, or at least he should be. But for me, who believe that I shall be able to lie contentedly on my deathbed, such scenes are secretly a game; indeed, in the death enacted I rejoice in my own death, hence calculatingly exploit the attention that the reader concentrates on death, have a much clearer understanding of it than he, of whom I suppose that he will loudly lament on his deathbed, and for these reasons my lament is as perfect as can be, nor does it suddenly break off, as is likely to be the case with a real lament, but dies beautifully and purely away. It is the same thing as my perpetual lamenting to my mother over pains that were not nearly so great as my laments would lead one to believe. With my mother, of course, I did not need to make so great a display of art as with the reader.

14 December. My work goes forward at a miserable crawl, in what is perhaps its most important part, where a good night would stand me in such stead.

At Baum's in the afternoon. He was giving a pale little girl with glasses a piano lesson. The boy sat quietly in the gloom of the kitchen, carelessly playing with some unrecognizable object. Impression of great ease. Especially in contrast to the bustling about of the tall housemaid, who was washing dishes in a tub.

15 December. Didn't work at all. For two hours now have been looking through new company applications for the office. The afternoon at B.'s. He was somewhat offensive and rude. Empty talk in consequence of my debility, blankness, and stupidity almost; was inferior to him in every respect; it is a long time now since I have had a purely private conversation with him, was happy to be alone again. The joy of lying on the sofa in the silent room without a headache, calmly breathing in a manner befitting a human being.

The defeats in Serbia, the stupid leadership.

19 December. Yesterday wrote 'The Village Schoolmaster'[88] almost without knowing it, but was afraid to go on writing later than a quarter to two; the fear was well founded, I slept hardly at all, merely suffered through perhaps three short dreams and was then in the office in the condition one would expect. Yesterday Father's reproaches on account of the factory: 'You talked me into it.' Then went home and calmly wrote for three hours in the consciousness that my guilt is beyond question, though not so great as Father pictures it. Today, Saturday, did not come to dinner, partly in fear of Father, partly in order to use the whole night for working; yet I wrote only one page that wasn't very good.

The beginning of every story is ridiculous at first. There seems no hope that this newborn thing, still incomplete and tender in every joint, will be able to keep alive in the completed organization of the world, which, like every completed organization, strives to close itself off. However, one should not forget that the story, if it has any justification to exist, bears its complete organization within itself even before it has been fully formed; for this reason despair over the beginning of a story is unwarranted; in a like case parents should have to despair of their suckling infant, for they had no intention of bringing this pathetic and ridiculous being into the world. Of course, one never knows whether the despair one feels is warranted or unwarranted. But reflecting on it can give one a certain support; in the past I have suffered from the lack of this knowledge.

20 December. Max's objection to Dostoyevsky, that he allows too

many mentally ill persons to enter. Completely wrong. They aren't ill. Their illness is merely a way to characterize them, and moreover a very delicate and fruitful one. One need only stubbornly keep repeating of a person that he is simple-minded and idiotic, and he will, if he has the Dostoyevskian core inside him, be spurred on, as it were, to do his very best. His characterizations have in this respect about the same significance as insults among friends. If they say to one another, 'You are a blockhead,' they don't mean that the other is really a blockhead who has disgraced them by his friendship; rather there is generally mixed in it an infinite number of intentions, if the insult isn't merely a joke, or even if it is. Thus, the father of the Karamazovs, though a wicked creature, is by no means a fool but rather a very clever man, almost the equal of Ivan, and in any case much cleverer than his cousin, for example, whom the novelist doesn't attack, or his nephew, the landowner, who feels so superior compared to him.

23 December. Read a few pages of Herzen's 'Fogs of London'. Had no idea what it was all about, and yet the whole of the unconscious man emerged, purposeful, self-tormenting, having himself firmly in hand and then going to pieces again.

26 December. In Kuttenberg with Max and his wife. How I counted on the four free days, how many hours I pondered how best to spend them, and now perhaps disappointed after all. Tonight wrote almost nothing and am in all likelihood no longer capable of going on with 'The Village Schoolmaster', which I have been working at for a week now, and which I should certainly have completed in three free nights, perfect and with no external defect; but now, in spite of the fact that I am still virtually at the beginning, it already has two irremediable defects and in addition is stunted – New schedule from now on! Use the time even better! Do I make my laments here only to find salvation here? It won't come out of this notebook, it will come when I'm in bed and it will put me on my back so that I lie there beautiful and light and bluish-white; no other salvation will come.

Hotel in Kuttenberg Moraṽetz, drunken porter, tiny, roofed court with a skylight. The darkly outlined soldier leaning against the railing on the second floor of the building across the court. The room they offered me; its window opened upon a dark, windowless corridor. Red sofa, candle light. Jacobskirche, the devout soldiers, the girls' voices in the choir.

27 December. A merchant was greatly dogged by misfortune. He bore it for a long time, but finally was convinced that he could not bear it any longer, and went to one learned in the law. He intended to ask his advice and learn what he might do to ward off misfortune or to acquire the strength to bear it. Now the scripture always lay open before this sage, that he might study it. It was his custom to receive everyone who sought advice from him with these words: 'I am just now reading of your case,' at the same time pointing with his finger to a passage of the page in front of him. The merchant, who had heard of this custom, did not like it; it is true that in this way the sage both asserted the possibility of his helping the supplicant, and relieved him of the fear that he had been visited with a calamity which worked in darkness, which he could share with no one and with which no one else could sympathize; but the incredibility of such a statement was after all too great and had in fact deterred the merchant from calling sooner on the man learned in the law. Even now he entered his house with hesitation, halting in the open doorway.

31 December. Have been working since August, in general not little and not badly, yet neither in the first nor in the second respect to the limit of my ability, as I should have done, especially as there is every indication (insomnia, headaches, weak heart) that my ability won't last much longer. Worked on, but did not finish: *The Trial*, 'Memoirs of the Kalda Railway', 'The Village Schoolmaster', 'The Assistant Attorney',[89] and the beginnings of various little things. Finished only: 'In the Penal Colony' and a chapter of *Der Verschollene*,[90] both during the two-week holiday. I don't know why I am drawing up this summary, it's not at all like me!

꜀ ꜀ ꜀

4 January. Great desire to begin another story; didn't yield to it. It is all pointless. If I can't pursue the stories through the nights, they break

away and disappear, as with 'The Assistant Attorney' now. And to-morrow I go to the factory, shall perhaps have to go there every after-noon after P. joins up. With that, everything is at an end. The thought of the factory is my perpetual Day of Atonement.

6 January. For the time being abandoned 'Village Schoolmaster' and 'The Assistant Attorney'. But almost incapable too of going on with *The Trial*. Thinking of the girl from Lemberg.[91] A promise of some kind of happiness resembles the hope of an eternal life. Seen from a certain distance it holds its ground, and one doesn't venture nearer.

17 January. Yesterday for the first time dictated letters in the factory. Worthless work (an hour), but not without satisfaction. Hor-rible afternoon previously. Continual headaches, so that I had con-stantly to hold my hand to my head to calm myself (condition in the Café Arco), and heart pains on the sofa at home.

Read Ottla's letter to E. I have really kept her down, and indeed ruthlessly, because of carelessness and incompetence on my part. F. is right about it. Happily, Ottla is strong enough, once she is alone in a strange city, to recover from my influence. How much of her talent for getting on with people lies unexploited because of me! She writes that she felt unhappy in Berlin. Untrue!

Realized that I have by no means made satisfactory use of the time since August. My constant attempts, by sleeping a great deal in the afternoon, to make it possible for myself to continue working late into the night were absurd; after the first two weeks I could already see that my nerves would not permit me to go to bed after one o'clock, for then I can no longer fall asleep at all, the next day is insupportable and I destroy myself. I lay down too long in the afternoon, though I seldom worked later than one o'clock at night, and always began about eleven o'clock at the earliest. That was a mistake. I must began at eight or nine o'clock; the night is certainly the best time (holiday!), but beyond my reach.

Saturday I shall see F. If she loves me, I do not deserve it. Today I think I see how narrow my limits are in everything, and consequently in my writing too. If one feels one's limits very intensely, one must burst. It is probably Ottla's letter that has made me aware of this. I have been very self-satisfied of late and knew a variety of arguments by which to defend and assert myself against F. A pity I had no time to write them down, today I should be unable to do it.

Strindberg's *Black Flags*. On far-away influences: You were certain that others disapproved of your behaviour without their having expressed their disapproval. In solitude you felt a quiet sense of well-being without having known why; some far-away person thought well of you, spoke well of you.

18 January. In the factory until half past six; as usual, worked, read, dictated, listened, wrote without result. The same meaningless satisfaction after it. Headache, slept badly. Incapable of sustained, concentrated work. Also have been in the open air too little. In spite of that began a new story; I was afraid I should spoil the old ones. Four or five stories now stand on their hindlegs in front of me like the horses in front of Schumann, the circus ringmaster, at the beginning of the performance.

19 January. I shall not be able to write so long as I have to go to the factory. I think it is a special inability to work that I feel now, similar to what I felt when I was employed by the Generali.[92] Immediate contact with the workaday world deprives me – though inwardly I am as detached as I can be – of the possibility of taking a broad view of matters, just as if I were at the bottom of a ravine, with my head bowed down in addition. In the newspaper today, for instance, there is an official statement by Sweden according to which it intends, despite threats by the Triple Entente, unconditionally to preserve its neutrality. At the end it says: The members of the Triple Entente will run their heads against a stone wall in Stockholm. Today I swallow it almost entirely the way it was meant. Three days ago I should have felt to my very marrow that a Stockholm ghost was speaking here, that 'threats by the Triple Entente', 'neutrality', 'official statement by Sweden', were only inspissated things of air of a certain shape, which

one can enjoy only with one's eye but can never succeed in touching with one's fingers.

I had agreed to go picknicking on Sunday with two friends, but quite unexpectedly slept past the hour when we were to meet. My friends, who knew how punctual I ordinarily am, were surprised, came to the house where I lived, waited outside awhile, then came upstairs and knocked on my door. I was very startled, jumped out of bed, and thought only of getting ready as soon as I could. When I emerged fully dressed from my room, my friends fell back in manifest alarm. 'What's that behind your head?' they cried. Since my awakening I had felt something preventing me from bending back my head, and I now groped for it with my hand. My friends, who had grown somewhat calmer, had just shouted 'Be careful, don't hurt yourself!' when my hand closed behind my head on the hilt of a sword. My friends came closer, examined me, led me back to the mirror in my room, and stripped me to the waist. A large, ancient knight's sword with a cross-shaped handle was buried to the hilt in my back, but the blade had been driven with such incredible precision between my skin and flesh that it had caused no injury. Nor was there a wound at the spot on my neck where the sword had penetrated; my friends assured me that there was an opening large enough to admit the blade, but dry and showing no trace of blood. And when my friends now stood on chairs and slowly, inch by inch, drew out the sword, I did not bleed, and the opening on my neck closed until no mark was left save a scarcely discernible slit. 'Here is your sword,' laughed my friends, and gave it to me. I hefted it in my two hands; it was a splendid weapon, Crusaders might have used it.

Who tolerates this gadding about of ancient knights in dreams, irresponsibly brandishing their swords, stabbing innocent sleepers who are saved from serious injury only because the weapons in all likelihood glance off living bodies, and also because there are faithful friends knocking at the door, prepared to come to their assistance?

20 January. The end of writing. When will it catch me up again? In what a bad state I am going to meet F.! The clumsy thinking that immediately appears when I give up my writing, my inability to prepare

for the meeting; whereas last week I could hardly shake off all the ideas it aroused in me. May I enjoy the only conceivable profit I can have from it – better sleep.

Black Flags. How badly I even read. And with what malice and weakness I observe myself. Apparently I cannot force my way into the world, but lie quietly, receive, spread out within me what I have received, and then step calmly forth.

24 January. With F. in Bodenbach. I think it is impossible for us ever to unite, but dare say so neither to her nor, at the decisive moment, to myself. Thus I have held out hope to her again, stupidly, for every day makes me older and crustier. My old headaches return when I try to comprehend that she is suffering and is at the same time calm and gay. We shouldn't torment each other again by a lot of writing, it would be best to pass over this meeting as a solitary occurrence; or is it that I believe I shall win freedom here, live by my writing, go abroad or no matter where, and live there secretly with F.?

We have found each other quite unchanged in other ways as well. Each of us silently says to himself that the other is immovable and merciless. I yield not a particle of my demand for a fantastic life arranged solely in the interest of my work; she, indifferent to every mute request, wants the average: a comfortable home, an interest on my part in the factory, good food, bed at eleven, central heating; sets my watch – which for the past three months has been an hour and a half fast – right to the minute. And she is right in the end and would continue to be right in the end; she is right when she corrects the bad German I used to the waiter, and I can put nothing right when she speaks of the 'personal touch' (it cannot be said any way but gratingly) in the furnishings she intends to have in her home. She calls my two elder sisters 'shallow', she doesn't ask after the youngest at all, she asks almost no questions about my work and has no apparent understanding of it. That is one side of the matter.

I am as incompetent and dreary as always and should really have no time to reflect on anything else but the question of how it happens that anyone has the slightest desire even to crook her little finger at me. In rapid succession I have blown upon three different kinds of people

328

with this cold breath. The people from Hellerau, the R. family in Bodenbach, and F. F. said, 'How well behaved we've been.' I am silent as if my hearing had suddenly failed me during this exclamation. We were alone two hours in the room. Round about me only boredom and despair. We haven't yet had a single good moment together during which I could have breathed freely. With F. I never experienced (except in letters) that sweetness one experiences in a relationship with a woman one loves, such as I had in Zuckmantel and Riva – only unlimited admiration, humility, sympathy, despair, and self-contempt. I also read aloud to her, the sentences proceeded in a disgusting confusion, with no relationship to the listener, who lay on the sofa with closed eyes and silently received them. A lukewarm request to be permitted to take a manuscript along and copy it. During the reading of the door-keeper story, greater attention and good observation. The significance of the story dawned upon me for the first time; she grasped it rightly too, then of course we barged into it with coarse remarks; I began it.

The difficulties (which other people surely find incredible) I have in speaking to people arise from the fact that my thinking, or rather the content of my consciousness, is entirely nebulous, that I remain undisturbed by this, so far as it concerns only myself, and am even occasionally self-satisfied; yet conversation with people demands pointedness, solidity, and sustained coherence, qualities not to be found in me. No one will want to lie in clouds of mist with me, and even if someone did, *I* couldn't expel the mist from my head; when two people come together it dissolves of itself and is nothing.

F. goes far out of her way to come to Bodenbach, goes to the trouble of getting herself a passport, after a night spent in sitting up must bear with me, must even listen to me read aloud, and all of it senseless. Does she feel it to be the same sort of calamity I do? Certainly not, even assuming the same degree of sensitivity. After all, she has no sense of guilt.

What I said was true and was acknowledged to be true: each loves the other person as he is. But doesn't think it possible to live with him as he is.

The group here: Dr W. tries to convince me that F. deserves to be hated, F. tries to convince me that W. deserves to be hated. I believe them both and love them both, or try to.

29 January. Again tried to write, virtually useless. The past two days went early to bed, about ten o'clock, something I haven't done for a long time now. Free feeling during the day, partial satisfaction, more useful in the office, possible to speak to people – Severe pain in my knee now.

30 January. The old incapacity. Hardly ten days interrupted in my writing and already cast aside. Once again prodigious efforts stand before me. You have to dive down, as it were, and sink more rapidly than that which sinks in advance of you.

7 February. Complete standstill. Unending torments.

At a certain point in self-knowledge, when other circumstances favouring self-security are present, it will invariably follow that you find yourself execrable. Every moral standard – however opinions may differ on it – will seem too high. You will see that you are nothing but a rat's nest of miserable dissimulations. The most trifling of your acts will not be untainted by these dissimulations. These dissimulated intentions are so squalid that in the course of your self-scrutiny you will not want to ponder them closely but will instead be content to gaze at them from afar. These intentions aren't all compounded merely of selfishness, selfishness seems in comparison an ideal of the good and beautiful. The filth you will find exists for its own sake; you will recognize that you came dripping into the world with this burden and will depart unrecognizable again – or only too recognizable – because of it. This filth is the nethermost depth you will find; at the nethermost depth there will be not lava, no, but filth. It is the nethermost and the uppermost, and even the doubts self-scrutiny begets will soon grow weak and self-complacent as the wallowing of a pig in muck.

9 February. Wrote a little today and yesterday. Dog story.[93]
Just now read the beginning. It is ugly and gives me a headache. In spite of all its truth it is wicked, pedantic, mechanical, a fish barely breathing on a sandbank. I write my *Bouvard et Pécuchet* prematurely. If the two elements – most pronounced in 'The Stoker' and 'In the Penal Colony' – do not combine, I am finished. But is there any prospect of their combining?

Finally took a room. In the same house on Bilekgasse.

10 February. First evening. My neighbour talks for hours with the landlady. Both speak softly, the landlady almost inaudibly, and therefore so much the worse. My writing, which has been coming along for the past two days, is interrupted, who knows for how long a time? Absolute despair. Is it like this in every house? Does such ridiculous and absolutely killing misery await me with every landlady in every city? My class president's two rooms in the monastery. It is senseless, however, to give way at once to despair; rather seek some means, much as – no, it is not contrary to my character, there is still some tough Jewishness in me, but for the most part it helps the other side.

14 February. The infinite attraction of Russia. It is best represented not by a troika but by the image of a vast river of yellowish water on which waves – but not too high ones – are everywhere tossing. Wild, desolate heaths upon its banks, blighted grass. But nothing can represent it; everything rather effaces it.

Saint-Simonism.

15 February. Everything at a halt. Bad, irregular schedule. This house spoils everything for me. Today again heard the landlady's daughter at her French lesson.

16 February. Can't see my way clear. As though everything I possessed had escaped me, and as though it would hardly satisfy me if it all returned.

22 February. Incapable in every respect, and completely so.

25 February. After days of uninterrupted headaches, finally a little easier and more confident. If I were another person observing myself and the course of my life, I should be compelled to say that it must all end unavailingly, be consumed in incessant doubt, creative only in its self-torment. But, an interested party, I go on hoping.

1 March. By a great effort, after weeks of preparation and anxiety, gave notice; not entirely with reason, it is quiet enough, but I simply

haven't done any good work yet and so haven't sufficiently tested either the quiet or the lack of it. I gave notice rather because of the lack of quiet in me. I want to torment myself, want continually to change my situation, believe I foresee my salvation in the change and in addition believe that by such petty changes, which others make while they doze but I make only after having roused up all my faculties, I shall be able to ready myself for the great change that I probably need. I am certainly changing for a room inferior in many ways. Nevertheless, today was the first (or the second) day on which I should have been able to work well, had I not had a very severe headache. Have written a page in haste.

11 March. How time flies; another ten days and I have achieved nothing. It doesn't come off. A page now and then is successful, but I can't keep it up, the next day I am powerless.

Eastern and Western Jews, a meeting.[94] The Eastern Jews' contempt for the Jews here. Justification for this contempt. The way the Eastern Jews know the reason for their contempt, but the Western Jews do not. For example, the appalling notions, beyond all ridicule, by which Mother tries to comprehend them. Even Max, the inadequacy and feebleness of his speech, unbuttoning and buttoning his jacket. And after all, he is full of the best good will. In contrast a certain W., buttoned into a shabby little jacket, a collar that it would have been impossible to make filthier worn as his holiday best, braying yes and no, yes and no. A diabolically unpleasant smile around his mouth, wrinkles in his young face, wild and embarrassed movements of his arms. But the best one is a little fellow, a walking argument, with a sharp voice impossible to modulate, one hand in his pocket, boring towards the listeners with the other, constantly asking questions and immediately proving what he sets out to prove. Canary voice. Tosses his head. I, as if made of wood, a clothes-rack pushed into the middle of the room. And yet hope.

13 March. An evening. At six o'clock lay down on the sofa. Slept until about eight. Couldn't get up, waited for the clock to strike, and in my sleepiness missed hearing it. Got up at nine o'clock. Didn't go home

for supper, nor to Max's either, where there was a gathering tonight. Reasons: lack of appetite, fear of getting back late in the evening; but above all the thought that I wrote nothing yesterday, that I keep getting farther and farther from it, and am in danger of losing everything I have laboriously achieved these past six months. Provided proof of this by writing one and a half wretched pages of a new story that I have already decided to discard and then in despair, part of the blame for which my listless stomach certainly shares, read Herzen in the hope that he might somehow carry me on. His happiness the first year after he was married, my horror of seeing myself in a similar happy state; the high life around him; Belinski; Bakunin in bed all day long with his fur coat on.

Occasionally I feel an unhappiness which almost dismembers me, and at the same time am convinced of its necessity and of the existence of a goal to which one makes one's way by undergoing every kind of unhappiness (am now influenced by my recollection of Herzen, but the thought occurs on other occasions too).

14 March. A morning: In bed until half past eleven. Jumble of thoughts which slowly takes shape and hardens in an incredible fashion. Read in the afternoon (Gogol, essay on the lyric), in the evening a walk, part of the time the defensible but untrustworthy ideas of the morning in my head. Was in Chotek Park. Most beautiful spot in Prague. Birds sang, the Castle with its arcade, the old trees hung with last year's foliage, the dim light. Later Ottla arrived with D.

17 March. Harassed by noise. A beautiful, much more friendly room than the one on Bilekgasse. I am so dependent on the view; there is a beautiful one here, the Teinkirche. But a great deal of noise from the carriages down below; however, I am growing quite used to it. But impossible for me to grow used to the noise in the afternoon. From time to time a crash in the kitchen or the corridor. Yesterday, in the attic above, perpetual rolling of a ball, as if someone for some incomprehensible reason were bowling, then a piano below me in addition. Yesterday evening a relative silence, worked somewhat hopefully ('Assistant Attorney'), today began with joy, suddenly, next door or

below me, a party taking place, loud and fluctuating as though I were in its midst. Contended with the noise awhile, then lay on the sofa with nerves virtually shattered, silence aften ten o'clock, but can't work any longer.

23 March. Incapable of writing a line. The feeling of ease with which I sat in Chotek Park yesterday and on the Karlsplatz today with Strindberg's *By the Open Sea*. My feeling of ease in my room today. Hollow as a clam-shell on the beach, ready to be pulverized by the tread of a foot.

25 March. Yesterday Max's lecture, 'Religion and Nation'. Talmudic Eastern Jews. The girl from Lemberg. The Western Jew who has become assimilated to the Hasidim, the plug of cotton in his ear. Steidler, a Socialist, long, shining, neatly cut hair. The delight with which the Eastern European Jewesses take sides. The group of Eastern Jews beside the stove. G. in a caftan, the matter-of-fact Jewish life. My confusion.

9 April. Torments of my apartment. Boundless. Worked well a few evenings. If I had been able to work at night! Today kept from sleep, from work, from everything by the noise.

14 April. The Homer class for the Galician girls. The one in the green blouse, sharp, severe face; when she raised her hand she held it straight out in front of her; quick movements when she put on her coat; if she raised her hand and was not called on, she felt ashamed and turned her face aside. The sturdy young girl in green at the sewing-machine.

27 April. In Nagy Mihály with my sister.[95] Incapable of living with people, of speaking. Complete immersion in myself, thinking of myself. Apathetic, witless, fearful. I have nothing to say to anyone – never.

Trip to Vienna. The much-travelled, all-knowing, all-judging Viennese, tall, blond-bearded, legs crossed, was reading *Az Est*; obliging, yet, as Elli and I (both of us equally on the watch) noted, reserved. I said, 'How much you must have travelled!' (He knew all

334

the train connexions I needed – as it turned out later, however, the particulars weren't entirely correct – knew all the tram routes in Vienna, advised how to telephone in Budapest, knew what the baggage arrangements were, knew that it was cheaper to take a taxi with your luggage.) He made no reply to this but sat motionless with bowed head. The girl from Žižkov, sentimental, talkative but seldom able to make herself heard, a poor, anaemic, undeveloped body no longer able to develop. The old woman from Dresden with a face like Bismarck's, let it be known later that she was a Viennese. The fat Viennese woman, wife of one of the editors of *Die Zeit*; knew all about newspapers, spoke clearly; to my extreme disgust usually expressed the very opinions I hold. I for the most part silent, had nothing to say; among such people the war doesn't call forth in me the slightest opinion worth expressing.

Vienna–Budapest. The two Poles, the lieutenant and the lady, soon got off, whispered at the window; she was pale, not quite young, almost hollow-cheeked, her hands often on her tight-skirted hips, smoked a great deal. The two Hungarian Jews; the one at the window, who resembles Bergmann, cushioned the head of the other, who was asleep, on his shoulder. Throughout the morning, from five on, talk about business, accounts and letters passing from hand to hand, samples of every kind of article were taken out of a handbag. Across from me a Hungarian lieutenant, in sleep a vacant, ugly face, open mouth, funny nose; earlier, when he had been describing Budapest, full of animation, bright-eyed; lively voice into which his whole personality entered. Near by in the compartment the Jews from Bistritz who were returning home. A man was accompanying several women. They learned that Körös Mesö had just been closed to civilians. They will have to travel twenty hours or more by car. They told a story of a man who stayed in Radautz until the Russians were so close that it was impossible for him to escape except by climbing on to the last Austrian piece of cannon that went through.

Budapest. Very contradictory reports about connexions with Nagy Mihály; I didn't believe the unfavourable ones, which then turned out to be true. At the railway station the hussar in the laced fur jacket danced and shifted his feet like a show horse. Was bidding good-bye to a lady going away. Chatted easily and uninterruptedly with her, if not by words then by dancing motions and manipulations of the hilt of his sabre. Once or twice, in fear lest the train be about to leave, escorted her up the steps to the car, his hand almost under her shoulder. He was of medium height, large, strong, healthy teeth, the cut and accentuated waistline of his fur jacket gave his appearance a somewhat feminine quality. He smiled a great deal in every direction, a really unwitting, meaningless smile, mere proof of the matter-of-fact, complete, and eternal harmony of his being which his honour as an officer almost demanded.

The old couple weeping as they said good-bye. Innumerable kisses senselessly repeated, just as when one despairs, one keeps picking up a cigarette over and over again without being aware of it. They behaved as if at home, without paying any attention to their surroundings. So it is in every bedroom. I couldn't make out her features at all, a homely old woman; if you looked at her face more closely, if you attempted to look at it more closely, it dissolved, so to speak, and only a faint recollection of some sort of homely little ugliness remained, the red nose or several pockmarks, perhaps. He had a grey moustache, a large nose, and real pockmarks. Cycling coat and cane. Had himself well under control, though he was deeply moved. In sorrowful jest chucked the old woman under the chin. What magic there is in chucking an old woman under the chin. Finally they looked tearfully into each other's eyes. They didn't mean this, but it could be interpreted to mean: Even this wretched little happiness, the union of us two old people, is destroyed by the war.

The huge German officer, hung with every kind of accoutrement, marched first through the railway station, then through the train. His height and military bearing made him stiff; it was almost surprising that he could move; the firmness of his waist, the breadth of his shoulders, the slimness of his body made one's eyes open in surprise in order to be able to take it all in at once.

Two Hungarian Jewesses in the compartment, mother and daughter. They resembled each other, and yet the mother was decent-looking, the daughter a miserable if self-conscious remnant. Mother – well-proportioned face, a fuzzy beard on her chin. The daughter was shorter; pointed face, bad complexion, blue dress, a white jabot over her pathetic bosom.

Red Cross nurse. Very certain and determined. Travelled as if she were a whole family sufficient to itself. She smoked cigarettes and walked up and down the corridor like a father; like a boy she jumped up on the seat to get something out of her knapsack; like a mother she carefully sliced the meat, the bread, the orange; like a flirtatious girl – what she really was – she showed off her pretty little feet, her yellow boots, and the yellow stockings on her trim legs against the opposite seat. She would have had no objections to being spoken to, and in fact began herself to ask about the mountains one could see in the distance, gave me her guidebook so that I could find the mountains on the map. Dejectedly I lay in my corner, a reluctance to ask her questions, as she expected me to, grew stronger, in spite of the fact that I rather liked her. Strong brown face of uncertain age, coarse skin, arched lower lip, travelling clothes with the nurse's uniform under them, soft peaked hat crushed carelessly over her tightly twisted hair. Since no one asked her a question, she herself started telling fragments of stories. My sister, who, as I learned later, didn't like her at all, helped her out a bit. She was going to Satvralja Ujhel, where she was to learn her ultimate destination; she preferred being where there was most to do because the time passed more quickly (my sister concluded from this that she was unhappy; I, however, didn't think so). You have all sorts of things happen to you; one man, for example, was snoring insufferably, they woke him, asked him to have some consideration for the other patients, he promised, but hardly had his head touched the pillow again when there was the horrible snoring again. It was very funny. The other patients threw their slippers at him, his bed stood in the corner of the room and he was a target impossible to miss. You have to be strict with sick people, otherwise you get nowhere, yes is yes, no is no, just don't be an easy mark.

At this point I made a stupid remark, but one very characteristic of me – servile, sly, irrelevant, impersonal, unsympathetic, untrue, fetched from far off, from some ultimate diseased tendency, influenced in addition by the Strindberg performance of the night before – to the effect that it must do a woman good to be able to treat men in that way. She did not hear the remark, or ignored it. My sister naturally understood it quite in the sense in which I made it, and by laughing made it her own. More stories of a tetanus case who simply wouldn't die. The Hungarian station master who got on later with his little boy. The nurse offered the boy an orange. He took it. Then she offered him a piece of marzipan, touched it to his lips, but he hesitated. I said: He can't believe it. The nurse repeated this word for word. Very pleasant.

Outside the window Theiss and Bodrog with their huge spring floods. Lake views. Wild ducks. Mountains with Tokay vines. Suddenly, near Budapest, among ploughed fields, a semicircular fortified position. Barbed-wire entanglements, carefully sand-bagged shelters with benches, looked like models. The expression that was a riddle to me: 'adapted to the terrain'. To know the terrain requires the instinct of a quadruped.

Filthy hotel in Ujhel. Everything in the room threadbare. The cigar ashes left by the previous occupant of the bed still on the night table. The beds freshly made only in appearance. Attempted to get permission to travel on a military train, first from the squad headquarters, then from the rear headquarters. Each located in a pleasant room, especially the latter. Contrast between the military and the bureaucracy. Proper estimate of paper work: a table with inkwell and pen. The door to the balcony and the window open. Comfortable sofa. In a curtained compartment on the balcony facing the yard, the clatter of dishes. Lunch was being served. Someone – the first lieutenant, as it later turned out – raised the curtain to see who was waiting. With the words, 'After all, you have to earn your salary,' he interrupted his lunch and approached me. I got nowhere, in spite of the fact that I had to go back to the hotel to fetch my other identification card. All I had written on my identification card was military permission to use the next day's mail train, permission that was entirely superfluous.

The neighbourhood around the railway station like a village, neglected Ringplatz (Kossuth memorial; coffee-houses with gipsy music; pastry shop; an elegant shoe store; newsboys crying the *Az Est*, a one-armed soldier proudly walking around with exaggerated movements; whenever, in the court of the last twenty-four hours, I passed by a crude coloured poster announcing a German victory, there was a crowd gathered closely scrutinizing it; met P.), the suburbs cleaner. Evening in the coffee-house; only civilians from Ujhel, simple people and yet strange, partly suspect, suspect not because there was a war on but because no one could make them out. An army chaplain sitting by himself was reading newspapers.

In the morning the handsome young German soldier in the tavern. Had a great quantity of food served him, smoked a fat cigar, then wrote. Sharp, stern, but youthful eyes, clear, regular, clean-shaven face. Then pulled on his knapsack. Saw him again later saluting someone, but don't remember where.

3 May. Completely indifferent and apathetic. A well gone dry, water at an unattainable depth and no certainty it is there. Nothing, nothing. Don't understand the life in Strindberg's *Separated*; what he calls beautiful, when I relate it to myself, disgusts me. A letter to F., all wrong, impossible to mail it. What is there to tie me to a past or a future? The present is a phantom state for me; I don't sit at the table but hover round it. Nothing, nothing. Emptiness, boredom, no, not boredom, merely emptiness, meaninglessness, weakness. Yesterday in Dobřichovice.[96]

4 May. In a better state because I read Strindberg (*Separated*). I don't read him to read him, but rather to lie on his breast. He holds me on his left arm like a child. I sit there like a man on a statue. Ten times I almost slip off, but at the eleventh attempt I sit there firmly, feel secure, and have a wide view.

Reflection on other people's relationship to me. Insignificant as I may be, nevertheless there is no one here who understands me in my entirety. To have someone possessed of such understanding, a wife perhaps, would mean to have support from every side, to have God. Ottla understands many things, even a great many; Max, Felix, many things; others, like E., understand only details, but with dreadful intensity; F. in all likelihood understands nothing, which, because of our undeniable inner relationship, places her in a very special position. Sometimes I thought she understood me without realizing it; for instance, the time she waited for me at the U-Bahn station – I had been longing for her unbearably, and in my passion to reach her as quickly as possible almost ran past her, thinking she would be at the top of the stairs, and she took me quietly by the hand.

5 May. Nothing, dull slight headache. Chotek Park in the afternoon, read Strindberg, who sustains me.

The long-legged, black-eyed, yellow-skinned, childlike girl, merry, pert, and lively. Saw a friend who was carrying her hat in her hand. 'Do you have two heads?' Her friend immediately understood the joke, in itself a rather feeble one, but alive with the voice and all of the little personality that had been put into it. Laughing, she repeated it to another friend whom she met a few steps farther on: 'She asked me whether I have two heads!'

Met Miss R.[97] in the morning. Really an abysmal ugliness, a man could never change so. Clumsy body, limp as if still asleep; the old jacket that I knew; what she was wearing under the jacket was as indeterminable as it was suspect, probably only her slip; and apparently she was disturbed by being discovered in this state, but she did the wrong thing – instead of concealing what it was that had given rise to her embarrassment, she reached as if guiltily inside the neck of her jacket and jerked it into place. Heavy down on her upper lip, but only in one spot; an exquisitely ugly impression. In spite of it all, I like her very much, even in all her undoubted ugliness; the beauty of her smile hasn't changed, the beauty of her eyes has suffered from the falling-off of the whole. As for the rest, we are continents apart, I certainly don't understand her; she on the other hand was satisfied with the first superficial impression she got of me. In all innocence she asked me for a bread card.

Read a chapter of *The New Christians*[98] in the evening.

Old father and his elderly daughter. He reasonable, slightly stooped, with a pointed beard, a little cane held behind his back. She broad-nosed, with a strong lower jaw, round, distended face; turned clumsily on her broad hips. 'They say I don't look well. But I do look well.'

14 May. Lost all regularity in writing. In the open a great deal. Walk to Troja with Miss St., to Dobřichovice, Častalice with Miss R., her sister, Felix, his wife and Ottla. As though on the rack. Church services on Teingasse today, then Tuckmachergasse, then the soup kitchen. Read old portions of 'The Stoker' today. A strength that seems unattainable (is already unattainable) today. Afraid I am unfit because of a bad heart.

27 May. A great deal of unhappiness in the last entry. Going to pieces. To go to pieces so pointlessly and unnecessarily.

13 September. Eve of Father's birthday, new diary. I don't need it as much as I used to, I mustn't upset myself, I'm upset enough, but to what purpose, when will it come, how can one heart, one heart not entirely sound, bear so much discontent and the incessant tugging of so much desire?

Distractedness, weak memory, stupidity!

14 September. With Max and Langer[99] at the wonder-rabbi's on Saturday. Žižkov,[100] Harantova street. A lot of children on the pavement and stairs. An inn. Completely dark upstairs, groped blindly along with my hands for a few steps. A pale, dim room, whitish-grey walls, several small women and girls standing around, white kerchiefs on their heads, pale faces, slight movements. An impression of lifelessness. Next room. Quite dark, full of men and young people. Loud praying. We squeezed into a corner. We had barely looked round a bit when the prayer was over, the room emptied. A corner room, windows on both sides, two windows each. We were pushed toward a table on the rabbi's right. We held back. 'You're Jews too, aren't you?' A nature as strongly paternal as possible makes a rabbi. All rabbis look like savages, Langer said. This one was in a silk caftan, trousers visible under it. Hair on the bridge of his nose. Furred cap which he kept tugging back and forth. Dirty and pure, a characteristic of people who think intensely. Scratched in his beard, blew his nose through his fingers, reached into the food with his fingers; but when his hand rested on the table for a moment you saw the whiteness of his skin, a whiteness such as you remembered having seen before only in your childhood imaginings – when one's parents too were pure.

16 September. Humiliation at X.'s. Wrote the first line of a letter to him because a dignified letter had taken shape in my head. None the less gave up after the first line. In the past I was different. Besides, how lightly I bore the humiliation, how easily I forgot it, how little impression even his indifference made on me. I could have floated

unperturbed down a thousand corridors, through a thousand offices, past a thousand former friends now grown indifferent, without lowering my eyes. Imperturbable but also unawakeable. And in one office Y. could have been sitting, in another Z., etc.

A new headache of a kind unknown so far. Short, painful stab above and to the right of my eye. This morning for the first time, more frequently since.

The Polish Jews going to Kol Nidre. The little boy with prayer shawls under both arms, running along at his father's side. Suicidal not to go to temple.

Opened the Bible. The unjust Judges. Confirmed in my own opinion, or at least in an opinion that I have already encountered in myself. But otherwise there is no significance to this, I am never visibly guided in such things, the pages of the Bible don't flutter in my presence.

Between throat and chin would seem to be the most rewarding place to stab. Lift the chin and stick the knife into the tensed muscles. But this spot is probably rewarding only in one's imagination. You expect to see a magnificent gush of blood and a network of sinews and little bones like you find in the leg of a roast turkey.

Read *Förster Fleck in Russland*. Napoleon's return to the battlefield of Borodino. The cloister there. It was blown up.

28 September.   Completely idle. Memoirs of General Marcellin de Marbot, and Holzhausen, *Leiden der Deutschen 1812*.

Pointless to complain. Stabbing pains in my head by way of reply.

A little boy lay in the bathtub. It was his first bath at which – as he had so long wished – neither his mother nor the maid was present. In obedience to the command now and then called out to him from the next room by his mother, he hastily passed the sponge over his body; then he stretched out and enjoyed his immobility in the warm water.

The gas flame steadily hummed and in the stove the dying fire crackled. It had long been quiet now in the next room, perhaps his mother had already gone away.

Why is it meaningless to ask questions? To complain means to put a question and wait for the answer. But questions that don't answer themselves at the very moment of their asking are never answered. No distance divides the interrogator from the one who answers him. There is no distance to overcome. Hence meaningless to ask and wait.

29 September. All sorts of vague resolves. That much I can do successfully. By chance caught sight on Ferdinandstrasse of a picture not entirely unconnected with them. A poor sketch of a fresco. Under it a Czech proverb, something like: Though dazzled you desert the wine-cup for the maid, you shall soon come back the wiser.

Slept badly, miserably, tormenting headaches in the morning, but a free day.

Many dreams. A combination of Marschner the director and Pimisker the servant appeared. Firm red cheeks, waxed black beard, thick unruly hair.

At one time I used to think: Nothing will destroy you, not this tough, clear, really empty head; you will never, either unwittingly or in pain, screw up your eyes, wrinkle your brow, twitch your hands, you will never be able to do more than act such a role.

How could Fortinbras say that Hamlet had prov'd most royally?

In the afternoon I couldn't keep myself from reading what I had written yesterday, 'yesterday's filth'; didn't do any harm, though.

30 September. Saw to it that Felix didn't disturb Max. Then at Felix's.

Rossman and K., the innocent and the guilty, both executed without distinction in the end, the guilty one with a gentler hand, more pushed aside than struck down.[101]

1 October. Volume III, Memoirs of General Marcellin de Marbot. Polotsk–Beresina–Leipzig–Waterloo.

Mistakes Napoleon made:

1. Decision to wage the war. What did he wish to achieve by that? Strict enforcement of the Continental Blockade in Russia. That was impossible. Alexander I could not comply without endangering his own position. His father, Paul I, had in fact been assassinated because of the alliance with France and the war with England, which had injured Russia's trade immeasurably. Yet Napoleon hoped Alexander would comply. He intended to march to the Niemen only in order to extort Alexander's compliance.

2. He could have known what awaited him. Lieutenant-Colonel de Pouthon, who had spent several years on military duty with the Russians, begged him on his knees to give it up. The obstacles he cited were: the apathy and lack of cooperation to be expected from the Lithuanian provinces, which had been subjugated by Russia many years ago; the fanaticism of the Muscovites; the lack of food and forage; the desolate countryside; roads that the lightest rain made impassable to artillery; the severity of the winter; the impossibility of advancing in the snow, which fell as early as the beginning of October – Napoleon allowed himself to be influenced in the contrary direction by Maret, the Duke of Bassano, and Davout.

3. He failed to appoint the Prussian Crown Prince to his head-quarters' staff, despite his having been asked to do so. He should have weakened Austria and Prussia as much as possible by demanding large contingents of additional troops from them, instead asked only 30,000 men from each. He should have used them in the front ranks, instead placed them on his flanks, the Austrians under Schwarzenberg facing Volhynia, the Prussians under Macdonald at the Niemen; in this way they were spared and he made it possible for them to block, or at least to endanger, his retreat, which is what actually happened – in November, after England had arranged peace between Russia and Turkey, so freeing Chichekov's army for service elsewhere, the Austrians permitted

344

it to move north through Volhynia unmolested, and this was responsible for the disaster at the Beresina.

4. In each corps were included great numbers of the untrustworthy allies (Badenese, Mecklenburgers, Hessians, Bavarians, Württembergers, Saxons, Westphalians, Spaniards, Portuguese, Illyrians, Swiss, Croats, Poles, Italians) and in that way the corps' unity was weakened. Good wine spoiled by mixing it with murky water.

5. He set his hopes on Turkey, Sweden, and Poland. The first made peace because England paid it to do so. The treacherous Bernadotte deserted him and with England's aid concluded an alliance with Russia; Sweden, it is true, lost Finland, but was promised Norway in return – Norway would be taken from the Danes, who remained devoted to Napoleon. The Poles: Lithuania was too closely tied to them by its forty years' annexation to the Russian state. The Austrian and Prussian Poles did go with him, but without enthusiasm; they feared for the devastation of their country; only what was now the Saxon Grand Duchy of Warsaw could be counted upon to some extent.

6. From Vilna he wanted to organize conquered Lithuania to his own advantage. He might perhaps have received assistance, 300,000 men, if he had proclaimed a Kingdom of Poland (including Galicia and Posen) – a national assembly in Warsaw had in fact already issued proclamations to that effect – but that would have meant war with Prussia and Austria (and would have made peace with Russia more difficult). Besides, even then the Poles would probably have been undependable. The Vilna district mustered only twenty men as bodyguard for Napoleon. Napoleon chose the middle road, promised a kingdom if they cooperated, and so achieved nothing. In any case Napoleon would not have been able to equip a Polish army, for he had had no supplies of weapons and clothing sent to the Niemen after him.

7. He gave Jerome Bonaparte, who had no military experience, the command of an army of 60,000 men. Immediately upon entering Russia Napoleon had split the Russian army. Tsar Alexander and Field Marshal Barclay marched north along the Dvina. Bagration's corps was still at Mir on the lower Niemen. Davout had already occupied Minsk, and he threw Bagration, who sought to pass north that way, back toward Bobruisk in the direction of Jerome. If Jerome had cooperated with Davout – but he did not find that compatible with his

royal dignity – Bagration would have been destroyed or forced to capitulate. Bagration escaped, Jerome was sent to Westphalia, Junot replaced him, only shortly to commit a serious error too.

8. He appointed the Duke of Bassano civil governor and General Hogendorp military governor of the province of Lithuania. Neither knew how to create a reserve force for the army. The Duke was a diplomat, understood nothing of administration; Hogendorp was unacquainted with French customs and military regulations. He spoke French very badly, thus found sympathy neither with the French nor with the local nobility.

9. He spent nineteen days in Vilna, seventeen in Vitebsk, until 13 August, thus lost thirty-six days (a reproach that other writers make against him, not Marbot). But it can be explained: he had still hoped to come to terms with the Russians, wanted to hold a central position from which to command the corps occupying the country behind Bagration, and wanted to spare his troops. Difficulties of supply developed too; every evening, at the end of their day's march, the troops were compelled to fetch their own provisions, often over very great distances. Only Davout had a supply train and cattle for his corps.

10. Unnecessarily great losses at the siege of Smolensk, 12,000 men. Napoleon had expected no such energetic defence. If they had bypassed Smolensk and pressed along Barclay de Tolly's line of retreat, they could have taken it without a struggle.

11. He has been reproached for his failure to act during the Battle of Borodino (7 September). He walked back and forth in a gully all day long, only twice climbing to a hilltop. In Marbot's opinion this was no error; Napoleon had been ill that day, had had severe migraine. On the evening of the 6th he had received reports from Portugal. Marshal Marmont, one of the generals in whom Napoleon had been mistaken, had been badly defeated by Wellington at Salamanca.

12. In principle the retreat from Moscow had been quickly decided upon. Many things made it necessary: the fires, the fighting in Kaluga, the cold, the desertions, the menace to his line of retreat, the situation in Spain, a conspiracy that was uncovered in Paris – but in spite of all this Napoleon remained in Moscow from 15 September until 19 October, still hoping to come to terms with Alexander. Kutusov did not even reply to his last offer to negotiate.

13. He tried to withdraw by way of Kaluga, though that meant taking the roundabout route. He hoped to get provisions there, his line of retreat through Mozhaisk extended a great distance on either side. After a few days, however, he realized that he could not continue this route without giving battle to Kutusov. He therefore turned back along the former line of retreat.

14. The big bridge across the Beresina was covered by a fort and protected by a Polish regiment. Confident that he would be able to use the bridge, Napoleon had all the pontoons burned to lighten and speed the march. But meanwhile Chichekov had taken the fort and burned the bridge. In spite of the extreme cold the river had not frozen. The lack of pontoons was one of the chief causes of the disaster.

15. The crossing over the two bridges thrown across at Studzianka was badly organized. The bridges were thrown across on 26 November, at noon. (If they had had pontoons they could have begun the crossing at daybreak.) They were unmolested by the Russians until the morning of the 28th. Nevertheless, only part of the corps had crossed by then and thousands of stragglers had been left two days on the left bank. The French lost 25,000 men.

16. The line of retreat was not protected. Except at Vilna and Smolensk, there were no garrisoned towns, no depots, no hospitals, from the Niemen to Moscow. The Cossacks were roving all through the intervening countryside. Nothing could reach or leave the army without running the danger of capture. And for that reason not one of the approximately 100,000 Russian prisoners of war was brought across the frontier.

17. Scarcity of interpreters. The Partouneaux division lost its way on the road from Borisov to Studzianka, ran into Wittgenstein's army, and was destroyed. They simply could not understand the Polish peasants who should have served as guides.

Paul Holzhausen, *Die Deutschen in Russland 1812*. Wretched condition of the horses, their great exertions; their fodder was wet green straw, unripe grain, rotten roof thatchings. Diarrhoea, loss of weight, constipation. Used smoking tobacco for enemas. One artillery officer said his men had to ram the length of their arms into the horses' rumps to relieve them of the mass of excrement accumulated in their bowels. Their bodies were bloated from the green fodder. Galloping them could sometimes cut it. But many succumbed; there were hundreds with burst bellies on the bridges of Pilony.

They lay in ditches and holes with dim, glassy eyes and weakly struggled to climb out. But all their efforts were in vain; seldom did one of them get a foot up on the road, and when it did, its condition was only rendered worse. Unfeelingly, service troops and artillery men with their guns drove over it; you heard the leg being crushed, the hollow sound of the animal's scream of pain, and saw it convulsively lift up its head and neck in terror, fall back again with all its weight and immediately bury itself in the thick ooze.

Despair even when they set out. Heat, hunger, thirst, disease. A non-commissioned officer who was exhorted to set an example. The next day a Württemberger first-lieutenant, after a dressing-down by the regimental commander, tore a bayonet out of the hands of the nearest soldier and ran himself through the breast.

Objection to the tenth mistake. Because of the sorry condition of the cavalry and the lack of scouts, the fords about the city were discovered too late.

6 October. Various types of nervousness. I think noises can no longer disturb me, though to be sure I am not doing any work now. Of course, the deeper one digs one's pit, the quieter it becomes, the less fearful one becomes, the quieter it becomes.

Langer's stories: A Zaddik is to be obeyed more than God. The Baal Shem once commanded a favourite disciple to have himself baptized. He was baptized, earned great esteem, became a bishop. Then the Baal Shem had him come to him and gave him his permission to return to Judaism. Again he obeyed and did great penance for his sin. The Baal Shem explained his command by saying that, because of his exceptional qualities, his disciple had been greatly set upon by the Evil One, whom it was the purpose of the baptism to divert. The Baal Shem himself cast the disciple into the midst of evil; it was not the disciple's own fault that he took this step, but because he was commanded to do so, and there seemed nothing more the Evil One could do.

Every hundred years a supreme Zaddik appears, a Zaddik Hador.

He need not be a wonder-rabbi, nor even be known, and yet he is supreme. The Baal Shem was not the Zaddik Hador of his day; it was rather an unknown merchant of Drohobycz. The latter heard that the Baal Shem inscribed amulets – as did other Zaddiks too – and suspected him of being an adherent of Sabbatai Zvi and of inscribing his name on amulets. Therefore, from afar, without knowing him personally, he took away from him the power to bestow amulets. The Baal Shem at once perceived the lack of power in his amulets – he had never inscribed anything but his own name on them – and after some time also learned that the man in Drohobycz was the cause of it. Once, when the man from Drohobycz came to the Baal Shem's town – it was on a Monday – the Baal Shem caused him to sleep an entire day without his being aware of it; as a result the man from Drohobycz fell behind one day in his estimation of the time. Friday evening – he thought it was Thursday – he wanted to depart in order to spend the holiday at home. Then he saw the people going to temple and realized his error. He resolved to remain where he was and asked to be taken to the Baal Shem. Early in the afternoon already, the latter had instructed his wife to prepare a meal for thirty people. When the man from Drohobycz arrived, he sat down to eat immediately after prayers and in a short time finished all the food that had been prepared for thirty people. But he had not eaten his fill, and demanded more food. The Baal Shem said: 'I expected an angel of the first rank, but was not prepared for an angel of the second rank.' Everything in the house that could be eaten he now had brought in, but even that was insufficient.

The Baal Shem was not the Zaddik Hador, but was even higher. Witness for this is the Zaddik Hador himself. For one evening the latter came to the place where lived the future wife of the Baal Shem. He was a guest in the house of the girl's parents. Before going up to the attic to sleep he asked for a light, but there was none in the house. He went up therefore without a light, but later, when the girl looked up from the yard, his room was as bright as a ballroom. Whereupon she recognized that he was an unusual guest, and asked him to take her for his wife. This she was permitted to ask, for her exalted destiny was revealed by her having recognized him. But the Zaddik Hador said: 'You are destined for one even higher.' This is proof that the Baal Shem was higher than a Zaddik Hador.

7 October. Was a long time with Miss R. in the lobby of the hotel yesterday. Slept badly. Headaches.

I frightened Gerti by limping; the horror in a clubfoot.[102]

Yesterday a fallen horse with a bloody knee on Niklasstrasse. I looked away and uncontrollably grimaced in the broad daylight.

Insoluble problem: Am I broken? Am I in decline? Almost all the signs speak for it (coldness, apathy, state of my nerves, distractedness, incompetence on the job, headaches, insomnia); almost nothing but hope speaks against it.

3 November. Went about a great deal lately, fewer headaches. Walks with Miss R. With her at *Er und seine Schwester*, played by Girardi. ('Have you talent then?' – 'Permit me to intervene and answer for you: Oh yes, oh yes.') In the municipal reading-room. Saw the flag at her parents'.

The two wonderful sisters, Esther and Tilka; they are like the contrast between a light on and a light off. Tilka especially is beautiful; olive-brown, lowered, curving eyelids, heart of Asia. Both with shawls drawn about their shoulders. They are of average height, short even, and appear as erect and tall as goddesses; one on the round cushion of the sofa, Tilka in a corner on some unrecognizable seat, perhaps on a box. Half asleep, I had a long vision of Esther, who, with the passion she impresses me as having for everything spiritual, had the knot of a rope firmly between her teeth and swung energetically back and forth in the empty room like the clapper of a bell (a film poster I remember).

The two L.'s. The little devil of a teacher whom I also saw in my half-sleep; how she flew furiously along in a dance, a Cossack-like but floating dance, up and down over a somewhat sloping, rough, dark brown brick pavement lying there in the twilight.

4 November. I remember a corner in Brescia were, on a similar pavement but in broad daylight, I distributed *soldi* to the children. And a church in Verona I forlornly and reluctantly went into, only because of the slight compulsion of duty that a tourist feels, and the heavy com-

pulsion of a man expiring of futility; saw an overgrown dwarf stooped under the holy water font, walked around a bit, sat down; and as reluctantly went out again, as if just such a church as this one, built door to door with it, awaited me outside.

The recent departure of the Jews from the railway station. The two men carrying a sack. The father loading his possessions on his many children, the smallest one as well, in order to mount the platform more quickly. The strong, healthy, young, but already shapeless woman sitting on a trunk holding a suckling infant, surrounded by acquaintances in lively conversation.

5 November. State of excitement in the afternoon. Began with my considering if and how many war bonds I should buy. Twice went to the office to give the necessary order and twice returned without having gone in. Feverishly computed the interest. Then asked my mother to buy a thousand kronen worth of bonds, but raised the amount to two thousand kronen. In the course of all this it was revealed that I knew nothing of an investment I possessed amounting to some three thousand kronen, and that it had almost no effect at all on me when I learned of it. There was nothing in my head save my doubts about the war bonds, which didn't cease plaguing me even after a half-hour's walk through the busiest streets. I felt myself directly involved in the war, weighed the general financial prospects, at least according to what information I possessed, increased or diminished the interest that would some day come to me, etc. But gradually my excitement underwent a transformation, my thoughts turning to writing, I felt myself up to it, wanted nothing save the opportunity to write, considered what nights in the future I could set aside for it, with pains in my heart crossed the stone bridge at a run, felt what I had already experienced so often, the unhappy sense of a consuming fire inside me that was not allowed to break out, made up a sentence – 'Little friend, pour forth' – incessantly sang it to a special tune, and squeezed and released a handkerchief in my pocket in accompaniment as if it were a bagpipe.

6 November. View of the antlike movements of the crowd in front of and in the trench.[103]

At the home of Oskar Pollak's[104] mother. His sister made a good impression on me. Is there anyone, by the way, to whom I don't bow down? Take Grünberg,[105] for instance, who in my opinion is a very remarkable person and almost universally depreciated for reasons which are beyond me – if it were a question, let's say, of which of the two of us should have to die immediately (no great improbability in his case, for they say he is in an advanced stage of tuberculosis), and the decision lay with me as to which it should be, then I should find the question a preposterous one, so long as it was looked at merely theoretically; for as a matter of course Grünberg, a far more valuable person than I, should have been spared. Grünberg too would agree with me. But in the final desperate moment I should, as everyone else would have done long before, invent arguments in my favour, arguments that at any other time, because of their crudity, nakedness, and falsity, would have made me vomit. And these final moments I am surely undergoing now, though no one is forcing a choice upon me; they are those moments when I put off all external distracting influences and try really to look into myself.

'Silently the "black ones" sit around the fire. The light of the flames flickers on their sombre, fanatic faces.'

19 November. Days passed in futility, powers wasting away in waiting, and, in spite of all this idleness, throbbing, gnawing pains in my head.

Letter from Werfel. Reply.

At Mrs M-T.'s, my defencelessness against everything. My malicious remarks at Max's. Disgusted by them the next morning.[106]

With Miss F. R. and Esther.

In the Altneu Synagogue at the Mishnah services. Home with Dr Jeiteles.[107] Greatly interested in certain controversial issues.

Self-pity, because it is cold, because of everything. Now, at half past nine at night, someone in the next apartment is hammering a nail into the wall between us.

21 November. Complete futility. Sunday. A more than ordinary sleepless night. In bed in the sunshine until a quarter past eleven. Walk. Lunch. Read the paper, leafed through some old catalogues. Walk, Hybernerstrasse, City Park, Wenzelsplatz, Ferdinandstrasse, then in the direction of Podol. Laboriously stretched out to two hours. Now and then felt severe pains in my head, once a really burning pain. Had supper. Now at home. Who on high could behold all this with open eyes from beginning to end?

25 December. Open the diary only in order to lull myself to sleep. But see what happens to be the last entry and could conceive of thousands of identical ones I might have entered over the past three or four years. I wear myself out to no purpose, should be happy if I could write, but don't. Haven't been able to get rid of my headaches lately. I have really wasted my strength away.

Yesterday spoke frankly to my boss; my decision to speak up and my vow not to shrink from it had made it possible for me to enjoy two – if restless – hours of sleep the night before last. Put four possibilities to him: (1) Let everything go on as it has been going this last tortured week, the worst I've undergone, and end up with brain fever, insanity, or something of the like; (2) out of some kind of sense of duty I don't want to take a vacation, nor would it help; (3) I can't give notice now because of my parents and the factory; (4) only military service remains. Answer: One week's holiday and hematogen treatment, which my boss intends to take with me. He himself is apparently very sick. If I went too, the department would be deserted.

Relief to have spoken frankly. For the first time, almost caused an official convulsion in the atmosphere of the office with the word 'notice'.

Nevertheless, hardly slept at all today.

Always this one principal anguish: If I had gone away in 1912, in full possession of all my forces, with a clear head, not eaten by the strain of keeping down living forces!

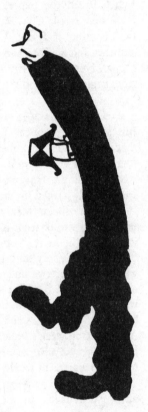

Kafka Sketch

With Langer: He will only be able to read Max's book thirteen days from now. He could have read it on Christmas Day – according to an old custom you are not allowed to read Torah at Christmas (one rabbi made a practice of cutting up his year's supply of toilet paper on that evening), but this year Christmas fell on Saturday. In thirteen days, however, the Russian Christmas will be here, he'll read it then. According to a medieval tradition you may take an interest in *belles-lettres* and other worldly knowledge only after your seventieth year, according to a more liberal view only after your fortieth year. Medicine was the only science in which you were allowed to take an interest. Today not even in that, since it is now too closely joined with the other sciences – You are not allowed to think of the Torah in the toilet, and for this reason you may read worldly books there. A very pious man in Prague, a certain K., knew a great deal of the worldly sciences, he had studied them all in the toilet.

✻ ✻ ✻

19 April. He attempted to open the door to the corridor, but it resisted. He looked up and down but could not discover what the obstacle was. Nor was the door locked; the key in the lock on the inside, if anyone had tried to lock it from the outside the key would have been pushed out. And after all, who could have locked it? He pushed against the door with his knee, the frosted glass rang, but the door stuck fast. How odd.

He went back into the room, stepped out on the balcony, and looked down into the street. But before he had given a thought to the usual afternoon activity below, he again returned to the door and once more attempted to open it. This time, however, it proved more than an attempt, the door immediately opened, hardly any pressure was needed, the draught blowing in from the balcony made it fly right open; he gained entry into the corridor as effortlessly as a child who is playfully allowed to touch the latch at the same time actually that an older person presses it down.

I shall have three weeks to myself. Do you call that inhuman treatment?

A short time ago this dream: We were living on the Graben near the Café Continental. A regiment turned in from Herrengasse on its way to the railway station. My father: 'That's something to look at as long as one can'; he swings himself up on the sill (in Felix's brown bathrobe, the figure in the dream was a mixture of the two) and with outstretched arms sprawls outside on the broad, sharply sloping window ledge. I catch hold of him by the two little loops through which the cord of his bathrobe passes. Maliciously, he leans even farther out, I exert all my strength to hold him. I think how good it would be if I could fasten my feet by ropes to something solid so that my father could not pull me out. But to do that I should have to let go of my father, at least for a short time, and that's impossible. Sleep – my sleep, especially – cannot withstand all this tension and I wake up.

20 April. The landlady came down the corridor towards him with a letter. He scrutinized the old lady's face, not the letter, as he opened it. Then he read:

My dear Sir: For several days you have been living across the way from me. Your close resemblance to an old friend of mine attracted my attention. Do me the honour of paying me a visit this afternoon. With best regards, Louise Halka.

'All right,' he said, as much to the landlady, who had not budged, as to the letter. It was a welcome opportunity to make what might perhaps be a useful acquaintance in this city where he was still a complete stranger.

'Do you know Mrs Halka?' asked the landlady, as he reached for his hat.

'No,' he said, questioningly.

'The girl who delivered the letter is her maid,' the landlady said, as though in apology.

'That may well be,' he said, annoyed at her interest, and hurried to leave the house.

'She is a widow,' the landlady breathed after him from the threshold.

A dream: Two groups of men were fighting each other. The group to which I belonged had captured one of our opponents, a gigantic naked man. Five of us clung to him, one by the head, two on either side by his arms and legs. Unfortunately we had no knife with which to stab him, we hurriedly asked each other for a knife, no one had one. But since for some reason there was no time to lose and an oven stood near by whose extraordinarily large cast-iron door was red-hot, we dragged the man to it, held one of his feet close to the oven until the foot began to smoke, pulled it back again until it stopped smoking, then thrust it close to the door again. We monotonously kept this up until I awoke, not only in cold sweat but with my teeth actually chattering.

Hans and Amalia, the butcher's two children, were playing marbles near the wall of the big warehouse – a large old fortress-like stone building with a double row of heavily barred windows – which extended a great distance along the riverbank. Hans took careful aim, intently regarding the marble, the path it must follow, and the hole, before he made his shot; Amalia squatted beside the hole, impatiently striking her little fists against the ground. But suddenly they both left off their play, slowly stood up, and looked at the nearest window of the warehouse. They heard a sound as if someone were trying to wipe the dirt off one of the many dim panes into which the window was divided; but the attempt failed and the pane was broken through, a thin face, smiling for no apparent reason, indistinctly appeared in the small rectangle; it seemed to be a man and he said, 'Come in, children, come in. Have you ever seen a warehouse?'

The children shook their heads, Amalia looked up in excitement at the man, Hans glanced behind him to see if anyone were near by, but saw only a man with bent back pushing a heavily laden wheelbarrow along the railing of the wharf, oblivious to everything. 'Then it will certainly be a surprise to you,' the man said very eagerly, as though by his eagerness he might overcome the unfortunate circumstance of the wall, bars, and window that separated him from the children. 'But come in now. It's getting late.'

'How shall we come in?' asked Amalia.

'I'll show you the door,' the man said. 'Just follow me, I'm going to the right now and will knock on every window.' Amalia nodded and ran to the next window, there was really a knock there and at all the others too. But while Amalia heeded the strange man and thoughtlessly ran after him as one might run after a hoop, Hans merely trailed slowly after her. He felt uneasy; the warehouse, which it had never before occurred to him to visit, was certainly very much worth seeing, but an invitation from any stranger you please by no means proved that you were really allowed inside it. It was unlikely, rather, for were it permissible, his father would surely have taken him there already, wouldn't he? – his father not only lived close by but even knew all the people a great distance round about, who bade him good day and treated him with respect. And it now occurred to Hans that this might also be the case with the stranger; he ran after Amalia to confirm this, catching up with her just as she, and the man with her, stopped at a small, low, galvanized-iron door level with the ground. It looked like a large oven door.

Again the man broke out a small pane in the last window and said, 'Here is the door. Wait a moment, I'll open the inner doors.'

'Do you know our father?' Hans at once asked, but the face had already disappeared and Hans had to wait with his question. Now they in fact heard the inner doors opening. At first the grating of the key in the lock was hardly audible, but it grew louder and louder as each successive door was opened. The aperture in the thick masonry at this point seemed to be filled by a great number of doors, one set closely behind the other. The last door finally opened inward, the children lay down on the ground to peer inside, and there in the gloom was the man's face. 'The doors are open, come along! Be quick though, quick!' With his arm he pushed all the doors against the wall.

As if the pause outside the door had made her recollect somewhat, Amalia now slipped behind Hans, not wanting to go first, but at the same time she pushed him forward in her eagerness to go with him into the warehouse. Hans was very close to the doorway, he felt the chill air that came through it; he had no desire to go inside, not inside to that strange man, behind all those doors which could be clapped together after him, not inside the huge, cold old building. He asked, only because he already lay in front of the opening: 'Do you know our father?'

'No,' the man replied, 'but come on in, will you? I am not allowed to leave the doors open so long.'

'He doesn't know our father,' Hans said to Amalia, and stood up; he felt relieved, now he would certainly not go in.

'But of course I know him,' said the man, poking his head farther forward in the aperture; 'naturally I know him, the butcher, the big butcher near the bridge, I sometimes get meat there myself; do you think I should let you into the warehouse if I didn't know your family?'

'Then why did you first say that you didn't know him?' asked Hans, who, with his hands in his pockets, had already turned his back on the warehouse.

'Because here, in this position, I don't want to carry on any long discussions. First come inside, then we can talk everything over. Besides, boy, you don't have to come in at all; on the contrary, with your bad manners I should prefer you to stay outside. But your sister now, she's more reasonable, she shall come in and is entirely welcome.' And he held out his hand to Amalia.

'Hans,' Amalia said, reaching out her hand to the stranger's – without taking it, however – 'why don't you want to go in?'

Hans, who after the man's last reply could give no definite reason for his disinclination, merely said softly to Amalia, 'He hisses so.' The stranger in fact did hiss, not only when he spoke but even when he was silent.

'Why do you hiss?' asked Amalia, who wished to intercede between Hans and the stranger.

'I will answer you, Amalia,' the stranger said. 'My breathing is heavy, it is the result of having been here in this damp warehouse for so long; and I shouldn't advise you to stay here too long either, though for a little while it's quite extraordinarily interesting.'

'I'm going,' Amalia said with a laugh, she was now won over completely; 'but,' she then added, more slowly again, 'Hans must come too.'

'Of course,' the stranger said and, lunging forward with the upper part of his body, grabbed Hans, who was taken completely unawares, by the hands so that he tumbled down at once, and with all his strength the man pulled him into the hole. 'This way in, my dear Hans,' he said, and dragged the struggling, screaming boy inside, heedless of the fact that one of Hans's sleeves was being torn to shreds on the sharp edges of the doors.

'Mali,' Hans suddenly cried out – his feet had already vanished within the hole, it went so quickly despite all the resistance he put up – 'Mali, get Father, get Father, I can't get out, he's pulling me so hard!'

But Mali, completely disconcerted by the stranger's rude onslaught – and with some feeling of guilt besides, for to a certain extent she had provoked the offence, though in the final analysis also quite curious, as she had been from the very beginning – did not run away but held on to Hans's feet and let –

It soon became known, of course, that the rabbi was working on a clay figure. Every door of every room in his house stood open night and day, it contained nothing whose presence was not immediately known to everybody. There were always a few disciples, or neighbours, or strangers wandering up and down the stairs of the house, looking into all the rooms and – unless they happened to encounter the rabbi himself – going anywhere they pleased. And once, in a washtub, they found a large lump of reddish clay.

The liberty the rabbi allowed everyone in his house had spoiled people to such a degree that they did not hesitate to touch the clay. It was hard, even when one pressed it one's fingers were hardly stained by it, its taste – the curious even had to touch their tongue to it – was bitter. Why the rabbi kept it in the washtub they could not understand.

Bitter, bitter, that is the most important word. How do I intend to solder fragments together into a story that will sweep one along?

A faint greyish-white smoke was lightly and continuously wafted from the chimney.

The rabbi, his sleeves rolled up like a washerwoman, stood in front of the tub kneading the clay which already bore the crude outline of a human form. The rabbi kept constantly before him the shape of the whole even while he worked on the smallest detail, the joint of a finger, perhaps. Though the figure obviously seemed to be acquiring a human likeness, the rabbi behaved like a madman – time and again he thrust out his lower jaw, unceasingly passed one lip over the other, and when he wet his hands in the bucket of water beside him, thrust them in so violently that the water splashed to the ceiling of the bare vault.

11 May. And so gave the letter to the Director. The day before yesterday. Asked either for a long leave later on, without pay of course, in the event of the war ending by autumn; or, if the war goes on, for my exemption to be cancelled. It was a complete lie. It would have been half a lie if I had asked for a long leave at once, and, if it were refused, for my dismissal. It would have been the truth if I had given notice. I dared neither, hence the complete lie.

Pointless discussion today. The Director thought I wanted to extort the usual three weeks' holiday, which in my exempted status I am not entitled to, offered me them accordingly without further ado, claimed he had decided on it even before the letter. He said nothing at all of the army, as though there had been nothing in my letter about it. When I mentioned it he didn't hear me. He seemed to find a long leave without pay funny, cautiously referred to it in that tone. Urged me to take the three weeks' holiday at once. Made incidental remarks in the role of a lay psychiatrist, as does everyone. After all, I don't have to bear the responsibilities he does, a position like his could really make one ill. And how hard he had had to work even before, when he was preparing for his bar examination and at the same time working in the Institute. Eleven hours a day for nine months. And then the chief difference – have I ever in any way had to be afraid of losing my job? But he had had to worry about that. He had had enemies in the Institute who had tried everything possible, even, as he had said, to deprive him of his means of livelihood, to throw him on the junk heap.

Remarkably enough, he did not speak of my writing.

I was weak, though I knew that it was almost a life-and-death matter for me. But insisted that I wanted to join the army and that three weeks were not enough. Whereupon he put off the rest of the discussion. If he were only not so friendly and concerned!

I will stick to the following: I want to join the army, to give in to a wish I've suppressed for two years; I should prefer to have a long leave for various reasons that have nothing to do with me personally. But because of office as well as military considerations, it is probably impossible. By a long leave I understand – the official is ashamed to say it, the invalid is not – a half or an entire year. I want no pay because it is not a matter of an organic illness that can be established beyond a doubt.

All this is a continuation of the lie; but if I am consistent in it, approximates the truth in its effect.

2 June. What a muddle I've been in with girls, in spite of all my headaches, insomnia, grey hair, despair. Let me count them: there have been at least six since the summer. I can't resist, my tongue is fairly torn from my mouth if I don't give in and admire anyone who is admirable and love her until admiration is exhausted. With all six my guilt is almost wholly inward, though one of the six did complain of me to someone.

From *Das Werden des Gottesglaubens* by N. Söderblom, Archbishop of Upsala; quite scientific, without his being personally or religiously involved.
The primordial divinity of the Mesai: how he lowered the first cattle down from heaven on a leather strap to the first kraal.
The primordial divinity of some Australian tribes: he came out of the west in the guise of a powerful medicine man, made men, animals, trees, rivers, mountains, instituted the sacred ceremonies, and determined from which clan a member of another clan was to take his wife. His task completed, he went away. The medicine men could climb up to him on a tree or a rope and receive their power from him.
Other tribes: during their creative wanderings from place to place they also performed the sacred dances and rites for the first time.
Others: in primordial times men themselves created their totem animals by their ceremonies. The sacred rites thus of themselves begot the object of their veneration.
The Bimbiga near the coast tell of two men who in primordial times created springs, forests, and ceremonies in the course of their wanderings.

19 June. Forget everything. Open the windows. Clear the room. The wind blows through it. You see only its emptiness, you search in every corner and don't find yourself.

With Ottla. Called for her at the English teacher's. Home by way of the quay, the stone bridge, a short stretch of the Kleinseite, the new bridge. Was excited by the statues of saints on the Karlsbrücke. The remarkable light of the summer evening together with the nocturnal emptiness of the bridge.

Joy over Max's liberation. I had believed in its possibility, but now see the reality as well. But again see no possibility for myself.

And they heard the voice of the Lord God walking in the garden towards the cool of the day.

The calm of Adam and Eve.

And the Lord God made for Adam and for his wife garments of skins, and clothed them.

God's rage against the human race. The two trees, the unexplained prohibition, the punishment of all (snake, woman, man), the favour granted Cain, who is nevertheless provoked by God's speaking to him.

My spirit shall not always strive with man.

Then began men to call upon the name of the Lord.

And Enoch walked with God, and he was not; for God took him.

3 July. First day in Marienbad with F. Door to door, keys on either side.

Three houses adjoined each other, forming a little yard. There were also two workshops under sheds in this yard, and in one corner stood a high pile of small boxes. One very stormy night – the wind drove the rain in sheets over the lowest of the houses into the yard – a student still sitting over his books in an attic room heard a loud groan in the yard. He jumped up and listened, but there was silence, unbroken silence. 'I was probably mistaken,' the student told himself, and resumed his reading.

'Not mistaken,' this, after a moment, was what the letters in his book seemed to spell out.

'Mistaken,' he repeated, and moved his index finger along the lines to calm their restlessness.

4 July. I awoke to find myself imprisoned in a fenced enclosure which allowed no room for more than a step in either direction. Sheep

are folded into pens of this kind, though theirs are not so narrow. The direct rays of the sun beat down on me; to shield my head I pressed it against my breast and squatted down with hunched back.

What are you? I am miserable. I have two little boards screwed against my temples.

5 July. The hardships of living together. Forced upon us by strangeness, pity, lust, cowardice, vanity, and only deep down, perhaps, a thin little stream worthy of the name of love, impossible to seek out, flashing once in the moment of a moment.

Poor F.
6 July. Unhappy night. Impossible to live with F. Intolerable living with anyone. I don't regret this; I regret the impossibility for me of not living alone. And yet how absurd it is for me to regret this, to give in, and then finally to understand. Get up from the ground. Hold to the book. But then I have it all back again: insomnia; headaches; jump out of the high window but on to the rain-soaked ground where the fall won't be fatal. Endless tossing with eyes closed, exposed to any random glance.

Only the Old Testament knows – say nothing yet on it.

Dreamed of Dr H. – he sat behind his desk, somehow leaning back and bending forward at the same time; limpid eyes; slowly and precisely, as is his way, pursuing an orderly train of thought to its end; even in the dream hear almost nothing of his words, simply follow the logic by which it is carried on. Then found myself beside his wife, who was carrying a lot of luggage and (what was astonishing) playing with my fingers; a patch was torn out of the thick felt of her sleeve, her arms took up only a small part of the sleeve, which was filled with strawberries.

That they laughed at him troubled Karl not a whit. What kind of fellows were they and what did they know? Smooth American faces having only two or three wrinkles, but these two or three tumid and deeply graven in their brows or down one side of their nose and mouth. Native Americans, in order to know them for what they were it would almost suffice to hammer on their stony brows. What did they know –

A man lay in bed, seriously ill. The doctor sat at the little table that had been pushed next to the bed and watched the sick man, who looked at him in return. 'No help,' said the sick man, not as if he were asking but as if he were answering a question. The doctor partly opened a large medical work lying on the edge of the little table, hurriedly glanced into it from afar, and, clapping the book shut, said, 'Help is coming from Bregenz.' When the sick man, with an effort, squinted his eyes, the doctor added: 'Bregenz in Vorarlberg.'
'That is far away,' the sick man said.

Receive me into your arms, they are the depths, receive me into the depths; if you refuse me now, then later.

Take me, take me, web of folly and pain.

The Negroes came out of the thicket. They leaped into a dance which they performed around a wooden stake encircled by a silver chain. The priest sat to one side, a little rod raised above the gong. The sky was overcast and silent; no rain fell.

I have never yet been intimate with a woman apart from that time in Zuckmantel. And then again with the Swiss girl in Riva. The first was a woman, and I was ignorant; the second a child, and I was utterly confused.

13 July. Then open yourself. Let the human person come forth. Breathe in the air and the silence.

It was an open-air restaurant in a spa. The afternoon had been rainy, not one customer had put in an appearance. The sky cleared only towards evening, the rain gradually stopped, and the waitresses began to wipe off the tables. The manager stood under the arch of the gate and looked out for customers. And in fact one was already coming up the path through the woods. He wore a long-fringed plaid over his shoulders, his head was bowed down on his breast, and at every step his outstretched arm brought his stick down on the ground far in front of him.

14 July. Isaac denies his wife before Abimelech, as Abraham earlier had denied his wife.
Confusion of the wells in Gerar. Verse repeated.
Jacob's sins. Esau's predestination.

A clock strikes gloomily. Listen to it as you enter the house.

15 July. He ran to the woods to look for help, he crossed the first hill almost in a bound, he sped up to the sources of the downward-flowing brooks, he beat the air with his hands, his breath came thickly through his nose and mouth.

19 July.

> Träume und weine, armes Geschlecht,
> findest den Weg nicht, hast ihn verloren.
> Wehe! ist dein Gruss am Abend. Wehe! am Morgen.
>
> Ich will nichts, nur mich entreissen
> Händen der Tiefe, die sich strecken,
> mich Ohnmächtigen hinabzunehmen.
> Schwer fall ich in die bereiten Hände.
>
> Tönend erklang in der Ferne der Berge
> langsame Rede. Wir horchten.
>
> Ach, sie trugen, Larven der Hölle,
> verhüllte Grimassen, eng an sich gedrückt den Leib.
>
> Langer Zug, langer Zug trägt den Unfertigen.[108]

A singular judicial procedure. The condemned man is stabbed to death in his room by the executioner with no other person present. He is seated at his table finishing a letter in which he writes: O loved ones, O angels, at what height do you hover, unknowing, beyond the reach of my earthly hand —

20 July. A small bird flew out of a near-by chimney, perched on its edge, looked about, soared, and flew away. It is no ordinary bird that flies out of a chimney. From a window on the first floor a girl looked up at the sky, saw the bird's upward flight, and cried: 'There it goes, quick, there it goes!' and two children at once crowded to her side to see the bird.

Have mercy on me, I am sinful in every nook and cranny of my being. But my gifts were not entirely contemptible; I had some small talents, squandered them, unadvised creature that I was, am now near my end just at a time when outwardly everything might at last turn out well for me. Don't thrust me in among the lost. I know it is my ridiculous love of self that speaks here, ridiculous whether looked at from a distance or close at hand; but, as I am alive, I also have life's love of self, and if life is not ridiculous its necessary manifestations can't be either – Poor dialectic!

If I am condemned, then I am not only condemned to die, but also condemned to struggle till I die.

Sunday morning, shortly before I left, you seemed to want to help me. I hoped. Until today a vain hope.

And no matter what my complaint, it is without conviction, even without real suffering; like the anchor of a lost ship, it swings far above the bottom in which it could catch hold.

Let me only have rest at night – childish complaint.

21 July. They called. The weather was fine. We stood up, a mixed lot of people, and assembled in front of the house. The street was silent as it always is in the early morning. A baker's boy put down his basket and watched us. All of us came running down the stairs at each other's heels, all the people living on the six floors were mingled indiscriminately together; I myself helped the merchant on the first floor put on the overcoat he had until then been dragging behind him. This merchant was our leader; that was only right, he had more experience of the world than any of us. First he arranged us in an orderly group, admonished the most restive of us to be quiet, took away the hat the bank clerk insisted on swinging and threw it across the street; each child's hand was taken by an adult.

22 July. A singular judicial procedure. The condemned man is stabbed to death in his cell by the executioner without any other person being permitted to be present. He is seated at the table finishing a letter or his last meal. A knock is heard, it is the executioner.

'Are you ready?' he asks. The content and sequence of his questions and actions are fixed for him by regulation, he cannot depart from it. The condemned man, who at first jumped up, now sits down again and stares straight before him or buries his face in his hands. Having received no reply, the executioner opens his instrument case on the cot, chooses the daggers, and even now attempts to touch up their several edges here and there. It is very dark by now, he sets up a small lantern and lights it. The condemned man furtively turns his head towards the executioner, but shudders when he sees what he is doing, turns away again, and has no desire to see more.

'Ready,' the executioner says after a little while.

'Ready?' screams the condemned man, jumps up and now, however, looks directly at the executioner. 'You're not going to kill me, not going to put me down on the cot and stab me to death, you're a human being after all, you can execute someone on a scaffold, with assistants and in the presence of magistrates, but not here in this cell, one man killing another!' And when the executioner, bent over his case, says nothing, the condemned man adds, more quietly: 'It is impossible.' And when the executioner even now says nothing, the condemned man goes on to say: 'This singular judicial procedure was instituted just because it is impossible. The form is to be preserved, but the death penalty is no longer carried out. You will take me to another jail; I shall probably have to stay there a long time, but they will not execute me.'

The executioner loosens a new dagger from its cotton sheath and says: 'You are probably thinking of those fairy tales in which a servant is commanded to expose a child but does not do so and instead binds him over as apprentice to a shoemaker. Those are fairy tales; this, though, is not a fairy tale' –

21 August. For the collection: 'All the beautiful phrases about

368

transcending nature prove ineffectual in face of the primordial forces of life' (Essays against Monogamy).

27 August. Final conclusion after two dreadful days and nights: you can thank your official's vices – weakness, parsimony, vacillation, calculation, caution, etc. – that you haven't sent F. the card. It is possible that you might not have retracted it, that, I grant, is possible. What would have been the result? Some decisive action on your part, a revival? No. You have acted decisively several times already and nothing was improved by it. Don't try to explain it; I am sure you can explain the past, down to the last detail, considering that you are too timid to embark upon a future without having it thoroughly explained in advance – which is plainly impossible. What seems a sense of responsibility on your part, and honourable as such, is at the bottom the official's spirit, childishness, a will broken by your father. Change this for the better, this is what to work at, this is what you can do at once. And that means, not to spare yourself (especially at the expense of a life you love, F.'s), for sparing yourself is impossible; this apparent sparing of yourself has brought you today to the verge of your destruction. It is not only the sparing of yourself so far as concerns F., marriage, children, responsibility, etc.; it is also the sparing of yourself so far as concerns the office you mope about in, the miserable room you don't stir out of. Everything. Then put a stop to all that. One cannot spare oneself, cannot calculate things in advance. You haven't the faintest idea of what would be better for you.

Tonight, for example, two considerations of equal strength and value battled in you at the expense of your brain and heart, you were equally worried on both their accounts; hence the impossibility of making calculations. What is left? Never again degrade yourself to the point where you become the battleground of a struggle that goes on with no regard as it were for you, and of which you feel nothing but the terrible blows of the warriors. Rise up, then. Mend your ways, escape officialdom, start seeing what you are instead of calculating what you should become. There is no question of your first task: become a soldier. Give up too those nonsensical comparisons you like to make between yourself and a Flaubert, a Kierkegaard, a Grillparzer. That is simply infantile. As a link in the chain of calculation, they undoubtedly serve as useful examples – or rather useless examples, for they are part of the whole useless chain of calculation; all by themselves, however, the comparisons are useless right off. Flaubert and Kierkegaard knew very clearly how matters stood with them, were men of decision, did not calculate but acted. But in your case – a perpetual succession of calculations, a monstrous four years' up and down. The comparison with Grillparzer is valid, perhaps, but you don't think Grillparzer a proper one to imitate, do you? an unhappy example whom future generations should thank for having suffered for them.

8 October. Förster: Wants the social relations that exist in school life to be made a subject of instruction.

The bringing up of children as a conspiracy on the part of adults. We lure them from their unconstrained rompings into our narrow dwelling by pretences in which we perhaps believe, but not in the sense we pretend. (Who would not like to be a nobleman? Shut the door.)

The incompensable value of giving free rein to one's vices consists in this, that they rise into view in all their strength and size, even if, in the excitement of indulgence, one catches only a faint glimpse of them. One doesn't learn to be a sailor by exercising in a puddle, though too much training in a puddle can probably render one unfit to be a sailor.

16 October. Among the four conditions that the Hussites proposed to the Catholics as basis for an agreement, there was one that made all mortal sins – by which they meant 'gluttony, drunkenness, unchastity, lying, perjury, usury, fee-taking for confessions, and mass' – punishable by death. One faction even wanted to grant each and every individual the right to exact the death penalty on the spot whenever he saw anyone besmirching himself with one of these sins.

Is it possible that reason and desire first disclose the bare outlines of the future to me, and that I actually move step by step into this same future only under their tugs and blows?

We are permitted to crack that whip, the will, over us with our own hand.

18 October. From a letter to F.:

The matter is not so simple that I can accept without correction what you say of your mother, parents, flowers, the New Year, and the dinner company. You say that for you too it 'would not be the greatest of pleasures to sit at table at home with your whole family'. Of course, you merely express your own opinion when you say this, and are perfectly right not to consider whether or not it pleases me. Well, it doesn't please me. But it would certainly please me even less had you written the contrary. Please tell me as plainly as you can in what this unpleasantness consists and what you regard as its reasons. I know that we have already often spoken of the matter from my side, but it is difficult to grasp even a little of the truth of the matter.

Baldly put – hence with a harshness that doesn't quite correspond to the truth – my position is about as follows: I, who for the most part have been a dependent creature, have an infinite yearning for independence and freedom in all things. Rather put on blinkers and go my way to the limit than have the familiar pack mill around me and distract my gaze. For that reason it is easy for every word I say to my parents or they to me to become a stumbling block under my feet. Every relationship that I don't create or conquer by myself, even though it be in part to my own detriment, is worthless, it hinders my walking, I hate it or am close to hating it. The way is long, my strength is little, there is abundant reason for such hatred. However, I am descended from my parents, am linked to them and my sisters by blood, am sensible of it neither in my everyday affairs nor, as a result of their inevitable familiarity to me, in my special concerns, but at bottom have more respect for it than I realize. Sometimes this bond of blood too is the target of my hatred; the sight of the double bed at home, the used sheets, the nightshirts carefully laid out, can exasperate me to the point of nausea, can turn me inside out; it is as if I had not been definitely born, were continually born anew into the world out of the stale life in that stale room, had constantly to seek confirmation of myself there, were indissolubly joined with all that loathsomeness, in part even if not entirely, at least it still clogs my feet which want to run, they are still stuck fast in the original shapeless pulp. That is how it sometimes is.

But at other times again, I know that they are my parents after all, indispensable elements of my own being from whom I constantly draw strength, essential parts of me, not only obstacles. At such times I want them to be the best parents one could wish for: if I, in all my viciousness, rudeness, selfishness, and lack of affection, have nevertheless always trembled in front of them (and in fact do so today – such habits aren't broken), and if they again, Father from one side, Mother from the other, have inevitably almost broken my spirit, then I want them at least to be worthy of their victory. They have cheated me of what is mine and yet, without going insane, I can't revolt against the law of nature – and so hatred again and only hatred. (At times Ottla seems to me to be what I should want a mother to be: pure, truthful, honest, consistent. Humility and pride, sympathetic understanding and distance, devoting and independence, vision and courage in unerring balance. I mention Ottla because Mother is in her too, though it is impossible to discern.) Very well then, I want them to be worthy of it.

You belong to me, I have made you mine. I can't believe that there was ever a woman in a fairy tale fought for harder and more desperately than I have fought for you within myself, from the beginning, and always anew, and perhaps forever. You belong to me then, and so my relation to your people is similar to my relation to my own, although incomparably less intense, of course, both for good and for bad. They constitute a tie that hinders me (hinders me even if I should never exchange a word with them), and they are not – in the sense I have used the word above – worthy. I speak as frankly to you as I should to myself; don't take it amiss or look for arrogance in it, it isn't there, at least not where you might look for it.

When you are here, sitting at my parents' table, my vulnerability to what is hostile to me in my father and mother is of course much greater. My connexion with the whole family seems to them to have grown much stronger (but it hasn't and shouldn't); I seem to them part of the chain one link of which is the bedroom near by (but I am not); they hope to have found an accomplice in you against my opposition (they haven't found one); and they appear more ugly and contemptible in my eyes in the degree that I expect more from them under such circumstances.

If all this is as I say, then why don't I rejoice at your remark? Because I confront my family unceasingly flailing about me in a circle with knives, as it were, in order simultaneously to injure and defend them. Let me be entirely your representative in this, without your representing me in the same sense to your family. Is this too great a sacrifice for you, darling? It is a tremendous one, I know, and will be made easier for you only by the knowledge that my nature is such that I must take it from you by force if you do not voluntarily make me it. But if you do make it, then you have done a great deal for me. I will purposely refrain from writing to you for a day or two so that you can think it over undisturbed by me and give me your reply. A single word – so great is my confidence in you – will serve as answer.

20 October. Two gentlemen in the paddock were discussing a horse whose hindquarters a stable boy was rubbing down. 'I haven't,' said the white-haired elder man, squinting one eye somewhat as he gently gnawed his lower lip, 'I haven't seen Atro for a week now, one's memory for horses is an uncertain thing no matter how much practice one has had. I miss qualities in Atro, now, that I distinctly remember him to have had. It is the total impression I speak of – the details, I am sure, are correct, though I do notice a flabbiness of his muscles here and there. Look here and here.' His lowered head moved from side to side in scrutiny and his hands groped in the air.[109]

ɯ ɯ ɯ

6 April. Today, in the tiny harbour where save for fishing boats only two ocean-going passenger steamers used to call, a strange boat lay at anchor. A clumsy old craft, rather low and very broad, filthy, as if bilge water had been poured over it, it still seemed to be dripping down the yellowish sides; the masts disproportionately tall, the upper third of the mainmast split; wrinkled, coarse, yellowish-brown sails stretched anyhow between the yards, patched, too weak to stand against the slightest gust of wind.

I gazed in astonishment at it for a time, waited for someone to show himself on deck; no one appeared. A workman sat down beside me on the harbour wall. 'Whose ship is that?' I asked; 'this is the first time I've seen it.'

'It puts in every two or three years,' the man said, 'and belongs to the Hunter Gracchus.'

29 July. Court yester. Essay on court jesters.

The great days of the court jesters are probably gone never to return. Everything points in another direction, it cannot be denied. I at least have thoroughly delighted in the institution, even if it should now be lost to mankind.

My place was always far in the rear of the shop, completely in the dark, often you had to guess what it was that you held in your hand; in spite of this every bad stitch brought you a blow from the master.

Our King made no display of pomp; anyone who did not know him from his pictures would never have recognized him as the King. His clothes were badly made, not in our shop, however, of a skimpy material, his coat forever unbuttoned, flapping, and wrinkled, his hat crumpled, clumsy, heavy boots, broad, careless movements of his arms, a strong face with a large, straight, masculine nose, a short moustache, dark, somewhat too sharp eyes, a powerful, well-shaped neck. Once he stopped in passing in the doorway of our shop, put his right hand up against the lintel of the door, and asked, 'Is Franz here?' He knew everyone by name. I came out of my dark corner and made my way through the journeymen. 'Come along,' he said, after briefly glancing at me. 'He's moving into the castle,' he said to the master.

30 July. Miss K. Coquetry that ill suits the kind of person she is. She spreads, points, pouts her lips as if her fingers were invisibly shaping them. Makes sudden, probably nervous, though controlled movements which always take one by surprise – the way she arranges her skirt over her knees, for instance, or changes her seat. Her conversation contains a minimum of words and ideas, is unassisted by other people, is chiefly produced by turns of her head, gesticulations, various pauses, lively glances; if necessary, by clenching her little fists.

He disengaged himself from their midst. Mist blew about him. A round clearing in the woods. The phoenix in the underbrush. A hand continually making the sign of the cross on an invisible face. A cool, perpetual rain, a changing song, as if from a heaving breast.

A useless person. A friend? If I attempt to summon to mind what those attributes are which he possesses, what remains, even after the most charitable verdict, is only his voice, somewhat deeper than mine. If I cry out, 'Saved!' – I mean if I were Robinson Crusoe and cried out, 'Saved!' – he would echo it in his deeper voice. If I were Korah and cried out, 'Lost!' he would promptly be there with his deeper voice to echo it. One eventually grows weary of perpetually leading this bass fiddler around with one. He himself by no means does this cheerfully, he echoes me only because he must and can do nothing else. Occasionally, during a holiday, when for once I have time to turn my attention to such personal matters, I consult with him, in the garden perhaps, as to how I might get rid of him.

31 July. Sit in a train, forget the fact, and live as if you were at home; but suddenly recollect where you are, feel the onward-rushing power of the train, change into a traveller, take a cap out of your bag, meet your fellow travellers with a more sovereign freedom, with more insistence, let yourself be carried towards your destination by no effort of your own, enjoy it like a child, become a darling of the women, feel the perpetual attraction of the window, always have at least one hand extended on the window sill. Same situation, more precisely stated: Forget that you forgot, change in an instant into a child travelling by itself on an express train around whom the speeding, trembling car materializes in its every fascinating detail as if out of a magician's hand.

1 August. Dr O.'s stories at the swimming-pool of old Prague. The wild speeches Friederich Adler[110] made against the rich during his student days, which everyone laughed at so; later he made a wealthy match and spoke no more – When Dr O. was a little boy and came from Amschelberg to attend the Gymnasium at Prague, he lived with a Jewish scholar whose wife was a saleswoman in a second-hand clothing store. Meals were brought in from a tavern. At half past five every day, O. was awakened for prayers – He provided for the education of all his younger brothers and sisters; it caused him a great deal of labour but gave him confidence and satisfaction. A certain Dr A., who later became a treasury official and has long been retired (a great egoist),

once advised him at that time to go away, hide, simply run away from his family, for otherwise they would be the ruin of him.

I tighten the reins.

2 August. Usually the one whom you are looking for lives next door. This isn't easy to explain, you must simply accept it as a fact. It is so deeply founded that there is nothing you can do about it, even if you should make an effort to. The reason is that you know nothing of this neighbour you are looking for. That is, you know neither that you are looking for him nor that he lives next door, in which case he very certainly lives next door. You may of course know this as a general fact in your experience; only such knowledge doesn't matter in the least, even if you expressly keep it forever in mind. I'll tell you of one such case –

Pascal arranges everything very tidily before God makes his appearance, but there must be a deeper, uneasier scepticism than that of a man cutting himself to bits with – indeed – wonderful knives, but still, with the calm of a butcher. Whence this calm? this confidence with which the knife is wielded? Is God a theatrical triumphal chariot that (granted the toil and despair of the stage-hands) is hauled on to the stage from afar by ropes?

3 August. Once more I screamed at the top of my voice into the world. Then they shoved a gag into my mouth, tied my hands and feet, and blindfolded me. I was rolled back and forth a number of times, I was set upright and knocked down again, this too several times, they jerked at my legs so that I jumped with pain; they let me lie quietly for a moment, but then, taking me by surprise, stabbed deep into me with something sharp, here and there, at random.

For years I have been sitting at the great intersection, but tomorrow, because the new Emperor is arriving, I intend to leave my post. As much on principle as from disinclination, I meddle in nothing that goes on around me. For a long time now I have even stopped begging; old passers-by give me something out of habit, out of loyalty, out of friendship, and the newcomers follow their example. I have a little basket beside me, and everybody tosses as much as he thinks proper into it. But for that very reason, because I bother with no one and in the tumult and absurdity of the street preserve the calmness of my outlook and the calmness of my soul, I understand better than anyone else everything that concerns me, my position, and what is rightfully my due. There can be no dispute about these questions, here only my opinion is of consequence. And therefore when a policeman, who naturally knows me very well but whom I just as naturally never noticed, halted beside me this morning and said, 'Tomorrow the Emperor will arrive; see to it that you're not here tomorrow,' I replied by asking him, 'How old are you?'

The term 'literature', when uttered in reproach, is a conversational catch-all for so much, that – there was probably some such intention in its usage from the very first – it has gradually become a catch-all for ideas as well; the term deprives one of right perspective and causes the reproach to fall short and wide of its mark.

The alarm trumpets of the void.

A: I want to ask your advice.
B: Why mine?
A: I have confidence in you.
B: Why?
A: I have often seen you at our gatherings. And among us it is ultimately always a matter of gathering together to seek advice. We agree on that, don't we? No matter what sort of gathering it may be, whether we want to put on theatricals, or drink tea, or raise up spirits, or help the poor, it is always ultimately a matter of seeking advice. So many people with no one to advise them! And even more than would appear, for those who proffer advice at meetings of this kind do so only with their voices, in their hearts they desire to be advised themselves. Their double is always among the listeners, their words are particularly aimed at him. But he, more than anyone else, departs unsatisfied, disgusted, and drags his adviser after him to other meetings and the same game.

B: That's how it is?

A: Certainly, you see it yourself, don't you? But there is no particular merit in your discernment; all the world sees it, and its plea is so much more insistent.

5 August. The afternoon in Radešovicz with Oskar. Sad, weak, made frequent efforts to keep track of the main question.

A: Good day.

B: You've been here once before? Right?

A: You recognize me? How surprising.

B: Several times already I've spoken to you in my thoughts. Now what was it you wanted the last time we met?

A: To ask your advice.

B: Correct. And was I able to give it to you?

A: No. Unfortunately, we couldn't agree even on how to put the question.

B: So that's how it was.

A: Yes. It was very unsatisfactory, but only for the moment, after all. One can't just get at the thing all at once. Couldn't we repeat the question once again?

B: Of course. Fire away.

A: Well then, my question is –

B: Yes?

A: My wife –

B: Your wife?

A: Yes, of course.

B: I don't understand. You have a wife?

A: –

6 August.

A: I am not satisfied with you.

B: I won't ask why. I know.

A: And?

B: I am so powerless. I can change nothing. Shrug my shoulders and screw up my mouth, that's all; I can't do more.

378

A: I'll take you to my Master. Will you go?

B: I feel ashamed. How will he receive me? Go straight to the Master! It's not right.

A: Let me bear the responsibility. I'm taking you. Come.

[*They go along a corridor. A knocks on a door. A voice calls out, 'Come in.' B wants to run away, but A catches hold of him and they enter.*]

C: Who is the Master?

A: I thought – At his feet! throw yourself at his feet!

A: No way out, then?

B: I've found none.

A: And you're the one who knows the neighbourhood best of all.

B: Yes.

7 August.

A: You're always hanging around the door here. Now what do you want?

B: Nothing, thank you.

A: Really! Nothing? Besides, I know you.

B: You must be mistaken.

A: No, no. You are B and went to school here twenty years ago. Yes or no?

B: All right, yes. I didn't dare introduce myself.

A: You do seem to have grown timid with the years. You weren't then.

B: Yes, then I wasn't. I repent me of everything as if I had done it this very hour.

A: You see, everything is paid for in this life.

B: Alas!

A: I told you so.

B: You told me so. But it *isn't* so. Things aren't paid for directly. What does my employer care if I chattered in school. That was no obstacle to my career, no.

The explorer felt too tired to give commands or to do anything. He merely took a handkerchief from his pocket, gestured as if he were dipping it in the distant bucket, pressed it to his brow, and lay down beside the pit. He was found in this position by the two men the Commandant had sent out to fetch him. He jumped up when they spoke to him as if revived. With his hand on his heart he said, 'I am a cur if I allow that to happen.' But then he took his own words literally and began to run around on all fours. From time to time, however, he leaped erect, shook the fit off, so to speak, threw his arms around the neck of one of the men, and tearfully exclaimed, 'Why does all this happen to me!' and then hurried to his post.[111]

8 August. And even if everything remained unchanged, the spike was still there, crookedly protruding from his shattered forehead as if it bore witness to some truth.[112]

As though all this were making the explorer aware that what was still to follow was solely his and the dead man's affair, he dismissed the soldier and the condemned man with a gesture of his hand; they hesitated, he threw a stone at them, and when they still deliberated, he ran up to them and struck them with his fists.
'What?' the explorer suddenly said. Had something been forgotten. A last word? A turn? An adjustment? Who can penetrate the confusion? Damned, miasmal tropical air, what are you doing to me? I don't know what is happening. My judgement has been left back at home in the north.

'What?' the explorer suddenly said. Had something been forgotten? A word? A turn? An adjustment? Very likely. Very probably. A gross error in the calculation, a fundamental misconception, the whole thing is going wrong. But who will set it right? Where is the man who will set it right? Where is the good old miller back home in the north who would stick these two grinning fellows between his millstones?

'Prepare the way for the snake!' came the shout. 'Prepare the way for the great Madame!'
'We are ready,' came the answering shout, 'we are ready!' And we who were to prepare the way, renowned stone-crushers all, marched out of the woods. 'Now!' our Commandant called out, blithely as always, 'go to it, you snake-fodder!' Immediately we raised our

hammers and for miles around the busiest hammering began. No pause was allowed, only a change from one hand to the other. The arrival of our snake was promised for the evening, by then everything had to be crushed to dust, our snake could not stand even the tiniest of stones. Where is there another snake so fastidious? She is a snake without peer, she has been thoroughly pampered by our labour, and by now there is no one to compare with her. We do not understand, we deplore the fact that she still calls herself a snake. She should call herself Madame at least – though as Madame she is of course without peer too. But that is no concern of ours; our job is to make dust.

Hold the lamp up high, you up front there! The rest of you without a sound behind me! All in single file! And quiet! That was nothing. Don't be afraid, I'm responsible. I'll lead you out.

9 August. The explorer made a vague movement of his hand, abandoned his efforts, again thrust the two men away from the corpse and pointed to the colony where they were to go at once. Their gurgling laughter indicated their gradual comprehension of his command; the condemned man pressed his face, which had been repeatedly smeared with grease, against the explorer's hand, the soldier slapped the explorer on the shoulder with his right hand – in his left hand he waved his gun – all three now belonged together.

The explorer had forcibly to ward off the feeling coming over him that in this case a perfect solution had been effected. He was stricken with fatigue and abandoned his intention of burying the corpse now. The heat, which was still on the increase – the explorer was unwilling to raise his head towards the sun only lest he grow dizzy – the sudden, final silence of the officer, the sight of the two men opposite staring strangely at him, and with whom every connexion had been severed by the death of the officer, and lastly, the smooth, automatic refutation which the officer's contention had found here, all this – the explorer could no longer stand erect and sat down in the cane chair.

If his ship had slithered to him across this trackless sand to take him aboard – that he would have preferred to everything. He would have climbed aboard, except that from the ladder he would have once more denounced the officer for the horrible execution of the condemned man. 'I'll tell them of it at home,' he would have said, raising his voice so that the captain and the sailors bending in curiosity over the rail might hear him. 'Executed?' the officer would have asked, with reason. 'But here he is,' he would have said, pointing to the man carrying the explorer's baggage. And in fact it was the condemned man, as the explorer proved to himself by looking sharply at him and scrutinizing his features.

'My compliments,' the explorer was obliged to say, and said it gladly. 'A conjuring trick?' he asked.

'No,' the officer said, 'a mistake on your part; I was executed, as you commanded.' The captain and the sailors now listened even more attentively. And all saw together how the officer passed his hand across his brow to disclose a spike crookedly protruding from his shattered forehead.

It was during the period of the last great battles that the American government had to wage against the Indians. The fort deepest in Indian territory – it was also the best fortified – was commanded by General Samson, who had often distinguished himself in this place and possessed the unswerving confidence of the population and his soldiers. The shout, 'General Samson!' was almost as good as a rifle against a single Indian.

One morning a scouting party out in the woods captured a young man, and in accordance with the standing order of the General – he took a personal interest even in the most trivial matters – brought him to headquarters. As the General was in conference at that moment with several farmers from the border district, the stranger was first brought before the adjutant, Lieutenant-Colonel Otway.

'General Samson!' I cried, and staggered back a step. It was he who stepped out of the tall thicket. 'Be quiet!' he said, pointing behind him. An escort of about ten men stumbled after him.

10 August. I was standing with my father in the lobby of a building; outside it was raining very hard. A man was about to hurry into the lobby from the street when he noticed my father. That made him

stop. 'Georg,' he said slowly, as though he had gradually to bring old memories to the surface, and, holding out his hand, approached my father from the side.

'No, let me alone! No, let me alone!' I shouted without pause all the way along the streets, and again and again she laid hold of me, again and again the clawed hands of the siren struck at my breast from the side or across my shoulder.

15 September.[118] You have the chance, as far as it is at all possible, to make a new beginning. Don't throw it away. If you insist on digging deep into yourself, you won't be able to avoid the muck that will well up. But don't wallow in it. If the infection in your lungs is only a symbol, as you say, a symbol of the infection whose inflammation is called F. and whose depth is its deep justification; if this is so then the medical advice (light, air, sun, rest) is also a symbol. Lay hold of this symbol.

O wonderful moment, masterful version, garden gone to seed. You turn the corner as you leave the house and the goddess of luck rushes towards you down the garden path.

Majestic presence, prince of the realm.

The village square abandoned to the night. The wisdom of the children. The primacy of the animals. The women. Cows moving across the square in the most matter-of-fact way.

18 September. Tear everything up.

19 September. Instead of the telegram – Very Welcome Michelob Station Feel Splendid Franz Ottla – which Mařenka twice took to Flöhau claiming not to have been able to send it because the post office had closed shortly before she arrived, I wrote a farewell letter and once again, at one blow, suppressed the violent beginnings of torment. Though the farewell letter is ambiguous, like my feelings.

It is the age of the infection rather than its depth and festering which makes it painful. To have it repeatedly ripped open in the same spot, though it has been operated on countless times, to have to see it taken under treatment again – that is what is bad.

The frail, uncertain, ineffectual being – a telegram knocks it over, a letter sets it on its feet, reanimates it, the silence that follows the letter plunges it into a stupor.

The cat's playing with the goats. The goats resemble: Polish Jews, Uncle S., I., E.W.

The manservant H. (who today left without dinner or saying good-bye; it is doubtful whether he will come tomorrow), the young woman and Mařenka are unapproachable in different but equally severe ways. I really feel constrained in their presence, as in the presence of animals in stalls when you tell them to do something and, surprisingly, they do it. Their case is the more difficult only because they so often seem approachable and understandable for a moment.

Have never understood how it is possible for almost everyone who writes to objectify his sufferings in the very midst of undergoing them; thus I, for example, in the midst of my unhappiness, in all likelihood with my head still smarting from unhappiness, sit down and write to someone: I am unhappy. Yes, I can even go beyond that and with as many flourishes as I have the talent for, all of which seem to have nothing to do with my unhappiness, ring simple, or contrapuntal, or a whole orchestration of changes on my theme. And it is not a lie, and it does not still my pain; it is simply a merciful surplus of strength at a moment when suffering has raked me to the bottom of my being and plainly exhausted all my strength. But then what kind of surplus is it?

Yesterday's letter to Max. Lying, vain, theatrical. A week in Zürau.

In peacetime you don't get anywhere, in wartime you bleed to death.

Dreamed of Werfel: He was saying that in Lower Austria, where he is stopping at present, by accident he lightly jostled against a man on

the street, whereupon the latter swore at him shamefully. I have forgotten the precise words, I remember only that one of them was
'barbarian' (from the World War), and that it ended with 'you proletarian Turch'. An interesting combination: 'Turch' is a dialect word
for 'Turk'; 'Turk' is a curse word apparently still part of a tradition
deriving from the old wars against the Turks and the sieges of Vienna,
and added to that the new epithet, 'proletarian'. Excellently char-
acterizes the simplicity and backwardness of his insulter, for today
neither 'proletarian' nor 'Turk' is a real curse word.

21 September. F. was here, travelled thirty hours to see me; I
should have prevented her. As I see it, she is suffering the utmost misery
and the guilt is essentially mine. I myself am unable to take hold of
myself, am as helpless as I am unfeeling, think of the disturbance of a
few of my comforts, and, as my only concession, condescend to act my
part. In single details she is wrong, wrong in defending what she calls –
or what are really – her rights, but taken all together, she is an innocent
person condemned to extreme torture; I am guilty of the wrong for
which she is being tortured, and am in addition the torturer – With her
departure (the carriage in which she and Ottla are riding goes around
the pond, I cut across and am close to her once more) and a headache
(the last trace in me of my acting), the day ends.

A dream about my father: There was a small audience (to characterize it, Mrs Fanta was there) before which my father was making
public for the first time a scheme of his for social reform. He was
anxious to have this select audience, an especially select one in his
opinion, undertake to make propaganda for his scheme. On the surface
he expressed this much more modestly, merely requesting the audience,
after they should have heard his views, to let him have the address of
interested people who might be invited to a large public meeting soon
to take place. My father had never yet had any dealings with these
people, consequently took them much too seriously, had even put on a
black frock coat, and described his scheme with that extreme solicitude
which is the mark of an amateur. The company, in spite of the fact
that they weren't at all prepared for a lecture, recognized at once that
he was offering them, with all the pride of originality, what was nothing

more than an old, outworn idea that had been thoroughly debated long ago. They let my father feel this. He had anticipated the objection, however, and, with magnificent conviction of its rutility (though it often appeared to tempt even him), with a faint bitter smile, put his case even more emphatically. When he had finished, one could perceive from the general murmur of annoyance that he had convinced them neither of the originality nor the practicability of his scheme. Not many were interested in it. Still, here and there someone was to be found who, out of kindness, and perhaps because he knew me, offered him a few addresses. My father, completely unruffled by the general mood, had cleared away his lecture notes and picked up the piles of white slips that he had ready for writing down the few addresses. I could hear only the name of a certain Privy Councillor Střižanowski, or something similar.

Later I saw my father sitting on the floor, his back against the sofa, as he sits when he plays with Felix.[114] Alarmed, I asked him what he was doing. He was pondering his scheme.

22 September. Nothing.

25 September. On the way to the woods. You have destroyed everything without having really possessed it. How do you intend to put it together again? What strength still remains to the roving spirit for the greatest of all labours?

Das neue Geschlecht by Tagger – miserable, loud-mouthed, lively, skilful, well written in spots, with faint tremors of amateurishness. What right has he to make a big stir? At bottom he is as miserable as I and everybody else.

Not entirely a crime for a tubercular to have children. Flaubert's father was tubercular. Choice: either the child's lungs will warble (very pretty expression for the music the doctor puts his ear to one's chest to hear), or it will be a Flaubert. The trembling of the father while off in the emptiness the matter is being discussed.

I can still have passing satisfaction from works like *A Country*

Doctor, provided I can still write such things at all (very improbable). But happiness only if I can raise the world into the pure, the true, and the immutable.

The whips with which we lash each other have put forth many knots these five years.

28 September. Outline of my conversations with F.

I: This, then, is what I have come to.

F.: This is what *I* have come to.

I: This is what I have brought you to.

F.: True.

I would put myself in death's hands, though. Remnant of a faith. Return to a father. Great Day of Atonement.[115]

From a letter to F., perhaps the last (1 October):

If I closely examine what is my ultimate aim, it turns out that I am not really striving to be good and to fulfil the demands of a Supreme Judgement, but rather very much the contrary: I strive to know the whole human and animal community, to recognize their basic predilections, desires, moral ideals, to reduce these to simple rules and as quickly as possible trim my behaviour to these rules in order that I may find favour in the whole world's eyes; and, indeed (this is the inconsistency), so much favour that in the end I could openly perpetrate the iniquities within me without alienating the universal love in which I am held – the only sinner who won't be roasted. To sum up, then, my sole concern is the human tribunal, which I wish to deceive, moreover, though without practising any actual deception.

8 October. In the meantime: letter of complaint from F.; G.B. threatens me with writing a letter. Disconsolate state (lumbago). Feeding the goats; field tunnelled by mice; digging potatoes ('How the wind blows up our arses'); picking hips; the peasant F. (seven girls, one of them short, a sweet look, a white rabbit on her shoulder); a picture in the room, *Emperor Franz Josef in the Capuchin Tomb*; the peasant K. (a powerful man; loftily recited the whole history of his farm, yet

friendly and kind). General impression given one by peasants: noble-men who have escaped into agriculture, where they have arranged their work so wisely and humbly that it fits perfectly into everything and they are protected against all insecurity and worry until their blissful death. True dwellers on this earth – The boys who ran over the broad fields in the evening in pursuit of the fleeing, scattered herds of cattle, and who at the same time had to keep yanking round a young fettered bull that refused to follow.

Dickens's *Copperfield*. 'The Stoker' a sheer imitation of Dickens, the projected novel even more so. The story of the trunk, the boy who delights and charms everyone, the menial labour, his sweetheart in the country house, the dirty houses, *et al.*, but above all the method. It was my intention, as I now see, to write a Dickens novel, but enhanced by the sharper lights I should have taken from the times and the duller ones I should have got from myself. Dickens's opulence and great, careless prodigality, but in consequence passages of awful insipidity in which he wearily works over effects he has already achieved. Gives one a barbaric impression because the whole does not make sense, a bar-barism that I, it is true, thanks to my weakness and wiser for my epigonism, have been able to avoid. There is a heartlessness behind his sentimentally overflowing style. These rude characterizations which are artificially stamped on everyone and without which Dickens would not be able to get on with his story even for a moment. (Walser resembles him in his use of vague, abstract metaphors.)

9 October. At the peasant Lüftner's. The great hall. All of it quite theatrical. His nervous hee-hee and ha-ha, banged on the table, raised his arms, shrugged his shoulders and lifted his beer glass like one of Wallenstein's men. His wife beside him, an old woman whom he mar-ried ten years ago when he was her hired hand. Is a passionate hunter, neglects the farm. Two huge horses in the stable, Homeric figures in a fleeting ray of sunshine coming through the stable windows.

15 October. On the highway to Oberklee in the evening; went because the housekeeper and two Hungarian soldiers were sitting in the kitchen.

The view from Ottla's window in the twilight, yonder a house and immediately behind it the open fields.

K. and his wife in their fields on the slope opposite my window.

21 October. Beautiful day, sunny, warm, no wind.

Most dogs bark pointlessly, even if someone is just walking by in the distance; but some, perhaps not the best watchdogs, yet rational creatures, quietly walk up to a stranger, sniff at him, and bark only if they smell something suspicious.

6 November. Sheer impotence.

10 November. I haven't yet written down the decisive thing, I am still going in two directions. The work awaiting me is enormous.

Dreamed of the battle of the Tagliamento. A plain, the river wasn't really there, a crowd of excited onlookers ready to run forwards or backwards as the situation changed. In front of us a plateau whose plainly visible edge was alternately bare and overgrown with tall bushes. Upon the plateau and beyond Austrians were fighting. Everyone was tense; what would be the outcome? By way of diversion you could from time to time look at isolated clumps on the dark slope, from behind which one or two Italians were firing. But that had no importance, though we did take a few steps backwards in flight. Then the plateau again: Austrians ran along the bare edge, pulled up abruptly behind the bushes, ran again. Things were apparently going badly, and moreover it was incomprehensible how they could ever go well; how could one merely human being ever conquer other human beings who were imbued with a will to defend themselves? Great despair, there will have to be a general retreat. A Prussian major appeared who had been watching the battle with us all the while; but when he calmly stepped forward into the suddenly deserted terrain, he seemed a new apparition. He put two fingers of each hand into his mouth and whistled the way one whistles to a dog, though affectionately. This was a signal to his detachment, which had been waiting close by and now marched forward. They were Prussian Guards, silent young men, not many, perhaps only a company, all seemed to be officers, at least they carried long sabres and their uniforms were dark. When they marched by us, with short steps, slowly, in close order, now and then looking at us, the matter-of-factness of their death march was at once stirring, solemn, and a promise of victory. With a feeling of relief at the intercession of these men, I woke up.

[*Final entry of 1917. There are no entries for 1918.*]

☙ ☙ ☙

27 June. A new diary, really only because I have been reading the old ones. A number of reasons and intentions, now, at a quarter to twelve, impossible to ascertain.

30 June. Was in Rieger Park. Walked up and down with J.[116] beside the jasmine bushes. False and sincere, false in my sighs, sincere in my feelings of closeness to her, in my trustfulness, in my feeling of security. Uneasy heart.

6 July. The same thought continually, desire, anxiety. Yet calmer than usual, as if some great development were going forward the distant tremor of which I feel. Too much said.

5 December. Again pulled through this terrible, long, narrow crack; it can only be forced through in a dream. On purpose and awake, one could certainly never do it.

8 December. Spent Monday, a holiday, in the park, the restaurant, and the Gallerie. Sorrow and joy, guilt and innocence, like two hands indissolubly clasped together; one would have to cut through flesh, blood, and bones to part them.

9 December. A lot of Eleseus.[117] But wherever I turn, the black wave rushes down on me.

11 December. Thursday. Cold. With J. in Rieger Park, said not a word. Seduction on the Graben. All this is too difficult. I am not suffi-

ciently prepared. It is the same thing, in a certain sense, as twenty-six years ago my teacher Beck saying, of course without realizing the prophetic joke he was making: 'Let him continue in the fifth grade for a while, he still isn't strong enough; rushing him in this way will have its consequences later on.' And in fact such has been my growth, like a shoot forced too soon and forgotten; there is a certain hothouse delicacy in the way in which I shrink from a puff of wind, if you like, even something affecting in it, but that is all. Like Eleseus and his spring trips to the cities. By the way, he is not to be underestimated: Eleseus could have become the hero of the book, and in Hamsun's youth such would probably have happened.

☙ ☙ ☙

6 January. His every action seems extraordinarily new to him. If it had not this fresh and living quality, of itself it would inevitably be something out of the old swamp of hell, this he knows. But this freshness deceives him: it allows him to forget his knowledge, or be heedless of it, or, though he see through the freshness, see without pain.

Today is undoubtedly the day, is it not, on which progress prepares to progress farther?

9 January. Superstition and principle and what makes life possible: Through a heaven of vice a hell of virtue is reached. So easily? So dirtily? So unbelievably? Superstition is easy.

A segment has been cut out of the back of his head. The sun, and the whole world with it, peep in. It makes him nervous, it distracts him from his work, and moreover it irritates him that just he should be the one to be debarred from the spectacle.

It is no disproof of one's presentiment of an ultimate liberation if the next day one's imprisonment continues on unchanged, or is even made straiter, or if it is even expressly stated that it will never end. All this can rather be the necessary preliminary to an ultimate liberation.[118]

☙ ☙ ☙

15 October [1921]. About a week ago gave M.[119] all the diaries. A little freer? No. Am I still able to keep a diary? It will in any case be a different kind of diary, or rather it will hide itself away, there won't be any diary at all; only with the greatest of effort could I note something down on Hardt, for example, though I was rather taken with him. It is as if I had already written everything there was to write about him long ago, or, what is the same thing, as if I were no longer alive. I could probably write about M., but would not willingly do it, and moreover it would be aimed too directly at myself; I no longer need to make myself so minutely conscious of such things, I am not so forgetful as I used to be in this respect, I am a memory come alive, hence my insomnia.

16 October. Sunday. The misery of having perpetually to begin, the lack of the illusion that anything is more than, or even as much as, a beginning, the foolishness of those who do not know this and play football, for example, in order at last 'to advance the ball', one's own foolishness buried within one as if in a coffin here, hence a coffin that one can transport, open, destroy, exchange.

Among the young women up in the park. No envy. Enough imagination to share their happiness, enough judgement to know I am too weak to have such happiness, foolish enough to think I see to the bottom of my own and their situation. Not foolish enough; there is a tiny crack there, and wind whistles through it and spoils the full effect.

Should I greatly yearn to be an athlete, it would probably be the same thing as my yearning to go to heaven and to be permitted to be as despairing there as I am here.

No matter how sorry a constitution I may have, even if – 'given the same circumstances' – it be the sorriest in the world (particularly in view of my lack of energy), I must do the best I can with it (even in my sense of the word) – it is hollow sophistry to argue that there is only one thing to be done with such a constitution, which must perforce be its best, and that that one thing is to despair.

17 October. There may be a purpose lurking behind the fact that I

never learned anything useful and – the two are connected – have allowed myself to become a physical wreck. I did not want to be distracted, did not want to be distracted by the pleasures life has to give a useful and healthy man. As if illness and despair were not just as much of a distraction!

There are several ways in which I could complete this thought and so reach a happy conclusion for myself, but don't dare, and don't believe – at least today, and most of the time as well – that a happy solution exists.

I do not envy particular married couples, I simply envy all married couples together; and even when I do envy one couple only, it is the happiness of married life in general, in all its infinite variety, that I envy – the happiness to be found in any one marriage, even in the likeliest case, would probably plunge me into despair.

I don't believe people exist whose inner plight resembles mine; still, it is possible for me to imagine such people – but that the secret raven forever flaps about their heads as it does about mine, even to imagine that is impossible.

It is astounding how I have systematically destroyed myself in the course of the years, it was like a slowly widening breach in a dam, a purposeful action. The spirit that brought it about must now be celebrating triumphs; why doesn't it let me take part in them? But perhaps it hasn't yet achieved its purpose and can therefore think of nothing else.

18 October. Eternal childhood. Life calls again.

It is entirely conceivable that life's splendour forever lies in wait about each one of us in all its fullness, but veiled from view, deep down, invisible, far off. It *is* there, though, not hostile, not reluctant, not deaf. If you summon it by the right word, by its right name, it will come. This is the essence of magic, which does not create but summons.

19 October. The essence of the Wandering in the Wilderness. A man

who leads his people along this way with a shred (more is unthinkable) of consciousness of what is happening. He is on the track of Canaan all his life; it is incredible that he should see the land only when on the verge of death. This dying vision of it can only be intended to illustrate how incomplete a moment is human life, incomplete because a life like this could last forever and still be nothing but a moment. Moses fails to enter Canaan not because his life is too short but because it is a human life. This ending of the Pentateuch bears a resemblance to the final scene of *L'Éducation sentimentale*.

Anyone who cannot come to terms with his life while he is alive needs one hand to ward off a little his despair over his fate – he has little success in this – but with his other hand he can note down what he sees among the ruins, for he sees different (and more) things than do the others; after all, dead as he is in his own lifetime, he is the real survivor. This assumes that he does not need both hands, or more hands than he has, in his struggle against despair.

20 October. In the afternoon Langer, then Max, who read *Franzi* aloud.

A short dream, during an agitated, short sleep, in agitation clung to it with a feeling of boundless happiness. A dream with many ramifications, full of a thousand connexions that became clear in a flash; but hardly more than the basic mood remains: My brother had committed a crime, a murder, I think, I and other people were involved in the crime; punishment, solution, and salvation approached from afar, loomed up powerfully, many signs indicated their ineluctable approach; my sister, I think, kept calling out these signs as they appeared and I kept greeting them with insane exclamations, my insanity increased as they drew nearer. I thought I should never be able to forget my fragmentary exclamations, brief sentences merely, because of their succinctness, and now don't clearly remember a single one. I could only have uttered brief exclamations because of the great effort it cost me to speak – I had to puff out my cheeks and at the same time contort my mouth as if I had a toothache before I could bring a word out. My feeling of happiness lay in the fact that I welcomed so freely, with such conviction and such joy, the punishment that came, a sight that must have moved the gods, and I felt the gods' emotion almost to the point of tears.

21 October. It had been impossible for him to enter the house, for he had heard a voice saying to him: 'Wait till I lead you in!' And so he continued to lie in the dust in front of the house, although by now, probably, everything was hopeless (as Sarah would say).

All is imaginary – family, office, friends, the street, all imaginary, far away or close at hand, the woman; the truth that lies closest, however, is only this, that you are beating your head against the wall of a windowless and doorless cell.

22 October. A connoisseur, an expert, someone who knows his field, knowledge, to be sure, that cannot be imparted but that fortunately no one seems to stand in need of.

23 October. A film about Palestine in the afternoon.

25 October. Ehrenstein yesterday.

My parents were playing cards; I sat apart, a perfect stranger; my father asked me to take a hand, or at least to look on; I made some sort of excuse. What is the meaning of these refusals, oft repeated since my childhood? I could have availed myself of invitations to take part in social, even, to an extent, public life; everything required of me I should have done, if not well, at least in middling fashion; even card-playing would probably not have bored me overmuch – yet I refused. Judging by this, I am wrong when I complain that I have never been caught up in the current of life, that I never made my escape from Prague, was never made to learn a sport or trade, and so forth – I should probably have refused every offer, just as I refused the invitation to play cards. I allowed only absurd things to claim my attention, my law studies, the job at the office, and later on such senseless additional occupations as a little gardening, carpentering, and the like; these later occupations are to be looked on as the actions of a man who throws a needy beggar out the door and then plays the benefactor by himself by passing alms from his right hand to his left.

I always refused, out of general weakness, probably, and in particular out of weakness of will – it was rather a long time before I understood as much. I used to consider this refusal a good sign (misled by the vague great hopes I cherished for myself); today only a remnant of this benevolent interpretation remains.

29 October. A few evenings later I did actually join in, to the extent of keeping score for my mother. But it begot no intimacy, or whatever trace there was of it was smothered under weariness, boredom, and regret for the wasted time. It would always have been thus. I have seldom, very seldom crossed this borderland between loneliness and fellowship, I have even been settled there longer than in loneliness itself. What a fine bustling place was Robinson Crusoe's island in comparison!

30 October. In the afternoon to the theatre, Pallenberg.

The possibilities within me, I won't say to act or write *The Miser*, but to be the miser himself. It would need only a sudden determined movement of my hands, the entire orchestra gazes in fascination at the spot above the conductor's stand where the baton will rise.

Feeling of complete helplessness.

What is it that binds you more intimately to these impenetrable, talking, eye-blinking bodies than to any other thing, the penholder in your hand, for example? Because you belong to the same species? But you don't belong to the same species, that's the very reason why you raised this question.

The impenetrable outline of human bodies is horrible.

The wonder, the riddle of my not having perished already, of the silent power guiding me. It forces one to this absurdity: 'Left to my own resources, I should have long ago been lost.' My own resources.

1 November. Werfel's *Goat Song*.

Free command of the world at the expense of its laws. Imposition of the law. The happiness in obeying the law.

But the law cannot merely be imposed upon the world, and then everything left to go on as before except that the new lawgiver be free to do as he pleases. Such would be not law, but arbitrariness, revolt against law, self-defeat.

2 November. Vague hope, vague confidence.

An endless, dreary Sunday afternoon, an afternoon swallowing down whole years, its every hour a year. By turns walked despairingly down empty streets and lay quietly on the couch. Occasionally astonished by the leaden, meaningless clouds almost uninterruptedly drifting by. 'You are reserved for a great Monday!' Fine, but Sunday will never end.

7 November. This inescapable duty to observe oneself: if someone else is observing me, naturally I have to observe myself too; if none observes me, I have to observe myself all the closer.

I envy the ease with which all those who fall out with me, or grow indifferent, or find me a nuisance, can shake me off – provided, probably, that it is not a life-and-death matter for me; once, with F., when it seemed to be a matter of life and death, it was not easy to shake me off, though of course I was young then, and strong, with strong desires.

1 December. After paying four calls on me, M. left; she goes away tomorrow. Four calmer days in the midst of tormented ones. I feel no sorrow at her departure, no real sorrow; it is a long way from this unconcern to the point where her departure would cause me endless sorrow. Sorrow, I confess it, is not the greatest evil.

2 December. Writing letters in my parents' room – the forms my decline takes are inconceivable! This thought lately, that as a little child I had been defeated by my father and because of ambition have never been able to quit the battlefield all these years despite the perpetual defeats I suffer – Always M. or not M. – but a principle, a light in the darkness!

6 December. From a letter: 'During this dreary winter I warm

myself by it.' Metaphors are one among many things which make me despair of writing. Writing's lack of independence of the world, its dependence on the maid who tends the fire, on the cat warming itself by the stove; it is even dependent on the poor old human being warming himself by the stove. All these are independent activities ruled by their own laws; only writing is helpless, cannot live in itself, is a joke and a despair.

Two children, alone in their house, climbed into a large trunk; the cover slammed shut, they could not open it, and suffocated.

20 December. Suffered in my thoughts.
I was startled out of a deep sleep. By the light of a candle I saw a strange man sitting at a little table in the centre of the room. Broad and heavy, he sat in the dim light, his unbuttoned winter coat making him appear even broader.

Don't forget:
Raabe, while dying, when his wife stroked his forehead: 'How pleasant.'
The toothless mouth of the grandfather laughing at his grandchild.

Undeniably, there is a certain joy in being able calmly to write down: 'Suffocation is inconceivably horrible.' Of course it is inconceivable – that is why I have written nothing down.

23 December. Again sat over *Náš Skautík*.[120] Ivan Ilyich.[121]

✄ ✄ ✄

16 January. This past week I suffered something very like a breakdown; the only one to match it was on that night two years ago; apart from then I have never experienced its like. Everything seemed over with, even today there is no great improvement to be noticed. One can put two interpretations on the breakdown, both of which are probably correct.
First: breakdown, impossible to sleep, impossible to stay awake, impossible to endure life, or, more exactly, the course of life. The clocks

are not in unison; the inner one runs crazily on at a devilish or demoniac or in any case inhuman pace, the outer one limps along at its usual speed. What else can happen but that the two worlds split apart, and they do split apart, or at least clash in a fearful manner. There are doubtless several reasons for the wild tempo of the inner process; the most obvious one is introspection, which will suffer no idea to sink tranquilly to rest but must pursue each one into consciousness, only itself to become an idea, in turn to be pursued by renewed introspection.

Secondly: this pursuit, originating in the midst of men, carries one in a direction away from them. The solitude that for the most part has been forced on me, in part voluntarily sought by me – but what was this if not compulsion too? – is now losing all its ambiguity and approaches its dénouement. Where is it leading? The strongest likelihood is, that it may lead to madness; there is nothing more to say, the pursuit goes right through me and rends me asunder. Or I can – can I? – manage to keep my feet somewhat and be carried along in the wild pursuit. Where, then, shall I be brought? 'Pursuit,' indeed, is only a metaphor. I can also say, 'assault on the last earthly frontier', an assault, moreover, launched from below, from mankind, and since this too is a metaphor, I can replace it by the metaphor of an assault from above, aimed at me from above.

All such writing is an assault on the frontiers; if Zionism had not intervened, it might easily have developed into a new secret doctrine, a Kabbalah. There are intimations of this. Though of course it would require genius of an unimaginable kind to strike root again in the old centuries, or create the old centuries anew and not spend itself withal, but only then begin to flower forth.

17 January. Hardly different.

18 January. A moment of thought: Resign yourself, learn (learn, forty-year-old) to rest content in the moment (yes, once you could do it). Yes, in the moment, the terrible moment. It is not terrible, only your fear of the future makes it so. And also looking back on it in retrospect. What have you done with your gift of sex? It was a failure, in the end that is all that they will say. But it might easily have

succeeded. A mere trifle, indeed so small as not to be perceived, decided between its failure and success. Why are you surprised? So it was with the greatest battles in the history of the world. Trifles decide trifles.

M. is right: fear means unhappiness but it does not follow from this that courage means happiness; not courage, which possibly aims at more than our strength can achieve (there were perhaps only two Jews in my class possessed of courage, and both shot themselves while still at school or shortly after); not courage, then, but fearlessness with its calm, open eye and stoical resolution. Don't force yourself to do anything, yet don't feel unhappy that you force yourself, or that if you were to do anything, you would have to force yourself. And if you don't force yourself, don't hanker after the possibilities of being forced. Of course, it is never as clear as all that, or rather, it is; it is always as clear as all that; for instance: sex keeps gnawing at me, hounds me day and night, I should have to conquer fear and shame and probably sorrow too to satisfy it; yet on the other hand I am certain that I should at once take advantage, with no feeling of fear or sorrow or shame, of the first opportunity to present itself quickly, close at hand, and willingly; according to the above, then, I am left with the law that fear, etc., should not be conquered (but also that one should not continually dally with the idea of conquest), but rather take advantage of opportunities as they come (and not complain if none should come). It is true that there is a middle ground between 'doing' and the 'opportunity to do', namely this, to make, to tempt one's 'opportunities' to one, a practice I have unfortunately followed not only in this but everything. As far as the 'law' is concerned, there is hardly anything to be said against this, though this 'tempting' of opportunities, especially when it makes use of ineffectual expedients, bears a considerable resemblance to 'dallying with the idea of conquest', and there is no trace in it of calm, open-eyed fearlessness. Despite the fact that it satisfies the 'letter' of the 'law', there is something detestable in it which must be unconditionally shunned. To be sure, one would have to force oneself to shun it – and so I shall never have done with the matter.

19 January. What meaning have yesterday's conclusions today? They have the same meaning as yesterday, are true, except that the blood is oozing away in the chinks between the great stones of the law.

The infinite, deep, warm, saving happiness of sitting beside the cradle of one's child opposite its mother.

There is in it also something of this feeling: matters no longer rest with you, unless you wish it so. In contrast, this feeling of those who have no children: it perpetually rests with you, whether you will or no, every moment to the end, every nerve-racking moment, it perpetually rests with you, and without result. Sisyphus was a bachelor.

Evil does not exist; once you have crossed the threshold, all is good. Once in another world, you must hold your tongue.

The two questions:[122]
Because of several piddling signs I am ashamed to mention, it was my impression that your recent visits were indeed kind and noble as ever but somewhat tiresome to you nevertheless, somewhat forced, too, like the visits one pays an invalid. Is my impression correct?
Did you find in the diaries some final proof against me?

20 January. A little calmer. How needed it was. No sooner is it a little calmer with me than it is almost too calm. As though I have the true feeling of myself only when I am unbearably unhappy. That is probably true too.

Seized by the collar, dragged through the streets, pushed through the door. In abstract, that is how it is; in reality, there are counterforces, only a trifle less violent than the forces they oppose – the trifle that keeps life and torment alive. I the victim of both.

This 'too calm'. It is as if the possibility of a calm creative life – and so creativity in general – were somehow closed to me because of physical reasons, because of year-long physical torments (confidence! confidence!) – for torment has no meaning for me beyond itself, is closed off against everything.

The torso: seen in profile, from the top of the stocking up, knee, thigh, and hip of a dark woman.

Longing for the country? It isn't certain. The country calls forth the longing, the infinite longing.

M. is right about me: 'All things are glorious, only not for me, and rightly so.' I say rightly, and show that I am sanguine at least to this extent. Or am I? For it is not really 'rightness' that I am thinking of; life, because of its sheer power to convince, has no room in it for right and wrong. As in the despairing hour of death you cannot meditate on right and wrong, so you cannot in the despairing hour of life. It is enough that the arrows fit exactly in the wounds that they have made.

On the other hand, there is no trace in me of a general condemnation of my generation.

21 January. As yet, it is not too calm. In the theatre suddenly, when I see Florestan's prison, the abyss opens. Everything – singers, music, audience, neighbours, everything – more remote than the abyss.

No one's task was as difficult, so far as I know. One might say that it is not a task at all, not even an impossible one, it is not even impossibility itself, it is nothing, it is not even as much of a child as the hope of a barren woman. But nevertheless it is the air I breathe, so long as I shall breathe at all.

I fell asleep past midnight, awoke at five, a remarkable achievement for me, remarkable good fortune; apart from that I still felt sleepy. My good fortune, however, proved my misfortune, or now the inevitable thought came: you don't deserve so much good fortune; all the venging furies flung themselves upon me, I saw their enraged chieftain widely spread her fingers and threaten me, or horribly strike cymbals. The excitement of the two hours until seven o'clock not only devoured what benefit I had got from sleep but made me tremulous and uneasy all day.

Without forebears, without marriage, without heirs, with a fierce longing for forebears, marriage, and heirs. They all of them stretch out their hands to me: forebears, marriage, and heirs, but too far away for me.

There is an artificial, miserable substitute for everything, for forebears, marriage, and heirs. Feverishly you contrive these substitutes, and if the fever has not already destroyed you, the hopelessness of the substitutes will.

22 January. Nocturnal resolve.

The remark about 'bachelors remembered from our youth' was clairvoyant, though of course under very favourable circumstances.[128] My resemblance to Uncle Rudolf, however, is even more disconcerting: both of us quiet (I less so), both dependent on our parents (I more so), at odds with our fathers, loved by our mothers (he in addition condemned to the horror of living with his father, though of course his father was likewise condemned to live with him), both of us shy, excessively modest (he more so), both regarded as noble, good men – there is nothing of these qualities in me and, so far as I know, very little in him (shyness, modesty, timidity are accounted noble and good because they offer little resistance to other people's aggressive impulses) – both hypochrondriacal at first, then really ill, both, for do-nothings, kept fairly well by the world (he, because he was less of a do-nothing, kept much more poorly, so far as it is possible to make a comparison now), both officials (he a better one), both living the most unvarying lives, with no trace of any development, young to the end of our days ('well-preserved' is a better expression), both on the verge of insanity; he, far away from Jews, with tremendous courage, with tremendous vitality (by which one can measure the degree of the danger of insanity) escaped into the church where, so far as one could tell, his tendencies to madness were somewhat held in check, he himself had probably not been able for years to hold himself in check. One difference in his favour, or disfavour, was his having had less artistic talent than I, he could therefore have chosen a better path in life for himself in his youth, was not inwardly pulled apart, not even by ambition. Whether he had had to contend (inwardly) with women I do not know, a story by him that I read would indicate as much; when I was a child, moreover, they spoke of something of the sort. I know much too little about him, I don't dare ask about it. Besides, up to this point I have been writing about him as irreverently as if he were alive. It isn't true that he was not good, I never found a trace of niggardliness, envy, hate, or greed in him; he was probably too unimportant a person to be able to help others. He was infinitely more innocent than I, there is no comparison. In single details he was my caricature, in essentials I am his.

23 January. A feeling of fretfulness again. From what did it arise? From certain thoughts which are quickly forgotten but leave my fretfulness unforgettably behind. Sooner than the thoughts themselves I could list the places in which they occurred to me; one, for example, on the little path that passes the Altneu Synagogue. Fretful too because of a certain sense of contentment that now and then drew near me, though timidly enough and sufficiently far off. Fretful too that my nocturnal resolve remains merely a resolve. Fretful that my life till now has been merely marking time, has progressed at most in the sense that decay progresses in a rotten tooth. I have not shown the faintest firmness of resolve in the conduct of my life. It was as if I, like everyone else, had been given a point from which to prolong the radius of a circle, and had then, like everyone else, to describe my perfect circle round this point. Instead, I was forever starting my radius only constantly to be forced at once to break it off. (Examples: piano, violin, languages, Germanics, anti-Zionism, Zionism, Hebrew, gardening, carpentering, writing, marriage attempts, an apartment of my own.) The centre of my imaginary circle bristles with the beginnings of radii, there is no room left for a new attempt; no room means old age and weak nerves, and never to make another attempt means the end. If I sometimes prolonged the radius a little farther than usual, in the case of my law studies, say, or engagements, everything was made worse rather than better just because of this little extra distance.

Told M. about the night, unsatisfactory. Accept your symptoms, don't complain of them; immerse yourself in your suffering.

Heart oppression.

The second opinion kept in reserve. The third opinion: already forgotten.

24 January. How happy are the married men, young and old both,

in the office. Beyond my reach, though if it were within my reach I should find it intolerable, and yet it is the only thing with which I have any inclination to appease my longing.

Hesitation before birth. If there is a transmigration of souls then I am not yet on the bottom rung. My life is a hesitation before birth.

Steadfastness. I don't want to pursue any particular course of development, I want to change my place in the world entirely, which actually means that I want to go to another planet; it would be enough if I could exist alongside myself, it would even be enough if I could consider the spot on which I stand as some other spot.

My development was a simple one. While I was still contented I wanted to be discontented, and with all the means that my time and tradition gave me, plunged into discontent – and then wanted to turn back again. Thus I have always been discontented, even with my contentment. Strange how make-believe, if engaged in systematically enough, can change into reality. Childish games (though I was well aware that they were so) marked the beginning of my intellectual decline. I deliberately cultivated a facial tic, for instance, or would walk across the Graben with arms crossed behind my head. A repulsively childish but successful game. (My writing began in the same way; only later on its development came to a halt, unfortunately.) If it is possible so to force misfortune upon oneself, it is possible to force anything upon oneself. Much as my development seems to contradict me, and much as it contradicts my nature to think it, I cannot grant that the first beginnings of my unhappiness were inwardly necessitated; they may have indeed had a necessity, but not an inward one – they swarmed down on me like flies and could have been as easily driven off.

My unhappiness on the other shore would have been as great, greater probably (thanks to my weakness); after all, I have had some experience of it, the lever is still trembling somewhat from the time when I last tried to shift it – why then do I add to the unhappiness that this shore causes me by longing to cross over to the other?

Sad, and with reason. My sadness depends on this reason. How easy it was the first time, how difficult now! How helplessly the tyrant looks at me: 'Is that where you are taking me!' And yet no peace in spite of everything; the hopes of the morning are buried in the afternoon. It is impossible amicably to come to terms with such a life; surely there has never been anyone who could have done so. When other people approached this boundary – even to have approached it is pitiful enough – they turned back; I cannot. It even seems to me as if I had not come by myself but had been pushed here as a child and then chained to this spot; the consciousness of my misfortune only gradually dawned on me, my misfortune itself was already complete; it needed not a prophetic but merely a penetrating eye to see it.

In the morning I thought: 'There is a possibility that I could go on living in this fashion, only guard such a way of life against women.' Guard it against women – why, they are already lurking in the 'in-this-fashion'.

It would be very unjust to say that you deserted me; but that I *was* deserted, and sometimes terribly so, is true.

Even in the sense of my 'resolve' I have a right to despair boundlessly over my situation.

27 January. Spindelmühle. I must be above such mixtures of bad luck and clumsiness on my own part as the mistake with the sledge, the broken trunk, the rickety table, the poor light, the impossibility of having quiet in the hotel during the afternoon, etc. Such superiority cannot be got by not caring, for one cannot remain indifferent to such things; it can only be got by summoning up new strength. Here, indeed, surprises await one, this the most despairing person will allow; experience proves that something can come of nothing, that the coachman and his horses can crawl out of the tumble-down pig-sty.[124]

My strength crumbling away during the sleigh ride. One cannot make a life for oneself as a tumbler makes a handstand.

The strange, mysterious, perhaps dangerous, perhaps saving comfort that there is in writing: it is a leap out of murderers' row; it is a seeing of what is really taking place. This occurs by a higher type of observation, a higher, not a keener type, and the higher it is and the less within reach of the 'row', the more independent it becomes, the more obedient to its own laws of motion, the more incalculable, the more joyful, the more ascendant its course.

Despite my having legibly written down my name, despite their having correctly written to me twice already, they have Joseph K.[125] down in the directory. Shall I enlighten them, or shall I let them enlighten me?

28 January. A little dizzy, tired from the tobogganing; weapons still exist for me, however seldom I may employ them; it is so hard for me to lay hold of them because I am ignorant of the joys of their use, never learned how when I was a child. It is not only 'Father's fault' that I never learned their use, but also my wanting to disturb the 'peace', to upset the balance, and for this reason I could not allow a new person to be born elsewhere while I was bending every effort to bury him here. Of course, in this too there is a question of 'fault', for why did I want to quit the world? Because 'he' would not let me live in it, in his world. Though indeed I should not judge the matter so precisely, for I am now a citizen of this other world, whose relationship to the ordinary one is the relationship of the wilderness to cultivated land (I have been forty years wandering from Canaan); I look back at it like a foreigner, though in this other world as well – it is the paternal heritage I carry with me – I am the most insignificant and timid of all creatures and am able to keep alive thanks only to the special nature of its arrangements; in this world it is possible even for the humblest to be raised to the heights as if with lightning speed, though they can also be crushed forever as if by the weight of the seas. Should I not be thankful despite everything? Was it certain that I should find my way to this world? Could not 'banishment' from one side, coming together with rejection from this, have crushed me at the border? Is not Father's power such that nothing (not I, certainly) could have resisted his decree? It is indeed a kind of Wandering in the Wilderness in reverse that I am undergoing: I think that I am continually skirting the wilderness and am full of childish hopes (particularly as regards women)

that 'perhaps I shall keep in Canaan after all' – when all the while I have been decades in the wilderness and these hopes are merely mirages born of despair, especially at those times when I am the wretchedest of creatures in the desert too, and Canaan is perforce my only Promised Land, for no third place exists for mankind.

29 January. Suffered some attacks on the road through the snow in the evening. There are conflicting thoughts always in my head, something like this: My situation in this world would seem to be a dreadful one, alone here in Spindelmühle, on a forsaken road, moreover where one keeps slipping in the snow in the dark, senseless road, moreover, without an earthly goal (to the bridge? Why there? Besides, I didn't even go that far); I too forsaken in this place (I cannot place a human, personal value on the help the doctor gives me, I haven't earned it; at bottom the fee is my only relationship to him), incapable of striking up a friendship with anyone, incapable of tolerating a friendship, at bottom full of endless astonishment when I see a group of people cheerfully assembled together (here in the hotel, indeed, there is little that is cheerful; I won't go so far as to say that I am the cause of this, in my character, perhaps, as 'the man with the too-great shadow', though my shadow in this world *is* too great – with fresh astonishment I observe the capacity for resistance some people have, who, 'in spite of everything', want to live under this shadow, directly under it; but there is much more than this to be said on the matter), or especially when I see parents with their children; forsaken, moreover, not only here but in general, even in Prague, my 'home', and, what is more, forsaken not by people (that would not be the worst thing, I could run after them as long as I was alive), but rather by myself *vis-à-vis* people, by my strength *vis-à-vis* people; I am fond of lovers but I cannot love, I am too far away, am banished, have – since I am human after all and my roots want nourishment – my proxies 'down' (or up) there too, sorry, unsatisfactory comedians who can satisfy me (though indeed they don't satisfy me at all and it is for this reason that I am so forsaken) only because I get my principal nourishment from other roots in other climes, these roots too are sorry ones, but nevertheless better able to sustain life.

This brings me to the conflict in my thoughts. If things were only as they seem to be on the road in the snow, it would be dreadful; I should be lost, lost not in the sense of a dreadful future menacing me but in the sense of a present execution. But I live elsewhere; it is only that the attraction of the human world is so immense, in an instant it can make one forget everything. Yet the attraction of my world too is strong; those who love me love me because I am 'forsaken' – not, I feel sure, on the principle of a Weissian vacuum, but because they sense that in happy moments I enjoy on another plane the freedom of movement completely lacking to me here.

If M., for example, should suddenly come here, it would be dreadful. Externally, indeed, my situation would at once seem comparatively brighter. I should be esteemed as one human being among others, I should have words spoken to me that were more than merely polite. I should sit at the actors' table (less erect, it is true, than now, when I am sitting here alone, though even now I am slumped down); outwardly, I should be almost a match in conviviality for Dr H. – yet I should be plunged into a world in which I could not live. It only remains to solve the riddle of why I had fourteen days of happiness in Marienbad, and why, consequently, I might perhaps also be able to be happy here with M. (though of course only after a painful break-down of barriers). But the difficulties would probably be much greater than in Marienbad, my opinions are more rigid, my experience larger. What used to be a dividing-thread is now a wall, or a mountain range, or rather a grave.

30 January. Waiting for pneumonia. Afraid, not so much of the illness, as for and of my mother, my father, the director, and all the others. Here it would seem clear that the two worlds do exist and that I am as ignorant in face of the illness, as detached, as fearful, as, say, in face of a headwaiter. And moreover the division seems to me to be much too definite, dangerous in its definiteness, sad, and too tyrannical. Do I live in the other world, then? Dare I say that?

Someone makes the remark: 'What do I care about life? It is only on my family's account that I don't want to die.' But it is just the family that is representative of life, and so it is on life's account that he wants to stay alive. Well, so far as my mother is concerned, this would seem to be the case with me as well, though only lately. But is it not gratitude and compassion that have brought this change about in me? Yes, gratitude and compassion, because I see how, with what at her age is inexhaustible strength, she bends every effort to compensate me for my isolation from life. But gratitude too is life.

31 January. This would mean that it is on my mother's account that I am alive. But it cannot be true, for even if I were much more important than I am, I should still be only an emissary of Life, and, if by nothing else, joined to it by this commission.

The Negative alone, however strong it may be, cannot suffice, as in my unhappiest moments I believe it can. For if I have gone the tiniest step upwards, won any, be it the most dubious kind of security for myself, I then stretch out on my step and wait for the Negative, not to climb up to me, indeed, but to drag me down from it. Hence it is a defensive instinct in me that won't tolerate my having the slightest degree of lasting ease and smashes the marriage bed, for example, even before it has been set up.

1 February. Nothing, merely tired. The happiness of the truck driver, whose every evening is as mine has been today, and even finer. An evening, for example, stretched out on the stove. A man is purer than in the morning; the period before falling wearily asleep is really the time when no ghosts haunt one; they are all dispersed; only as the night advances do they return, in the morning they have all assembled again, even if one cannot recognize them; and now, in a healthy person, the daily dispersal of them begins anew.

Looked at with a primitive eye, the real, incontestable truth, a truth marred by no external circumstance (martyrdom, sacrifice of oneself for the sake of another), is only physical pain. Strange that the god of pain was not the chief god of the earliest religions (but first became so in the later ones, perhaps). For each invalid his household god, for the tubercular the god of suffocation. How can one bear his approach if one does not partake of him in advance of the terrible union?

2 February. Struggle on the road to Tannenstein in the morning,

struggle while watching the ski-jumping contest. Happy little B. in all his innocence somehow shadowed by my ghosts, at least in my eyes, his aimless wandering glance, his aimless talk. In this connexion it occurs to me – but this is already forced – that towards evening he wanted to go home with me.

The 'struggle' would probably be horrible if I were to learn a trade.

The Negative having been in all probability greatly strengthened by the 'struggle', a decision between insanity and security is imminent.

The happiness of being with people.

3 February. Almost impossible to sleep; plagued by dreams, as if they were being scratched on me, on a stubborn material.

There is a certain failing, a lack in me, that is clear and distinct enough but difficult to describe: it is a compound of timidity, reserve, talkativeness, and half-heartedness; by this I intend to characterize something specific, a group of failings that under a certain aspect constitute one single clearly defined failing (which has nothing to do with such grave vices as mendacity, vanity, etc.). This failing keeps me from going mad, but also from making any headway. Because it keeps me from going mad, I cultivate it; out of fear of madness I sacrifice whatever headway I might make and shall certainly be the loser in the bargain, for no bargains are possible at this level. Provided that drowsiness does not intervene and with its nocturnal-diurnal labour break down every obstacle and clear the road. But in that event I shall be snapped up by madness – for to make headway one must want to, and I did not.

4 February. In the terrible cold, my changed face, the incomprehensible faces of the others.

What M. said, without being able completely to understand the truth of it (there is a type of sad conceit that is wholly justified), about the joy of merely talking with people. How can talking delight anyone but me! Too late, probably, and returning by a queer roundabout way to people.

5 February. Escape them. Any kind of nimble leap. At home beside the lamp in the silent room. Incautious to say this. It calls them out of the woods as if one had lit the lamp to help them find the way.

6 February. The comfort in hearing that someone had served in Paris, Brussels, London, Liverpool, had gone up the Amazon on a Brazilian steamer as far as the Peruvian border, with comparative ease had borne the dreadful sufferings of the winter campaign of the Seven Communities[126] because he had been accustomed to hardship since his childhood. The comfort consists not only in the demonstration that such things are possible, but in the pleasure one feels when one realizes that with these achievements on the one level, much at the same time must have necessarily been achieved on the other level, much must have been wrung from clenched fists. It *is* possible, then.

7 February. Shielded and exhausted by K. and H.

8 February. Horribly taken advantage of by both and yet – I surely could not live like that (it is not living, it is a tug-of-war in which the other person keeps straining and winning and yet never pulls me across); I sink into a peaceful numbness, as I did that time with W.

9 February. Two days lost; used the same two days, however, to get settled.

10 February. Can't sleep; have not the slightest relationship with people other than what their initiative creates, which then persuades me for the moment, as does everything they do.

New attack by G. Attacked right and left as I am by overwhelming forces, it is as plain as can be that I cannot escape either to the right or to the left -- straight on only, starved beast, lies the road to food that will sustain you, air that you can breathe, a free life, even if it should take you beyond life. Great, tall commander-in-chief, leader of multitudes, lead the despairing through the mountain passes no one else can find beneath the snow. And who is it that gives you your strength? He who gives you your clear vision.

The commander-in-chief stood at the window of the ruined hut and looked outside with wide, unclosing eyes at the column of troops marching by in the snow under the pale moonlight. Now and then it seemed to him that a soldier out of ranks would halt by the window, press his face against the pane, look at him for a moment, and then go on. Though always a different soldier, it always seemed to him to be the same one; a big-boned face with fat cheeks, round eyes, and coarse sallow skin; each time that the man walked away he would straighten the straps of his pack, shrug his shoulders, and skip his feet to get back into step with the mass of troops marching by as always in the background. The commander-in-chief had no intention of tolerating this game any longer; he lay in wait for the next soldier, threw open the window in his face, and seized the man by the front of his coat. 'Inside with you!' he said, and made him climb through the window. He pushed the man into a corner, stood in front of him, and asked: 'Who are you?'

'Nobody,' the soldier said, fearfully.

'One might have expected as much,' the commander-in-chief said. 'Why did you look inside?'

'To see if you were still here.'

12 February. The gesture of rejection with which I was forever met did not mean: 'I do not love you,' but: 'You cannot love me, much as you would like; you are unhappily in love with your love for me, but your love for me is not in love with you.' It is consequently incorrect to say that I have known the words, 'I love you'; I have known only the expectant stillness that should have been broken by my 'I love you', that is all that I have known, nothing more.

The fear I have tobogganing, my nervousness in walking on the slippery snow; a little story I read today revived in me the long unheeded, ever-present question of whether the cause of my downfall was not insane selfishness, mere anxiety for self; not, moreover, anxiety for a higher self, but vulgar anxiety for my well-being; such that it would seem that I have dispatched my own avenger from myself (a special instance of the-right-hand-not-knowing-what-the-left-hand-does). In the Great Account of my life, it is still reckoned as if my life were first beginning tomorrow, and in the meantime it is all over with me.

13 February. The possibility of serving with all one's heart.

14 February. The power comfort has over me, my powerlessness without it. I know no one in whom both are so great. Consequently everything I build is insubstantial, unstable; the maid who forgets to bring me my warm water in the morning overturns my world. At the same time I have been under comfort's constant harassment; it has deprived me not only of the strength to bear up under anything, but also the strength myself to create comfort; it creates itself about me of itself, or I achieve it by begging, crying, renouncing more important things.

15 February. A bit of singing on the floor below, an occasional door slamming in the corridor, and all is lost.

16 February. The story of the crevice in the glacier.

18 February. The theatre director who must himself create everything from the ground up, has even first to beget the actors. A visitor is not admitted; the director has important theatrical work in hand. What is it? He is changing the diapers of a future actor.

19 February. Hopes?

20 February. Unnoticeable life. Noticeable failure.
25 February. A letter.
26 February. I grant – to whom do I grant it? the letter? – that possibilities exist in me, possibilities close at hand that I don't yet know of; only to find the way to them! and when I have found it, to dare! This signifies a great many things: that possibilities do exist; it even signifies that a scoundrel can become an honest man, a man happy in his honesty.

Your drowsy fantasies recently.

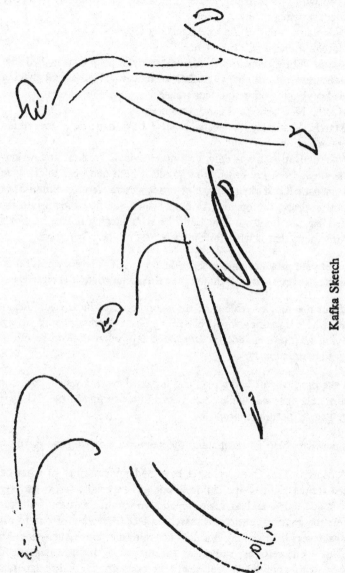

Kafka Sketch

27 February. Slept badly in the afternoon; everything is changed; my misery pressing me hard again.

28 February. View of the tower and the blue sky. Calming.

1 March. *Richard III*. Impotence.

5 March. Three days in bed. A small party of people at my bedside. A sudden reversal. Flight. Complete surrender. These world-shaking events always going on within four walls.

6 March. New seriousness and weariness.

7 March. Yesterday the worst night I have had; as if everything were at an end.

9 March. But that was only weariness; today a fresh attack, wringing the sweat from my brow. How would it be if one were to choke to death on oneself? If the pressure of introspection were to diminish, or close off entirely, the opening through which one flows forth into the world. I am not far from it at times. A river flowing upstream. For a long time now, that is what for the most part has been going on.

Mount your attacker's horse and ride it yourself. The only possibility. But what strength and skill that requires! And how late it is already!

Life in the jungle. Jealous of the happiness and inexhaustibility of nature, whose impelling force (like mine) is yet distress, though always satisfying all the demands its antagonist lays upon it. And so effortlessly, so harmoniously.

In the past, when I had a pain and it passed away, I was happy; now I am merely relieved, while there is this bitter feeling in me: 'Only to be well again, nothing more.'

Somewhere help is waiting and the beaters are driving me there.

13 March. This pure feeling I have and my certainty of what has caused it: the sight of the children, one girl especially (erect carriage, short black hair), and another (blonde; indefinite features, indefinite smile); the rousing music, the marching feet. A feeling of one in distress who sees help coming but does not rejoice at his rescue – nor is he rescued – but rejoices, rather, at the arrival of fresh young people imbued with confidence and ready to take up the fight; ignorant,

indeed, of what awaits them, but an ignorance that inspires not hopelessness but admiration and joy in the onlooker and brings tears to his eyes. Hatred too of him whom the fight is against is mingled in it (but little Jewish feeling, or so I think).

15 March. Objections to be made against the book: he has popularized it, and with a will, moreover – and with magic. How he escapes the dangers (Blüher).[127]

To flee to a conquered country and soon find it insupportable there, for there is nowhere else to flee.

16 March. The attacks, my fear, rats that tear at me and whom my eyes multiply.

17 March. 99·3°.

Still unborn and already compelled to walk around the streets and speak to people.

19 March. Hysteria making me surprisingly and unaccountably happy.

20 March. Yesterday an unsuccessful, today a lost (?) evening. A hard day.

The conversation at dinner on murderers and executions. The placidly breathing breast knows no fear. Knows no difference between murder planned and murder executed.

23 March. In the afternoon dreamed of the boil on my cheek. The perpetually shifting frontier that lies between ordinary life and the terror that would seem to be more real.

24 March. How it lies in wait for me! On the way to the doctor, for example, so often there.

29 March. In the stream.

4 April. How long the road is from my inner anguish to a scene like

that in the yard – and how short the road back. And since one has now reached one's home, there is no leaving it again.

6 April. Yesterday an outbreak I had been afraid of for two days; further pursuit; the enemy's great strength. One of the causes: the talk with my mother, the jokes about the future – Planned letter to Milena.

The three Erinyes. Flight into the grove. Milena.

7 April. The two pictures and the two terra-cotta figures in the exhibition.

Fairy princess (Kubin), naked on a divan, looks out of an open window; the landscape prominently looming up, has a kind of airiness like that in Schwind's picture.

Nude girl (Bruder)[128] German-Bohemian, her unmatchable grace faithfully caught by a lover; noble, convincing, seductive.

Pietsch: Seated peasant girl; luxuriously resting with one leg under her, her ankle bent. Standing girl, her right arm clasping her body across her belly; left hand supporting her head under the chin; broad-nosed, simple, and pensive, unique face.

Letter by Storm.

10 April. The five guiding principles on the road to hell (in genetic succession):

1. 'The worst lies outside the window.' All else is conceded to be angelic either openly or (more often) by silently ignoring it.

2. 'You must possess every girl!' not in Don Juan fashion, but according to the devil's expression, 'sexual etiquette'.

3. 'This girl you are not permitted to possess!' and for this very reason cannot. A heavenly *fata Morgana* in hell.

4. 'All comes back to mere needs.' Since you have needs, resign yourself to the fact.

5. 'Needs are all.' But how could you have all? Consequently you have not even needs.

As a boy I was as innocent of and uninterested in sexual matters (and would have long remained so, if they had not been forcibly thrust on me) as I am today in, say, the theory of relativity. Only trifling things (yet even these only after they were pointedly called to my attention) struck me, for example that it was just those women on the street who seemed to me most beautiful and best dressed who were supposed to be bad.

11 April. 'All that he deserves is the dirty unknown old woman with shrunken thighs who drains his semen in an instant, pockets the money, and hurries off to the next room where another customer is already waiting for her.'

Eternal youth is impossible; even if there were no other obstacle introspection would make it impossible.

13 April. Max's grief. Morning in his office.
Afternoon in front of the Thein Church (Easter Sunday).

My fear of being disturbed; my insomnia because of this fear. A nightmare recently because of M.'s letter in my portfolio.

1. Young little girl, eighteen years old; nose, shape of head, blonde; seen fleetingly in profile; came out of the church.

16 April. Max's grief. A walk with him. Tuesday he leaves.

2. Five-year-old girl; orchard, little path to the main alley; hair, nose, shining face.

23 April. 3. Fawn-coloured velvet jacket in the distance in the direction of the fruit market.

Helpless days; yesterday evening.

27 April. Yesterday a Makkabi girl in the office of *Selbstwehr* telephoning: '*Přišla jsem ti pomoct.*'[129] Clear, cordial voice and speech.
Shortly thereafter opened the door to M.

8 May. Work with the plough. It digs in deep and yet goes easily

along. Or it just scratches the ground. Or it moves along with the plough-share drawn uselessly up; with it or without it, it is all the same.

The work draws to an end in the way an unhealed wound might draw together.

Would you call it a conversation if the other person is silent and, to keep up the appearance of a conversation, you try to substitute for him, and so imitate him, and so parody him, and so parody yourself.

M. was here, won't come again; probably wise and right in this, yet there is perhaps still a possibility whose locked door we both are guarding lest it open, or rather lest we open it, for it will not open of itself.

Maggid.[180]

12 May. The constant variety of the form it takes, and once, in the midst of it all, the affecting sight of a momentary abatement in its variations.

From *Pilger Kamanita*, from the Vedas: 'O beloved, even as a man brought blindfold from the land of the Gandharians and then set free in the desert will wander east or north or south, for in blindness was he brought there and in blindness was set free; yet after someone has struck the blindfold from his eyes and said to him: "Thither dwell the Gandharians, go ye thither," after having asked his way from village to village, enlightened and made wise he comes home to the Gandharians – so too a man who has found a teacher here below knows: "I shall belong to this earthly coil until I am redeemed, and then I shall return home."'

In the same place: 'Such a one, so long as he dwells in the body, is seen by men and gods; but after his body is fallen to dust, neither men nor gods see him more. And even nature, the all-seeing, sees him no more: he has blinded the eye of nature, he has vanished from the sight of the wicked.'

19 May. He feels more deserted with a second person than when alone. If he is together with someone, this second person reaches out for

him and he is helplessly delivered into his hand. If he is alone, all mankind reaches out for him – but the innumerable outstretched arms become entangled with one another and no one reaches to him.

20 May. The Freemasons on Altstädter Ring. The possible truth
that there is in every discourse and doctrine.

The dirty little barefoot girl running along in her shift with her hair
blowing.

23 May. It is incorrect to say of anyone: Things were easy for him,
he suffered little; more correct: His nature was such that nothing could
happen to him; most correct: He has suffered everything, but all in a
single all-embracing moment; how could anything have still happened
to him when the varieties of sorrow had been completely exhausted
either in actual fact or at his own peremptory command? (Two old
Englishwomen in Taine.)

25 May. Day before yesterday 'H. K.' Pleasant walk today. Everywhere people sitting, wearily standing, dreamily leaning – Much disturbed.

26 May. The severe 'attacks' during the evening walk (resulting
from four tiny vexations during the day: the dog in the summer resort;
Mars's book; enlistment as a soldier; lending the money through Z.);
momentary confusion, helplessness, hopelessness, unfathomable abyss,
nothing but abyss; only when I turned in at the front door did a thought
come to my assistance – during the entire walk none came to me, apparently because, in my complete hopelessness, I had made no attempt at
all to seek it out, though otherwise its possibility is always close at
hand.

5 June. Myslbeck's funeral. Talent for 'botch work'.

16 June. Quite apart from the insuperable difficulties always presented by Blüher's philosophical and visionary power, one is in the
difficult position of easily incurring the suspicion, almost with one's

every remark, of wanting ironically to dismiss the ideas of this book. One is suspect even if, as in my case, there is nothing farther from one's mind, in face of this book, than irony. This difficulty in reviewing his book has its counterpart in a difficulty that Blüher, from his side, cannot surmount. He calls himself an anti-Semite without hatred, *sine ira et studio*, and he really is that; yet he easily awakens the suspicion, almost with his every remark, that he is an enemy of the Jews, whether out of happy hatred or unhappy love. These difficulties confront each other like stubborn facts of nature, and attention must be called to them lest in reflecting on this book one stumble over these errors and at the very outset be rendered incapable of going on.

According to Blüher, one cannot refute Judaism inductively, by statistics, by appealing to experience; these methods of the older anti-Semitism cannot prevail against Judaism; all other peoples can be refuted in this way, but not the Jews, the chosen people; to each particular charge the anti-Semites make, the Jew will be able to give a particular answer in justification. Blüher makes a very superficial survey, to be sure, of the particular charges and the answers given them.

This perception, in so far as it concerns the Jews and not the other peoples, is profound and true. Blüher draws two conclusions from it, a full and a partial one –

23 June. Planá.[131]

27 July. The attacks. Yesterday a walk with the dog in the evening. Tvrz Sedlec. The row of cherry trees where the woods end; it gives one almost the same sense of seclusion as a room. The man and woman returning from the fields. The girl in the stable door of the dilapidated farmyard seems almost at odds with her big breasts; an innocently attentive animal gaze. The man with glasses who is pulling the heavy cartload of fodder; elderly, somewhat hunchbacked, but nevertheless very erect because of his exertions; high boots; the woman with the sickle, now at his side and now behind him.

26 September. No entries for two months. With some exceptions, a good period thanks to Ottla. For the past few days collapse again. On one of the first days made a kind of discovery in the woods.

14 November. Always 99·6°, 99·9° in the evening. Sit at the desk, get nothing done, am hardly ever in the street. Nevertheless, tartuffism to complain of my illness.

18 December. All this time in bed. Yesterday *Either/Or*.

❦ ❦ ❦

12 June. The horrible spells lately, innumerable, almost without interruption. Walks, nights, days, incapable of anything but pain.

And yet. No 'and yet', no matter how anxiously and tensely you look at me; Krizanovskaya on the picture postcard in front of me.

More and more fearful as I write. It is understandable. Every word, twisted in the hands of the spirits – this twist of the hand is their characteristic gesture – becomes a spear turned against the speaker. Most especially a remark like this. And so *ad infinitum*. The only consolation would be: it happens whether you like or no. And what you like is of infinitesimally little help. More than consolation is: You too have weapons.

TRAVEL
DIARIES

I SHOULD write the whole night through, so many things occur to me, but all of it rough. What a power this has come to have over me, whereas in the past I was able, so far as I remember, to elude it by a turn, a slight turn which by itself had been enough to make me happy.

A Reichenberg Jew in the compartment called attention to himself by uttering brief exclamations over expresses that are expresses only in so far as the fare is concerned. Meanwhile a very thin passenger was rapidly wolfing down ham, bread, and two sausages, the skins of which he kept scraping with a knife until they were transparent; finally he threw all the scraps and paper under the seat behind the steampipe. While eating in all this unnecessary heat and haste (a practice with which I am sympathetic, but cannot successfully imitate), he read through two evening papers that he held up in my direction. Protruding ears. A nose that seemed broad only by comparison. Wiped hair and face with his greasy hands without getting himself dirty, another thing I should not succeed in.

Across from me a deaf gentleman with a piping voice and a pointed beard and moustache laughed derisively at the Reichenberg Jew, silently at first, without betraying himself; after exchanging understanding glances with him, I joined in, always with a certain repugnance but out of some kind of feeling of deference. Later it turned out that this man, who read the *Montagsblatt*, ate something, bought wine at one stop and drank in the way I do, in gulps, was nobody.

Then too a red-cheeked young fellow who spent a great deal of time reading the *Interessantes Blatt*, the pages of which he carelessly cut open with the edge of his hand only finally to fold it up again, as if it were a piece of silk, with that painstaking solicitude people who have nothing to do display and which always arouses my admiration; he folded it together, creased it on the inside, straightened it out on the outside, smoothed the surfaces, and, bulky as it was, stuffed it into his breast pocket. Thus he intended to read it again at home. I don't know where he got off.

The hotel in Friedland. The great entrance hall. I remember a Christ on the Cross that perhaps wasn't there at all – No water closet; the snowstorm came up from below. For a while I was the only guest. Most of the weddings in the neighbourhood take place in the hotel. Very indistinctly I recall glancing into a room the morning after a wedding. It was very cold throughout the entrance hall and corridor. My room was over the hotel entrance; I felt the cold at once, how much more so when I became aware of the reason. In front of my room was a sort of alcove off the entrance hall; there on a table, in vases, were two bouquets left over from a wedding. The window closed top and bottom not with latches but with hooks. I now recollect that once I heard music for a short while. However, there was no piano in the guest room; perhaps there was one in the room where the wedding took place. Every time I went to close the window I saw a grocery store on the other side of the market place. My room was heated by burning logs. Chambermaid with a large mouth; once her throat was bare and her collar open, in spite of the cold; at times she was withdrawn in her manner, at other times surprisingly friendly; I was always respectful and embarrassed, as I usually am in the presence of friendly people. While she was fixing the fire she noticed with pleasure the brighter light I had had put in so that I could work in the afternoon and evening. 'Of course, it was impossible to work with the other light,' she said. 'And with this one too,' I said, after a few jaunty exclamations of the sort that unfortunately always come into my mouth when I am embarrassed. And I could think of nothing else but to express an opinion that electric light is at once too harsh and too weak. Whereupon she went silently on with the fire. Only when I said, 'Besides, I have only turned the old lamp up,' did she laugh a little, and we were in accord.

On the other hand, I can do things like the following very well: I had always treated her like a lady and she acted accordingly. Once I came back at an unexpected hour and saw her scrubbing the floor in the cold entrance hall. It gave me not the slightest difficulty to spare her whatever embarrassment she mày have felt by saying hello to her and making some request about the heating.

Beside me on the return trip from Raspenau to Friedland the rigid, corpse-like man whose beard came down over his open mouth and who, when I asked him about a station, cordially turned towards me and with great animation gave me the information.

The castle in Friedland.[188] The different ways there are to view it: from the plain, from a bridge, from the park, through bare trees, from the woods through tall firs. The castle astonishes one by the way it is built one part above the other; long after one has entered the yard it still presents no unified appearance, for the dark ivy, the dark grey walls, the white snow, the ice covering the slate-coloured glacis enhance the heterogeneity of its aspect. The castle is really built not on a plateau but around the rather steep sides of a hilltop. I went up by a road, slipping all the time, while the castellan, whom I encountered farther up, came up without difficulty by two flights of stairs. A wide view from a jutting coign. A staircase against the wall came pointlessly to an end halfway up. The chains of the drawbridge dangled in neglect from their hooks.

Beautiful park. Because it is laid out terrace-fashion on the slope, with scattered clumps of trees, but part of it too extending down around the pond below, it was impossible to guess what it looked like in summer. On the icy water of the pond floated two swans, one of them put its head and neck into the water. Uneasy and curious, but also undecided, I followed two girls who kept looking uneasily and curiously back at me; I was led by them along the mountain, over a bridge, a meadow, under a railway embankment into a rotunda unexpectedly formed by the wooded slope and the embankment, then higher up into a wood with no apparent end to it. The girls walked slowly at first, by the time I began to wonder at the extent of the wood they were walking more quickly, and by then we were already on the plateau with a brisk wind blowing, a few steps from the town.

The Emperor's Panorama, the only amusement in Friedland. Didn't feel quite at ease because I hadn't been prepared for so elegantly furnished an interior as I found inside, had entered with snow-covered boots, and, sitting in front of the glass showcases, touched the rug only with my boot toes. I had forgotten how such places are arranged and for a moment was afraid I should have to walk from one chair to another. An old man reading a volume of the *Illustrierte Welt* at a little table lighted by a lamp was in charge of everything. After a while he showed magic-lantern slides for me. Later two elderly ladies arrived, sat down at my right, then another one at my left. Brescia, Cremona, Verona. People in them like wax dolls, their feet glued to the pavement. Tombstones; a lady dragging the train of her dress over a low staircase opens a door part way, looking backward all the while. A family, in the foreground a boy is reading, one hand at his brow; a boy on the right is bending an unstrung bow. Statue of the hero, Tito Speri: his clothes flutter in enthusiastic neglect about his body. Blouse, broad-brimmed hat.

The pictures more alive than in the cinema because they offer the eye all the repose of reality. The cinema communicates the restlessness of its motion to the things pictured in it; the eye's repose would seem to be more important. The smooth floors of the cathedrals at the tip of our tongues. Why can't they combine the cinema and stereoscope in this way? Posters reading 'Pilsen Wührer', familiar to me from Brescia.[184] The gap between simply hearing about a thing and seeing lantern slides of it is greater than the gap between the latter and actually seeing the thing itself. Alteisenmarkt in Cremona. At the end wanted to tell the old gentleman how much I enjoyed it, did not dare. Got the next programme. Open from ten to ten.

I had noticed the *Literarischen Ratgeber* of the Dürer Society in the window of the bookshop. Decided to buy it, but changed my mind, then once again returned to my original decision; while this went on I kept halting in front of the shop window at every hour of the day. The bookshop seemed so forlorn to me, the books so forlorn. It was only here that I felt a connexion between Friedland and the world, and it was such a tenuous one. But since all forlornness begets in me a feeling of warmth in return, I at once felt what must be this bookshop's joy, and once I even went in to see the inside. Because there is no need for scientific works in Friedland, there was almost more fiction on its shelves than on those of metropolitan bookshops. An old lady sat under a green-shaded electric light. Four or five copies of *Kunstwart*, just unpacked, reminded me that it was the first of the month. The woman, refusing my help, took the book, of whose existence she was hardly aware, out of the display, put it into my hand, was surprised that I had noticed it behind the frosted pane (I had in fact already noticed it before), and began to look up its price in the ledgers, for she didn't know it and her husband was out. I'll return later on in the evening, I said (it was 4 p.m.), but did not keep my promise.

Reichenberg.

One is completely in the dark as to what real object people have in hurrying through a small town in the evening. If they live outside the town, then they surely have to use the tram, because the distances are too great. But if they live in the town itself, there are really no great distances to go and thus no reason to hurry. And yet people hurry with lengthened strides across this square which would not be too large for a village and which is made to seem even smaller by the unexpected size of the town hall (its shadow can more than cover the square). At the same time, because the square is so small, one can't quite believe that the town hall is as large as it is, and would like to attribute his first impression of its size to the smallness of the square.

One policeman did not know the address of the workmen's compensation office, another where its exhibition was taking place, a third did not even know where Johannesgasse was. This they explained by their having been in the force only a short time. For directions I was obliged to go to the police station, where there were a great many policemen lounging about, all in uniforms whose beauty, newness, and colour surprised one, for otherwise one saw nothing but dark winter coats on the street.

The narrow streets allowed for the laying of only a single line of track. This is why the tram going to the railway station ran on different streets than the one coming from the railway station. From the railway station through Wiener Strasse (where I was living in the Hotel Eiche); to the railway station through Stückerstrasse.

Went to the theatre three times. *Des Meeres und der Liebe Wellen*. I sat in the balcony, an actor who was much too good made too much noise in the part of Naukleros; I had tears in my eyes several times, as at the end of the first act when Hero and Leander could not take their eyes away from one another. Hero stepped out of the temple doorway through which you saw something that could have been nothing else but an ice-box. In the second act, forests of the kind you see pictured in old de luxe editions, it was very affecting, creepers twined from tree to tree. Everything mossy and dark green. The backdrop of the wall of the tower chamber turned up again in *Miss Dudelsack* a few evenings later. From the third act on, the play fell off, as though an enemy had been after it.

TRIP TO SWITZERLAND, ITALY, PARIS AND ERLENBACH

AUGUST–SEPTEMBER 1911

DEPARTED 28 August 1911. Noon. Our idea is a poor one: to describe the trip and at the same time our feelings towards each other during the trip.[135] How impossible it is, proved when a wagon full of peasant women passed by. The heroic peasant woman (Delphic Sibyl). One of them was laughing and another, who had been sleeping in her lap, woke up and waved. If I should describe the way Max waved to them a false enmity would enter the description.

A girl (who later turned out to be Alice R.[136]) got on at Pilsen. (During the trip you ordered coffee from the steward by putting a little green sticker up on the window. However, you didn't have to take the coffee even if there was a sticker on your window, and could get it even if there was none.) At first I couldn't see her because she was sitting next to me. Our first social contact: her hat, which had been put away on the rack above, fell down on Max. Thus do hats come in with difficulty through the carriage doors and fly out with ease through the large windows.

Max probably made it impossible to give a true description of the scene later; he is a married man and had to say something that would deprive the incident of all its risk, and in doing so passed over what was important, emphasized what was didactic and made it all a little ugly.

'Perfect aim!' 'Fire away!' 'Rate of fall zero point five'; our joking about the card she'd write in Munich, we agreed to post it for her, but from Zürich, and it will read: 'The expected, alas, has happened . . . wrong train . . . now in Zürich . . . two days of the trip lost.' Her delight. But she expected that as gentlemen we should add nothing to it. Motor-car in Munich. Rain, fast ride (twenty minutes), a view as if from a basement apartment, the driver called out the names of the invisible sights, the tyres hummed on the wet asphalt like a film projector. My clearest recollection: of the uncurtained window of

433

the Vier Jahreszeiten, the reflection of the lights on the asphalt as if in a river.

Washing hands and face in the men's room in the station in Munich.

Baggage left on the train. A place provided for Alice in a car where a lady (who was more to be feared than we) offered to take her under her protection. Offer enthusiastically accepted. Suspicious.

Max asleep in the compartment. The two Frenchmen, the dark one laughed continually; once because Max left him hardly enough room in which to sit (he was so sprawled out), and then because he seized his opportunity and Max could no longer stretch out. Max under the hood of his ulster. Eating at night. An invasion by three Swiss. One of them was smoking. One, who stayed on after the other two got off, was at first inconspicuous, grew expansive only towards morning. Bodensee.

Switzerland left to itself in the first hours of the morning. I woke Max when I caught sight of such a bridge[137] and then got from it my first impression of Switzerland, despite the fact that I had been peering out into the grey daybreak at it for a long time from the inner obscurity of the train – The impression the houses in St Gallen give one of standing boldly upright in defiance of any arrangement into streets – Winterthur – The man leaning over the porch railing of the lighted villa in Württemberg at two o'clock in the morning. Door to the study open – The cattle already awake in sleeping Switzerland – Telegraph poles: cross-sections of clothes-hooks – The meadows paling under the rising sun – My recollection of the prison-like station at Cham, with its name inscribed on it with biblical solemnity. The window decorations, despite their meagreness, seemed to be contrary to regulations.

Tramp in the station at Winterthur with cane, song, and one hand in his trouser pocket.

Business carried on in villas.

A lot of singing in the station at Lindau during the night.

Patriotic statistics: the area of Switzerland, were it spread out level on a plain.

Foreign chocolate companies.

Zürich. The station loomed up before us like a composite of several stations recently seen – Max took possession of it for $A + x$.[138]

The impression foreign soldiers made on one of being out of the past. The absence of it in one's own. Anti-militarist argument.

Marksmen in the station at Zürich. Our fear lest their guns go off when they ran.

Bought a map of Zürich.

Back and forth on a bridge in indecision as to the order in which to have a cold bath, a warm bath, and breakfast.

In the direction of Limmat, Urania Observatory.

Main business artery, empty tram, pyramids of cuffs in the foreground of an Italian haberdasher's window.

Only fancy posters (spas, festival performance of *Marignano* by Wiegand, music by Jermoli).

Enlargement of the premises of a department store. Best advertisement. Watched for years by all the townspeople. (Dufayel.)

Postmen, looked as though they were wearing night-shirts. Carried small boxes in front, in which they sorted their letters like the 'planets'[139] at the Christmas Fair. Lake view. If you imagine you live here, a strong sense of its being Sunday. Horseman. Frightened horse. Pedagogic inscription, possibly a relief of Rebecca at the well. The inscription's serenity above the flowing water.

Altstadt: Narrow, steep street which a man in a blue blouse was laboriously descending. Down steps.

I remember the traffic-menaced lavatory in front of Saint Roche in Paris.

Breakfast in the temperance restaurant. Butter like egg yolk. *Zürcher Zeitung.*

Large cathedral, old or new? Men are supposed to sit at the sides. The sexton pointed out some better seats to us. We walked after him in that direction, since it was on our way to the door. When we were already at the exit, he apparently thought we couldn't find the seats and came diagonally across the church towards us. We pushed each other out. Much laughter.

Max: Scrambling languages together as the solution for national difficulties; the chauvinist would be at his wits' end.

Swimming-pool in Zürich: For men only. One man next to the

other. Swiss: German poured out like lead. There weren't enough lockers for everyone; republican freedom of undressing in front of your own clothes-hook, as well as the swimming master's freedom to clear the crowded solarium with a fire hose. Moreover, clearing the solarium in this way would be no more senseless than the language was incomprehensible. Diver: his feet outspread on the railing, he jumped down on the springboard, thus adding to his spring — It's only possible to judge the conveniences of a bathing establishment after long use. No swimming lessons. A long-haired nature-healer looking lonesome. Low banks of the lake.

Free concert by the Officers' Tourist Club. A writer in the audience, surrounded by companions, was noting something down in a closely written notebook; after one number on the programme was finished, he was pulled away by his companions.

No Jews. Max: The Jews have let this big business slip from their hands. Began with the *Bersaglieri March*. Ended with the *Pro Patria March*. In Prague there are no free concerts for the sake of the music alone (Jardin de Luxembourg); republican, according to Max.

Keller's room closed. Travel Bureau. Bright house behind a dark street. Houses with terraces on the right bank of the Limmat. Window shutters a brilliant blue-white. The soldiers walking slowly along serve as policemen. Concert hall. Polytechnic institute not looked for and not found. City Hall. Lunch on the first floor. Meilen wine. (Sterilized wine made of fresh grapes.) A waitress from Lucerne told us what trains run there. Pea soup with sago, beans with baked potatoes, lemon crème — Decent-looking buildings in Arts-and-Crafts style.

Left about three o'clock for Lucerne, going around the lake. The empty, dark, hilly, wooded shore of the Lake of Zug with its many peninsulas. Had an American look. During the trip, my distaste for making comparisons with countries not yet seen. To the right of the railway station a skating rink. We walked into the midst of the hotel employees and called out: Rebstock. A bridge (so Max said) divides the lake from the river, as in Zürich.

Where is the German population that warrants the German signs? Casino. The [German] Swiss you see everywhere in Zürich don't seem to have any aptitude for hotel-keeping; here, where they do run hotels, they have disappeared from view, the hotel-keepers may even be French.

The empty balloon hangar opposite. Hard to imagine how the airship glides in. Roller-skating rink, Berlin-like appearance. Fruit. The dark outlines of the Strand Promenade still clearly apparent under the tree-tops in the evening. Men with their daughters or prostitutes. Boats rocking so steeply their undermost ribs were visible.

Ridiculous lady receptionist in the hotel; a laughing girl showed people to their rooms; a serious, red-cheeked chambermaid. Small stair-case. Bolted, walled-in chest in the room. Happy to be out of the room. Would have liked to dine on fruit. Gotthard Hotel, girls in Swiss costume. Apricot compote, Meilen wine. Two elderly ladies and a gentleman talking about growing old.

Discovered the gambling house in Lucerne. Admission one franc. Two long tables. It is unpleasant to describe anything really worth seeing, people impatiently expect, as it were, to see the thing before them. At each table a croupier in the middle with an observer on either side. Betting limit five francs. 'The Swiss are requested to give pre-cedence to foreigners as the game is intended for the entertainment of our visitors.' One table with balls, one with toy horses. Croupiers in Prince Alberts. *'Messieurs faites votre jeu'* – *'Marquez le jeu'* – *'Les jeux sont faits'* – *'Sont marqués'* – *'Rien ne va plus.'* Croupiers with nickelled rakes at the end of wooden sticks. The things they can do with them: rake the money on to the right squares, sort it, draw money to them, catch the money they toss on the winning squares. The influence the different croupiers have on your chances, or rather: you like the croupier with whom you win. Our excitement when we both of us decided to play; you feel entirely alone in the room. The money (ten francs) disappeared down a gently sloping incline. The loss of ten francs was not enough temptation to go on playing, but still, a temptation. Rage at everything. The day prolonged by the gambling.

Monday, 28 August. Man in high boots breakfasting against the wall. Second-class steamer. Lucerne in the morning. Poorer appearance of the hotels. A married couple reading letters from home with news-paper clippings about cholera in Italy. The beautiful homes that you could only see from a boat on the lake. Changing shapes of the

mountains. Vitznau. Rigi railways. Lake seen through leaves. Feeling of
the south. Your surprise when you suddenly catch sight of the broad surface of the Lake of Zug. Woods like at home. Railway built in '75; look
it up in the old copy of *Über Land und Meer*. Old stamping-ground
for the English. They still wear checks and sideburns here. Telescope.
Jungfrau in the distance, rotunda of the Monk, shimmering heat waves
lent movement to the picture. The outstretched palm of the Titli. A
snow field sliced through life a loaf of bread. False estimates of the
altitudes from above as well as from below. Unsettled dispute as to
whether the railway station at Arth-Goldau rested on slanting or on
level ground. *Table d'hôte*. Dark woman, serious, sharp mouth – had
already seen her below near the carriage – sat in the hall. English girl
at the departure, her teeth even all round. A short Frenchwoman got
into the next compartment, with outstretched arm announced that our
full compartment was not '*complet*', and pushed in her father and her
older, shorter sister, who looked at once innocent and lewd and who
tickled my hips with her elbow. Some more English, toothily spoken
by the old lady at Max's right. We tried to guess what part of England.
Route from Vitznau to Flüelen – Gersau, Beckenried, Brunnen (nothing but hotels), Schillerstein, Tellplatte, Rütli, two loggias on Axenstrasse (Max imagined there were several of them, because in photographs you always see these two), Urnser Becken, Flüelen. Hotel
Sternen.

Tuesday, 29 August. This beautiful room with a balcony. The
friendliness. Too much hemmed in by mountains. A man and two girls,
in raincoats, one behind the other, walked through the hall in the evening carrying alpenstocks; when all of them were already on the steps
they were stopped by a question from the chambermaid. They thanked
her, they knew about it. In reply to a further question about their
mountain excursion: 'And it wasn't so easy either, I can tell you that.'
In the hall they seemed to me to be out of *Miss Dudelsack*; on the staircase they seem to Max to be out of Ibsen, then to me too. Forgotten
binoculars. Boys with Swiss flags. Bathing in Lake Lucerne. Married
couple. Life preserver. People walking on Axenstrasse. Fisherwoman in
light yellow dress.

Boarding the Gotthard train, Reuss. Milky water of our rivers. The
Hungarian flower. Thick lips. Exotic curve from the back to the but-

tocks. The handsome man among the Hungarians. Jesuit general in the railway station at Göschenen. Italy suddenly, tables placed haphazardly in front of taverns; an excited young man dressed in all colours who couldn't contain himself; the women with high-piled black hair waving their hands in good-bye (a kind of pinching motion) beside a station; bright pink houses, blurred signs. Later the landscape lost its Italian aspect, or the underlying Swiss quality emerged. Ticino Falls, off and on we saw waterfalls everywhere. German Lugano. Noisy palestra. Post office recently built. Hotel Belvedere. Concert in the assembly room. No fruit.

30 August. From four in the evening to eleven at the same table with Max;[140] first in the garden, then in the reading-room, then in my room. Bath in the morning and mail.

31 August. The snowcaps on the Rigi rose up into view like the hands of a clock.

Friday, 1 September. Left at 10.05 from Place Guglielmo Tell – Awning frames on the boats like on milk wagons – Every debarkation an attack.

No luggage on the trip, hand free to prop up my head.

Gandria [near Lugano]: one house stuck behind the other; loggias hung with coloured cloths; no bird's-eye view; streets, then no streets. St Margarita, a fountain on the landing-stage. Villa in Oria with twelve cypresses. You cannot, dare not imagine a house in Oria that has a porch in front with Greek pillars. Mamette: medieval magician's cap on a belfry. Earlier, a donkey in the arboured walk, along one side of the harbour. Osteno. The clergyman among the ladies. The shouting more than ordinarily incomprehensible. Child in the window behind the passage to the *pissoir*. Shivery feeling at the sight of lizards wriggling on a wall. Psyche's falling hair. Soldiers riding by on bicycles and hotel employees dressed up as sailors.

Children on the landing-stage at Menaggio; their father; the pride in her children expressed in the woman's body.

Passers-by in a carriage pointed out the Italian boys to one another. Statesman with half-opened mouth (Villa Carlotta).

Frenchwoman with my aunt's voice and a straw parasol with a thick fibre edge was writing something down about *montagne*, etc., in a small notebook. Dark man framed by the arching ribs of his boat, bent over the oars. Customs official rapidly examined a little basket, rummaging through it as if it all had been a present for him. Italian on the Porlezza–Menaggio train. Every word of Italian spoken to one penetrates the great void of one's own ignorance and, whether understood or not, lengthily engages one's attention; one's own uncertain Italian cannot prevail against the speaker's fluency and, whether understood or not, is easily disregarded – Joke about the train going backward at Menaggio, nice matter for a conversation – On the other side of the street, in front of the villas, decorated stone boat-houses. Thriving business in antiques. Boatman: *Peu de commerce* – Revenue cutter ('Story of Captain Nemo' and *A Journey through Planetary Space*).

2 September, Saturday. My face was twitching on board the small steamer. Draped curtains (brown, edged in white) in front of the stores (Cadenabbia). Bees in the honey. Lonely, peevish, short-waisted woman, a language teacher. The punctiliously dressed gentleman in high-drawn trousers. His forearms were suspended over the table as though he were clasping not the handles of a knife and fork but the end of an arm rest. Children watching the weak rockets: *Encore un* – hiss – arms stretched up.

Bad trip on the steamer, too much a part of the rocking of the boat. Not high enough to smell the fresh air and have an unobstructed view around, somewhat like the situation of the stokers. A passing group: man, cow, and woman. She was saying something. Black turban, loose dress – The heartbeat of lizards – Host's little boy, without my having spoken to him previously, under the urging of his mother held his mouth up to me for a good-night kiss. I enjoyed it.

Gandria: instead of streets, cellar steps and cellar passageways. A boy was being whipped; the hollow sound of beds being beaten. House overgrown with ivy. Seamstress in Gandria at the window without shutters, curtains, or panes. We were so tired we had to hold one another up on the way from the bathing place to Gandria. Solemn procession of boats behind a small black steamer. Young men looking at pictures, kneeling, lounging about on the wharf in Gandria, one of them a rather pale person well known to us as a ladies' man and buffoon.

On the quay in the evening in Porlezza. At the William Tell monument a full-bearded Frenchman we had already forgotten reminded us again of what had been memorable about him.

3 September, Sunday. A German with a gold tooth who because of it would have stuck in the memory of anyone describing him, though the impression he made was otherwise an indeterminate one, bought a ticket for the swimming-pool as late as a quarter to twelve, despite its closing at twelve; the swimming master inside immediately called this to his attention in an incomprehensible Italian which for this reason sounded rather stern. Flustered by it even in his own language, the German stammeringly asked why in that case they had sold him a ticket at the entrance booth, complained that they should have sold him a ticket, and protested at its having been sold to him so late. From the Italian reply you could make out that he still had almost a quarter of an hour in which to swim and get dressed, didn't he? Tears – Sat on the barrel in the lake. Hotel Belvedere: 'With all due respect to the manager, the food is miserable.'

4 September. Cholera reports: travel bureau, *Corriere della Sera*, North German Lloyd, *Berliner Tageblatt*, chambermaid brought us reports from a Berlin doctor; the general character of the reports varied according to the group and one's physical condition; when we left Lugano for Porto Ceresio, at 1.05, they were fairly favourable – Felt a passing enthusiasm for Paris in the wind blowing on the third of September *Excelsior*, which we held open in front of us and ran off to a bench to read. There was still some advertising space to let on the bridge across Lake Lugano.

Friday. Three crew members chased us away from the ship's bow on the pretext that the helmsman had to have an unobstructed view forward of the light, and then pushed a bench over and sat down themselves. I should have liked to have sung.

Under the eyes of the Italian who advised us to make the trip to Turin (*exposition*) and to whom we nodded agreement, we shook hands in confirmation of our common decision not to go to Turin at any price. Praised the cut-rate tickets. Cyclist circling about on the lake terrace of a house in Porto Ceresio. Whip that had only a little tail of horse-hair instead of a strap. A cyclist pedalling along with a rope in his hand, leading a horse that trotted beside him.

Milan: Forgot guidebook in a store. Went back and stole it. Ate apple strudel in the courtyard of the Mercanti. Health cake. Teatro Fossati. Every hat and fan in motion. A child laughing up above. An elderly lady in the male orchestra. *Poltrone – Ingresso* – Pit on a level with the orchestra. All the windows in the back wall open. Tall, vigorous actor with delicately painted nostrils; the black of the nostrils continued to stand out even when the outline of his upturned face was lost in the light. Girl with a long slender neck ran off-stage with short steps and rigid elbows – you could guess at the high heels that went with the long neck. The importance of the laughter exaggerated, for there is a greater gap between laughter and uncomprehending gravity than between it and the gravity of an initiated spectator. Significance of every piece of furniture. Five doors in each of the two plays for any emergency. Nose and mouth of a girl shadowed by her painted eyes. Man in a box opened his mouth when he laughed until a gold molar became visible, then kept it open like that for a while. That kind of unity of stage and audience which is created for and against the spectator does not understand the language, a unity impossible to achieve in any other way.

Young Italian woman whose otherwise Jewish face became non-Jewish in profile. How she stood up, leaned forward with her hands on the ledge so that only her narrow body could be seen, her arms and shoulders being concealed; how she extended her arms to either side of the window; how she clung in the breeze with both hands to one side of the window, as though to a tree. She was reading a paper-bound detective story that her little brother had been vainly begging from her for some time. Her father, near by, had a hooked nose whereas hers, at the same place, curved gently, was therefore more Jewish. She looked at me often, curious to see whether I shouldn't finally stop my annoying staring. Her dress of raw silk. Tall, stout, perfumed woman near me scattering her scent into the air with her fan. I felt myself shrivel up next to her – In the baggage room the tin plate over the gas flame was shaped like a girl's flat-brimmed hat. Pleasant variety of lattice-work on the houses. We had been looking for the Scala right under the arch of its entrance; when we came out on the square and saw its simple, worn façade we were not surprised at the error we had made.

Pleased by the connexion a pair of folding doors affords between the two rooms. Each of us can open a door. A good arrangement for married people too, Max thinks.

First write down a thought, then recite it aloud; don't write as you recite, for in that case only the beginning already inwardly pondered will succeed, while what is still to be written will be lost. A discussion of asphyxia and [lethal] heart injection at a little table in a coffeehouse on the Cathedral Square. Mahler asked for a heart injection too. As the discussion went on, I felt the time that we had planned to spend in Milan rapidly dwindling away, in spite of some resistance on my part – The Cathedral with its many spires is a little tiresome.

Genesis of our decision to go to Paris: the moment in Lugano with the *Excelsior*; trip to Milan in consequence of our not altogether voluntary purchase of the Porto Ceresia–Milan tickets; from Milan to Paris out of fear of the cholera and the desire to be compensated for this fear. In addition, our calculation of the time and money this trip would save us.

1. Rimini–Genoa–Nervi (Prague).

2. Upper Italian lakes, Milan–Genoa (wavering between Locarno and Lugano).

3. Omit Lago Maggiore, Lugano, Milan, trip through the cities as far as Bologna.

4. Lugano–Paris.

5. Lugano–Milan (several days)–Maggiore.

6. In Milan: directly to Paris (possibly Fontainebleau).

7. Got off at Stresa. Here, for the first time, we were at a point in our trip where it was possible to look backwards and forwards along it; it had passed out of its infant stages and there was something there to take by the waist.

I have never yet seen people looking so small as they did in the Galleria in Milan. Max thought the Galleria was only as high as the other houses you saw outside; I denied it with some objection I have since forgotten, for I will always come to the defence of the Galleria. It had almost no superfluous ornamentation, there was nothing to arrest the sweep of the eye, seemed little because of this, as well as because of its height, but could afford that too. It was shaped like a cross, through which the air blew freely. From the roof of the Cathedral the people seemed to have grown bigger as against the Galleria. The Galleria consoled me completely for the fact that I did not see the ancient Roman ruins.

Transparent inscription deep in the tiles over the brothel: *Al vero Eden.* Heavy traffic between there and the street, mostly single persons. Up and down the narrow streets of the neighbourhood. They were clean, some had pavements in spite of their narrow width; once we looked from one narrow street down another that ran into it at right angles and saw a woman leaning against the window-grating on the top floor of a house. I was lighthearted and unhesitating in everything at the time, and, as always in such moods, felt my body grow heavier. The girls spoke their French like virgins. Milanese beer smells like beer, tastes like wine. Max regrets what he writes only during the writing of it, never afterwards. Somewhat apprehensively, Max took a cat for a walk in the reading-room.

A girl with a belly that had undoubtedly spread shapelessly over and between her outspread legs under her transparent dress while she had been sitting down; but when she stood up it was pulled in, and her body at last looked something like what a girl's body should. The Frenchwoman whose sweetness, to an analytical eye, chiefly showed in her round, talkative, and devoted knees. An imperious and monumental figure that thrust the money she had just earned into her stocking – The old man who lay one hand atop the other on one knee – The woman by the door, whose sinister face was Spanish, whose manner of putting her hands on her hips was Spanish and who stretched herself in her close-fitting dress of prophylactic silk – At home it was with the German bordello girls that one lost a sense of one's nationality for a moment, here it was with the French girls. Perhaps insufficiently acquainted with the conditions here.

My passion for iced drinks punished: one grenadine, two aranciatas in the theatre, one in the bar on the Corso Emmanuele, one sherbet in the coffee-house in the Galleria, one French Thierry mineral water that all at once disclosed what had been the effect of everything that I had had before. Sadly went to bed, looking out from it on a sweeping, very Italianate prospect framed in the shallow bay window of a side-wall. Miserably awoke with a dry pressure against the walls of my mouth – The very unofficial elegance of the police who make their rounds carrying their knit gloves in one hand and their canes in the other.

444

5 September. Banca Commerciale on Scala Square. Letters from home – Card to my boss – Our astonishment when we entered the Cathedral – Wanted to make an architectural sketch of it; the Cathedral interior was purely architectural, there were no benches for the most part, few statues on the pillars, a few dim pictures on the distant walls; the individual visitors on the Cathedral floor provided a measure of its height, and their walking about provided a measure of its extent. Sublime, but recalled the Galleria too directly.

Inexcusable to travel – or even live – without taking notes. The deathly feeling of the monotonous passing of the days is made impossible.

Climbed to the roof of the Cathedral. A young Italian in front made the climb easier for us by humming a tune, trying to take off his coat, looking through cracks through which only sunlight could be seen, and continually tapping at the numerals that showed the number of steps – View from the roof: something was wrong with the tram-cars down below, they moved so slowly, only the curve of the rails carried them along. A conductor, distorted and foreshortened from where we stood, hurried to his tram and jumped in. A fountain shaped like a man, spinal column and brain removed to make a passage for the rainwater – Each of the great stained-glass windows was dominated by the colour of some one piece of clothing that recurred over and over again in the individual panes.

Max: Toy railway station in the display of a toy store, rails that formed a circle and led nowhere; is and will remain his strongest impression of Milan. An attempt to show the variety of the stock could account for placing the railway station and Cathedral side by side in the display – From the back portal of the Cathedral you looked right into the face of a large clock on a roof – Teatro Fossati – Trip to Stresa. The people turning in their sleep in the crowded compartment. The two lovers – Afternoon in Stresa.

Thursday, 7 September. Bath, letters, departure – Sleeping in public –

Friday, 8 September. Trip [to Paris]. Italian couple. Clergyman. American. The two little Frenchwomen with their fat behinds. Montreux. Your legs parted company on the broad Parisian streets –

Japanese lanterns in the garden restaurants – The Place de la Concorde is arranged so that its sights are off in the distance, where one's eye can easily find them out, but only if it looks for them.

École Florentine (fifteenth century), apple scene – Tintoretto: *Suzanne* – Simone Martini: (1285, école de Sienne) *Jésus Christ marchant au Calvaire* – Mantegna: *La Sagesse victorieuse des Vices* 1431–1506, école Vénétienne – Titian: *Le Concile de Trente 1477– 1576* – Raphael: *Apollo and Marsyas* – Velázquez: *Portrait de Philippe IV roi d'Espagne* 1599–1600. Jacob Jordaens 1593–1678: *Le Concert après le repas* – Rubens: *Kermesse.*[141]

Confiserie de l'enfant gâté, rue des Petits Champs. Washerwoman in morning undress – rue des Petits Champs so narrow it was entirely in the shade. *Le sou du soldat, société anonyme.* Capital one mill., avenue de l'Opéra – Robert, Samuel. *Ambassadeur:* a roll of the drums followed by brasses (the double *s*), with the *eur* the drumsticks are lifted up in the midst of their flourish and are silent – Gare de Lyon. The construction workers' substitute for braces is a coloured sash worn round the waist; here, where sashes have an official meaning, it gives it a democratic effect.

I didn't know whether I was sleepy or not, and the question bothered me all morning on the train. Don't mistake the nursemaids for French governesses of German children.

Prise de Salins, 17 May 1668, par M. Lafarge. In the background a man dressed in red on a white horse and a man in dark clothes on a dark horse catch their breath after the siege of a city by going for a ride while a storm approaches – *Voyage de Louis XVI à Cherbourg*, 23 juin 1786 – *Bivouac de Napoléon sur le champ de bataille de Wagram, nuit de 5 au 6 juillet 1809.*[142] Napoleon is sitting alone, one leg propped on a low table. Behind him a smoking campfire. The shadows of his right leg and of the legs of the table and camp stool lie in the foreground like rays about him. Peaceful moon. The generals, in a distant semi-circle, look into the fire or at him.

How easy it is for a grenadine and seltzer to get into your nose when you laugh (bar in front of the Opéra Comique).

Platform tickets – that vulgar intrusion on family life – are unknown.

Alone [in Erlenbach][143] in the reading-room with a lady who was hard of hearing; while she looked elsewhere, I vainly introduced myself to her; she considered the rain I pointed to outside as a continuing humidity. She was telling fortunes by cards according to the instructions given in a book beside her, into which she intently peered with her head propped against her fist. There must have been a hundred little miniature cards printed on both sides in her fist that she hadn't used yet. Near by, his back to me, an old gentleman dressed in black was reading the *Münchner Neueste Nachrichten*. A pouring rain. Travelled with a Jewish goldsmith. He was from Cracow, a little more than twenty years old, had been in America two and a half years, had been living in Paris for two months, and had had only fourteen days' work. Badly paid (only ten francs a day), no place to do business. When you've just come to a city you don't know what your work is worth. Fine life in Amsterdam. Full of people from Cracow. Every day you knew what was new in Cracow, for someone was always going there or coming back. There were entire streets where only Polish was spoken. Made a lot of money in New York because the girls earn a lot there and can deck themselves out. Paris wouldn't compare with it, the minute you stepped into the boulevards you could see that. Left New York because his people live here, after all, and because they wrote him: We're here in Cracow and still make a living too; how long are you going to stay in America? Quite right. Enthusiastic over the way the Swiss live. Living out in the country as they do and raising cattle, they must get to be as strong as giants. And the rivers. But the most important thing is, bathe in running water after you get up – He had long, curly hair, only occasionally ran his fingers through it, very bright eyes, a gently curving nose, hollows in his cheeks, a suit of American cut, a frayed shirt, falling socks. His bag was small, but when he got off he carried it as if it had been a heavy burden. His German was disturbed by an English pronunciation and English expressions; his English was so strong that his Yiddish was given a rest. Full of animation after a night spent in travelling. 'You're an Austrian, aren't you? You have one of those rain-capes too. All the Austrians have them.' By showing him the sleeves I proved that it was not a cape but a coat. He still maintained that every Austrian had a cape. This was how they threw it on. He turned to a third person and showed him how they did it. He pretended to fasten something behind on his shirt collar, bent his body to see whether it held, then pulled this something first over his right then over his left arm, until he was entirely enveloped in it and nice and warm, as you could see. Although he was sitting down, the movements of his legs showed how easily and unconcernedly an Austrian wearing a cape like that could walk. There was almost no mockery in all this, rather it was done as if by someone who had travelled around a bit and seen something of the world. There was a little child-like touch to it all.

My walk in the dark little garden in front of the sanatorium.

Morning setting-up exercises accompanied by the singing of a song from *Wunderhorn* which someone played on the cornet.

The secretary who went for walking trips every winter, to Budapest, southern France, Italy. Barefoot, ate raw food only (whole-wheat bread, fish, dates), lived two weeks with two other people in the region around Nice, mostly naked, in a deserted house.

Fat little girl who was always picking her nose, clever but not especially pretty, had a nose with no expectations, was called Waltraute and, according to a young woman, there was something radiant about her.

I dreaded the pillars of the dining-room in advance, because of the pictures (tall, shining, solid marble) I had seen in the prospectus, and cursed myself during the trip across on the little steamer. But they turned out to be made of very unpretentious brick painted in bad imitation of marble, and unusually low.

Lively conversation between a man in the pear tree opposite my window and a girl on the ground floor whom I couldn't see.

A pleasant feeling when the doctor listened over and over again to my heart, kept asking me to change my position, and couldn't make up his mind. He tapped the area around my heart for an especially long time; it lasted so long he seemed almost absent-minded.

The quarrel at night between the two women in the compartment, the lamp of which they had covered over. The Frenchwoman lying down screamed out of the darkness, and the elderly woman whom her feet were pressing against the wall and who spoke French badly didn't know what to do. According to the Frenchwoman she should have left the seat, carried all her luggage over to the other side, the back seat, and permitted her to stretch out. The Greek doctor in my compartment said she was definitely in the wrong, in bad, clear French that was apparently based on German. I fetched the conductor, who settled matters between them.

Again encountered the lady, who is a fanatical writer too. She carried with her a portfolio full of stationery, cards, pens, and pencils, all of which was an incitement to me.

This place looks like a family group now. Outside it is raining, the mother has her fortune-telling cards in front of her and the son is writing. Otherwise the room is empty. Since she is hard of hearing, I could also call her mother.

In spite of my great dislike for the word 'type', I think it is true that nature-healing and everything associated with it is producing a new human type represented in a person such as Mr Fellenberg (of course, I only know him superficially). People with thin skins, rather small heads, looking exaggeratedly clean, with one or two incongruous little details (in the case of Mr F., some missing teeth, the beginning of a paunch), a greater spareness than would seem appropriate to the structure of their bodies, that is, every trace of fattiness is suppressed, they treat their health as if it were a malady, or at least something they had acquired by their own merit (I'm not reproaching them), with all the other consequences of an artificially cultivated feeling of good health.

In the balcony at the Opéra Comique. In the front row a man in a frock coat and top hat; in one of the rear rows, a man in his shirt sleeves (with his shirt even turned in in front in order to leave his chest free), all prepared to go to bed.

National quarrels in Switzerland. Biel, a wholly German city a few years ago, is in danger of becoming gallicized because of the heavy immigration of French watchmakers. Ticino, the only Italian canton, wants to secede from Switzerland. An irredenta exists. The reason is that the Italians have no representation in the Federal Council (it has seven members); with their small number (perhaps 180,000) it would need a council of nine members to give them representation. But they don't want to change the number. The St Gotthard railway was a private German enterprise, had German officials who founded a German school in Bellinzona; now that it has been taken over by the state the Italians want Italian officials and the suppression of the German school. And education is actually a matter in which only the government of the canton is authorized to make decisions. Total population: two thirds German, one third French and Italian.

The ailing Greek doctor who drove me out of the compartment with his coughing during the night can only – so he said – digest mutton. Since he had to spend the night in Vienna, he asked me to write the German word down for him.

Though it was raining and later on I was left completely to myself, though my misery is always present to me, though group games were going on in the dining-hall in which I took no part because of my lack of skill, and even though in the end everything I wrote was bad, I still had no feeling for either what was ugly or degrading, sad or painful in this lonely state of mine, a loneliness, moreover, that is organic with me – as though I consisted only of bones. At the same time I was happy to think that I had detected the trace of an appetite in the region above my clogged intestines. The old lady, who had gone to fetch some milk for herself in a tin pot, returned, and before losing herself in her cards again asked me: 'What are you writing? Notes? A diary?' And since she knew she would not understand my answer, she went right on with her questions: 'Are you a student?' Without thinking of her deafness, I replied: 'No, but I was one'; and while she was already laying out her cards again, I was left alone with my sentence, the weight of which compelled me to go on looking at her for a while.

We are two men sitting at a table with six or seven Swiss women. When my plate is half empty, or when I stare in boredom round me in the dining-hall, I see plates rise up far off in the distance, rapidly draw near me in the hands of women (sometimes I call them Mrs, sometimes Miss), and slowly go back the way they came when I say, 'No, thank you.'

Le Siège de Paris par Francisque Sarcey: 19 July 1870, declaration of war. Those who were famous for a few days – Changing character of the book as it describes the changing character of Paris – Praise and blame for the same things. The calm of Paris after the surrender is sometimes French frivolity, sometimes French ability to resist – 4 September, after Sedan, the Republic – workers and national guardsmen on ladders hammer the *N* off the public buildings – eight days after the Republic was proclaimed the enthusiasm still ran so high that they could get no one to work on the fortifications – The Germans are advancing.

Parisian jokes: MacMahon was captured at Sedan, Bazaine surrendered Metz, the two armies have at last established contact – The destruction of the suburbs ordered – no news for three months – Paris never had such an appetite as at the beginning of the siege. Gambetta organized the rising of the provinces. Once, by good fortune, a letter from him arrived. But instead of giving the exact dates everyone was on fire to know, he wrote only *que la résistance de Paris faisait l'admiration de l'univers* – Insane club meetings. A meeting of women in the Triat school. 'How should the women defend their honour against the enemy?' With the *doigt de Dieu*, or rather *le doigt prussique. Il consiste en une sorte de dé en caoutchouc que les femmes se mettent au doigt. Au bout de ce dé est un petit tube contenant de l'acide prussique.* If a German soldier comes along, he is extended a hand, his skin is pricked, and the acid is injected – The Institute sends a scholar out by balloon to study the eclipse of the sun in Algeria – They ate last year's chestnuts and the animals of the Jardin des Plantes – There were a few restaurants where everything was to be had up to the last day – Sergeant Hoff, who was so famous for murdering a Prussian to avenge his father, disappeared and was considered a spy – State of the army: several of the outposts have a friendly drink with the Germans – Louis Blanc compares the Germans to Mohicans who have studied technology – On 5 January the bombardment begins. Doesn't amount to much. People were told to throw themselves on the ground when they heard the shelling. Street boys, grown-ups too, stood in the mud and from time to time shouted *gare l'obus* – For a while General Chauzy was the hope of Paris, but met defeat like all the others; even at that time there was no reason for his renown, nevertheless, so great was the enthusiasm in Paris that Sarcey, even when writing his book, feels a vague, unfounded admiration for Chauzy.

A day in Paris at the time: Sunny and fine on the boulevards, people strolling placidly along; the scene changes near the Hôtel de Ville where the Communards are in revolt, many dead, troops, excesses. Prussian shells whistle on the Left Bank. Quays and bridges are quiet. Back to the Théâtre Français. The audience is leaving after a performance of the *Mariage de Figaro*. The evening papers are just coming out, the playgoers collect in groups around the kiosks, children are playing in the Champs-Élysées, Sunday strollers curiously watch a squadron of cavalry riding by with trumpets blowing – From a German soldier's letter to his mother: *Tu n'imagines pas comme ce Paris est immense, mais les Parisiens sont de drôles de gens; ils trompettent toute la journée* – For fourteen days there was no hot water in Paris – At the end of January the four-and-a-half-month siege ended.

The comradely way old women behave to one another in a compartment. Stories about old women who were run over by motor-cars; the rules they follow on a journey: never eat gravy, take out the meat, keep your eyes closed during the trip; but at the same time eat fruit down to the core, no tough veal, ask men to escort you across the street, cherries are the best fruit for roughage, the salvation of old women.

The young Italian couple on the train to Stresa joined another couple on the train to Paris. One of the husbands merely submitted to being kissed, and while he looked out of the window gave her only his shoulder to rest her cheek against. When he took off his coat because of the heat and closed his eyes, she seemed to look at him more intently. She wasn't pretty, there were only some thin curls around her face. The other woman wore a veil with blue dots one of which would frequently obscure her eye, her nose seemed to come too abruptly to an end, the wrinkles of her mouth were youthful ones, by which she could give expression to her youthful vivacity. When she bent her head her eyes moved back and forth in a way that I have observed at home only in people who wear eyeglasses.

The efforts made by all the Frenchmen one meets to improve one's bad French, at least temporarily.

Sitting inside our carriage, uncertain as we were of which hotel to choose, we seemed to be driving our carriage uncertainly too; once we turned into a side-street, then brought it back on the right road; and this is in the morning traffic of the rue de Rivoli near the markets.

Stepped out on the balcony and looked around for the first time as though I had just awakened in this room, when in fact I was so tired from the night's journey that I didn't know whether I would be able to dash around in these streets the whole day, especially in view of the way they now looked to me from above, with me not yet on them.

Beginning of our Parisian misunderstandings. Max came up to my hotel room and was upset that I wasn't ready. I was washing my face, whereas I had previously said that we should just wash up a little and leave at once. Since by 'washing up a little' I had only meant to exclude washing one's whole body, and on the other hand it was precisely the washing of my face that I had meant by it, which I hadn't finished yet, I didn't understand his complaints and went right on washing, even if not with quite the same solicitude; while Max, with all the dirt of the night's journey on his clothes, sat down on my bed to wait. Whenever Max finds fault with someone he has the trick of knitting his mouth, and even his whole face together in a sweet expression, he is doing it this very moment, as if on the one hand he intended by this to make his reproaches more understandable, and as if he wanted to indicate on the other hand that only the sweetness of his present expression keeps him from giving me a box on the ear. In the fact that I force him into a hypocrisy unnatural to him there is contained a further reproach which I feel him to be expressing when he falls silent and the lines of his face draw apart in a contrary direction – that is, away from his mouth – in order to recover from the sweetness they had expressed, which of course has a much stronger effect than did his first expression. I, on the other hand, out of weariness can retreat so deeply inside myself that these various expressions never reach to me (such was the case in Paris); which is why I can then behave in so lordly a fashion in my misery (out of a feeling of completest indifference and without a trace of guilt) as to apologize at once. This pacified him at the time in Paris, or so at least it seemed to, and he stepped out on the balcony with me and remarked on the view, chiefly on how Parisian it was. What I really saw was only how fresh Max was; how assuredly he fitted into a Paris of some sort that I couldn't even perceive; how, emerging from his dark back room, he stepped out on a Paris balcony in the sunlight for the first time in a year and knew that he was deserving of it, while I, unfortunately, was noticeably more tired than when I had first come out on the balcony shortly before Max. And my tiredness in Paris cannot be got over by sleep, but only by going away. Sometimes I even consider this one of the characteristics of Paris.

This was really written without ill will, but he was at my heels at every word.

At first I was against the Café Biard because I thought you could only get black coffee there. It turned out that they have milk too, even if only with bad, spongy pastry. Almost the only way to improve Paris that I can think of is to provide better pastry in these cafés. Later, just before breakfast, when Max had already sat down at the table, I hit upon the idea of going about the side-streets to look for fruit. On the way to the café I kept eating a little of the fruit, so that Max would not be too astonished. After a successful attempt, in an excellent café near the Versailles railway station under the eyes of a waiter leaning over us in the doorway, to eat apple strudel and almond cake bought by us in a bakery, we do the same thing in the Café Biard, and in this way discover that, apart from enjoying fine pastry, you more decidedly enjoy the café's real advantages; such as the complete lack of attention paid to you in the relative emptiness of the place, the good service, and your position near the people passing by the open door and standing at the counter. You have only to put up with the floor's being swept – something they do frequently because the customers come in directly from the street and mill back and forth at the counter – and their habitual disregard of their customers while they do it.

Looking at the tiny bars that line the route of the Versailles railway, you would think it simple for a young couple to open one up and so lead a fine, interesting life involving no risk and no hard work except at certain hours of the day. Even on the boulevards you find cheap bars of this kind cropping up in the shadow at the corner of a wedge-shaped block of houses between two side-streets.

The customers in whitewash-spotted shirts around little tables in the suburban inns.

The woman with a little barrow of books calling out her wares on the boulevard Poissonière in the evening. Look through them, gentlemen, look through them, take your pick, they're all for sale. Without urging him to buy it, even without watching obtrusively, in the midst of her cries she at once quotes the price of the book that one of the bystanders picks up. She seems to ask only that the books be looked through with more speed, more speedily exchanged for others, all of which a person can understand when he watches the way here and there someone, myself, for instance, will slowly pick up a book, slowly leaf through it a little, slowly put it down and finally walk slowly away. The solemn way she quotes the prices of the books, which are full of such ludicrous indecencies that at first you can't imagine your ever deciding to buy a book under the eyes of all the people.

How much more decision is required to buy a book from a pavement stall than inside the store, for choosing a book in this way is really nothing but a free deliberation in the accidental presence of the books on display.

Sitting on two little chairs facing each other on the Champs-Élysées. Children up much too late were still playing in the dusk and could no longer clearly see the lines they had drawn in the dirt.

A fat usherette at the Opéra Comique rather condescendingly accepted our tip. The reason for it, I thought, was our somewhat too hesitant approach one behind the other with the theatre tickets in our hand, and I inwardly resolved the following evening to refuse a tip to the usherette at the Comédie to her face; stricken by shame in her presence and mine, however, I then gave her a large tip, though everyone else came in without giving one. I even said something at the Comédie to the effect that in my opinion tips were something 'not indispensable', but nevertheless had to pay again when the usherette, this time a thin one, complained that she was not paid by the management and hung her head on her breast.

Boot-polishing scene at the beginning. How the children accompanying the watch walked down the stairs in step. The overture played perfunctorily to make it easy for the latecomers to take their seats. They used to do that only to operettas. A nice simplicity of scenery. Lethargic extras, as in every performance I have seen in Paris, whereas at home they can hardly contain their high spirits. The donkey for the first act of *Carmen* was waiting in the narrow street outside the entrance to the theatre, surrounded by theatre people and a small pavement audience, until the little entrance door was clear. On the steps outside I bought, almost purposely, one of those fake programmes which are sold in front of every theatre. A ballerina substituted for Carmen in the dance in the smugglers' inn. How her mute body laboured during Carmen's song. Later Carmen's dance, which seemed much prettier than it really was because of the merits of her previous performance. It was as if she had taken a few hasty lessons from the leading ballerina before the performance. The footlights whitened her soles when she leaned against the table, listening to someone, and crossed and uncrossed her feet below her green skirt.

Man in the lobby talking to two ladies; had a somewhat loosely hanging frock coat which, had it not been new, had it fitted better and had he not been wearing it here, could have come right out of the past. Monocle allowed to fall and raised again. Tapped uncertainly with his stick when the conversation halted. His arm continually trembled as if at any moment he intended to put it out and escort the ladies through the centre of the crowd. Worn, bloodless skin of his face.

We were too tired to sit out the last act (I was too tired even for the next to the last), went off, and sat down in a bar opposite the Opéra Comique; where Max out of weariness sprayed soda over me and I out of weariness couldn't keep from laughing and got grenadine in my nose. Meanwhile the last act was probably beginning; we walked home.

The German language's faculty of sounding beautiful in the mouths of foreigners who haven't mastered it, and for the most part don't intend to, either. So far as we have observed, we never could see that Frenchmen took any delight in the errors we committed in French, or even so much as deigned to notice them, and even we, whose French has little feeling for the language –

The very fortunate (from my point of view) cooks and waiters: after the general meal they eat lettuce, beans, and potatoes mixed in large bowls, take only small portions of each dish though a great deal is served them, and from the distance look like the cooks and waiters at home – The waiter with the elegantly contracted mouth and little beard who one day waited on me, I think, only because I was tired, awkward, abstracted, and disagreeable, and for this reason was unable to serve myself, whereas he brought the food to me almost without being aware of it.

At Duval's on the boulevard Sébastopol at twilight. Three customers scattered about the place. The waitresses murmuring quietly to each other. The cashier's cage still empty. I ordered a yogurt, then another. The waitress silently brought it to me, the semi-darkness of the place added to the silence too, silently she took away the silver that had been laid at my place in preparation for the evening meal and that might be in my way. It was very pleasant to have been able to sense a tolerance and understanding for my sufferings in this woman moving so silently about me.

In the Louvre from one bench to the next. Pang if one was skipped – Crowd in the Salon Carré, the excitement and the knots of people, as if the Mona Lisa had just been stolen – In front of the pictures the cross-bars that you could conveniently lean upon, especially in the gallery where the Primitives were hung – This compulsion I have to look with Max at his favourite pictures, though I am too tired to look by myself – Looking up admiringly – The vigour of a tall young Englishwoman who walked up and down the length of the longest gallery with her escort.

Max's appearance as he was reading *Phèdre* under a street lamp in front of the Aristede, ruining his eyes on the small print. Why does he never listen to me? – But I profited from it, unfortunately, for on the way to the theatre he told me everything he had read in his *Phèdre* on the street while I had been having supper. A short distance; Max's effort to tell me everything, everything; an effort on my part too. The military show in the lobby. The crowd had been pushed back several yards, and soldiers in military fashion were regulating the flow to the box office.

Apparently a claqueur in our row. Her applause seemed to follow the regular outbursts of the head claqueur busy in the last row above us. She clapped with her face absent-mindedly bent so far forward that when the applause stopped she stared in astonished concern at the palms of her mesh gloves. But at once recommenced when it was called for. But in the end clapped on her own too, and so was no claqueur after all.

The feeling theatregoers must have of being on an equal footing with the play in order to arrive towards the end of the first act and make a whole row of people stand up.

A stage set that was never changed during the five acts made the performance more impressive, and was, even if only made of paper, more solid than one of wood and stone that is continually changed.

A group of pillars facing the sea and blue sky, overgrown by creepers. Direct influence of Veronese's *Banquet*, of Claude Lorrain too.

Oenone readily passed from one rigid pose into another; once, standing erect, her robe tightly wound about her legs, her arm raised and her fist steady, she delivered herself of a verse. Often veiled the expression of her face in her hands.

I was dissatisfied with the actress playing *Phèdre* when I remembered what satisfaction I had got from reading about Rachel in the period when she had been a member of the Comédie Française.

At a sight as surprising as the first scene offered, when Hippolyte, with his man-sized bow motionless at his side, was on the point of confiding in the Pedagogue, looking directly at the audience in quiet pride while he declaimed his verses as if they had been a holiday recitation, I had the impression – a slight one, though, as often in the past – that all this was taking place for the first time, and in my general admiration there was mingled admiration for something that had succeeded at its first attempt.

Sensibly conducted brothels. Clean shutters lowered everywhere over the large windows of the house. In the concierge's box, instead of a man, a decently dressed woman who would have been at home anywhere. In Prague already, I had often taken casual notice of the Amazonian character of brothels. Here it was even more pronounced. The female concierge who rang her electric bell, detained us in her box when she was notified that two visitors were just coming down the stairs; the two respectable-looking women upstairs (why two?) who received us; the light switched on in the adjoining room in the darkness or semi-darkness of which were sitting the unengaged girls; the three-quarter circle (we made it a full circle) in which they stood around us, drawn up in postures calculated to reveal them to best advantage; the long stride with which the girl who had been chosen came forward; the grasp with which the madam urged me on, while I felt myself impelled towards the exit. I cannot imagine how I got to the street, it happened so quickly. It was difficult to see the girls clearly because there were too many of them, they blinked their eyes, but most of all because they crowded too closely around one. One would have had to keep one's eyes wide open, and that takes practice. I really only remember the one who stood directly in front of me. She had gaps in her teeth, stretched herself to her full height, her clenched fist held her dress together over her pudenda, and she rapidly opened and shut her large eyes and large mouth. Her blonde hair was dishevelled. She was thin. Anxious lest I should forget and take off my hat. Lonely, long, absurd walk home.

The assembled visitors waiting for the Louvre to open. Girls sat among the tall columns, read their Baedekers, wrote postcards.

Even when you walked round the Venus de Milo as slowly as possible, there was a rapid and surprising alteration in its appearance. Unfortunately made a forced remark (about the waist and drapery), but several true ones too. I should need a plastic reproduction to remember them, especially one about the way the bended left knee affected her appearance from every side, though sometimes only very slightly. My forced remark: One would expect the body to grow slimmer above where the drapery leaves off, but at first it is even broader. The falling robe held up by the knee.

The front view of the Borghese Wrestler isn't the best one, for it makes the spectator recoil and presents a disjointed appearance. Seen from the rear, however, where for the first time you see his foot touching the ground, your eye is drawn in delight along the rigid leg and flies safely over the irresistible back to the arm and sword raised towards the front.

The Métro seemed very empty to me then, especially in comparison with the time when, sick and alone, I had ridden out to the races. Even apart from the number of passengers, the fact that it was Sunday influenced the way the Métro looked. The dark colour of the steel sides of the carriages predominated. The conductors did their work – opening and closing carriage doors and swinging themselves in and out between times – in a Sunday-afternoon manner. Everyone walked the long distances between branch connexions in leisurely fashion. The unnatural indifference with which passengers submit to a ride in the Métro was more noticeable. People seemed to face the door, or get off at unfamiliar stations far from the Opéra, as the impulse moved them. In spite of the electric lights you can definitely see the changing light of day in the stations; you notice it immediately after you've walked down, the afternoon light particularly, just before it gets dark. Arrival at the empty terminal of Porte Dauphine, a lot of tubes became visible, view into the loop where the trains make the curve they are permitted after their long trip in a straight line. Going through railway tunnels is much worse; in the Métro there isn't that feeling of oppression which a railway passenger has under the weight – though held in check – of mountains. Then, too, you aren't far off somewhere, away from people; it is rather an urban contrivance, like water pipes, for example. Tiny offices, most of them deserted, with telephones and bell systems, control the traffic. Max liked to look into them. The first time in my life I rode the Métro, from Montmartre to the main boulevards, the noise was horrible. Otherwise it hasn't been bad, even intensifies the calm, pleasant sense of speed. Métro system does away with speech; you don't have to speak either when you pay or when you get in and out. Because it is so easy to understand, the Métro is a frail and hopeful stranger's best chance to think that he has quickly and correctly, at the first attempt, penetrated the essence of Paris.

You recognize strangers by the fact that they no longer know their way the moment they reach the top step of the Métro stairs, unlike the Parisians, they don't pass from the Métro without transition into the bustle of the street. In addition, it takes a long time, after coming up, for reality and the map to correspond; we should never have been able, on foot or by carriage, to have reached the spot we stood on without the help of a map.

It is always pleasant to remember walks in parks: one's joy that the day was still so light, watching out that it didn't get dark suddenly – this and fatigue governed one's manner of walking and looking about. The motor-cars pursuing their rigid course along the wide, smooth streets. In the little garden restaurant, the red-uniformed band, unheard amidst the noise of the motor-cars, labouring at its instruments for the entertainment of those in its immediate vicinity only. Parisians never previously seen walking hand in hand. Men in shirt sleeves, with their families, in the semi-darkness under the trees amid the flower beds, notwithstanding the 'keep off' signs. There the absence of Jews was most noticeable. Looking back at the tiny train, which seemed to have rolled off a merry-go-round and puffed away. The path to the lake of the Bois de Boulogne. My most vivid recollection of the first sight of the lake is the bent back of a man stooping down to us under the canopy of our boat to give us tickets. Probably because of my anxiety about the tickets and my inability to make the man explain whether the boat went around the lake or across to the island, and whether it stopped off anywhere. And for this reason I was so taken by him that I often see him, with equal vividness, bent all by himself over the lake without there being any boat. A lot of people in summer clothes on the dock. Boats with unskilful rowers in them. The low bank of the lake, it had no railing. A slow trip, reminding me of walks I used to take alone every Sunday several years ago. Lifting our feet out of the water in the bottom of the boat. The other passengers' astonishment, when they heard our Czech, at finding themselves in the same boat with foreigners such as we were. A lot of people on the slopes of the western bank, canes planted in the ground, outspread newspapers, a man and his daughters flat in the grass, some laughter, the low eastern bank; the paths bounded by a low fence of curving sticks linked together, to keep the lap dogs off the lawns, something we did away with long ago back home; a stray dog was running across the meadow; rowers toiling solemnly at their oars, a girl in their heavy boat. I left Max over his grenadine, looking particularly lonely in the shadow at the edge of the half-empty garden café past which went a street that was intersected as if by chance by another street unknown to me. Motor-cars and carriages drove out from the shadowy crossing into even more desolate-looking regions. Saw a large iron fence that was probably a part of the food-tax bureau; it was open, however, and everyone could go through. Near by you saw the glaring light of Luna Park, which only added to the twilight confusion. So much light and so empty. I stumbled perhaps five times on the way to Luna Park and back to Max.

Monday, 11 September. Motor-cars are easier to steer on asphalt surfaces, but also harder to bring to a stop. Especially when the gentleman at the wheel, taking advantage of the wide streets, the beautiful day, his light motor-car and his skill as a driver to make a little business trip, at the same time weaves his car in and out at crossings in the manner of pedestrians on the pavements. This is why such a motor-car, on the point of turning off into a side-street and while yet on the large square, runs into a tricycle; it comes gracefully to a halt, however, does little damage to the tricycle, has only stepped on its toe, as it were; but whereas a pedestrian having his toe stepped on in such fashion only hurries on all the faster, the tricycle remains where it is with a bent front wheel.

The baker's boy, who until this point had been riding along on his vehicle (the property of the N. Co.) without a thought, in that clumsy wobble peculiar to tricycles, climbs down, walks up to the motorist – who likewise climbs out – and upbraids him in a manner that is subdued by his respect for the owner of a motor-car and inflamed by his fear of his boss. It is first a question of explaining how the accident happened. The motor-car owner with raised palms simulates the approaching motor-car; he sees the tricycle cutting across his path, detaches his right hand, and gesticulates back and forth in warning to it, a worried expression on his face – what motor-car could apply its brakes in time in so short a distance? Will the tricycle understand this and give the motor-car the right of way? No, it is too late; his left hand ceases its warning motions, both hands join together for the collision, his knees bend to watch the last moment. It has happened, and the bent, motionless tricycle standing there can now assist in the description.

The baker's boy is hardly a match for the motorist. First of all, the motorist is a brisk, educated man; secondly, until now he has been sitting in the motor-car at his ease, can go right back in and sit at his ease again; and thirdly, he really had had a better view from the height of the motor-car of what had happened. Some people have collected together in the meantime who don't stand in a circle round him but rather before him, as only befits the motorist's performance. The traffic meanwhile must manage without the space these people occupy, who in addition move back and forth with every new idea occurring to the motorist. Thus, for example, at one point they all march over to the tricycle to have a closer look at the damage that is so much under discussion. The motorist doesn't think it very serious (a number of people, all engaged in fairly loud discussion, agree with him), though he is not satisfied with just a glance but walks around it, peers into it from above and through it from below. One person, wanting to shout, sides with the tricycle, for the motorist is in no need of anyone's shouts; but is answered very well and loudly by an unknown man who has just come up, and who, if one were to believe him, had been with the motorist in the car. Every once in a while several spectators laugh aloud together but then grow quiet at the thought of some new, weighty point.

Now there is really no great difference of opinion between the motorist and the baker's boy; the motorist sees around him a small, friendly crowd of people whom he has convinced, the baker's boy gradually stops monotonously stretching out his arms and uttering his protests, the motorist does not as a matter of fact deny that he has caused a little damage and by no means puts all the blame on the baker's boy, both are to blame, therefore none, such things just happen, etc. In short, the affair would finally have become embarrassing, the votes of the spectators, already conferring together over the costs of the repairs, would have had to be called for, if they hadn't remembered that they could call a policeman. The baker's boy, whose position in respect to the motorist is more and more a subordinate one, is simply sent off by him to fetch a policeman, his tricycle being entrusted to the motorist's protection. Without any dishonourable intention, for he has no need to build a faction for himself, the motorist goes on with his story even in his adversary's absence. Because you can tell a story better while you smoke, he rolls a cigarette for himself. He has a supply of tobacco in his pocket.

Uninformed newcomers, even if only errand boys, are systematically conducted first to the motor-car, then to the tricycle, and only then instructed in all the details. If the motorist catches an objection from someone standing far back in the crowd, he answers him on tiptoe so as to look him in the face. It proves too much trouble to conduct the people back and forth between the motor-car and the tricycle, so the motor-car is driven nearer to the pavement of the side-street. An undamaged tricycle stops and the rider has a look at things. As if to teach one a lesson in the difficulties of driving a motor-car, a large bus has come to a halt in the middle of the square. The motor is being worked on at the front. The passengers, alighting from the bus, are the first to bend down around it, with a real feeling of their more intimate relationship to it. Meanwhile the motorist has brought a little order into things and pushed the tricycle, too, closer to the pavement. The affair is losing its public interest. Newcomers now have to guess at what has happened. The motorist has withdrawn completely with several of the original onlookers, who are important witnesses, and is talking quietly to them.

But where in the meantime has the poor boy been wandering about? At last he is seen in the distance, starting to cut across the square with the policeman. No one had displayed any impatience, but interest is at once revived. Many new onlookers appear who will enjoy at no expense the extreme pleasure of seeing statements taken. The motorist leaves his group and walks over to the policeman, who has at once accepted the situation with a degree of calm that the parties involved were able to attain only after a half-hour's lapse. He begins taking statements without any lengthy preliminary investigation. With the speed of a carpenter, the policeman pulls an ancient, dirty, but blank sheet of paper out of his notebook, notes down the name of the baking company, and to make certain of the latter walks around the tricycle as he writes. The unconscious, unreasonable hope of those present that the policeman will bring the whole matter to an immediate and objective conclusion is transformed into an enjoyment of the details of the statement-taking. The taking of the statements occasionally flags. Something has gone wrong with the policeman's notes, and for a while, in his effort to set it right, he hears and sees nothing further. He had, that is, begun to write on the sheet of paper at a point where for some reason or other he should not have begun. But now it is done in any case and his astonishment finds perpetual renewal. He has to keep turning the paper around over and over again to persuade himself of his having incorrectly begun the statements. He had, however, soon left off this incorrect beginning and begun to write in some other place, and so when he has finished a column he cannot tell – without much unfolding and careful scrutiny of the paper – where is the right place for him to go on. The calm the whole affair acquires in this way is not to be compared with that earlier calm which it had achieved solely through the parties involved.

FRIDAY, 28 June. Left from the Staatsbahnhof. Felt fine. Sokols[145] delayed the departure of the train. Took off my jacket, stretched out full length on the seat. Bank of the Elbe. The beautifully situated villages and villas, as on lake shores. Dresden. Clean, punctilious service. Calmly spoken words. Massive look of the buildings as a result of the use of concrete; though in America, for example, it hasn't this effect. The Elbe's placid waters marbled by eddies.

Leipzig, conversation with the porter. Opel's Hotel. The half-built new railway station. Beautiful ruins of the old one. Room together. Buried alive from four o'clock on, for the noise made Max close the window. Great deal of noise, sounded like one wagon pulling another behind it. The horses on the asphalt like galloping saddle horses. The receding bell of the tram by its pauses marking off the streets and squares.

Evening in Leipzig. Max's sense of direction, I was lost. But I discovered a beautiful oriel on the Fürstenhaus and was later confirmed by the guidebook. Night work on a construction job, probably on the site of Auerbach's Keller. A dissatisfaction with Leipzig that I couldn't throw off. The attractive Café Oriental. Dovecot, a beer parlour. The slow-moving, long-bearded proprietor. His wife drew the beer. Their two tall robust daughters served. Drawers in the tables. Lichtenhain beer in wooden jugs. Disgraceful smell when the lid was opened. An infirm habitué of the place, reddish, pinched cheeks, wrinkled nose; he sat with a large group of people, then stayed on alone; the girl joined him with her beer glass. The picture of the habitué, dead twelve years ago, who had been going there for fourteen years. He is lifting his glass, behind him a skeleton. Many heavily bandaged students in Leipzig. Many monocles.

Friday, 29 June. Breakfast. The man who wouldn't sign the receipt for a money order on Saturday. Walk. Max to Rowohlt. Museum of the book trade. Couldn't contain myself in the presence of all the books.

The ancient look of the streets of the publishing quarter, though there were straight streets too, and newer but less decorative houses. Public reading-room. Lunch in the Manna. Bad. Wilhelm's winehouse; dimly lit tavern in a courtyard. Rowohlt: young, red-cheeked, beads of sweat between his nose and cheeks, moved only above the hips. Count Basse-witz, author of *Judas*, large, nervous, expressionless face. The move-ment in his waist, a strong physique carried well. Hasenclever, a lot of shadow and highlights in a small face, bluish colours too. All three flourished sticks and arms. Queer daily lunch in the winehouse. Large, broad wine cups with slices of lemon. In the Café Français, Pinthus, correspondent for the *Berliner Tageblatt*, a round, rather flat face, correcting the typescript of a review of *Johanna von Neapel* (première the previous evening). Café Français. Rowohlt was rather serious about wanting a book from me. Publishers' personal obligations and their effect on the average of the present-day German literature. In the publishing house.

Left for Weimar at five o'clock. The old maid in the compartment. Dark skin. Beautiful contours of her chin and cheeks. The twisted seams of her stockings; her face was concealed by the newspaper and we looked at her legs. Weimar. She got off there too, after putting on a large old hat. Later on I saw her again while looking at the Goethehaus from the market place.

Long way to the Hotel Chemnitius. Almost gave up. Search for a place to swim. Public beach on the Kirschberg. Schwanensee. Walked at night to the Goethehaus. Recognized it at once. All of it a yellowish-brown colour. Felt the whole of our previous life share in the im-mediate impression. The dark windows of the uninhabited rooms. The light-coloured bust of Juno. Touched the wall. White shades pulled part way down in all the rooms. Fourteen windows facing on the street. The chain on the door. No picture quite catches the whole of it. The uneven surface of the square, the fountain, the irregular alignment of the house along the rising slope of the square. The dark, rather tall windows in the midst of the brownish-yellow. Even without knowing it was the Goethehaus, the most impressive middle-class house in Weimar.

Sunday the 30th. Morning. Schillerhaus. The hunch-backed woman who came forward and in a few words, but mostly by the tone of her voice, seemed to be apologizing for the fact that these souvenirs still existed. On the steps, Clio, as diarist. Picture of the centennial birthday celebration, 10 November 1859; the decorated, enlarged house. Italian views, Bellagio, presents from Goethe. Locks of hair no longer human, yellow and dry as the beard on grain. Maria Pavlovna, slender neck, her face no broader, large eyes. Various Schiller heads. Well-arranged house for a writer. Waiting-room, reception room, study, sleeping alcoves. Frau Junot, his daughter, resembled him. *Large-Scale Arboriculture Based on Small-Scale Experiments*, his father's book.

Goethehaus. Reception rooms. Quick look into the study and bedroom. Sad, reminding one of dead grandfathers. The garden that had gone' on growing since Goethe's death. The beech tree darkening his study.

While we were still sitting below on the landing, she ran past us with her little sister. The plaster greyhound on the landing is associated in my memory with this running. Then we saw her again in the Juno room, and again when we were looking out of the garden room. There were many other times I thought I heard her step and voice. Two carnations handed through the balcony railing. Went into the garden too late. I caught sight of her on a balcony. She came down only later on, with a young man. In passing I thanked her for having called our attention to the garden. But we did not leave yet. Her mother came up, a conversation sprang up in the garden. She stood next to a rosebush. Urged on by Max, I went over to her, learned of the excursion to Tiefurt. I'll go too. She's going with her parents. She mentioned an inn from where you can see the door of the Goethehaus. Gasthaus zum Schwan. We were sitting among strands of ivy. She came out of the house. I ran over, introduced myself to everyone, received permission to accompany them, and ran back again. Later the family arrived, without the father. I wanted to join them; no, they were going to have coffee first, I was supposed to follow with the father. She told me to go into the house at four. I called for the father after taking leave of Max.

Conversation with the coachman outside the gate. Walk with the father. Talked about Silesia, the Grand Duke, Goethe, the National

Museum, photography and drawing, and our nervous age. Stopped in front of the house where they were drinking coffee. He ran up and called them all to the bay window; he was going to take a picture. Out of nervousness played ball with a little girl. Walked with the men, the two women in front of us, the three girls in front of them. A small dog scampered in and out among us. Castle in Tiefurt. Sightseeing with the three girls. She has a lot of those things in the Goethehaus too, and better. Explanations in front of the Werther pictures. Fräulein von Göchhausen's room. Walled-up door. Imitation poodle. Then left with her parents. Twice took picture in the park; one on a bridge, it won't come out. At last, on the way home, a definite contact but without establishing any real relationship. Rain. Breslau carnival jokes told in the Archives. Took leave in front of the house. I stood around on Seifengasse. Max had meanwhile napped.

In the evening, incomprehensibly, ran into her three times. She with her girl friend. The first time we escorted them on their way. I can come to the garden any time after six in the evening. Now she had to go home. Then met her again on the Rundplatz, which had been got ready for a duel. They were talking to a young man in a manner more hostile than friendly. But then why hadn't they stayed home, since we had already escorted them to the Goetheplatz? They had had to go home as quickly as possible, hadn't they? Why were they now running out of Schillerstrasse down the small flight of steps into the out-of-the-way square, pursued by the young man or on their way to meet him, apparently without having been home at all? Why, after speaking a few words to the young man at a distance of ten paces and apparently refusing his escort, did they turn around again and run back alone? Had we, who had passed by with only a simple greeting, disturbed them? Later we walked slowly back; when we came to the Goetheplatz they once more came running out of another street almost into our arms, evidently very frightened. To spare them, we turned away. But they had already gone a roundabout way.

Monday, 1 July. Gartenhaus am Stern. Sat in the grass in front of it and sketched. Memorized the verse on the Ruhesitz. Box bed. Slept. Parrot in the court calling Grete. Went without success to the Erfurter Allee, where she is learning to sew. Bathing.

Tuesday, 2 July. Goethehaus. Garrets. Looked at the photographs in the custodian's quarters. Children standing around. Talked about photography. Continually on the alert for a chance to speak to her. She went off to her sewing with a friend. We stayed behind.

In the afternoon, Liszthaus. A virtuoso's place. Old Pauline. Liszt worked from five to eight, then church, then slept a second time, visitors from eleven on. Max took a bath, I went for the photographs, ran into her just before, walked up to the gate with her. Her father showed me the pictures, but finally I had to go. She smiled at me meaninglessly, purposelessly, behind her father's back. Sad. Thought of having the photographs enlarged. To the chemist. Back to the Goethehaus again for the negatives. She saw me from the window and opened the door.

Often ran into Grete. At the strawberry festival, in front of Werther's Garden, where there was a concert. The suppleness of her body in its loose dress. The tall officers who came out of the Russischen Hof. Every kind of uniform. Strong slender fellow in dark clothes.

The brawl on the side-street. 'You're the biggest *Dreckorsch* there is!' The people at the windows. The departing family, a drunk, an old woman with a rucksack, and two boys tagging along.

I choke up at the thought of my having to leave soon. Discovery of the Tivoli. The old snake charmer; her husband who acts as the magician. The women German teachers.

Wednesday, 3 July. Goethehaus. Photographs were to be taken in the garden. She was nowhere in sight so I was sent to fetch her. She is always all atremble with movement, but stirs only if you speak to her. They snapped the photographs. The two of us on the bench. Max showed the man how to do it. She agreed to meet me the next day. Öttingen was looking through the window and forbade Max and me, who happened to be standing alone at the apparatus, to take photographs. But we weren't taking photographs at all! Her mother was still friendly then.

Not counting the schools and those who don't pay, there are thirty thousand visitors every year – Swim. The children boxing seriously and calmly.

Grand-ducal library in the afternoon. The praise of it in the guidebook. The unmistakable Grand Duke. Massive chin and heavy lips.

Hand inside his buttoned coat. Bust of Goethe by David, with hair bristling backward and a large, tense face. The transformation of a palace into a library, which Goethe undertook. Busts by Passow (pretty, curly-haired boy), Zach. Werner, narrow, searching, out-thrust face. Gluck. Cast from life. The holes in the mouth from the tubes through which he breathed. Goethe's study. You passed through a door straight into Frau von Stein's garden. The staircase that a convict fashioned from a giant oak without using a single nail.

Walk in the park with the carpenter's son, Fritz Wenski. His earnest speech. At the same time he kept striking at the shrubbery with a branch. He is going to be a carpenter too, and do his *Wanderjahre*. They no longer travel now in the way they did in his father's time, the railway is spoiling people. To become a guide you would have to know languages, hence you must either learn them in school or buy the necessary books. Whatever he knew about the park he either learned in school or heard from the guides. Remarks plainly picked up from the guides which didn't fit in with the rest of his conversation; for instance, of the Roman house nothing but: This was the tradesmen's entrance – Borkenhäuschen. Shakespeare monument.

Children around me on Karlsplatz. They discussed the navy. The children's earnestness. Ships going down. The children's air of superiority. Promise of a ball. Distribution of cookies. *Carmen* garden concert. Completely under its spell.

Thursday, 4 July. Goethehaus. The promised appointment confirmed with a loud yes. She was looking out through the gate. I misinterpreted this, for she continued to look out even when we were there. I asked once more: 'Even if it rains?' 'Yes.'

Max went to Jena, to Diederich's. I to the Fürstengruft. With the officers. Above Goethe's coffin a golden laurel wreath, donated by the German women of Prague in 1882. Met everyone again in the cemetery. The Goethe family vault. Walter von Goethe, b. Weimar, 9 April 1818, d. Leipzig, 15 April 1885: 'With him the house of Goethe ceased to be, whose name shall outlive the ages.' Inscription over the grave of Frau Karoline Falk: 'Though God took seven of her children, she was a mother to the children of strangers. God shall dry all her tears.' Charlotte von Stein: 1742–1827.

Swim. Didn't sleep in the afternoon in order to keep an eye on the uncertain weather. She didn't keep the appointment.

Found Max in bed with his clothes on. Both of us unhappy. If a person could only pour sorrow out the window.

In the evening Hiller, with his mother. I dashed away from the table because I thought I saw her. Mistake. Then all of us went to the Goethehaus. Said hello to her.

Friday, 5 July. Walked to no avail to the Goethehaus – Goethe-Schiller Archives. Letters from Lenz. Letter from the citizens of Frankfort to Goethe, 28 August 1830:

A number of citizens of the old city on the Mayn, long wont to greet the twenty-eighth of August with beakers in their fist, would commend the favour of heaven could they welcome in person within the precincts of the Free City that rare Frankfort man whom this day saw come into the world.

But as one year follows the next and they continue to hope and wait and wish, they must for the present be content to extend the gleaming bumper across woods and plains, frontiers and boundaries, to the lucky city on the Ilm, begging their honoured fellow townsman the favour of clinking glasses with him and singing:

> Willst Du Absolution
> Deinen Treuen geben,
> Wollen wir nach Deinem Wink
> Unablässig streben,
> Uns vom Halben zu entwöhnen
> Und im Ganzen Guten Schönen
> Resolut zu leben. [146]

1757 'Sublime Grossmama! . . .'

Jerusalem to Kestner: 'Might I make so bold as humbly to ask to borrow Your Excellency's pistols for a journey I intend?'

Song of Mignon, without a single change.

Went for the photographs. Took them there. Waited around to no avail, delivered only three of the six photographs. And just the worst ones, in the hope that the custodian, to vindicate himself, would again take photographs. Not a chance.

Swim. Straight from there to Erfurter Strasse. Max for lunch. She came with two friends. I drew her aside. Yes, she had to leave ten minutes earlier yesterday, she just now learned from her friends that I had waited yesterday. She also had some difficulty with her dancing lessons. She certainly doesn't love me, but does respect me a little. I gave her the box of chocolates with the little heart and chain twined about it, and walked on with her a short distance. A few words between us about a meeting. Tomorrow at eleven, in front of the Goethehaus. It can only be an excuse, she has to do the cooking, I'm sure, and then – in front of the Goethehaus! Nevertheless I agreed to it. Sad agreement. Went into the hotel, sat a little while with Max, who was lying in bed.

In the afternoon, an excursion to Belvedere. Hiller and his mother. Beautiful ride in the carriage along the single alley. The castle's surprising plan, which consists of a main section and four small buildings disposed along its sides, everything low and in muted colours. A low fountain in the middle. The front faces in the direction of Weimar. The Grand Duke hadn't been there for a number of years now. He hunts, and there is no hunting to be had here. Placid footman with clean-shaven, angular face who came to meet us. Sad, as perhaps all people who move among masters. The sadness of domestic animals. Maria Pavlovna, daughter-in-law of the Grand Duke Karl August, daughter of Maria Fedorovna and of Tsar Paul who was strangled. Many Russian things. Cloisonné, copper vessels with wires hammered on between which the enamel is poured. The bedrooms with their domed sky-painted ceilings. Photographs in the still habitable rooms were the only modern touch. How they too fell unnoticed into their proper places! Goethe's room, a corner room on the ground floor. Several ceiling paintings by Oeser, restored past all recognition. Many Chinese things. The 'dark Kammerfrauenzimmer'. Open-air theatre with two rows of seats. The carriage with benches placed back to back, *dos à dos*, in which the ladies sat while their cavaliers rode in attendance beside them. The heavy carriage drawn by three teams of horses in which Maria Pavlovna and her husband drove from Petersburg to Weimar in twenty-six days on their wedding journey. Open-air theatre and park were laid out by Goethe.

In the evening to Paul Ernst. (On the street asked two girls for the house of the writer, P. E. First they looked at us reflectively, then one nudged the other as if she wanted to remind her of a name she couldn't at the moment recall. Do you mean Wildenbruch? the other then asked us.) Moustache falling over his mouth and a pointed beard. Clasped his chair or his knees, and even when he had been angered (by his critics) wouldn't let go. Lives on the Horn. A villa, seemed to be entirely filled with his family. A dish of strong-smelling fish that they were about to carry upstairs was taken back into the kitchen when we appeared – Father Expeditus Schmidt, whom I had already met once before on the steps of the hotel, came in. Is working in the Library on an edition of Otto Ludwig. Wanted to bring narghiles into the Archives. Reviled a newspaper as a 'pious snake in the grass' because it attacked his *Heiligenlegenden.*

Saturday, 6 July. To Johannes Schlaf's.[147] An elderly sister who looked like him received us. He wasn't in. We will return in the evening.

Walked for an hour with Grete. It would seem that she came with her mother's consent, whom she continued speaking to through the window even from the street. Pink dress, my little heart. Restless because of the big ball in the evening. Had nothing in common with her. Conversation broke off and kept resuming again. Our pace now very fast, now very slow. Straining at any cost to conceal the fact that there was not the slightest thread of a relation between us. What was it that drove us through the park together? Only my obstinacy?

Towards evening at Schlaf's. A visit to Grete before that. She was standing in front of the partly opened kitchen door in the ball dress whose praises she had already sung and which wasn't at all as beautiful as her usual dress. Eyes red from weeping, apparently because of her dancing partner, who had already caused her great distress. I said good-bye forever. She didn't know it, nor would it have mattered to her had she known. A woman bringing roses disturbed even this little farewell. Men and women from the dancing school everywhere on the streets.

Schlaf. Doesn't precisely live in a garret, as Ernst, who has fallen out with him, tried to persuade us. A man of great animation, his stout chest enclosed in a tightly buttoned jacket. His eyes only had a sick and nervous twitch. Talked mostly of astronomy and his geocentric system. Everything else, literature, criticism, painting, still clung to him only because he hadn't thrown it off. Besides, everything will be decided by Christmas. He hadn't the slightest doubt of his victory. Max said his position in relation to the astronomers was similar to Goethe's position in relation to the opticists. 'Similar,' he replied, continually taking hold of the table with his hand, 'but much more favourable, for I have incontestable facts on my side.' His small telescope for four hundred marks. He hadn't needed it to make his discovery, or mathematics either. He is entirely happy. The sphere of his activity is infinite, for his discovery, once recognized, will have great consequences in every field (religion, ethics, aesthetics, etc.) and he will naturally be the first to be called upon to reinterpret them. When we arrived he had just been pasting notices published on the occasion of his fiftieth birthday into a large book. 'On such occasions they go easy on one.'

Before that, a walk with Paul Ernst in the Webicht. His contempt for the present, for Hauptmann, Wassermann, Thomas Mann. In a little subordinate clause which you only caught long after it was said, with no regard for what our opinion might be, he called Hauptmann a scribbler. Otherwise vague utterances on the Jews, Zionism, races, etc., in all of which he showed himself remarkable only as being a man who had energetically used his time to good purpose – Dry, automatic 'yes, yes' at short intervals when someone else was speaking. Once he repeated it so often that I no longer believed my ears.

7 July. Twenty-seven, number of the porter in Halle – Now at half past six drop down on a long-sought bench near the Gleim Memorial. If I were a child, I should have to be carried, my legs ache so. No feeling of loneliness long after saying good-bye to you. And then fell into such an apathy again that it still wasn't loneliness.

Halle, a little Leipzig. These pairs of church towers here and in Halle which are connected by small wooden bridges in the sky. Even my feeling that you won't read these things right away, but only later, makes me so uncertain – The cyclists' club meeting on the market place in Halle for an excursion. How difficult it is to go sight-seeing in a city, or even along a single street, by oneself.

A good vegetarian lunch. Unlike other innkeepers, it is just the vegetarian innkeepers with whom the vegetarian diet doesn't agree. Timid people who approach from the side.

Trip from Halle with four Jews from Prague: two pleasant, cheerful, robust elderly men, one resembling Dr K., one my father, but much shorter; then a weak-looking young married man, exhausted by the heat, and his dreadful, stoutly built young wife whose face was somehow derived from the X family. She was reading a three-mark Ullstein novel by Ida Boy-Ed with a gem of a title that Ullstein had probably thought up: *One Moment in Paradise*. Her husband asked her how she liked it. She had only begun it. 'Can't say just yet.' A nice German with dry skin and a whitish-blond beard beautifully parted over his cheeks and chin took a noticeably friendly interest in everything that went on among the four.

Railway hotel [in Jungborn], room down on the street with a little garden in front. Went off into the city. A thoroughly ancient city. Timber framework seems to be the type of construction calculated to last the longest. The beams warp everywhere, the panelling sinks in or buckles out, but the whole keeps together; at most it shrinks a little with time and becomes even more solid. I have never seen people leaning so beautifully in windows. The centre posts of most of the windows were immovable. People propped their shoulders against them, children swung from them. Sturdy girls were sitting on the bottom steps of the broad landing of a staircase, the skirts of their Sunday dresses spread out around them. Drachenweg Katzenplan. In the park on a bench with some little girls; we called it a girls' bench and defended it against some boys. Polish Jews. The children called them Itzig and didn't want to sit down on the bench right after them.

Jewish hotel N.N. with a Hebrew inscription. It is a neglected, castle-like building with a wide flight of stairs in front that stands out in the narrow streets. I walked behind a Jew who came out of the hotel and spoke to him. After nine. I wanted to know something about the community. Learned nothing. Looked too suspicious to him. He kept looking at my feet. But after all, I'm a Jew too. Then I can put up at N.N. – No, I already have a place to stay – So – Suddenly he moved close to me. Whether I wasn't in Schöppenstedt a week ago. We said good-bye in front of the gate of his house, he was happy to be rid of me; without my even asking about it, he told me how to get to the synagogue.

People in bathrobes on the doorsteps. Old, meaningless inscriptions. Pondered the possibilities offered me, on these streets, squares, garden benches, and brooksides, of feeling thoroughly unhappy. Whoever can cry should come here on Sunday. In the evening, after walking around for five hours, on the terrace of my hotel in front of a little garden. At the table near by the landlord's family with a young, lively woman who looked like a widow. Unnecessarily thin cheeks. Hair parted and fluffed out.

8 July. My house is called 'Ruth'. Practically arranged. Four dormers, four windows, one door. Fairly quiet. Only in the distance they are playing football, the birds are loudly singing, several naked people are lying motionless in front of my door. All except me without swimming trunks. Wonderful freedom. In the park, reading room, etc., there are pretty, fat little feet to be seen.

9 July. Slept well in the cabin, which is open on three sides. I can lean against my door like a householder. Woke up at all hours of the night and kept hearing rats or birds gurgling or flitting in the grass around the hut. The man who was freckled like a leopard. Yesterday evening lecture on clothing. The feet of Chinese women are crippled in order to give them big buttocks.

The doctor, an ex-officer; affected, insane, tearful, jovial laughter. Buoyant walk. A follower of Mazdaznan. A face created to be serious. Clean-shaven, lips made to be compressed. He steps out of his examination room, you go past him to enter. 'Please step in!' he laughs after you. Forbade me to eat fruit, with the proviso that I needn't obey him. I'm an educated man, I should listen to his lectures, they have even been published, should study the question, draw my own conclusions, and then act accordingly.

From his lecture yesterday: 'Though your toes may be completely crippled, if you tug at one of them and breathe deeply at the same time, after a while it will straighten out.' A certain exercise will make the sexual organs grow. One of his health rules: 'Atmospheric baths at night are highly recommended' – (whenever it suits me, I simply slip out of bed and go out into the meadow in front of my cabin) – 'but you shouldn't expose yourself too much to the moonlight, it has an injurious effect.' It is impossible to clean the kind of clothes we wear today!

This morning: washing, setting-up exercises, group gymnastics (I am called the man in the swimming trunks), some hymn singing, ball playing in a big circle. Two handsome Swedish boys with long legs. Concert by a military band from Goslar. Pitched hay in the afternoon. In the evening my stomach so upset that out of irritation I refused to walk a step. An old Swede was playing tag with several little girls and was so caught up in the game that once, while running, he shouted: 'Wait, I'll block these Dardanelles for you.' Meant the passage between two clumps of bushes. When an old, unattractive nursemaid went by: That's something you could really tap on (her back, in the black dress with white polka dots). Constant, senseless need to confide in someone. Looks at each person to see whether there is a possibility there, and whether an opportunity will present itself.

10 July. Sprained my ankle. Pain. Loaded new hay. In the afternoon walked to Ilsenburg with a very young Gymnasium professor from Nauheim; he may go to Wickersdorf[148] next year. Co-education, nature cure, Cohen, Freud. Story about the group of boys and girls he took on an excursion. Storm, everyone soaked through, had to strip completely in a room in the nearest inn.

A fever during the night because of my swollen ankle. The noise the rabbits made running past. When I got up during the night three of these rabbits were sitting in the meadow in front of my door. I dreamt that I heard Goethe reciting, with infinite freedom and arbitrariness.

11 July. Talked to a Dr Friedrich Sch., a municipal official of Breslau, had been in Paris for a long time to study municipal institutions. Lived in a hotel with a view into the court of the Palais Royal. Before that in a hotel near the Observatoire. One night there were two lovers in the next room. The girl shamelessly screamed with joy. Only when he spoke through the wall and offered to call a doctor did she grow quiet, and he was able to sleep.

My two friends disturb me; their path goes past my cabin and they always pause a moment at my door for a short chat or an invitation to take a walk. But I am also grateful to them for it.

In the *Evangelischen Missionzeitung*, July 1912, about missions in
Java: 'Much as may justly be urged against the amateur medical
activities extensively engaged in by missionaries, it is nevertheless the
principal resource of their missionary work and cannot be dispensed
with.'

When I see these stark-naked people moving slowly past among the
trees (though they are usually at a distance), I now and then get light,
superficial attacks of nausea. Their running doesn't make things any
better. A naked man, a complete stranger to me, just now stopped at
my door and asked me in a deliberate and friendly way whether I lived
here in my house, something there couldn't be much doubt of, after all.
They come upon you so silently. Suddenly one of them is standing
there, you don't know where he came from. Old men who leap naked
over haystacks are no particular delight to me, either.

Walked to Stapelburg in the evening. With two people I introduced
and recommended to one another. Ruins. Back at ten. Some nudists
prowling about among the haystacks on the meadow in front of my
cabin, disappeared into the distance. At night, when I walked across
the meadow to the toilet, there were three of them sleeping in the
grass.

12 July. Dr Sch.'s stories. Travelled for one year. Then a long
debate in the grass on Christianity. Old, blue-eyed Adolf Just who
cures everything with clay and warns me against the doctor who had
forbidden me fruit. The defence of God and the Bible by a member
of the 'Christian Community'; as the proof he needed at the moment,
he read a Psalm. My Dr Sch. made a fool of himself with his atheism.
Foreign words – illusion, auto-suggestion – didn't help him a bit.
Someone we didn't know asked how it was that everything goes so well
with the Americans, though they swear at every second word. With
most of them it was impossible to discover what their real opinions
were, though they all took a lively part in the discussion. The one who
spoke so passionately of Flower Day and how it was just the Metho-
dists who held back. The one from the 'Christian Community' who
lunches with his pretty little boy on cherries and dry bread wrapped
in a small paper bag; otherwise he lies in the grass all day, three
Bibles open before him, and takes notes. It has only been three years

that he has been on the right path. Dr Sch.'s oil sketches from Holland. Pont Neuf.

Two sisters, little girls. One with a narrow face, easy posture, nose coming delicately to a point, clear, not entirely candid eyes. Her face shone with so much intelligence that I found myself looking excitedly at her for several minutes. Something moved me when I looked at her. Her more womanly little sister intercepted my glances – A newly arrived prim miss with a bluish look. The blonde with short, dishevelled hair. Supple and lean as a leather strap. Coat, blouse, and skirt, nothing else. Her stride!

With Dr Sch. (forty-three years old) on the meadow in the evening. Going for a walk, stretching, rubbing, slapping, and scratching. Stark naked. Shameless – The fragrance when I stepped out of the writing-room in the evening.

13 July. Picked cherries. Lutz read Kinkel's *Die Seele* to me. After eating I always read a chapter from the Bible, a copy of which is in every room. Evening, the children at play. Little Susanne von Puttkammer, nine years old, in pink drawers.

14 July. Picked cherries on the ladder with a little basket. Was high up in the tree. Religious services in the morning on Eckarplätzen. Ambrosian chant. In the afternoon sent the two friends to Ilsenburg.

I was lying in the grass when the man from the 'Christian Community' (tall, handsome body, sunburned, pointed beard, happy appearance) walked from the place where he reads to the dressing-cabin; I followed him unsuspectingly with my eyes, but instead of returning to his place he came in my direction, I closed my eyes, but he was already introducing himself: H., land surveyor, and gave me four pamphlets as reading matter for Sunday. When he left he was still speaking about 'pearls' and 'casting', by which he meant to indicate that I was not to show the pamphlets to Dr Sch. They are: 'The Prodigal Son', 'Bought, or No Longer Mine (for Unbelieving Believers)', 'Why Can't the Educated Man Believe in the Bible?' and 'Three Cheers for Freedom: But What Is True Freedom?' I read a little in them and then went back to him and, hesitant because of the respect in which I held him, tried to make it clear why there was no prospect of grace for me at present. Exercising a beautiful mastery over every word, something that only sincerity makes possible, he discussed this with me for an hour and a half (towards the end an old, thin, white-haired, red-nosed man in linen joined in with several indistinct remarks). Unhappy Goethe, who made so many other people unhappy. A great many stories. How he, H., forbade his father to speak when he blasphemed God in his house. 'Oh, Father, may you be stricken with horror, by your own words and be too terrified to speak further, I wouldn't care one bit.' How his father heard God's voice on his deathbed. He saw that I was close to grace. I interrupted all his arguments and referred him to the inner voice. Successfully.

15 July. Read Kühnemann's *Schiller* – The man who always carries a card in his pocket to his wife in case of accident – The Book of Ruth – I read Schiller. Not far away a naked old man was lying in the grass, an umbrella open over his head.

Plato's *Republic* – Posed for Dr Sch. – The page in Flaubert on prostitution – The large part the naked body plays in the total impression an individual gives.

A dream: The sunbathers destroyed one another in a brawl. After the two groups into which they were divided had joked with one another, someone stepped out in front of one group and shouted to the others: 'Lustron and Kastron!' The others: 'What? Lustron and Kastron?' He: 'Right.' Beginning of the brawl.

16 July. Kühnemann – Herr Guido von Gillshausen, captain, retired, writes poetry and music. A handsome man. Out of respect for his noble birth didn't dare look up at him; broke out in a sweat (we were naked) and spoke too softly. His seal ring – The bowing of the Swedish boys – Talked in the park with my clothes on to a man with his clothes on. Missed the group excursion to Harzburg.

Evening. Rifle meet in Stapelburg. With Dr Sch. and a Berlin hairdresser. The wide plain rising gently to the Burgberg, bordered by ancient linden trees, incongruously traversed by a railway embankment. The platform from which they shot. Old peasants made the entries in the scorebook. The three fife players with women's kerchiefs hanging down their backs. Old, inexplicable custom. Several of them in old, simple blue smocks, heirlooms made of the finest linen and costing fifteen marks. Almost everyone had his gun. Muzzle-loaders. You had the impression that they were all somehow bent from work in the fields, especially when they lined up in double file. Several former meet-masters in top hats with sabres buckled round them. Horses' tails and other old emblems were carried past; excitement; then the band played, greater excitement; then silence and drumming and fife playing, still greater excitement; finally, as the drums and fifes sounded for the last time, three flags were brought out, climax of the excitement. Forward march and off they went. Old man with a black suit, black cap, a somewhat pinched face, and a not too long, thick, silky, unsurpassable white beard encircling his face. The former champion shot, also in a top hat and a sash like a curtain around his body; the sash had little metal shields sewn all over it on each of which was engraved the name of the champion of a given year together with the symbol of his trade. (The master baker had a loaf of bread, etc.) Marching off in the dust to music under the changing light of the thickly clouded sky. Doll-like appearance of a soldier marching with them (a rifleman now in the army) and his hopping step. People's armies and peasant wars. We followed them through the streets. Sometimes they were closer, some-times farther away, since they stopped at the houses of the various champion shots, played, and were given some refreshments. The dust cleared towards the end of the column. The last pair could be seen most distinctly. From time to time we lost sight of them entirely. Tall peasant with somewhat sunken chest, eternal face, top boots, clothes that seemed made of leather; how ceremoniously he detached himself from the gatepost. The three women who were standing one behind the other in front of him. The one in the centre dark and beautiful. The two women at the gate of the farmyard opposite. In each of the two farmyards there was a giant tree that united with the other above the wide road. The large targets on the houses of the former champions.

The dance floor, in two parts, divided down the middle, the band in a fenced-off section having two rows of seats. Empty as yet, little girls slide across the smooth boards. (Chess players, relaxing from their play and talking, disturb me as I write.) I offer them my soda, they drink, the oldest first. Lack of a really common language. I ask whether they have already eaten dinner [*genachtmahlt*], complete lack of under-standing; Dr Sch. asks whether they have already had supper [*Abendbrot*], they begin to have a vague understanding (he doesn't speak clearly, breathes too hard); they are able to give an answer only when the hairdresser asks whether they have had their grub [*gefuttert*]. They didn't want the second soda I ordered for them, but they wanted to ride on the merry-go-round; I, with the six girls (from six to thirteen) around me, flew to the merry-go-round. On the way the girl who suggested the ride boasted that the merry-go-round belonged to her parents. We sat down and went around in a coach. Her friends around me, one on my knees. Girls crowding about who wanted to have some fun out of my money too, but my girls pushed them away against my will. The proprietor's daughter superintended the reckoning so that I shouldn't have to pay for strangers. If they wished, I was ready to go for another ride, but the proprietor's daughter herself said that it was enough; instead, she wanted to go to the sweet tent. In my stupidity and curiosity I led the way to the wheel of fortune. As far as it was possible, they were very sparing of my money. Then off for the sweets. The tent had a large stock, and was as clean and neat as a store on the main street of a city. At the same time the prices were low, just as they are at our fairs. Then we went back to the dance floor. In all this I was more sensible of the girls than of my own bounty. Now they were ready for soda again, and thanked me prettily, the oldest for all of them and each for herself. When the dance began we had to leave, it was already a quarter to ten.

The hairdresser talking incessantly. Thirty years old, with a square beard and pointed moustache. Ran after girls but loved his wife, who was at home running the business and couldn't travel because she was fat and couldn't stand riding. Even when they once went to Rixdorf, she twice got out of the tram to walk for a while and recover. She didn't need a holiday, she was satisfied just to sleep late once in a while. He was faithful to her, she provided him with everything he needed. The temptations to which a hairdresser is exposed. The young wife of a restaurateur. The Swedish woman who had to pay more for everything. He bought hair from a Bohemian Jew named Puderbeutel. When a delegation from the Social Democrats came to him and demanded that he take in the *Vorwärts* too, he said: 'If that's what you're here for, then I didn't send for you.' But finally gave in. When he was a 'junior' (assistant) he was in Görlitz. He was an organized bowler. Was at the big bowlers' convention in Braunschweig a week ago. There are some 20,000 organized German bowlers. They bowled for three days until far into the night on four championship alleys. But you couldn't say that any one person was the best German bowler.

When I entered my cabin in the evening I couldn't find the matches, borrowed some in the next cabin and made a light under the table to see if they might have fallen down there. They hadn't, but the water tumbler was standing there. Gradually I discovered that my sandals were behind the wall mirror, the matches on a window sill, the hand mirror was hanging on a projecting corner. The chamber pot rested on top of the closet, my *Éducation sentimentale* was in the pillow, a clothes-hook under the sheet, my traveller's inkwell and a wet wash-cloth in the bed, etc. All this as a punishment for my not having gone to Harzburg.

19 July. Rainy day. You lie in bed and the loud thrumming of the rain on the cabin roof is as if it were beating against one's own breast. Drops appear at the edge of the eaves as mechanically as a row of lights lit along a street. Then they fall. An old man suddenly charges across the meadow like a wild animal, taking a rain bath. The drumming of the drops in the night. As though one were sitting in a violin case. Running in the morning, the soft earth underfoot.

20 July. Morning in the woods with Dr Sch. The red earth and the light diffused from it. The upward soar of the trunks. The broad, over-hanging, flat-leaved limbs of the beeches.

In the afternoon a group of maskers arrived from Stapelburg. The giant with the man dressed up as a dancing bear. The swing of his thighs and back. March through the garden behind the music. Specta-tors running over the turf, through the shrubbery. Little Hans Eppe when he saw them. Walter Eppe on the mail-box. The men dressed as women, with curtains as veils. An indecent sight when they danced with the kitchenmaids, who yielded seemingly without knowing that they were men in disguise.

In the morning read the first chapter of *L'Éducation sentimentale* to Dr Sch. A walk with him in the afternoon. Stories about his lady friend. He is a friend of Morgenstern, Baluschek, Brandenburg, Pop-penberg. His horrid complaining in the cabin in the evening, on the bed with his clothes on. Talked to Miss Pollinger for the first time, but she already knew all there was to know about me. Prague she knew from *Die Zwölf aus der Steiermark*. An ash-blonde, twenty-two years old, looks like a seventeen-year-old, always worrying about her deaf mother; engaged and a flirt.

At noon the departure of Frau von W., the Swedish widow who resembles a leather strap. Only a grey jacket over her usual clothes, a little grey hat with a bit of a veil. Her brown face looked very delicate in such a frame; only distance and concealment exercise an effect on regular features. Her luggage consisted of a small knapsack, there was not much more than a nightgown in it. This is the way she always travels, came from Egypt, is going to Munich.

Dance at Stapelburg in the evening. The celebration lasts four days, hardly any work is done. We saw the new champion shot, and on his back read the names of the champions from the beginning of the nineteenth century on. Both dance floors full. Couple stood behind couple around the hall. Each had only a short dance every fifteen minutes. Most of them were silent, not from embarrassment or any other reason, but simply silent. A drunken man was standing at the edge of the dance floor, knew all the girls, lunged for them or at least stretched out his arms to hug them. Their dancing partners didn't budge. There was a great deal of noise, from the music, and the shouting of the people at the tables down below and those standing at the bar. We walked vainly around for some time (I and Dr Sch.). I was the one who accosted a girl. I had already noticed her outside when she and two friends were eating frankfurters with mustard. She was wearing a white blouse with flowers embroidered over her arms and shoulders. Her head was bent forward in a sweet and melancholy way, so that her breast was squeezed and her blouse puffed out. Her turned-up little nose, in such a posture, added to the melancholy. Patches of reddish brown here and there on her face. I accosted her just as she was descending the two steps from the dance floor. We stood face to face and she turned around. We danced. Her name was Auguste A., she was from Wolfenbüttel and had been employed on the farm of a certain Klaude in Appenroda for a year and a half. My peculiarity of not understanding names even after they have been repeated many times, and then not remembering them. She was an orphan and would enter a convent on 1 October. She hadn't told her friends about it yet. She had already intended to enter in April but her employers wouldn't let her go. She was entering the convent because of the bad experiences she had had. She couldn't tell me about them. We walked up and down in the moonlight in front of the dance hall, my little erstwhile friends pursued me and my 'bride'. Despite her melancholy she liked to dance very much, what was especially evident later on when I temporarily gave her over to Dr Sch. She was a farm worker. She had to go home at ten o'clock.

22 July. Miss G., teacher, owl-like, vivacious young face with animated and alert features. Her body is more indolent. Mr Eppe, private-school headmaster from Braunschweig. A man who gets the better of me. His speech is authoritative, impassioned if necessary, considered, musical – even hesitant, for form's sake. Soft face, a soft beard growing over his cheeks and chin. Mincing walk. I found myself diagonally across from him when he and I sat down together (it was his first time) at the common table. A silently chewing lot of people. He scattered words here and there. If the silence continued unbroken, there wasn't anything he could do. But if someone down the table said a word, he at once took it up, with no great to-do, however; rather to himself as though he had been the one addressed and was now being listened to, and at the same time looked down at the tomato he was peeling. Everyone paid attention except those who felt shamed and were defiant, like me. He laughed at no one, but when he spoke acknowledged all opinions. If one stirred, then he continued humming softly while he cracked nuts or performed all those little preliminaries which are necessary when eating vegetables and fruit. (The table was covered with bowls and you mixed the foods as you pleased.) Finally he involved everyone in his own affairs on the pretext that he had to make a note of all the foods and send the list to his wife. After he had beguiled us with his wife for several days, he began all over again with some new stories about her. She suffers from melancholia, he said, has to go to a sanatorium in Goslar, will be accepted only if she pledges herself to stay for eight weeks, brings a nurse, etc.; the whole thing, as he had worked it out and as he once more worked it out for us at the table, will cost more than 1,800 marks. But no trace of an intention to excite sympathy. But still, anything as expensive as this needs to be

thought over, everybody thinks things over. A few days later we heard that his wife was coming, perhaps this sanatorium will do for her. During the meal he received the news that his wife had just arrived with her two boys and was waiting for him. He was happy but ate calmly to the end, though there is no end to these meals, for they put all the courses on the table at the same time. His wife is young, fat, with a waist marked only by her clothes, clever blue eyes, high-combed blonde hair, can cook, market, etc., very well. At breakfast – his family hadn't arrived at the table yet – while cracking nuts, he told Miss G. and me: His wife suffers from melancholia, weak kidneys, her digestion is bad, she suffers from agoraphobia, falls asleep only towards five o'clock in the morning; then if she is awakened at eight 'she naturally frets herself into a temper' and becomes 'furious'. She has a very serious heart disorder, a severe asthma. Her father died in a madhouse.

POSTSCRIPT

THE text of the *Diaries* is as complete as it was possible to make it. A few passages, apparently meaningless because of their fragmentary nature, are omitted. In most instances no more than a few words are involved. In several (rare) cases I omitted things that were too intimate, as well as scathing criticism of various people that Kafka certainly never intended for the public. Living persons are usually identified by an initial or initials – that is, when they are not artists or political figures who because of their public activity must always anticipate criticism. Although I have used the blue pencil in the case of attacks on people still alive, I have not considered this sort of censorship necessary in the little that Kafka has to say against myself (partly in lighthearted playful mockery, and partly in earnest). The reader himself will know how to correct the false impression naturally arising out of this, that I was the only person against whom Kafka harboured anything. On this, as on many other points, I have followed the example of V. Chertkov in his editing of Tolstoy's diaries (cf. Chertkov's preface to that edition).

One must in general take into consideration the false impression that every diary unintentionally makes. When you keep a diary, you usually put down only what is oppressive or irritating. By being put down on paper painful impressions are got rid of. Pleasant impressions for the most part do not have to be counteracted in this way; you make note of them, as many people should know from experience, only in exceptional cases, or when (as in the case of a travel diary) it is your express purpose to do so. Ordinarily, however, diaries resemble a kind of defective barometric curve that registers only the 'lows', the hours of greatest depression, but not the 'highs'.

This rule also holds true for the thirteen quarto notebooks that constitute Kafka's true diary. In the 'Travel Diaries' of the same period a relatively brighter mood prevails. His good humour is seen with even more distinctness in his letters. A gloom begins to settle on the letters only as his illness grows worse, though then, to be sure, they are coloured the deepest black of despair. For the most part, however, one can distinguish forms of *personal* utterance (each of his *literary* works, of course, runs the gamut of the scale): the quarto notebooks show up as the darkest band of the spectrum; his travel notes are somewhat brighter; many of the letters (roughly, until the Zürau period, and even into it) are brighter still; in his conversations and daily intercourse there was often – even most often, during the early periods of his life – a gay ingenuousness one would scarcely credit to the author of the *Diaries*.

The bulk of the *Diaries* is contained in thirteen notebooks of quarto size.

The first, third, fourth, and fifth notebooks Kafka numbered himself, in Roman numerals (the second notebook bears no number). Pages are numbered consecutively throughout, although a second pagination, also by Kafka, makes for some confusion. There was a further difficulty in arranging the material chronologically in the fact Kafka would occasionally, in the same notebook, write from the last page backwards as well as from the first page forwards, so that the entries met in the middle. Nevertheless, it was possible to establish the correct chronological order.

The first notebook begins with several undated entries. The first date noted is 17–18 May 1910. A few pages later there are entries for the period from 19 February 1911 to 24 November 1911. Notebook II, embracing the period from 6 November 1910 to May 1911, fills in the interval between May 1910 and February 1911, and also contains part of the first chapter of *Amerika*, 'The Stoker'. Notebook III goes from 26 October 1911 to 24 November 1911. Thus the first three notebooks dovetail – what is also the case with Notebooks VIII and IX. Notebook IV embraces the period from 28 November 1911 to the end of that year; Notebook V (in which several obviously erroneous dates had to be corrected) goes from 4 January 1912 to 8 April 1912; Notebook VI from 6 May 1912 to September 1912. Notebook VI contains 'The Judgement' and the second part of 'The Stoker'. After an interval the diary is continued in Notebook VII from 2 May 1913 to 14 February

1914, and in Notebook VIII from 16 February 1914 to 15 August 1914. Notebook VIII, however, also contains (beginning on the last page and going backwards) entries for the month of February 1913, and Notebook IX belongs to the period covered by the eighth notebook. Many pages have been torn out of the ninth and tenth notebooks. The latter notebook goes from 21 August 1914 (thus it follows directly after Notebook VIII) to 27 May 1915. Notebook XI contains entries for the period from 13 September 1915 to 30 October 1916, as well as a few from April to August 1917. Notebook XII, many of whose pages likewise were torn out by the author, begin in Zürau on 15 September 1917 and goes to 10 November 1917; after a lengthy interval it resumes with the entry of 27 June 1919, continuing on until 10 January 1920. The last – the thirteenth – notebook embraces the period between 15 October 1921 and November 1922, and also contains a few notes dated 12 June 1923. A part of the incomplete 'Investigations of a Dog' (not the beginning, however) is sketched out in it in minuscule characters. In the earlier notebooks (the first eight) Kafka writes a large and swinging hand; later it gradually grows smaller and pointed.

These thirteen notebooks form a stylistic whole that I have tried to preserve. The writer notes down literary ideas, the beginnings of stories, or reflections passing through his head. The principles that guide him; the manner in which he looks to his literary efforts for a counterweight against the unfriendly world around him; the hated, arduous, indeed exhausting job – all this is repeatedly shown in detail in the entries themselves. In addition to the inspiration of his imagination, Kafka notes down occurrences in the workaday world, and also dreams – there are sketches where dreams predominate over relatively 'realistic' entries; often they are the starting-point for literary creation. In exceptionally happy cases the result, whether long or short, is a finished literary work in every respect. From these Kafka later chose a few for publication; they are to be found in Vol. I* of the *Gesammelte Schriften*. In the context of the *Diaries* an unexpected light is very often cast on the content of these pieces.

Thus, amid daily notations which served the writer as a kind of springboard for literary creation, one sees many things that could have

* Published in translation under the title of *The Penal Colony*.

been published as independent fragments. One has the half-finished figure and the unworked marble before one at the same time.

These thirteen quarto notebooks thus have a composition different from the 'blue octavo notebooks', which are made up almost entirely of literary ideas, fragments, and aphorisms (without reference to the everyday world). The octavo notebooks will be included in a future publication. Notations of a diary nature, dates, are found in them only as a rare exception. The three 'Travel Diaries', on the other hand, have an entirely different character again: occurrences and experiences are noted in bare matter-of-fact fashion, in a way that would apparently provide no starting-point for later work – just as a tourist would do. Of course, this tourist is Franz Kafka, and though his manner of observing things seems thoroughly natural, in a mysterious way it departs from everything customary.

Both – the bare factual and the partially wrought (which in happy cases became a finished work) – are uniquely mingled in the thirteen notebooks.

MAX BROD

Tel Aviv, 1948

NOTES

1. A member of the Russian Ballet during its guest appearance at the German theatre in Prague.
2. This remark is connected with the entry of 16 December 1910, concerning Gerhart Hauptmann's comedy, *Jungfern vom Bischofsberg*.
3. Kafka was twenty-eight years old at the time.
4. The story 'Unhappiness', from *Meditation*, follows here, without title. This particular draft breaks off several lines before the end. Only a title, 'The Little Dweller in the Ruins', follows on a fresh page; this, apparently, is related to the preceding fragments of Kafka's critique of his education. The fragments that now follow form a mosaic difficult to arrange, since many things are repeated several times. The tale begins over and over again with the same words, and ripples of it are still to be seen in 1911.

The whole has many points of contact with several chapters of 'Description of a Struggle', cf. especially that part of it called 'Conversation with the Supplicant'. See also the sketch, 'Unmasking a Confidence Trickster', from *Meditation*.
5. The poet Paul Claudel, who at that time was the French consul in Prague. Kafka never met him.
6. Paul Wiegler, the translator of *Moralités légendaires* by Jules Laforgue. The reading of this translation (and later of the original as well) was an important experience for Kafka and the Editor.
7. Kafka was survived by three sisters. All three sisters, including Kafka's favourite, Ottla, and the larger part of their families, were killed by the Nazis.
8. Oscar Baum, the blind author of *Das Volk des harten Schlafes*, one of the closest friends of Kafka and the Editor.
9. The paragraph ending at this point was crossed out by Kafka.
10. A reminiscence of the journey to Paris during the previous year (1910).
11. The title (*Wie erlangt man Erkenntnisse der höherern Welten*) of a book by Dr Rudolf Steiner.
12. Another fragment of the story begun on p. 21.
13. The diary of the Lugano–Erlenbach–Paris journey follows at this point in the manuscript. For the 'Travel Diaries', see pp. 425 ff.

14. This entry is connected with the plan that Kafka and the Editor developed, during the Lugano–Erlenbach–Paris trip, to write together the novel, *Richard and Samuel*, one chapter of which has been preserved under the title, 'The First Long Train Journey'. See *The Penal Colony* (New York, 1947), Appendix.

15. Longen is the biographer of Jaroslav Hašek, author of *The Good Soldier Schweik*.

16. The prayer that opens the service on the Day of Atonement.

17. A Yiddish theatre troupe from Eastern Europe. The troupe performed in a small café. Another troupe had performed in the same café in 1910.

18. 'The Apostate'. It is probably not unjustified to see in the two figures described here, who act as a sort of chorus, the first sketch of the two 'assistants' in *The Castle*.

19. A Czech folk dance.

20. *Mezuzah* ('doorpost'), a small roll of parchment inscribed with certain biblical verses (Deut. 6: 4–9, 11, 20) and encased in a small wood or metal box. It hangs on the doorpost of the home of every orthodox Jew.

21. Preliminary work on the novel, *Richard and Samuel*. R. is the woman who appears in the first chapter as Dora Lippert.

22. The Czech word *pavlač* means 'balcony' and has passed into the German of Prague and Vienna. It refers to the characteristic open balcony running the entire length of an upper storey on the side of a house facing the court.

23. Kafka was actually twenty-eight years old at the time.

24. Otto Brod, the writer, and brother of the Editor. The three of us took a trip together to Riva and Brescia in 1909. Otto Brod, his wife and child were murdered by the Nazis in 1944.

25. The Editor's future wife.

26. A novel by Wilhelm Schäfer. Kafka had a great deal of respect for this writer. He later went over to the Nazis.

27. One of Kafka's sisters.

28. A rough translation of the Yiddish would be: 'crazy hothead'.

29. 'Enough for *parnusse*', enough to live on.

30. 'The Aeroplanes at Brescia'. See *The Penal Colony*, Appendix.

31. This entry appeared later, with a few changes and omissions, in *Meditation*, under the title, 'Bachelor's Ill Luck'. For the version Kafka published, in the translation of Willa and Edwin Muir, see *The Penal Colony*. The translation appearing here is by the Muirs, except in those

places where the German text of the published version and the version in the *Diaries* differ.

32. Written at the time Kafka was studying for his bar examination.

33. Emil Utitz, later a professor of philosophy, a fellow student of Kafka's at the Gymnasium.

34. The family of Egon Erwin Kisch, author of *Der rasende Reporter*. His brother, Paul Kisch, studied Germanics.

35. A toy through the aperture of which one perceived the successive positions of a figure affixed to a revolving wheel. It thus created the illusion of motion.

36. An uneducated person. Kafka acquired this and similar expressions from his conversations with the actor Löwy.

37. Felix Weltsch, the philosopher and author of *Gnade und Freiheit*.

38. Properly, *mohel* – 'circumciser'.

39. A novel by Emil Strauss, whom Kafka estimated highly.

40. This entry, slightly changed, appeared under the title of 'The Sudden Walk', in *Meditation*. The translation is based on one made by the Muirs (see *n*. 31 above).

41. Christian von Ehrenfels, the philosopher and originator of the *Gestalt* theory in psychology.

42. Cf. this entry with 'Resolutions', in *Meditation*. The translation is based on one made by the Muirs (see *n*. 31 above).

43. 'Schlaflied für Mirjam', by Richard Beer-Hofmann.

44. In *Hermann und Dorothea*.

45. From Goethe's 'Der Fischer'.

46. The distinguished Viennese novelist Otto Stössl, of whom Kafka had a very high opinion.

47. Willi Haas, the editor of *Die Literarische Welt*. At the time Kafka wrote this, Haas was editing *Die Herderblätter* in Prague, in which he published the first chapter of *Richard and Samuel*, and also some of Werfel's early work.

48. Kafka was then working on the novel, *Amerika*, the title of which at that time was *Der Verschollene* (*The Man Who Disappeared*).

49. Written during the holiday trip to Weimar and the Harz Mountains (28 June to 29 July 1912).

50. Kafka's first published work, *Meditation*, which I had urged him very strongly to finish – or, rather, to put together out of his prose pieces that for the most part were already finished. In the middle of August he finally gave me the finished manuscript, which I sent off to the Rowohlt Publishers (Kurt Wolff). The book was published early in 1913.

51. Two days earlier Kafka had met Miss F. B. of Berlin, later his fiancée.

52. This entry is preceded by the complete draft of 'The Judgement'.

53. This entry is followed by the final version, untitled, of 'The Stoker', chapter one of *Amerika*.

54. On a visit to F.B.

55. Kafka's governess in his childhood.

56. The writer and critic Otto Pick, later editor of the *Prager Presse*.

57. The very talented novelist and dramatist Ernst Weiss, who later was quite close to Kafka. His first novel, *Die Galeere*, was published in 1913. He fled to France in 1933 and took his own life when the Nazis occupied Paris.

58. An anthology of Kierkegaard's writings.

59. Kafka's trip to the Hartungen Sanatorium in Riva took place between this and the following entry.

60. Kropotkin's memoirs were among Kafka's favourite books, as were the memoirs of Alexander Herzen.

61. Of 'The Metamorphosis'. In the next entry is probably to be found the germ of 'The Hunter Gracchus' (in the book *The Great Wall of China*), the scene of which is Riva.

62. This remark which the boy addressed to Kafka was in commendation of the unhappy reading of Kleist's *Michael Kohlhaas* that Kafka mentions in the entry of 11 December 1913. Kafka told this anecdote with so much humour that among his friends the boy's remark became proverbial. Kafka said that the boy even added, quite precociously: 'Very good!' Whenever someone, haughtily, patronizingly, and with the air of a connoisseur, praised something he was entirely ignorant of, we liked to quote this 'very good' and everyone immediately knew what was meant.

Actually, the quite unimportant incident of the reading was a much less melancholy affair than Kafka's account would indicate. Kafka, needless to say, read wonderfully; I was present at the reading and remember it quite well. It was only that he had chosen a selection that was much too long, and in the end was obliged to shorten it as he read. In addition, there was the quite incongruous contrast between this great literature and the uninterested and inferior audience, the majority of whom came to benefit affairs of this kind only for the sake of the free cup of tea that they received.

63. A play by Paul Claudel. Fantl, as well as Claudel, belonged to the so-called Hellerau circle. In Hellerau, a garden suburb of Dresden, Jacques-Dalcroze had his school for dancing and rhythmic gymnastics. There, in 1913, Jakob Hegner founded his publishing house, around which a circle of writers and intellectuals gathered.

64. A quotation from *Das Erlebnis und die Dichtung*, by Wilhelm Dilthey. Tellheim is the hero of Lessing's *Minna von Barnhelm*.

65. Kafka's eldest sister.

66. Czech writer and historian. Among other things he edited (in collaboration with Otto Pick) the Bohemian National Museum's manuscript letters of the correspondence between Casanova and J. F. Opiz.

67. This is the concluding entry of the seventh manuscript notebook of the *Diaries*. It began with the entry of 2 May 1913 (see p. 219).

68. Robert Musil, who later won renown for his *Der Mann ohne Eigenschaften*, invited Kafka to collaborate in the publication of a literary magazine.

69. This and the two entries that follow were written almost two months before the war broke out. Soon thereafter, when the Russians conquered part of Austria, we witnessed scenes very like those Kafka describes here.

70. A preliminary sketch for *The Castle*; it was several years later that Kafka wrote the novel.

71. Kafka quotes P.'s remark ironically; P. in his innocence compared that rather important artist, Alfred Kubin, with an illustrator of pornographic books called 'Marquis Bayros' who was in vogue at the time.

72. The name of a theatre in a suburb of Prague.

73. Kafka, too was buried in the same grave with his parents.

74. E., several times referred to later, was the sister of F.B.

75. Bl. was a friend of F.B.'s.

76. After the first breaking-off of his engagement, Kafka went on a short trip to Denmark with Ernst Weiss and the latter's friend.

77. Probably *Franziska*, a novel by Ernst Weiss.

78. Beginning with 16 February 1914, Kafka had been making his diary entries in two notebooks instead of one, alternating from one to the other. This first sentence of 31 July followed directly after the last sentence of 29 July ('. . . I'll have the time') in the same notebook. The entries under 30 July were made in the other notebook.

79. Czech for 'cheers'.

80. The Czech diminutive for Adalbert.

81. Kafka had begun *The Trial*. Two years previously he had written 'The Judgement' and parts of *Amerika*.

82. Part of the manuscript page has been torn off, leaving lacunae here and at the end of the entry of 25 October.

83. A brother-in-law home from the front on leave.

84. The two sentences in parentheses were added as a kind of footnote.

85. Tabakskollegium, name of the place (in Königswusterhausen, near

Berlin) where Friedrich Wilhelm I of Prussia informally consorted with his ministers and advisers over beer and tobacco.

86. Published as a fragment in an appendix to the German edition of *The Trial*, under the title of 'Fahrt zur Mutter'.

87. Exegesis of 'Before the Law'; 'Before the Law' was originally published in the collection, *A Country Doctor*, and then incorporated into chapter II of *The Trial*. The 'Legend' and its exegesis are published in *Parables* (No. 7, Schocken Library).

88. Later published as 'The Giant Mole' in *The Great Wall of China*.

89. This story has not been preserved.

90. *The Man Who Disappeared*, the title Kafka first gave to *Amerika*.

91. Miss F. R., a young woman from Lemberg whom Kafka met at a lecture course on world literature that I gave in a school for refugee Jewish children. Cf. also the entry of 14 April 1915, p. 334.

92. The Assicurazioni Generali, an Italian insurance company; Kafka's first job. The work cost him a great deal of effort.

93. Not the 'Investigations of a Dog' in *The Great Wall of China*.

94. We Zionists took advantage of the presence of Eastern European Jewish war refugees to hold discussion evenings; it was our purpose to clarify the relations between the Jews of the East and the West. Needless to say, there were many misunderstandings at first; later, however, a fruitful collaboration ensued, and a mutual tempering of our views.

95. Kafka accompanied his elder sister Elli on a visit to her husband, a reserve officer, who had been moved up to the front.

96. An excursion spot near Prague.

97. A chance acquaintance we had made on our trip to Zurich in 1911 (see p. 433).

98. An unfinished novel of mine.

99. Georg Mordecai Langer of Prague. For years, in Eastern Europe, he had sought to lead the life of a Hasid; later he wrote in Czech, German and Hebrew on Kabbalah and related subjects. Among other things he published two small volumes of Hebrew poems.

The wonder-rabbi mentioned here, a relative of the Zaddik of Belz, had fled with his disciples before the Russians from Grodek to Prague.

100. A suburb of Prague.

101. Rossmann and K. are the heroes of *Amerika* and *The Trial*, respectively.

102. Gerti was Kafka's niece, a child at the time. [The German word *Pferdefuss* means both the devil's cloven foot and, colloquially, clubfoot – Trans.]

103. A model of a trench on exhibition near Prague.

104. A childhood friend of Kafka's; cf. Kafka's letters to him, in volume six of the first German edition (Schocken Verlag) of his works.

105. Abraham Grünberg, a young and gifted refugee from Warsaw whom we saw a great deal of at the time. He died of tuberculosis during the war.

106. Kafka gave a humorous report of his visit to Mrs M-T. Later he regretted his unintentional ridicule.

107. A talmudic scholar belonging to the pious Lieben family of Prague. Only two members of this extensive family were saved from the horrors of the Nazi occupation – the scholar mentioned here and a boy in a Palestinian kibbutz.

108. [Dream and weep, poor race of man, the way can't be found – you have lost it. With 'Woe!' you greet the night, with 'Woe!' the day.

I want nothing save to escape the hands that reach out for me from the depths to draw my powerless body down to them. I fall heavily into the waiting hands.

Words slowly spoken echoed in the distant mountains. We listened.

Horrors of hell, veiled grimaces, alas, they bore my body close-pressed to them.

The long procession bears the unborn along.]

109. Several entries in the octavo notebooks (see Postscript, p. 489] fill, chronologically, the gap that occurs at this point in the *Diaries*. These entries, however, have a different, more 'objective' character than the quarto notebooks of the *Diaries*; they are made up solely of short stories, the beginnings of stories, and meditations (aphorisms), but nothing that bears on the events of the day.

110. A Prague writer who (with Hugo Salus) had exercised a great influence on the generation that preceded ours. His poetic drama (adapted from the Spanish), *Don Gil von den grünen Hosen*, was famous.

111. This and a number of the succeeding entries are fragments of 'In the Penal Colony'.

112. The clause, 'as if it bore witness to some truth', was struck out by Kafka in the manuscript.

113. Between this and the preceding entry the following occurred: the first medical confirmation was made of Kafka's tuberculosis; he again decided to break off his engagement to F., took a leave of absence from his job, and went to live in the country, with his sister Ottla (in Zürau, Post Flöhau, about five kilometres east of Karlsbad). The trip to Ottla's house took place on 12 September 1917.

114. A nephew of Kafka's. He was murdered by the Nazis.

115. [The German word for atonement (*Versöhnung*) also means reconciliation – Trans.]

116. Kafka's second fiancée, Miss J. W. The engagement lasted only six months or so.

117. A character in Knut Hamsun's *Growth of the Soil*, which Kafka was reading at the time. Kafka particularly loved and admired this writer.

118. The twelfth manuscript notebook of the *Diaries*, which ends at this point, consists only of a number of loose leaves between covers. Much of it was torn out by Kafka and destroyed.

119. Mrs Milena Jesenská, whose acquaintance Kafka made at the beginning of 1920. She was a clever, able woman of liberal views; an excellent writer. A very intimate friendship developed between her and Kafka, one full of hope and happiness at first but which later turned into hopelessness. The friendship lasted a little more than two years. In 1939 Mrs Jesenská was thrown into prison by the Nazis in Prague and murdered.

120. The magazine of the Czech scout movement. All problems of education interested Kafka.

121. 'The Death of Ivan Ilyich' by Tolstoy. This and his *Folk Tales* ('The Three Old Men', particularly), were great favourites of Kafka's.

122. Addressed to Milena Jesenská.

123. This remark occurs in Kafka's first book, *Meditation*, in the piece entitled 'Bachelor's Ill Luck'. Cf. also p. 117.

124. The last clause of this sentence is a reference to a line in Kafka's story, 'A Country Doctor'.

125. Joseph K., the hero of *The Trial*; the novel, written in 1914 and 1915, remained unpublished during Kafka's lifetime.

126. The seven ancient Jewish communities in Burgenland.

127. The beginning of a polemic against Hans Blüher's *Secessio Judaica*. Here Kafka throws up to Blüher the very faults Blüher maintains he finds in Jewish books.

128. The name of one of the exhibiting painters.

129. Makkabi was the name of a Zionist sports club. *Selbstwehr* was a Prague Zionist weekly. The Czech means: 'I came to help you.'

130. *Der grosse Maggid* (*The Great Preacher*), title of a book by Martin Buber on the hasidic Rabbi Dow Baer of Mezritch, a disciple of the Baal Shem.

131. In south-eastern Bohemia, where Kafka was recuperating at his sister Ottla's house.

132. Frydlant and Liberic, two old towns in northern Bohemia. The text retains Kafka's German spelling of the names.

133. Judging from the last entry in the diary of this trip (p. 431), it seems

probable that Kafka visited these places on official business for the Workers' Accident Insurance Institute, by which he was employed.

This castle may perhaps have influenced Kafka's conception of the castle in his novel.

134. A recollection of the trip to Riva, Brescia, in 1909.

135. Kafka undertook this trip together with the Editor. We planned to write a novel together, called *Richard and Samuel*, one chapter of which has been preserved under the title of 'The First Long Train Journey'. (See *n.* 14.)

136. Alice R. is the woman who appears as Dora Lippert in 'The First Long Train Journey.' (See *n.* 21.)

137. As shown in a drawing in the manuscript.

138. An allusion to the theory of the 'Indistinct', with which the book *Anschauung und Begriff* by Felix Weltsch and myself begins. The 'Indistinct' is represented there by the graphic symbol, $A + x$.

139. A Czech expression for the little envelopes that contain fortunes; a trained parrot would draw one out of a heap.

140. Writing entries in our diaries.

141. Paintings in the Louvre.

142. Paintings in the palace of Versailles.

143. From this point on the entries were made at the Erlenbach Sanatorium, Switzerland, whither Kafka had gone on alone while I returned home. His leave of absence was a little longer than mine. The entries, however, soon revert to the impressions of Paris that he had just absorbed.

144. Kafka and I went to Weimar together during our holiday, staying there until 7 July. On 8 July Kafka left for the Jungborn nature therapy establishment in the Harz. Kafka was always interested in *Naturheilkunde* in all its various forms, such as the raw food diet, vegetarianism, Mazdaznan, nudism, gymnastics, and anti-vaccinationism. The curious mixture of irony and respect in his attitude to these cults, and his efforts over the years to live in accordance with several of them, defy all analysis. The 'Travel Diary' faithfully reflects Kafka's attitude.

145. Patriotic Czech gymnastic societies.

146. ['Confession', by Goethe. The following is a translation by Paul Dyrsen (1878):

> Absolution give to us!
>   And we shall forever
> To remember your command
>   Faithfully endeavour;

> Wholly love all worth and beauty
> And from doing half our duty
> Resolutely sever.]

147. Johannes Schlaf, with Arno Holz one of the first men in German literature to write in the genre of modern realism, was one of the forerunners of .Gerhart Hauptmann. In the years before our visit he had again made himself much talked about by advancing and vehemently defending an anti-Copernican theory according to which the sun moved round the earth.

148. Wickersdorf was a progressive country boarding school founded in Germany in 1906 in close conformity with the ideals of the German Youth Movement.

CHRONOLOGY
1883 – 1924

1883 Born 3 July in Prague.

1901 Graduates from the German Gymnasium. (Incorrectly given in *Diaries* as 1903.)

1906 Doctorate in jurisprudence from the Karl-Ferdinand University in Prague.

before 1907 Writes 'Description of a Struggle' and 'Hochzeitsvorbereitungen auf dem Lande'.

1907–08 Temporary employment in the Assicurazioni Generali, an Italian insurance company.

1908 Appointed to post with government-sponsored Arbeiter-Unfall-Versicherungs-Anstalt für das Königreich Böhmen in Prag.

1909 Publication of 'Conversation with the Supplicant' and 'Conversation with the Drunken Man', two dialogues from 'Description of a Struggle', in the literary periodical *Hyperion*. Publication of 'The Aeroplanes at Brescia' in the Prague newspaper *Bohemia*.

1910 Publication in *Bohemia* of several short pieces later included in *Meditation*.

1911 Trip to Frydlant and Liberic.
Trip to Switzerland, Italy, Paris, and Erlenbach.
Meets Yiddish theatre troupe in Prague.

1912 Publication in the literary periodical *Herderblätter* of 'The First Long Train Journey', first chapter of *Richard and Samuel*.
Trip to Weimar and Jungborn.
Meets F.B.
Begins *Amerika*.
Writes 'The Judgement'.

1913 Publication of *Meditation*.
Publication of 'The Judgement' in the literary year-book *Arkadia*.
Publication of 'The Stoker', first chapter of *Amerika*.
Trip to Riva.
Writes 'The Metamorphosis'.

1914 Formal engagement to F.B.
Begins *The Trial*.
Writes first draft of 'In the Penal Colony'.

Writes 'The Giant Mole'.

Trip to Denmark.

1915 Publication of 'The Metamorphosis'.

Completes *The Trial*.

Awarded the Fontane Prize for 'The Stoker'.

Moves from parental house into a rented room.

1917 Tuberculosis.

Sick leave from the Arbeiter-Unfall-Versicherungs-Anstalt.

Final break with F. B.

1918 Writes 'The Great Wall of China'.

1919 Publication of the collection of stories, *A Country Doctor*.

Short-lived second engagement to J.W.

1920 Publication of 'In the Penal Colony'.

Stay in Meran, Austria.

Resumes work at his office.

Meets Milena Jesenská.

1921 Stay in a sanatorium in the Tatra.

Writes *The Castle*.

Publication of 'The Bucket Rider' in *Prager Presse*.

1922 Publication of the story 'A Hunger Artist' in *Die Neue Rundschau*.

1923 Writes 'Investigations of a Dog', 'The Burrow', and 'Josephine the Singer'.

Meets Dora Dymant; goes with her to Berlin.

1924 Publication of the collection of stories, *A Hunger Artist*.

Dies 3 June in a sanatorium near Vienna.

Buried 11 June in the Jewish cemetery in Prague-Strashnitz.

LIST OF AUTHORS, ARTISTS, PERIODICALS, AND WORKS

Numerals preceded by an italic *n* refer to notes at the end of the book. A number in parentheses following a note reference indicates the text page to which the note refers.

It was not possible to identify all the authors and artists mentioned in the text. In such cases their names are not listed here.

* Listed only when mentioned in the text as author.

507

THE DIARIES OF FRANZ KAFKA
1910–23

Franz Kafka was born in Prague in 1883, the son of a rich Jewish Czech merchant. After studying literature and medicine for a short time, he turned to law, which he believed was the profession that would give him the greatest amount of free time for his private life and his writing. He took his doctorate in law at Prague University, got a job with an insurance company, and later became a clerk in the semi-governmental Workers' Insurance Office. In later years the necessity of earning his living by routine office work became an intolerable burden, and he broke away altogether, settling down in a Berlin suburb to devote himself to writing. In 1914 he became engaged, but broke it off, feeling unable to face marriage. He made one more attempt to marry, but it was discovered that he was suffering from tuberculosis and he went to a sanatorium. His unsatisfactory love affairs, his relationship with his father, a self-made man who cared nothing for his son's literary aspirations, and his own inflexible intellectual honesty and almost psychopathic sensitivity finally broke down his health, and the 'hunger years' of post-1918 Berlin added the finishing touches. He died in 1924. Although he was a Czech, Kafka's books were all written in German. Seven of them were published during his lifetime. *The Trial* first appeared after the author's death in 1925, *The Castle* in 1926, *Amerika* in 1927, and *The Great Wall of China* in 1931.

•

Max Brod was a close friend of Kafka in his youth, and wrote a well-known biography of him. Kafka left him all his papers to be destroyed, but Brod, as friend and executor, decided against it. He wrote a novel about their friendship, *The Kingdom of Love*. Max Brod died in 1968.

THE SCHOCKEN KAFKA LIBRARY

AMERIKA
a new translation by Mark Harman,
based on the restored text

Kafka's first and funniest novel tells the story of the young immigrant Karl Rossmann who, "packed off to America" by his parents, finds himself caught up in a whirlwind of dizzying reversals, strange escapades, and picaresque adventures.

"Almost ninety years after his death, Kafka continues to defy simplifications, to force us to consider him anew. That's the effect of Mark Harman's new translation."   —*Los Angeles Times*

THE CASTLE
a new translation by Mark Harman,
based on the restored text

This haunting tale of a man known only as K. and his endless struggle against an inscrutable authority to gain admittance to a castle is often cited as Kafka's most autobiographical work.

"Will be *the* translation of preference for some time to come."
—J. M. Coetzee, *The New York Review of Books*

THE COMPLETE STORIES
edited by Nahum N. Glatzer,
with a foreword by John Updike

All of Kafka's stories are collected here in one comprehensive volume; with the exception of the three novels, the whole of his narrative work is included.

"*The Complete Stories* is an encyclopedia of our insecurities and our brave attempts to oppose them."   —Anatole Broyard

DIARIES, 1910–1923
edited by Max Brod

For the first time in this country, the complete diaries of Franz Kafka are available in one volume. Covering the period from 1910 to 1923, the year before Kafka's death, they reveal the essential Kafka behind the enigmatic artist.

"It is likely that these journals will be regarded as one of [Kafka's] major literary works; in these pages, he reveals what he customarily hid from the world."   —*The New Yorker*

THE METAMORPHOSIS AND OTHER STORIES
translated by Willa and Edwin Muir

This powerful collection brings together all the stories Franz Kafka published during his lifetime, including "The Judgment," "The Metamorphosis," "In the Penal Colony," "A Country Doctor," and "A Hunger Artist."

"Kafka's survey of the insectile situation of young Jews in inner Bohemia can hardly be improved upon. There is a sense in which Kafka's Jewish question has become everybody's question, Jewish alienation the template for all our doubts. These days we all find our anterior legs flailing before us. We're all insects, all *Ungeziefer*, now."
—Zadie Smith

THE SONS
translations revised and updated by Arthur Wensinger,
with an introduction by Mark Anderson

Franz Kafka's three classic stories of filial revolt—"The Metamorphosis," "The Judgment," and "The Stoker"—grouped together with his own poignant "Letter to His Father," take on fresh, compelling meaning.

"Kafka is the author who comes nearest to bearing the same kind of relationship to our age as Dante, Shakespeare, and Goethe bore to theirs."
—W. H. Auden

THE TRIAL
a new translation by Breon Mitchell,
based on the restored text

The terrifying story of Joseph K., his arrest and trial, is one of the greatest novels of the twentieth century.

"Mitchell's translation is an accomplishment of the highest order—one that will honor Kafka far into the twenty-first century."
—Walter Abish, author of *How German Is It*